Sub

Copyright © 2014 by Tom Gallagher

Coast to Coast Publishing
Boston, New York, San Francisco

submyyearsundergroundinamericasschools.com

SubMyYearsUnder@aol.com

ISBN: 978-0-9916695-0-9

SUB:

My

Years

Tom Gallagher
(That's Mr. Gallagher to you)

Underground

in

America's

Schools

Dedicated to substitute teachers everywhere, whose skills will be needed so long as humanity remains in its fallen state.

With thanks to Jim Creamer for his vanguard action.

Homo sum: human nil a me alienum puto.
(I am a man: I consider nothing human foreign to me.)

                                                    Terentius (Terence)

One sings what is written for the voice. When my so-called "rivals" are willing to do that, then perhaps we can speak of my actually having rivals.

                                                    Maria Callas

Contents

P 9   PREFACE

P 15   SUB

P 309 EPILOGUE

P 311 APPENDIX: THE ANTI-SUSPENSION MOVEMENT

P 319 BIOGRAPHY

PREFACE

When asked what I do for a living, I often reply that I yell at children professionally – I am a substitute teacher. Five days a week I see children on their worst behavior. That's in a good week, of course – when I get five days work. I once thought of subbing as what I did in between other things; now it looks like the other things may have been what I did in between subbing. Whichever turns out to be the case, it was only during one of my non-subbing episodes that I came to understand just how well trained the American substitute teacher really is.

In the summer of 1997, I was an international voter registration supervisor in Ilidja, a suburb of Sarajevo, the capital of Bosnia-Herzogovina. I'd gone there on just two weeks notice, which subbing allows you to do (often used as justification for continuing this dubious "career path") and would be spending the next nine weeks in the re-registration of the entire country, the first post-civil war registration of the previous summer having been deemed irreparably flawed.

A lot of people had asked me didn't I consider this dangerous, but with my sub experience, I certainly never had doubts as to being up to the challenges of the job. After all, I typically started my day in pre-dawn hours listening to a recording asking me to accept a mission that began in an hour or two. Its purpose would be unclear even after all instructions were given. The possibility of communication with the population to which I would be assigned often ran from dim to nil. Outbreaks of hostility with no apparent cause were routine. How much different than that could Bosnia be? Plus, I'd have an interpreter.

But it wasn't until one particular day in Ilidja that I realized just how qualified I really was. This was my first trip to the country so I guess I just assumed that recent citizens of "communist" Yugoslavia would be okay at lining up. But they weren't. Perhaps it was a reaction against Communism, I don't know, but instead of forming a line, people would simply cluster outside the entrance and push their way in whenever the door opened.

We had just gone along with this until the day the crowd got so dense that a pregnant woman had to force her way out and a guy with two recent heart attacks had to fight his way in. As a matter of policy we international voter registration supervisors were always supposed to let the local Bosnian officials run things and intervene only in extreme situations. So I told the center director I figured we had to do something. He then called the local police who came and gave the crowd some guff. The crowd gave the police some guff back. The cops left. The scrum outside the door remained intact.

Moving up the line of authority, we agreed to call in the military police from the United Nations Protection Force (UNPROFOR) that was sent there to enforce the Dayton Peace Accords. A nice young Austrian captain showed up and told the crowd, through my interpreter, that it would be nice if they would stop blocking the doors. They probably thought he was a nice young man, too, but they didn't move. When he left I said to the director, "It's up to us." He said, "It's up to you."

So I went outside and shouted at the crowd in English, after which my interpreter shouted some version of what I'd said at them in Bosnian. They were going to have to form an orderly line, we told them. They replied and when my interpreter translated the lip they were giving back to me into English, I knew that while police and military methods might fail, sub methods would not. Time had come for the international equivalent of throwing the annoying student out of class. "Okay," I told them, "this registration center has just closed." By the time I got back inside they were already starting to form a line. In twenty minutes or so they were well lined up and we reopened.

I had to go out and repeat the performance a couple of more times over the next two days, but by the third morning, and every day thereafter, a line had already formed by the time we arrived. Apparently the word had gotten around the neighborhood that there was an American substitute teacher in the center and they'd have to shape up. I never said anything more to the local police or the military. It wasn't their fault they didn't have the proper training for the situation.

I made a number of subsequent trips to Bosnia and one to Macedonia, another country to emerge from the Yugoslav Civil Wars; on each of them "land mine awareness" was a regular part of the job orientation. Yet I never considered myself foolhardy. I won't do just anything – like sub in Oakland again, for instance.

My honeymoon in that city across the Bay was pretty much over by the end of the first period on my first – and last – day there, when a McClymonds High School student threw a metal wastepaper basket at me blind side. Now McClymonds is a school with a big sports history – alumni include baseball players like Vada Pinson, Frank Robinson and Curt Flood and basketball players Bill Russell and Paul Silas. Fortunately, the student I encountered on this particular day didn't appear to have that kind of talent. I only became aware of his intent when the book rack – which the wastebasket actually hit – struck me a harmless, glancing blow and a girl said, "Why'd you throw the garbage can at the teacher?" (The answer to that question, by the way, is that he was disappointed that I hadn't been able to mark him down as present after he'd shown up so late for class that the attendance form had already been collected. I had underestimated his sensitivity about his attendance record.)

The school administration assured me that day that they would let me know what the consequences turned out to be for that kid. They haven't gotten back to me yet and it's been well over a decade now. I remain optimistic, though, that they will do so in time for the second edition of this book. After all, chances are that guy probably hasn't graduated yet.

A friend of mine used to find it very funny that I was willing to go to Bosnia but wouldn't substitute teach in Oakland. I tried to explain that in Bosnia I had 40,000 UNPROFOR soldiers to protect me and what did I have in Oakland? The security guard working at McClymonds that day was big enough, all right.

My first thought at seeing him was to wonder how far his football career went – tight end, I figured. But so far as I could see, he wasn't armed. In Bosnia, on the other hand, the UN troops might not have been any good at classroom or voter registration center-control, but if you needed back-up, they did have tanks. And certainly I knew that any Bosnian who might attack me was in for a lot more trouble than some Oakland high school kid would be.

Later I worked on a foreign election that I actually did consider dangerous – the 1999 United Nations independence plebiscite in East Timor – the vote after which the losers burned the whole country down and killed upwards of a thousand people because the Timorese voted to leave Indonesia. Our security on that mission was provided by the Indonesian police which on first glance, you'd likely mistake for the army, as they carried rifles rather than handguns. And, since up until only a few months earlier they actually had been part of the army – which had killed tens of thousands of Timorese since invading in 1975, relying on them for security for allowing the Timorese to vote Indonesia out was actually pretty crazy. But I still won't sub in Oakland.

As you might imagine, though, there's a serious part to all of this. Substitute teaching has let me experience American public education in hundreds of classrooms, from kindergartners to seniors, in over a hundred schools. There's not a lot of teachers or administrators who see all of what a sub can. Naturally I've formed opinions about America's educational crisis, the first of which is that we don't fundamentally have an educational crisis in this country. For large parts of the population, the educational system is working pretty much okay. What I do believe we have is a social crisis.

There's actually more than one social crisis, of course, but if there's one impression I've taken away from hundreds of classroom days, it's been the difficulty of the plight of Black America. It's a subject I write about with great trepidation, however, particularly in a book whose outlook is fundamentally wry. But if you're teaching in an American city, you're thinking about it.

Of course, San Francisco, it turns out, is not just any city in that regard. The December 29, 2012 *San Francisco Chronicle* reported that the city (and county) had "a black infant mortality rate of 16.2 deaths per 1,000 births, compared with the white rate of 2.5," a sixfold disparity that "is one of the largest in the nation, and the largest for any county in the state." The article went on to acknowledge the imprecision of the calculation because the city's remaining African-American population of 50,000 no longer provides a sample large enough to determine an accurate infant mortality rate. There in a nutshell is the status of the Black population of San Francisco, which counterintuitively – given the city's overall affluence – has an income level lower than that of their counterparts in the state's other largest cities, the relentlessly increasing cost of housing tending to drive out all but the poorest, who hang on in public housing.

Nevertheless, the circumstances of San Francisco's black students' lives are much more similar to those elsewhere in the state and the country than not. As I grapple with figuring out the right touch for this topic, I find myself always reworking a couple of conversations. There was the one with my cousin, whose response to my take on the situation of black students was that she felt blacks faced obstacles just like any other group that came to this country and they just had to deal with them – like any other group. A normal, typical enough reaction, in other words.

Of course, the ancestors of most American blacks *didn't* come here like everyone else. They didn't come here to make a better life for themselves; they were brought here to make a better life for someone else – and a much, much worse life for themselves. Unhappily, it is my conclusion that this fact still matters – greatly. Much as we might hope to believe that the civil rights movement dealt with the problem, clearly this is not the case. (There is actually one other group with a history and life experience reasonably comparable to that of African-Americans – Native Americans – but those who have survived have been so marginalized that few other Americans have much awareness of their situation.)

This sort of argument is not necessarily an easy sell. I wrote a book review once that made the case for a form of educational reparations for Black America and I still find myself wishing I'd had *69 (a callback mechanism of the last millennium) capability on my phone when some guy looked up my number and called me just so he could hang up on me. Why, he even had a doctorate in education, he informed me before his outrage with my ideas simply became too much to bear. If I had his number I might have later treated him to a little of the language you hear in public school classrooms that he might not have heard so much of in his grad school classes. But, then I suppose not that many people like him are going to read this book anyhow.

On the other side, I think of conversation with friends whom, unlike my cousin, you'd probably call "liberals." One expressed surprise at my description of the dire situation of so many black students; she sort of thought blacks were educating their own and it was going okay. Yet she had moved from San Francisco to the suburbs at about the time her kids reached school age. Another time, to be a bit provocative, I mentioned to a different friend that the level of difficulty of whatever school I would encounter in the morning would likely be related to the proportion of black students there. This drew her up short, more or less as anticipated, and she informed me that I was one of the few people that she would even let get away with a statement like that. Her child had never attended public school, her explanation for which had to do with her perception that the San Francisco schools were screwed up because of their less-than-ideal administration. Whatever the reason, she was another person who seemed to have little idea what public school was actually like – and I thought she ought to know.

Over the years, I've told these stories because I thought that a lot of people needed to hear them, even if it made them uncomfortable. So far as the racial situation in schools and education went, they often thought they knew, but in most cases they didn't know. They knew the dire situation of blacks, particularly males, in relation to the criminal justice system and yet didn't seem to connect it very directly with the schools. Any time I venture into talking about what the schools can really be like, I fear I run the risk of appearing to "blame the victims" for their situation. America as a whole finds all of this extremely difficult to discuss, acknowledge, or even recognize. Much easier to talk about a more general "educational crisis" instead.

For whatever reasons, the United States has not yet decided to incorporate the same level of support for the well being of all of its citizens that some other countries have. Employment, for instance, is not considered a right in our country, nor is decent housing. Unemployment and job training benefits remain modest and it remains to be seen how far the recent national health care reform legislation will take us toward establishing health care as a right.

At the same time, the idea of the U.S. as a land of equal opportunity is closely held and education has come down to us as one of the few areas where a consensus exists that the government has an obligation to deliver for everyone (without being denounced as "socialistic.") The result has been wildly unrealistic expectations placed upon the public education system – expectations that simply can't be met. Yet, that's what we've got. And, oh yes, there's also these people trying to turn public education into a for-profit industry.

(Names of schools and persons have been changed to protect the innocent and guilty alike, with the exception of the kids with the cool names – they're all real.)

*****

AUTHOR'S DISPENSATION

There is something of a tradition of imposing a narrative arc on books like this. The author may find or lose God, love, family, vocation, career, success or the like. Nothing of that sort happens here. There are more tests, charter schools and cellphones at the end of this book than at the beginning, but basically the schools are the same. The reader, therefore, should not hesitate to read this book in serendipitous order.

SUB

DOUBLE COVERAGE – Language Arts, Samuel Adams Middle School, February 3, 1997

I often wonder what people really mean when they ask what I've been teaching lately. I once heard Milena Moser, a Swiss German writer describe moving to the Bay Area and learning that when Americans say, "Let's have lunch," they don't really mean that. They just mean, "Let's keep in touch." And they don't actually mean that either. They're just saying "Goodbye."

Likewise with these people asking what I've been teaching. Is this a real question or just their way of saying, "Hi, how are you?" – which they may not really want to know all that much about either, but seems friendlier than saying, "Hello." But sometimes a cigar is just a cigar; some people actually do want to meet for lunch; and occasionally people really want to know what I've been teaching. In those cases, I point out that I'm not actually a teacher, I'm a substitute. And the difference is what I'm going to tell you about.

How did I wind up in the ersatz teaching business? The eight years of Jesuit schooling may have contributed somehow. The Jesuits liked to think of themselves both as educators and as the marines of the Catholic Church. We substitute teachers like to think of ourselves as the marines of the public education system. Whenever a breach opens in our nation's educational front lines, off we go: The few, the brave, the stupid.

And majoring in philosophy in college may have been a factor: *What does permanence really mean anyhow? And isn't teaching a poor substitute for experience in the first place?*

Whatever the reason, this all started in Boston in the 1970s. At that point my profile was reasonably *normal* for a substitute teacher – I was a guy in his twenties sort of waiting for something to happen. The first recidivism occurred in 1980, the year I was elected to the Massachusetts Legislature. So now *something* had definitely happened in my life and subbing should have been relegated to the past along with jobs like affixing "Super Regular" stickers on gas pumps, raking leaves (within sight of the campus that had granted me my BA a couple of years earlier) and professional picketing.

Technically I would be elected in November of that year, but since Boston is a one-party city, as a practical matter the Democratic primary had decided the question in September – there wasn't even a token Republican opponent. So while I had a big deal, high profile job waiting for me in January, my meaningful campaigning was over and for the months of October, November and December I was flat broke, but in no position to be looking for other "real" work. I returned to subbing for the interim.

Since I myself didn't consider this situation particularly normal, I did it with some trepidation, wondering what other people might make of the new State Representative thrashing about at the bottom of the educational heap. Eventually the dreaded day that somebody recognized me came at "the Jerry," the Jeremiah Burke High School in Dorchester, generally considered the city's toughest school once Boston Trade shut down. One day's assignment at the

"Jerry" consisted of sitting out in the corridor on a folding chair set next to the fire alarm box, in order to prevent yet another false alarm from emptying out the school. On another day the students and I stood, dressed in hats, coats and gloves, clapping our arms for warmth throughout the day because the classroom, which was on the ground floor, had recently had all of its windows broken, and it was winter. The students, at least, got to switch rooms.

I forget whether or not it was the day I had the chair job but at some point Pam Hilton, a regular teacher there who had been a big campaign supporter, spotted me and blurted, "Now I know I voted for the right person." She no doubt figured that anyone willing to set foot in the Jerry probably wasn't likely to be daunted by anything he encountered in the Massachusetts House of Representatives.

That was then and this is now — my first day in the San Francisco schools. I've been doing some subbing in South San Francisco, but it actually proved difficult to get into San Francisco. (South San Francisco is a separate city, to which we shall return with great frequency.) I'm starting out in a middle school. The one way in which a middle school is preferable to a high school is that the kids are generally smaller, and therefore less dangerous. The average middle school guy throwing something at you is just not going to bring the same velocity as a high school kid might.

I actually never set foot in a middle school until I was in my twenties and writing an end-of-the-year story on the neighborhood schools for the *Allston Brighton Community News.* As I was interviewing a teacher at the Taft Middle School, I was slightly taken aback when he asked if I hadn't noticed that most of his peers looked like they were in some kind of state of shock. Well, yes, now that he mentioned it, they did look a little ill, but I would have thought it impertinent to mention their zombie-like appearance in my story if he hadn't brought it up. He said they hadn't looked like that back in September. It appeared that these could have been some of the best minds of my generation before they became middle school teachers, but there was no way of telling now.

I didn't attend middle school myself because I went to Catholic schools and there were no such things as Catholic middle schools — a matter in which the Church proved itself wiser than secular society. I'm not exactly sure what the Canon Law on this is, but my Church training tells me that middle schools might be deemed immoral on at least two counts. (Second Place – Boys, New York Archdiocese, Cardinal's Christian Doctrine Examination, 1962 – in case you were wondering about my credentials on the subject. And the gold medal winner was ordained a priest, so I just missed the cut.) The fundamental objection would likely be that middle schools constitute a crime against nature – a possibility that has at least passed through the mind of any reflective person experiencing the effects of isolating the age group for educational purposes. A second, more subtle theological objection might be that middle schools constitute an instance of the same cardinal sin of pride that brought down Lucifer – in this case forgetting that only God can create Purgatory (which, as we know, differs from Hell only in duration, not intensity), even in three-year terrestrial form.

Anyhow, here I am at Sam Adams, with these dark theological ruminations flooding my mind. Yet my first impressions are actually positive. The building is definitely "old school" – wide corridors, high ceilings and bad lighting. The broad corridors are nice things to have in a middle school because you want to give these kids a wide berth. Among the many things a lot of them don't know at this age is how big they actually are. A lot of bodies growing faster than the brains inside them can lead to a lot of bumping into things, but the corridors are pretty orderly here today. Back in Boston I'd found I could usually gauge what the classroom was going to be like even before I had opened the door just from the situation in the halls – when I walked into the Edison Middle School in Brighton after Joe Bage took over as principal and saw order where I'd seen none before, I knew his boosters were right about him. Likewise, there were days I pretty well knew I wouldn't be coming back to a particular school before I ever got into the classroom.

The reason it has taken me this long to get here, by the way, is that the Substitute Teacher Office told me they didn't hire subs who only had a 30-Day Emergency Credential, the kind that allows you to substitute but not to teach full time – which is what I have. But a teacher later told me this was no longer the case, if it had ever been – he actually didn't seem to consider the Sub Office a reliable source about its own policies. Today I can't complain about them though, since they've called two subs for the same class and, to my surprise, the school lets us both stay. The other guy has apparently been subbing here for years, so I gladly step back and let him preside while I take in the scene. There is really no substitute for a second substitute in the classroom, so this is a pretty good first day at school in San Francisco.

Plus I meet a particularly impressive person in the teachers' lunchroom, a Mrs. T who says she is the Dean, a position I'm surprised to find existing in middle school.

WRITING ON THE WALL – *Computer Lab, Gregor Mendel Middle, February 4, 1997*

Sorry to disappoint you if you were expecting a smooth narrative, but the sub's life is nothing like that. Work today usually has nothing to do with anything that happened yesterday or the day before. So that's the way I'm going to tell it.

Day Two of San Francisco. Honeymoon over. The first thing that goes wrong is that the Sub Office didn't call two subs for the job today, just me. The second problem is that they sent me here. Gregor Mendel Middle School is a little like Baffin Island – you won't hear a lot of people telling you, "Have a nice day" in either place. Talk about being able to figure out what the classrooms are going to be like before you even enter them – there's a sign on a wall here prohibiting urinating, and it's on an inside wall. How many kids have to piss in the halls before you decide to post a sign like that? And did they really think that part of the problem was that the kids didn't know they were required to use the lavatories? I really would love to see a transcript of the meeting at which the decision to post that sign was made. The sign isn't hand scrawled, either. Looks like a union job. Word would have gotten around about the job order on this one. Was the principal already looking at a career change by the time of that meeting?

The Computer Lab, where I am in one of my stints here, is off in a cul-de-sac and if this were a high school rather than a middle school, I might be nervous in this location. Rich D has told me that a teacher was raped at this school. Anyhow, close to the end of the last period, my entire class runs away. I feel duty-bound to give chase, but after turning a couple of corners these sweet children are gone from my life forever. Dang!

Gregor Mendel Middle School closed at the end of the 2005-2006 academic year.

CAN'T FAULT HIM – *Language Arts, Gettysburg Middle, February 12, 1997*
Fifth straight middle school assignment, so I see teacher absentee patterns haven't changed since I was doing this in Boston. But subbing is certainly much better organized nowadays, at least around here. In Boston in the 70s and 80s, you expected to wing it, but here and now you can normally assume that a teacher will actually leave you a lesson plan. Unfortunately, this is not a normal day, and I have to use the emergency plan that every teacher is supposed to have on file in the office for such situations. It's puzzles and word games, which these things tend to be because they have to be general enough to fit in anywhere in the year. I might as well announce to the students: "Today will be Doodle Day." Another big change in working conditions is that there's now a phone in every classroom, making reinforcements a lot more accessible than they used to be. I use that phone generously today and the Assistant Principal is up several times attempting to assert order. She's quite helpful and at one point says something about not wanting to insult my professionalism. *Insult my professionalism?* I think, "Just whom does she think she's calling a professional, anyhow?" but I keep my mouth shut.

After I've been here for a few hours, I learn that the reason there are no regular lesson plans is that the teacher was placed upon administrative leave yesterday for having laid hands upon a student. By this time, I've seen enough that I cannot fault him for that decision. This was actually supposed to be a three-day job, but I've seen enough in one. So when the South San Francisco machine calls me that night with a job for the 14th, I take it, telling myself that maybe when the machine said that this San Francisco job started on February 12 and ended on February 14, it meant that the 14th was the first day that it was over. Make sense to you? No? Well, it worked for me. Brain damage brought on by overexposure to middle schools? Merely evidence of the brain's fundamental drive to survive? Either way, I walked into the office at the end of my second day and rattled through this pathetic logic by way of explaining why I wouldn't be back the next day and walked, leaving the kids to chew on a new sub tomorrow.

And just to show this experience was no fluke for this place, the next time I come back here we have a little episode that a lot of subs'll probably go their whole career without experiencing — and it was a first for me: a boy and a girl duking it out in class. I am happy to say that actual fights inside a classroom are quite rare, so having to call the office to have someone come in and haul out two kids in mixed combat — well it was just a special day.

I'm asked to write a report on the incident but the fact is I was looking somewheres else at the moment these two started at it. These two kids were both pretty tall and they went at in a way that would not have been shocking in much smaller children, which they had no doubt been until recently. So the girl is just fighting with the boy like she might have in fourth grade.

TAKE YOUR BOOK HOME? – Science, J.P. Morgan Middle, February 17, 1997

Picked this up last week when I was here for a half-day job I only took because I didn't entirely realize it was a half day. During lunch I was assigned to guard the cafeteria door with instructions that once the kids are out, they're out. No one gets back in alive. Apparently I was pretty impressive at guarding that door, because a regular teacher who walked by asked if I'd be available to cover his science classes for the whole of the next week.

Mr. D is being treated for lymphoma. (He'll be dead in a year.) The kids keep asking why he's gone and I keep telling them they'll have to ask him when he gets back. Mr. D told me that kids were allowed to sign books out for the weekend to take them home to study. On the one hand, the idea that bringing schoolbooks home has become a special event seems strange, but then the thought of most of the kids I've been dealing with actually wanting to take a book home was even stranger, although this is easily the best of the San Francisco schools I've been to thus far. Anyhow, on Friday morning we do have a couple of Chinese boys asking if they can take their books home, please. *What? You want to do what? You want to take the books home? Well, I don't know – maybe if you're good.* Probably I'm required to file some report on these guys – middle school kids asking to take books home are likely at risk for something. They could turn out to be trench coat snipers or terrorists. But I don't ask and there wasn't anything in the newspaper afterwards, and no one called me, so I'm hoping it worked out okay.

These kids reminded me of another Chinese boy I had once in Daly City. This kid was in a fourth grade class that was reading something about Albert Einstein. This seemed remarkable enough in itself, but when recess arrived this kid says "Mr. Gallagher, can we talk about Einstein some more?" I had to shoo him outside to dumb down with his peers – as the law requires.

Mr. D's got one not-so-hot class, though, which has this one really nasty eighth grade girl who issues me an invitation to "Kiss my ass." When she repeats this upon request, I write her a "referral," which is what they call the piece of paper releasing a student from further obligation to be in your classroom. In today's world, you can't just throw this darling little bitch out. You've got to have paperwork, which is all well and good except for the fact that you've usually got to write these things while you're also trying to maintain order, frequently with kids who don't want to give you their names. Plus, this citation-writing process can also provide so-inclined ejectees with the opportunity for a parting peroration while your ability to compose a clever retort is hindered by bureaucratic responsibility.

And this time, we have something extra special to go with the paperwork – a conference with the little sweetheart and her guidance counselor, which is what they call the person you send the kids to in order to get rid of them. This is quite unusual for a sub to participate in and, by the end, I think the kid promised to never again tell me to kiss her ass, at least not while we were in the counselor's office, or something like that.

NOT A REGULAR – *Language Arts, Gilbert Middle, March 6, 1997*

There's probably not a lot of grown-ups who can remember the name of even a single day-to-day sub they had. They might remember a long-term substitute who finished out a semester for a regular teacher who was having a baby or something like that, but the day-to-day sub is neutrino-like, passing through classrooms leaving no trace of ever having been there at all. But this doesn't mean that people don't have memories of what went on when one of those unidentified subs was in their classroom on a day when a few students, or many of the students, or most of the students, or maybe even all of the students tried to see what they might be able to get away with.

From the point of view of the nameless sub, some of these nameless children must be eliminated – not permanently, mind you – or at least not necessarily permanently – but ejected from the classroom before the day develops into one of those stories that everyone's going to remember for years. This is the sub's basic weapon – I may not be able to get you to pay attention, behave, be quiet, or even sit down, but on the other hand I don't have to put up with you either. Without the power of ejection, I have nothing. Back in Boston, any school that ever sent me back a student that I'd gotten rid of had just gotten rid of me – I wouldn't be back. The principals, counselors or whoever had sent the kid back could damn well sit in that classroom themselves the next time.

The next level of schools I didn't return to in Boston were the ones where I had to call in outside assistance when even throwing several kids out of class did not bring order. So far, my South San Francisco subbing over the past few months has not crossed either threshold; San Francisco I'm still sorting out. The phones in every classroom here are a big help. Assuming that someone answers the phone when you call – not always the case – when you're ejecting a kid you can now tell the authorities that trouble's on its way and if they want it to go somewhere else they can tell you where. There's bound to be fewer kids just wandering the halls after they're ejected if they're expected somewhere, plus I figure that someone who talked to you is going to be less likely to send a student back to you. Anyhow, right now I don't want to make any quick decisions on individual schools before I get a better handle on the overall system, but I will say that if I stick to my Boston standards, Gilbert won't be on my regular itinerary.

NOT PYTHON COUNTRY – *Phys Ed, Annunciation Gulch Middle, April 7, 1997*

Oooeee, Phys Ed in Annunciation Gulch – for a week! The regular teacher here appears to have quit mid-year. Surprised she lasted this long. (And yes, in case you're wondering, other than in the matter of locker room duty, PE teachers are now interchangeable by gender, as all PE is coed.) This is the sort of job where it's a good day if you can just take attendance, since the absence of the usual restraints of desks and walls can make even this seemingly basic task quite difficult. In gym, you generally do this with the kids sitting on numbered spots on the floor, but some of the girls in my classes won't actually set foot in the gym for the entire week that I'm here. If and when I can get finished checking off attendance on the ones who are actually on their assigned number spots, or at least inside the building, I then have to check on the ones who've gone feral and spend the entire period outside the building. Some I can't get close get enough to to get a name.

The upside of PE, on the other hand, is that there's almost always at least one other class in the gym with yours, so there's another teacher who knows and is known by some of the students. Of course, once in a while the other gym teacher's going to be a sub too, in which case you might be better off being alone. Fortunately, this week there's a regular in here with me, a guy from the islands – Jamaican, I think – whom the kids call by his last name, no Mr. – something you sometimes get in PE. He's got a reasonable grip on his classes, although not so much that he can afford to divert any kind of time to keeping mine in line. No telling what they were doing before I came, but in all of my five classes combined there's really only one kid who does much of anything, which I let him know. It turns out he's only just recently transferred in from another school. I hope he holds up.

I broke up my first fight this week. At least I think it was my first, I can't ever remember doing in it Boston. Middle school would about be my limit for trying this sort of thing, as I'm not about to get into the middle of two high school guys. It's not actually clear to me what you're expected to do in these situations these days. The potential for parents getting litigious about your laying your hands on their child always looms, but are you supposed to just let them pound each other? Today's fight took place in the locker room too, where the situation can much more easily get way out of hand. One thing I did learn, though, is that a Full Nelson is not the right hold for breaking up a fight – they can kick backward at you.

I also resolved to be more selective with my humor this week. In addition to subbing, I have also been working evenings doing phone sales for the San Francisco Opera and sitting next to this really funny guy. We aren't making any money to speak of, but we do laugh an awful lot in between phone calls. Once in a while I have to hang up the phone because a prospective customer has picked up while I'm laughing too hard to break into a serious sales pitch. One night my co-worker was going on about this Monty Python routine in which one of them tells the other, "I'll shoot you," so the next day I used the line on one of the kids who was not being cooperative in my daily struggle to take attendance. This twelve-year-old from the projects apparently wasn't a big Python fan, and he responded by telling me who'd shoot me in response if I shot him. Since he appeared to be much more in earnest than I had been, I now mostly save any good Monty Python lines for kids more likely to be familiar with PBS and BBC broadcasting.

RAISED EYEBROW — *Science, J.P. Morgan Middle, April 21, 1997*

This will be my last time here for Mr. D. He asked me to do another week for him but I told him that I couldn't because I would be going to work on the upcoming election in Bosnia. He seemed a bit taken aback by my plans to go to a place that everyone considers really dangerous, but that may only be because he teaches at Morgan. He might not have questioned my judgment if he taught at Gregor Mendel or, say, if he were a sub. After a stint at Ishi Middle School a couple of days later, where just getting the kids to walk down the hall from the classroom to the library is a major undertaking, I can hardly wait to get to Bosnia.

*****

BACK TO COMBAT *– Phys Ed, Calvin Coolidge Middle, August 29, 1997*
August 29! This is not just school before Labor Day, it's in August! Is this even legal? Do we need further proof that the Communists have taken over in San Francisco – or California, for that matter?

The PE teachers here take my name down because they tell me there's a lot of subs who won't do PE, so they don't want to forget me. I'm doing them for now and the novelty of wearing sneakers and sweat pants to school will probably get me through a few more, anyhow. Not that that's so very different from what some regular, that is to say, non-PE teachers wear these days.

Used to be I'd do a lot of PE. I spent enough time in the Brighton High PE office to play on the faculty softball team. Still have my cloisonne key ring an Art class made for the team members when it won the Boston faculty championship. My teammates included Brighton's famous Mahoney brothers, the elder of whom managed a Park League baseball team named after him, and Crude McCool. Crude and I had lived on the same dorm corridor freshman year at Boston College, but, he being a football player and I pretty much the opposite of that, it wasn't until the Brighton High PE Office that we got to know each other. I still admire the camaraderie of PE departments I first experienced there. Plus, they played lacrosse in the gym, with a plastic trash can strung up for a goal, and a period or two of that has turned out to be my only experience with the game. Crude, by the way, left the planet some time back and if you want to know how he got the nickname, you'll have to ask me privately.

And while we're on the subject, then there was that day in swimming class at Cappuccino High School when my job essentially was to watch high school girls in bikinis. And I can't even swim. If they knew that they probably would have arrested me or something. I figured there must be a lot of middle-aged guys who'd *pay* to do this job. Anyhow, I have drifted steadily away from PE because my time there is essentially spent walking kids back and forth, standing, and watching – but I have not forgotten its appeals.

But no time for such reveries. I'm back from Bosnia to reality and ready for real combat. And today I'm breaking up my second school fight. This time it's in the gym and I now know to forget the Full Nelson and go straight to the headlock, so I'm soon holding one of the combatants in the crook of each arm until a real teacher comes along and takes them away. Never had to do that in Bosnia. We had troops backing us up there; no one tried nothing.

IN CHARGE *– Principal (!), Yi He Elementary School, September 2, 1997*
Today, the phone machine asks me if I would like to substitute for the principal of Yi He Elementary School. And why, yes, as a matter of fact, I would. Talk about rapid advancement – I'm only in this system for a few months and already I'm considered principal material. This never happened in Boston! Of course, the one thing that you know you won't be doing when you're called in to sub for the principal is actually sub for the principal. The reason for the call is that the union contract requires it, as insurance that classes do not go uncovered if some regular teacher steps in for the principal. You might actually

23

sub for the teacher who does that, but most likely you'll be filing, answering the phone, and the like.

Nevertheless, I do believe in taking my responsibilities seriously, even if the system doesn't, so I always try to ingratiate myself with my office staff by making a point of asking if there's anything special I can do for them while I'm in charge. Is there, for instance, any new office furniture they've had their eye that I could maybe order for them? Or do they have friends or relatives they'd like me to hire? Generally I receive blank stares in return and go on about my filing. But you never know.

ORIGINS – *Something or other, Gilbert Middle, September 24, 1997*

Who invented middle schools anyhow? I've only ever heard one person come up with any kind of reasonable justification for their existence – that they made life safer for the littler kids who otherwise might be injured by oblivious middle school-age kids running over them if they were all in the same building. But it seems to me that if we can develop space suits to keep men alive on the moon, we should be able to develop some kind of safety padding for these little kids.

I mean how can having kids of this age set off all by themselves possibly be a good thing for society? First of all, this gives them the idea that what they see around them all day is normal, perhaps even acceptable – not a message we should want to suggest to these kids. Whatever other criticisms we might make about the human race, it's simply not fair to characterize its behavior during grades six through eight as *normal*. So far as I can recall from those years, the hope of looking cool to littler kids, or at least not embarrassing yourself in front of them, was a very useful check on the powerful attraction idiotic behavior holds at that age. Odd, isn't it, that in the course of history no one appears to have ever stepped forward and claimed to be the one who thought up the idea of middle schools? Hitler, Stalin and Walter O'Malley owned up to their deeds, but the inventor of middle schools lived and died anonymously.

One too many twelve-year-old girls sucking her tongue in disgust at my mispronunciation of her name in roll call can get me to thinking thoughts like this.

PACKING – *Principal, Waterfront Middle, October 7, 1997*

Today, being substitute principal means boxing up the school's completed California state tests – in case you thought a middle school principal's work wasn't important. And the fact is that I do have the training for this job. I was once a Christmas season packer in the sub- basement at Macy's Herald Square – the largest store in the world, so I learned my packing with the best. How many middle school principals with this type of packing background could there be in San Francisco? These Waterfront kids have no way of knowing just what qualified hands their work is in. And how did the sub machine happen to call me out of the list of hundreds? Intelligent design?

I do a four-day stint for this guy later in the year. The best thing about subbing for the principal at Waterfront is that it means that he won't be here. Right now, he's with the eighth grade in Yosemite for four days. What fun; they deserve each other. My principal duties include standing in the lunchroom, monitoring an after-school street crossing, patrolling the yard during "nutrition break" (when the kids get to eat chocolate donuts and such) and the halls afterwards, packing thirteen boxes of material from the recently administered standardized "STAR" (Standardized Testing and Reporting) test, handing out late passes in the counselor's office, making up room-use folders for the next several months, and breaking up a fight between two girls (it's harder to get a bear hug on them in an appropriate place). Normally you need a special credential in administration to do this sort of stuff.

On my last day here I am called into the girls Gender Academy to fill in for another sub who's late arriving. The Gender Academy is an experiment in dividing the sexes within the same school. The experiment does not last long, and if my experience was typical, I can see why. Ultimately I have to call a counselor up to help bring order to the class. She seems surprised that I called and tells me this is the best group in the school. I might agree if the considerations were hair dressing, trying on clothes, or arm-wrestling. I grab the hands of the arm wrestlers to get them to stop, and one of them is later muttering about suing me if I touch her again. Another mutters about how I'm prejudiced. I am not sure what group she thinks I'm prejudiced against, unless maybe it's obnoxious pubescent girls and she may have me on that one. Let's say we don't like each other.

WAY OUT WEST – *This and that, Castillo Elementary, October 14, 1997*

Like Morgan, Castillo is "out on the Avenues," as they say in San Francisco – at least as they used to say. This is the Sunset District, a world apart from the places I've mostly been to lately. Historically, San Francisco has been the odd city where living on the ocean was considered déclassé. With the exception of a few spots like the Cliff House and the reopened Beach Chalet at the end of Golden Gate Park, not a lot of tourists get to the ocean in San Francisco. The San Francisco that people visit was built a couple of right turns off the Pacific, on the bay, a place where a ship might safely land, and where it happens to be sunnier.

This is the fog belt. And in a city where newcomers may ask one another if the neighborhoods they live in are sunny or cloudy, that is not a small matter. There's a monument on the Peninsula marking the spot where Spaniards first spotted San Francisco Bay, previous explorers having sailed up the coast past what we now call the Golden Gate because it was fogged in.

Anyhow, the eastern part of San Francisco is generally where the rich and poor live; the Avenues was for the "middle class." In 1940, Herb Caen, the columnist who told San Franciscans about themselves for over fifty years, described outer Geary Boulevard as "where a great city dissolves without self-consciousness into a small town." After World War II, block after perfectly rectangular block filled with $5,000 GI-Bill-financed "Sunset Specials" – one story above a garage, in three or four basic styles. Today, a lot of the signs Caen remembered as "'Jimmy's' and 'Pat and Johnny's' and 'Sam's,'" are in Chinese, and a house out there costs a whole lot more than it used to.

But it still ain't the San Francisco the tourists come to see. There's no cable cars, no drag queens, not many coffee houses, or hills, even. Just the Avenues gently rolling down to the Pacific Ocean and the fog rolling up them. It feels very quiet out in the Avenues on a foggy night. And Castillo is *way* out on the Avenues.

Today is a little-bit-of-this, little-of-that day. Go take Ms. So-and-so's class for an hour while she has a parent conference, sit here in the office until we think of something, and the like. For a while I have a first grade class. It is stunningly peaceful in this room compared to what I'm used to. The kids sit quietly at my feet as I read to them. They pass a stuffed kangaroo around to whichever student wants to talk. I tell them that a kangaroo is a marsupial. A lot of them repeat "marsupial," without my even prompting them. An older father comes in to read with some of the kids. You won't get that sort of thing in every neighborhood.

TOUGH SCHOLARS – *Something, Edward R. Murrow Middle, November 6, 1997*

Back on the east side of town and there's nothing at all peaceful about the Edward R. Murrow Middle School. This is the place where the principal calls the kids scholars – he's trying to convince them, presumably. A sub once discussed her month-long stint here at a union meeting. She filed a police report on one student and had her car window shot out. She concluded that "They've got some pretty tough little scholars there."

After you've been there, you realized that everything you needed to know about the place was on the recording on the school department machine. It went: "Edward R. Murrow Middle School, 1195 Hudsons Avenue, corner of Whitney Young Circle. It's near the east off of Third Street, about six blocks up from the Third Street, on the top end of the hill, next to the hill top part." In other words, nothing about this place is easy.

One time I came down here to pick up some surveys for the teachers union, because the deadline day had arrived but none of the surveys from Edward R. Murrow had. I walked in the front door to witness a boy throwing a girl down on the floor in front of the main office and an adult trying to explain that this is not acceptable behavior, even if it was the case, as the boy insisted, that he was "just playing." When someone finally got around to me, I asked after the surveys. There were none done. You could see how being here might make it difficult to keep up with non-essential paperwork.

I find myself continually having to remember that those patient, less harried administrators that I often encounter in the "better" schools are not necessarily any better or more concerned than the administrators in the "bad" schools, it's just that they have fewer things to worry about. So I guess I shouldn't be surprised when the poorly informed critics who've never spent any time in the schools think that the problem in a school like this is that the teachers or the administrators just don't care.

Edward R. Murrow College Preparatory Academy closed at the end of the 2006-2007 academic year.

WET – *Second Grade, Henry Ward Beecher Elementary, December 8, 1997*
      One tough elementary school here, or as the woman in the office puts it, "They're a handful." And this was second grade. The most noteworthy event of the day was a career-first in-class pants-wetting. Must remember to loosen the bathroom allowance threshold for the elementary school bladder.

MAS CHEVERE – *This and that, Buenos Dias Elementary, January 20, 1998*
      "Buenos Dias – la escuela mas chevere," according to the bumperstickers you see around town – maybe the trendiest public elementary school in San Francisco. To get their kids into the school, parents have to demonstrate a commitment to raise them bilingually in Spanish and English.

      If it does nothing else, any kind of "magnet school" sorts out the kids from families that, for whatever reason, are not organized enough to proceed through the application process. So if you've steered away the kids from dysfunctional households who will likely do worse at school and be more trouble than average, you've probably started with a boost above the average right there. At a place like Buenos Dias, when teachers call home they can expect to at least find someone in a position to try to deal with whatever a kid might be doing or not. Not so everywhere.

      The symbiosis here is that Latino kids – who I assume are mostly from the adjacent Mission District – are mixed with native-English speakers probably drawn by the appeal of the bilingual program from somewhat more affluent families whose presence will likely raise the level of academic expectation. And it comes with a touch of socialist ethos – at times the school has had a "head teacher" rather than an principal.

      Another day here, I'm subbing for a teacher who has a student teacher who wants to go it alone. So, although I think it's technically illegal not to have a credentialed person in the room, (though she could have the same Thirty Day Emergency Credential that I have, I suppose), I am doing office help like I did the last time I was here – xeroxing and delivering newsletters, answering phones, folding paper for classroom "books," sorting mail, delivering kids to class and issuing late passes to late students. My favorite reason for being late was "My mother took a bath and didn't know what to wear."

      Among my more traditional educational duties, I supervise the yard during recess where a couple of girls come up to me barking because they are playing dog. I'm also called in to play bad cop in a fourth grade Math class in the afternoon. When I tell a kid he's got to leave for disrupting the class, he knocks over a chair, tells me to stop yelling at him when I address him in a firm voice, tells me I look like Frankenstein, and runs away from me in the hall. Someone's pride and joy at home no doubt; just another rude little boy in school. At the end of the day I handle kindergarten dismissal, where the kids have to wait on a bench until their parents pick them up. So when people ask me what I've been teaching lately, well the question just doesn't begin to encompass the job.

TOO BAD – *Fourth Grade, Ernest Everett Just Elementary, January 27, 1998*

This was a very late call for a two-day fourth grade assignment. I generally try to avoid more-than-one day assignments at any school I haven't been to before, but I figured this is an elementary school and the call was so late that there would be only four hours left in the first day by the time I arrived and that included lunch. So how bad could this be? I had my answer before lunch.

The kids were horrible. That's plain HORRIBLE – rude, mean, nasty. They wouldn't shut up. They wouldn't do anything I tried to get them to do. They were just not going to cooperate no way A boy starts beating up a girl early on, so I have him removed, but this doesn't appreciably improve things. And here I'm just done claiming that actual in-classroom fights are rarities, but I do so few elementary schools that I'd forgotten that this sort of thing actually does happen there. And I've also been claiming that middle schools are the worst in every way. Okay, maybe not *every* way. And I certainly need to qualify my characterization of the Gettysburg Middle School fight – it was the only in-classroom, mixed gender fight I've experienced in one of the upper weight divisions.

Anyhow, very quickly I'm scrambling just to make it through to lunch without any more kids pounding each other. I'm taking names down for retribution real quick, which is accomplishing about nothing. After all, the kids no doubt knew before I did that I wouldn't be coming back tomorrow. Certainly they knew before I did that the reason I'd been called so late was that another teacher had already quit this morning.

I hated these kids, which a pretty amazing thing to say about a bunch of nine-year-olds, and I wasn't happy about feeling that way, but it was so. They were mean as middle school kids can be, and with significantly less maturity – this was seventh circle of hell stuff. And all of this chaos is happening in an "open classroom" setting – a very large room containing several classes. For the most part, distance and bookcases and such effectively separate one class from the other, but there are no walls. You're usually not seeing any other classes – but you sure can hear them. Any big disruption – such as we are having continuously – is common knowledge.

By lunchtime, it is clear that I won't be picking up my option on the second day, but I do still have the afternoon to get through. My only real shot at establishing any kind of order is having something clearly defined for them to work on individually, so I need to copy enough math papers for everyone. The secretary won't let me use the photocopier, though; she says she'll do it for me. And she doesn't. This place is starting to look like the Stanford Experiment.

With this type of support behind me, I battle on into the afternoon, until I decide I absolutely have to have someone come in here to bring these kids to some kind of order, probably by removing a few more of them. When I call the office looking for the person to do that, I am given another number to call. The person at that number says she'll come. And she doesn't. For all I know, the entire administration of this place walked out this morning, along with that other sub. And if it is still here, it apparently has more important things to do than helping a substitute get a runaway class in hand.

And then a *deus ex-machina* worthy of Euripides! There being effectively no administration in this school, I am not so surprised as I might have been in a real school when a woman not on the school staff suddenly appears in my classroom. She is the mother of one of the children. My immediate concern is whether she's going to be part of the solution or part of the problem. Is she going to help me with this mess, or blame me for it?

As it turns out, she is with me. The kids behave for her immediately. After she's there for a little while and some kind of order is achieved, she asks if I'll be back tomorrow, in which case she could give me some tips about dealing with them. But by then I have firmly decided that I don't want to see these kids or this school – again for, say, ten years. And there is really no reversing that feeling, so I just shake my head no. "They were too bad?" she says. I just nod, at which point she starts muttering to herself, "It's embarrassing. People come and try to help and they act this way." She asks if her daughter was bad. I have a list in my breast pocket of who was naughty (and nobody was nice) from the morning, which I take out and show her daughter's name with the check mark next to it for double bad. She has been about the rudest child of that age that I could ever remember having met.

I later regret not asking the daughter to repeat for her mother the story she had been telling the class earlier – at which point I could not get her to shut up – about her cousin with the gun in his closet and how cool that was, but I think that at the time I just did not want to add to this hardworking woman's troubles – she had just popped in on her lunchtime from San Francisco General Hospital wearing her purple SEIU jacket and hadn't been planning on doing riot control.

When I go to the office at the end of the day and tell the secretary that, like the first substitute, I also won't be coming back, her response is, "That's understandable." I guess there was no point getting the copying done or showing up in my classroom if they knew I wouldn't be coming back. However useless the people running this place might be, you couldn't say they were out of touch with reality.

TAPE – *Seventh Grade, Samuel Adams Middle, February 18, 1998*

A momentous day in this sub's life – the day I decided I'd start taking serious notes. (Henceforth, fewer days headed "something or other.") And the day my laptop was stolen, which is, I guess, what made me decide I'd better keep notes because I might want to tell this story sometime. And what better location than back at the first San Francisco school I subbed in?

By now kids in a number of schools know me as the sub with the laptop. I'm never without it, except in Physical Education classes and elementary school. You can't really pull it out in PE and in elementary school there is really no time to make any use of it. I've always preferred to be in high school than elementary, but a large part of why I put up with middle school is that there are prep periods and even classroom periods when you can read and write while maintaining order and keeping the kids on track. Of course I never had a laptop back when I subbed in Boston, but the ability to use a computer during slack time is probably my deal with the devil – the reason I've continued in this insane job.

I've got four regular classroom periods today, but fourth period goes downstairs to computer lab after first meeting in the classroom. My computer was open on my desk as it usually is, even if I can only look at in passing period or something. Naturally I thought about packing it up and bringing it down with me, except that I was only supposed to be delivering the kids to the computer room and would be coming right back up here. Since I had the key to the room, I decided I'd just lock the door and it wouldn't be a problem. But when I returned, no computer.

So, down to the principal's office. She is quite pleasant about the whole thing and immediately turns the case over to the Dean, Mrs. T, the woman who had previously impressed me. Over the course of the rest of the day, I learned that this was Mrs. T's thirty-sixth year in the San Francisco school system, and that it would be her last, and that they were going to miss her here – a lot.

When I brought the class down to the computer lab, two kids had shown up late and gave me some ragtime explanation about where they were, so I told them go to the office to get a pass. They returned empty handed a few minutes later, claiming that the principal told them to just go back to class without one. You can see how they might not have wanted to explain that they needed a pass for the span of time when they were stealing my computer. The amazing part, though, is that I ultimately let them in without it.

Later, when these same two guys seem to have trouble understanding me as I pass out their progress reports, although they have no problem with the English language, I'm pretty sure we have our perpetrators identified. The only questions are whether they have already gotten the computer out of the school, and whether Mrs. T can break them over the course of the last two periods of the day. And I actually don't have much doubt on the latter question.

Sure enough, after lunch comes the phone call telling me that Mrs. T has gotten the computer back. The kids' M.O. turns out to be taping the door so it wouldn't lock. They taped the door! They'd had larceny in their hearts for a couple of periods and silly me, I hadn't seen it, sedated, as I was, by the illusory security of having the key in my pocket. And when they swiped the computer, they'd passed it right off to someone else. A combination of ingenuity, sophistication and childishness that would probably lead to their first arrests in the not too distant future.

Mrs. T is in fine form at the end of the day. She's been pulling kids into her office all afternoon, telling them that she herself is at risk because the school has not reported the theft, and at any point I might just opt to tell the police myself. It worked. The principal suggests that I might want to get Mrs. T flowers or something, as she probably had reason to feel under-appreciated within the system. I return the next day with a bouquet.

MY FRIEND – Sixth Grade Guidance Counselor, J.P. Morgan Middle, February 23, 1998

Today I am a sixth grade guidance counselor which as practical matter is essentially a disciplinarian. When the probation officer comes to visit a school, he deals with the guidance counselor, so it's a sort of a gateway position to the criminal justice system. Today I will be on the receiving end of those "referral" slips I write up as student ejection tickets.

Now I have to introduce you to an old friend who has maybe been subbing a bit too long – mostly in middle schools, no less. His views have become so extreme over the years that I cannot mention his name – or even his initial in order to protect him from the disapprobation of family, friends, and decent society in general, so I shall refer to him only as My Friend the Evil Substitute Teacher.

My Friend The Evil Substitute Teacher says his favorite subbing assignment is actually sitting in for a middle school guidance counselors, as I am doing today. He believes that the first principle guiding a middle school counselor should be to encourage kids living through some of the most turbulent years of their lives to believe in themselves, to get in touch with themselves, to trust their own instincts. So when one of them gets sent out of class for his obsession with farting, say, and says no one likes him and that sort of thing, My Friend the Evil Substitute Teacher says he reaffirms his instincts, tells the student he understands why he feels that way and that he is right to feel that way. In fact, he is actually probably being very perceptive – it is likely the case that no one does like him, given how he probably generally behaves, and certainly how he's just been behaving. Even the suicidal ones My Friend the Evil Substitute Teacher tells to trust their feelings. (He claims he's tried to get Dr. Kevorkian appointed as consulting physician to one of the schools he subs at.) I don't know how frequently My Friend the Evil Substitute Teacher is called for counseling assignments, but he is not pursuing a counseling credential, at least so far as I know.

HERE'S JOHNNY – Special Ed, J.P. Morgan Middle, February 24, 1998

I'm not sure what all the rules and regulations actually say – this is pretty complicated stuff – but roughly speaking, "Special Education" students generally seem divided into two types: kids who test low on IQ tests and the like; and kids who "act out" in class. It can certainly be hard going with the first group, but if you can do it you always feel like you're doing God's work. A day with the second type usually feels more like Satan's work.

Today I am with a bunch of the latter and they are bad enough that I have the assistant principal sitting in for the entire last two periods – and the kids still aren't that good. And I already have a paraprofessional (generally referred to here as a teacher's aide or para) which is standard for Special Ed, so at this point there's three of us. I've been to schools where the whole place is like this class, mind you, but Morgan is out in the Sunset District and it's ranked second-best middle school in the city (big middle schools, anyhow – there's a couple of small ones also ranked better), so this class sticks out here. Unfortunately, the AP (Assistant Principal) wasn't in the classroom earlier in the day, when a mother arrived and took her daughter away over the objections of the para who understood the mother not to have legal custody of the child. She called security, but too late – they got away.

And a fire drill today. My Friend the Evil Substitute Teacher loves fire drills when he has bad classes. He says he makes a major effort to keep the kids calm and explains the importance of not running or panicking – in case it is a real fire. And he says that he also tries to keep them in the classroom, calm, as long as possible – in case it is a real fire, in which case he plans to run out at the last possible moment – by himself. Fortunately, My Friend the Evil Substitute Teacher has not yet been assigned to an actually burning school.

When I subbed in Boston, kids used to think I looked like George Carlin. A friend maintained that they just thought all white guys cracking one-liners looked the same, but whatever the reason then, no one says it now. His hair is a lot grayer now, and mine is a lot lesser, and besides no school kid knows who George Carlin is anymore. Nowadays it's Jack Nicholson, which is a very positive development from a professional point of view. The movie the kids are most likely to mention in this regard is *The Shining,* where Nicholson's character is positively demented.

Now, a sub is always looking for a little extra something and a persona with a certain deranged edge to it can be just that. If even just a couple of your middle school students subconsciously fear that you might have a knife with a ten inch blade in your briefcase, this is not a bad thing. One of many reasons I'll never sit through the education classes required for a real teaching certificate is that there are some things you've either got or you don't. They can't teach fear in a classroom.

I am offered the opportunity to return to this class on Friday, but I decline. I do feel bad about turning down these difficult classes, but my deal with myself on these is that after every other substitute in the system has been to them once, I'll come back.

ONE OUT OF FIVE AIN'T BAD – *Unknown, Osgood Conklin Elementary, March 21, 1998*

By the time Friday afternoon rolls around, there's a lot of people who have a hard time remembering exactly what they were doing at work on Monday morning. But by Friday I don't always even remember *where* I was working on Monday. In fact, I might have trouble remembering where I was on Wednesday without checking my "demand sheet," also known in San Francisco as the "green sheet" – the one the school secretary signs the principal's name to at the end of the day.

This week is slated to be different so far as remembering though, in that I've got a week-long assignment at Osgood Conklin. Not to be, though. As soon as I get there on Monday, the principal informs me that subs didn't usually stay more than one day with this class. Give her credit for full disclosure, anyhow. It seems that the regular teacher recently quit right in the middle of a school day and took her posters off the walls in front of the class before she left. The principal described the class as "wounded."

And the class is, in fact, off-the-wall nuts. For most of the morning there are two other adults in the room with me trying to keep the most minimal order. Teaching is simply impossible; our aspirations go only so far as keeping them in their seats. "Grief counselors" arrive in the afternoon, A girl in the back keeps asking them, "What are you doing here?" The counselors ignore her question.

I've seen enough by lunchtime. I'm not particularly looking forward to telling the principal that, but I needn't have worried. When I actually do tell her I won't be coming back tomorrow, her reaction is, "You will stay the afternoon?" And, yes, I was planning to do that. So I figure I got off pretty cheap in feeling like I was doing something positive by finishing one day out of five. The regular teacher hadn't finished her last day, after all. The way I figure, there is absolutely nothing I am going to be able to do with this class, so they won't be any worse off with someone else.

A friend of mine who lives near this school has several times mentioned that when he passes he notices the teachers have a hard time even getting the kids to line up, and that he's seen kids from the school chasing dogs around with sticks. Not coincidentally, this school lies catty-corner from a housing project that was dangerous to even go near – I recall reading of at least two instances of people being hit by stray bullets just passing by. The project has since been razed to the ground and rebuilt. We will hope for better luck next time.

SUNDAE SCHOOL – *Cooking, Waterfront Middle, March 23, 1998*

I used to get a lot more of these strange assignments in Boston. At one point I was the first sub off the bench in the Brighton High Automotive Program – in both classroom and shop programs. And I barely knew how to open the hood of a car, whereas, so far as this situation goes, I can use a toaster with the best of them. I actually have many fine memories of my 1970s *Welcome Back Kotter* days with the grease monkeys in Brighton. I'm not sure that "teachable moments" had actually been identified in the 70s, but one particularly stands out in hindsight.

It was a day when one of my budding mechanics decided that he would roll a joint during class. Having absorbed at least some of the lessons of serious craftsmen, he logically sought a level stable surface for his work. Since this was a classroom instruction day, rather than a shop day, that level surface was his desktop. For my part, being the level-headed, hip, 1970s substitute that I then was, I decided to reason with the boy and pointed out to him that his activity could be seen from the hall through the window in the classroom door. Acknowledging the logic of my argument, he transferred his materials to his lap and we proceeded with the class. After that day, I'll bet that no administrator ever looked through a door and caught that guy rolling a joint on his desk – and I'll take some credit for that. Of course, that was before decades of drug education created the unfortunate chasm between students and teachers that we live with today – and when marijuana was cheap enough for high school students to roll joints.

Of course, those kids were more in their element in the auto shop – that is, the garage – anyhow. They used to work on teachers' cars for practice. There'd always be another automotive teacher in with me, but the garage was pretty big, so that other teacher might be pretty far away. One day we had a kid screwing around with a screwdriver who managed to find a soft spot under the hood and puncture it. The other teacher on duty, that is, the actual mechanic on the premises, rushed over sputtering, but it was too late. I'm guessing the teacher who owned the car didn't come back for free servicing any more.

But enough of the flashbacks. Cooking is much more San Francisco-in-the-nineties than auto shop, anyhow. It's a partial-semester elective and today is the first meeting for this batch. I'm to show them a Ben & Jerry's video, and give them an assignment of designing a ice cream sundae and then a plan for promoting it on Chestnut Street, the nearby chic shopping area. And the winner will get – a sundae. Not a terribly tough assignment, nonetheless one guy does get thrown out of ice cream class. He tells me that he'll see me in hell, although he denies that he was actually speaking to me. No ice cream sundaes in hell they tell me. No freezers. There's middle school there, though, I imagine.

HI, TOM – *Kindergarten/First Grade, Benjamin Banneker Elementary, March 24, 1998*

Benjamin Banneker is an "alternative" school in the Bayview District, an area where the tourists never go unless they get lost, not too far from Candlestick Park (which these days is actually known as 3Com (sic) Park, the naming rights being available to the highest bidder as is now the custom). The school is racially-mixed and white parents try to get their kids into it because it's seen as successful.

There's quite a few "alternative" schools in San Francisco and as far as I can figure, the only thing they have in common is that parents have to request that their kids go there. Although this one doesn't have a specialty like the bilingual program at Buenos Dias, the same phenomenon is in play here as well – sorting out a lot of kids who don't have someone at home up to the task of analyzing alternative schools. There's a good number of "middle class" parents who might otherwise decide to send their kids to private schools who'd like to send them to an integrated school if they didn't think they were putting them at risk. (And, of course, they'd save a lot of money while feeling they were doing the right thing.) And the more of those kids you lose, the harder it becomes to keep the rest and the more isolated the black kids become. (I abstract, of course, from the actual four "race" make-up of the San Francisco system where Chinese and Latinos play as prominent a role, but historically, it's the black/white dynamic that has been defining in American public education and it's still the situation of the black kids that grabs your attention even in a more complex situation like San Francisco's.) These are the realities in a society of great inequality, with a "peculiar" history.

One unusual thing about Benjamin Banneker is that it is a first name school, that is, everyone here is called by their first name, including the principal. So I'll be walking down the hall here and kids I don't even recognize are saying, "Hi, Tom" as they pass. Takes a little getting used to. I've got a K-1 class today that I've had before. Not easy, but there's a para today, and she's big and tough, so things are manageable One kid gets put on the computer to keep him out of trouble. (This might be considered a reward in another setting, but hey, who knows, he might learn something this way.) Girls ask me to be their daddy; I'm guessing there might not be one at home. One little girl named Cassandra has the greatest whine. It gets frequent practice as she is often in trouble for throwing things at other kids, and the like.

Have my first pre-kindergarten class at Benjamin Banneker – for the last 40 minutes of the day only. This is in the company of another adult, of course. There is no way I'd take kids this little by myself; I don't even know if it'd be legal. The kids are all, "Look at what I'm making" and I'm giving them lifts in the playground to hang on the bars. Three of them are on the ground barking like dogs. They're so small that they've got their names pinned on them in case they get lost.

Student Name of the Day: Mae Bea (pronounced "maybe") Green

MEMORIAL – *First Grade, Pamplona Elementary, March 25, 1998*

Another first grade in an area equally obscure, but at the other end of town and toward the other end of the social structure from the Bayview District – Mt. Davidson, the tallest of San Francisco's hills, just across from the much better known Twin Peaks. Visually it's known for the cross where a crowd greets the dawn each Easter near the top of the hill. A few years ago the city thought it wise to sell off the patch of land the cross stands on in order to avoid the perception of public support of religion – a charge not that frequently made against San Francisco, at least not these days. Otherwise, unlike Twin Peaks, if you don't know someone on the hill there's not much up there that you'd be likely to visit. The principal tells me he's lived in San Francisco for 60 years and he's gotten lost around here.

On my way in, I notice a picture of a little girl in the foyer. Underneath is written the years of her life, ending this year. I figure a traffic accident or something, but she turns out to be a girl I read about in the newspaper. Her mother went off the edge just a couple of days ago, tied her three kids' hands, then covered their mouths and noses with duct tape. It happened in Daly City, so I didn't connect it, but this girl was one of those kids. The day started with an outdoor memorial service for her.

Two days later I'm back again for a third grade teacher who spotted me seeing the kids to their buses after school the first day. A girl named Sydney comes in before class to take down the chairs from the tables and tell me who is rough, who is gentle, who is nice, and who does their work.

I confiscate a lot of toys today. One girl asks if I have ever been to this class before. I tell her no, but ask why she asked. She says she wants to know, "Are you the sub who told the class to shut the hell up?" I tell her I am not; just some other Jack Nicholson look-alike, I guess. And I think, "Good for him." Was My Friend the Evil Substitute Teacher here and he didn't mention it?

In the teachers' lunchroom a particularly difficult student comes up in conversation. One teacher says, "Has anyone thought of binding and gagging her?" and immediately realizes that this was not the thing to say at this school at this time.

DOING TIME – Detention, Samuel Adams Middle, March 30, 1998

You read that right – detention. Sam Adams is the only school I've been to that runs an in-school detention program. There's actually a lot to be said for this. You can get kids out of classes they are disrupting and at the same time at least they won't just be at home watching TV or running the streets. Of course, you've got to have an available body to supervise this. The District's probably not going to knowingly fund a slot for it and teachers are probably not going to want to give up a prep period to do it. But today, somehow I am that available body.

So here I am in a room of wall-to-wall middle school pains-in-the-ass. The question of the day for these kids is whether they can manage to serve their time without getting in any further trouble. They may not be learning a tangible skill like license plate making, but they are at least learning how to do time. At one point, I look out the window and see a girl I let out to go to the bathroom out in the yard playing. She returns 53 minutes later. So she still hasn't learned her time-serving lesson and presumably will be invited back for more tomorrow. For all I know, she may still be studying in that detention room to this day. Is any Ed school yet offering a certificate program in Detention, I wonder.

I'm here another time on a three day assignment of subbing to the second degree, which is to say that I am subbing for another sub, when I witness Mrs. T do her stuff once again. I have to call her for help with a problem student and she tells me that she will hang up the phone, but that I should just keep talking as if she were still on and she'll be there before I know it. I do and she is. She gets 'em every time with this one. She takes two hostages and order is restored. The sub I'm replacing had to go to San Diego because her father had a heart attack and when it turns out that he will have open heart surgery, I'm offered the job for the week.

I tell them I'll get back to them on that, and by the time of my Honors class, which isn't even very good on the second day, I'm already pretty sure I won't be picking up my option. By lunchtime, I'm sure enough that I figure I ought to go to the office and tell them so they'll have more lead time to get another sub for the rest of the week. I just plain don't like these classes. Certainly if it weren't for Mrs. T, I wouldn't even be here today.

I do still have the rest of the day to do battle, though, and so I attempt the good fight, quieting them down by whatever means available. By this point, I'm beginning each class letting them know that I am already aggravated from the last class and intend to cut them no slack, which does have impact. By the end of seventh period the paraprofessional who's accompanying a Pakistani girl in the class tells me that she's never seen them so quiet before. It had occurred to me about half way through the period that things actually were going better than I thought they would and I thought about reneging on my decision to leave, but the price of bad vibing students all day long is more than I want to pay. And why not go out on top? I never feel great about deciding not to come back to a tough school – obviously these kids have greater need for whatever you might be able to give, but if I'm going to keep doing this, I figure I've got to minimize the situations that I think I'm going to hate.

So that was my last day at the first school I ever subbed at in San Francisco. It is, by the way, one of the relatively few upper schools where teachers still eat together. One teacher walks in with a Beatles book because Linda McCartney died yesterday. She has 33 Beatles books. The first "Who's your favorite Beatle?" discussion I've heard in a very long time ensues. So I'll miss that.

Samuel Adams Middle School closed at the end of the 2004-2005 academic year.

NICE? – *Fifth Grade, Benjamin Banneker Elementary, March 31, 1998*

I've got a student teacher with me today who thinks the kids are being quite bad. As a grizzled veteran sub, I feel obliged to tell her, honey, you ain't seen nothing yet. A few days later I learned that the daughter of someone I know was in this class. She had come home and told her mother that they had a sub that day who was really nice, unlike most of the subs, who she thinks are mean. Whoa! Think I better watch out here. I might be losing my edge. This must not be allowed to get around. Must call My Friend the Evil Substitute Teacher for his thoughts.
Student Name Of The Day: Precious McGee

BRUSHING UP – *Kindergarten to Second Grade Spanish Bilingual,*
 Benjamin Cardozo Elementary, April 1, 1998

This comes with a student teacher who takes over most of the show. One of the nicest classes I've ever had. They have a student maestro of the day. At one point one girl accuses another of hitting her. When I ask the alleged hitter if the charge is true, she covers her ears and won't answer. Hear no evil. When it's popcorn time, there'll be none for her. We teach tooth brushing in this class: the student teacher and I hand out tooth brushes and apply tooth paste. The whirl of activities in these early grades always amazes me. Next they're making Easter baskets. I've got to laugh when I hear the rap about failing schools. Failing at what? Solving all of society's problems?

NOW, THIS I KNOW – Music, Cabot High School, April 16, 1998

This job turns out better than advertised. It was supposed to be a Language Arts job at Sam Adams Middle School, but one of the flaws in the sub system is that it leaves it to individual teachers to update information on their recordings. So this guy's says he works at Sam Adams, but when I arrive they inform me he now teaches music at Cabot High School where I will have to go. Now, having to go to a second school because the teacher no longer works at the one that's on the machine can be a major annoyance on some days, but not today. I'd rather be in a high school in general and this one is considered the best public high school in northern California. I'm guessing this teacher's probably pretty pleased with his transfer too.

Cabot claims some type of continuous existence since 1854, almost since San Francisco was founded. Although there's no entrance exam so far as I know – it's all grades and recommendation, I gather – it's very much like the "exam schools" I knew in New York and Boston. When I lived in the Bronx, there was a trio of them in New York – Bronx Science, Brooklyn Tech and Peter Stuyvesant. Stuyvesant (the setting of *Angela's Ashes* author Frank McCourt's later memoir *Teacher Man*) is apparently the big one these days; back then it was Science.

There was also a Catholic exam school, Regis, in Manhattan, which I went to. Regis was, by virtue of an endowment from a secret founding family, an all-scholarship, all-boys Jesuit school that drew from the entire metropolitan area. Although it was considered harder to get into than Science, it was only open to, and therefore generally only known to the faithful. (After a visit to her old Catholic grammar school in Queens, novelist Mary Gordon once told my friend Josh that things were "the same – Regis for the boys, nothing for the girls.") Four years of Latin was mandatory and the two main tracks were Science and Ancient Greek, science apparently having recently attained parity with the classics.

There is a point to this rambling – that schools like Cabot are familiar and comfortable to me. (What's different here? Girls, Chinese kids, non-Catholics in general, wandering around the campus, no God, and the campus itself – of course, the Regis building, located between 84th, 85th, Park and Madison, would probably sell for more than the whole campus here.) I never subbed in New York, but I did go to Boston Latin a few times. Like Cabot, it's the city's oldest and most prestigious school and at both, Chinese-American parents have protested that their children's access to these schools was unfairly limited by efforts to replicate the city's overall racial/ethnic make-up within them.

There was also some similarity to their faculties, I'd say. When I subbed in Boston I always ate in the teachers' lunchroom and, in my memory's eye, so did a lot of people – a lot more than now – at least in middle and high schools, greater camaraderie still maintaining in elementary. Some schools don't even have faculty lunchrooms anymore – converted to counseling or photocopying. Anyhow, back in Boston, in general I might reasonably expect an interesting conversation in the lunch room, but I remember the Latin lunch room as an exception to that. The teachers I encounter today in a well-appointed lunch room are talking about retirement, prostate operations and such and that's pretty much how I remember the scene at Boston Latin. A lot less spunky at these places.

As for the students, they tell me they're allowed to leave about halfway through class and their story checks out. This surprises me at first, but then I realize that these kids are here because they *haven't* usually been trying to get away with whatever they could, so they are accorded much greater freedom. Now, if you could only explain this wonder of the world to the students who *do* spend all their time trying to figure out how to get away with things ...

My first earthquake drill today. We had no earthquake awareness to speak of at all back east. I'm supposed to say "Duck," and the students are supposed to duck under their desks. But there's only music stands here, so they line up along the walls. Not the class to be in when the Big One hits, I guess. I experienced my first ever earthquake at Appian Way High, actually. Sort of felt something in the lunchroom during a prep period, but wasn't really sure until I noticed the reflection in a plexiglass window going *wah-wah*. Meanwhile, a school lunch worker has been talking through all of this while walking about the room in search of something. When it ends, another luncher comes running in and says, "Did you feel that?" "Feel what?" says the first. You can get a little blase' about feeling the earth move in these parts.

RESPECT – Computer Lab, Nathaniel Hawthorne Middle, April 22, 1998

All Mac's here and I'm PC. One of the posters on the wall is a picture of an Indian saying, "Who's the illegal immigrant, pilgrim?" The regular teacher's name is Mr. Pilgrim, so this is apparently a bit of a joke, but there are also two Che posters, another Cuban poster, and one commemorating the 60th anniversary of the Abraham Lincoln Brigade. The teacher across the hall is wearing shorts. When I was in eighth grade, my teacher, Sister Acquin, wore a floor length black habit, I'll never get used to the dress code here.

Mr. Pilgrim has been very thoughtful. Not only has he has left me a filled-out referral form but also a list of the names most likely to be filled in. He's even left pictures so they can't give fake names! Now this guy is showing the proper respect for subs. And neither of my potential opponents comes girded for battle today, as it turns out.

Back here the next week for a seventh grade Science teacher who also has Salsa Dancing class, but she's coming back for that – fortunately, as I am a much better science sub than I would be a dance sub. The classes are real battles but not beyond the pale. We're doing the human reproductive system and it's very hard to get the kids to read out loud in the first class (it's not cool; many can't read well, etc.), but so far as the topic goes, I find they do remarkably well in the degree to which they are able to concentrate on it all. Sister Thomas certainly never discussed women in labor with us in seventh grade, although the topic would have been useful for one classmate's little sister who had to leave that class the next year to actually go into labor. And we never performed any plays at St. Athanasius like *Nightmare on Puberty Street*, which they're doing here. The kids need parental permission slips signed in order to attend, though. The aide, who's Chinese, says a lot of them are coming back with "No's" – the parents apparently don't want the kids to start practicing like my classmate's little sister did. Wonder what they make of the halls here being festooned with posters about sexual minorities. Very San Francisco.

DANGLING CONVERSATION – Math, Nathaniel Hawthorne Middle, April 23, 1998

A film record of the day would probably show me doing some kind of double take at my first sighting of the big uncombed, unbraided dreadlock mass on the head of the teacher across the hall. My first reaction is that it's a Halloween wig or something, but a quick glance at the calendar shows that we've got six months to go, so this is for real. Maybe Sister Rita had something like that under her bonnet back in sixth grade, but we'll never know.

I've actually got the first two periods off and third and fourth periods are team taught, which for a sub generally means carrying out the other teacher's instructions. Cruising right along here, but a regular teacher informs me that sixth and seventh are "rude and rowdy" – although she says they actually want to learn. And, sure enough, a great day at school is utterly destroyed when I actually meet my own students.

The most ridiculous point comes when the grandmother of a student calls him on the classroom phone to tell him he's to leave school early. I find it simply amazing that the administration would let *any* outside calls come through to a classroom during the school day, much less a call to a student. You'll have a hard time convincing me that anything but an emergency call is not a mistake. Take him out if you must, but don't interrupt the class – is anyone thinking about this? Grandma proceeds to talk to her young James for about a half an hour and I'd have to rip the phone out of his hands to get him off – he's talking to his grandmother, after all, and who am I to get in the middle of that? And what thought processes are going on in this woman's head, talking to him at this length in class? When he's through on the phone he then wants to play on the computer and tells me to shut up when I tell him to get off.

Off to the counselor with him and he slams the door on his way out. One of the kids I let go to the bathroom now shows up a half an hour later, telling me he needed to see the nurse and he's spent all this time looking for her. I send him down to the counselor to see if he can perhaps find her there. During homework period, six kids want to go to the library. I call the librarian who tells me she doesn't want them there. I inform them of this, but they leave anyway. Of course, I don't want them here either, so I shouldn't complain.

HMMM – Computer Lab, Shady Grove Elementary, April 28, 1998

Most elementary schools are very peaceful places compared to middle schools and a calm envelops me on the drive over here and hums on as I walk down the halls past the teachers chatting quietly before class, as I think of Sam Adams, Ghiradelli, and Hawthorne – places where I'm not and am glad I'm not. I work with a kindergarten girl on adding and subtracting on the computer until the numbers got too big – 53, whoa! Help another girl find aardvark in the dictionary. I staple booklets for first graders. All part of keeping America's educational machine humming.

BLINK – Language Arts, Calvin Coolidge Middle, May 1, 1998

The assignment in these Language Arts classes is to read a grammar book aloud, and to my surprise, the students actually do it. Even the bilingual teacher who comes in to borrow the TV seems surprised at this. I tell them they'll be well ahead of most of the rest of the country if they know the grammar rules they're going over. They don't seem impressed. I wish them a happy Mayday and ask if they know what Mayday means. None do. They need to catch up. They're living in a town where it's an actual holiday in at least a few places, like Rainbow Grocery, the city's foremost counter-cultural food emporium.

The last class is well-behaved almost to a fault. At one point I ask if they understand something one of them has read. No one answers. Then I ask them to blink their eyes if anyone can hear me. I think four do. I'm figuring I must be somewhere in *The Twilight Zone*, but I know none of them will know what that means, so I ask if I've entered the *X-Files*. There is no response. I'm starting to worry that some of them are going to go home to their Parental Units and report that a substitute teacher is somehow on to whatever mission they were sent to earth to carry out. I think maybe I shouldn't come back here tomorrow.

IT STINKS – Band, Nathaniel Hawthorne Middle, May 4, 1998

This is Band class and the assignment couldn't be simpler – I am to show them a video of *Jurassic Park*. And no, they didn't make a musical of it that you missed, this is just a situation where the teacher presumably doesn't figure on my being able to do anything with these guys – an assessment pretty much on the mark, if that's what it was. Lots of freelance percussion before I wise up and confiscate the drumming equipment. And all of these classes are flat out rude. Of course, what my assignment amounts to is trying to stop kids from listening to a Walkman while making them watch a monster movie instead. So none of this can exactly be taken seriously.

And these kids are having lots of emergencies – besides needing to go to the bathroom a lot, we've got a bunch of them who've sprained something or other and need to go to the office for ice. One girl tells me that they're taking advantage of me, even more so than with the usual sub; then she asks if she can borrow a quarter.

When I send two kids to the counselor, they are returned to me as I am writing up the next two to go. That counselor doesn't know it, but he's finished my career at this place. The second pair explodes some type of cap/stink bomb device after being told they will be thrown out if they do so. They've already tied one to the classroom doorknob at the beginning of class. They go through the usual routine of giving me false names and when one persists in talking in Spanish after I tell him to be quiet; he tells me I'm anti-Latino. He tells me that in English, though.

Adios, Nathaniel Hawthorne Middle. Another one down.

¡NO PASARON! – *Social Studies, Millard Fillmore High, May 5, 1998*

Three days here for my friend Rich D. This place starts at 7:15 AM – and they wonder why high schools produce mass murderers. I asked a girl who came in late for first period here what her last name was. She hesitated; told me she was thinking. Actually, I've read somewhere of a study that determined that the only thing known to improve high school performance *that didn't cost money* – lowering the student-teacher ratio would, but certainly costs money – is not starting the day before 9 AM, the reason presumably being that kids are just not going to go to bed correspondingly earlier for earlier school starts. (On the other hand, the early start does put the students at a serious first period disadvantage, meaning the teachers – or subs – only have to wage a fair fight for five periods rather than six.)

Fortunately, Rich doesn't have a first period. This is another video day, but these are actually educational. The Latin America class is finishing one on Fidel Castro and the History class is seeing *The Good Fight*, the film on the International Brigades in the Spanish Civil War which some old acquaintances of mine made back in Boston years ago. Much more civilized than my day in *Jurassic Park*.

There are kids in sixth and seventh periods who actually know all about the Spanish Civil War and I tell the rest of the class to listen to them. Both of them are from Russia – one of the things they did do right in the Soviet Union was the educational system. These kids understand the Spanish Civil War as one of the great tragedies of the twentieth century. Having been in love with this topic ever since I saw the French documentary *To Die In Madrid* when I was in college, I could go on all afternoon about this – but not to a group of American high school students, unfortunately.

Second day I talk to the class watching the Castro movie about yesterday's *New York Times* report on Jose Mas Canosa's attempts to assassinate Castro. I ask if Mr. D ever talked about this stuff and someone says, "probably," so I prattle on a bit longer and tell them the story was in the paper near the picture of the president standing on his head – just to see who's listening, you know. One or two heads turn up at that, but the main interest among the girls remains eye makeup.

Today's first is filling out a report for a probation officer. Our boy had 15 absences during the four-week period covered in the report.

I spend my last morning administering standardized tests to a freshman home room class, many of whom I'm sure could manage to flunk home room. Eventually we're running 20 minutes behind the rest of the school because some of these guys won't let me read the written instructions, as I am required to do, because they insist that I'm wasting their time. One of them then starts on her second test ahead of time, thereby invalidating it. She then asks if she can take it for fun, and I tell her yes, but after a few minutes of that she wants to go see her counselor. I tell her she needs to stay; she leaves

Student Names of the Day: Tijuana Jackson, Summer Harb, Lucky Vo

*****

PHILOSOPHY *– Book Room, Citadel Middle, August 24, 1998*

Ye gads! Rich D had e-mailed that school started on August 24th, but I'd figured it was probably like baseball spring training, where the pitchers and catchers come down before everyone else. Surely they wouldn't be having students – and substitutes – in on August 24, that's even more ridiculous than last year. But apparently so – when I flew back from Amsterdam Friday night, my phone machine told me that the sub machine had been trying to get me.

I was flying back from Amsterdam, by the way, because I've enjoyed a respite from the children since late May when I headed back to Bosnia for another voter registration stint. But now the peace and quiet of the Balkans – and the now 32,000 troops to protect me – are over.

The system started calling again on Monday morning – heavily. It calls out on ten or twenty lines, and it sometimes calls the same person for more than one job at the same time, so if you've got call waiting, you may find yourself putting one of the machine's calls on hold so you can take another one that turns out to be the machine calling about another job, which is what happens this morning. One of them is a week-long job at Citadel. Citadel's considered the city's best middle school, and the first day starts three hours late, so it was an easy decision.

I'm subbing for a teacher who hasn't actually been hired, a fact that intrigues me. Generally the essence of the regular teacher is assumed to precede the essence of his or her substitute, but what if the "regular" or "real" teacher does not actually yet exist? Does the substitute then precede the regular? I've never been able to get much work in my field, but it's moments like this that reassure me that philosophy was the right college major for me. So far as reality goes, though, what I'll actually be doing is spending the week stamping the school's name on textbooks, numbering them, and filling classroom orders from the book room in the basement. And talking politics: occasionally a security guard will pop in and talk about his summer as a "counselor" in Juvenile Hall, but my main companion is Y, a Palestinian who used to teach political science in a junior college in LA.

We do occasionally have to leave our lair to eat, though – and to watch students eat. So, after having to walk through the lunch line to get to my yard assignment one day, I can tell you that coming between middle school students and their feeding trough is not something for amateurs. Like the making of sausages and laws, middle school lunch is something you want to leave to the professionals. My yard assignment is to prevent kids from bringing food to the upper yard. Why can't kids bring food to the upper yard? Well, subs are not hired to ask questions like that. Maybe it's just my philosophy background that makes me even wonder. Anyhow, for the most part Y and I are really wrapped up in the Middle East most of the week.

ABC *– Counseling, Dayton Elementary, September 9, 1998*

An elementary school counseling job is not common in the San Francisco system, but this is one of a small number of Kindergarten-through-

Eighth Grade schools out there, and presumably the counseling position goes along with the sixth through eighth grade middle school students. But whatever it's for, the call doesn't come until almost nine and I'm doing my best to hustle out there, but I get stuck behind a car driven by a woman with a kerchief on her head, a "Pray to end abortion" sticker on her bumper, and her foot on the brake all the way across West Portal. When I do get there at almost 10:30, they still haven't figured out what to do with me, so I hurry up and wait.

We have then a perfect situation for practicing what I preach when I give the kids the spiel about always having a book with you so you'll never be forced to waste your time waiting for someone or something. On the rare occasion when my sermon provokes interest, I'll usually mention that Malcolm X made this point in his autobiography, figuring that having a name to associate with the idea might enhance the chance of its sinking in. Not bloody likely, but ... The fact is, though, that riding the New York Subway to high school formed the habit in me before I read Malcolm X. Anyway, any student who walks into the office now will see me with that book. The ideal book for this situation will look serious, preferably nonfiction, although Dostoyevsky will do. And never a newspaper or magazine, much more likely to be interpreted as an announcement of idleness that might present something of a challenge to the secretary to put me to work. Eventually they send me off to correct fourth grade papers on spelling and alphabetization – or "ABC order," as they call it these days.

Next day my car is in the shop, so I'm on the N-Judah, the streetcar line that tourists remember, San Francisco's version of a Streetcar Named Desire – which you can actually only ride in San Francisco now, New Orleans having gone to buses while San Francisco has scarfed up old streetcars from all sorts of places, including New Orleans, to run them on the new, retro Market Street line.

I digress, however. The afternoon secretary asked me back for today, and here I am. Unfortunately, she apparently hadn't known the proper procedure – and neither had I. The morning secretary informs me that they've called in a new job number on this one so maybe I'd best call downtown. The sub office has, in fact given the job to someone else, but ultimately they reroute the other sub and give me a lecture about never coming back to a job past its expiration date, unless I'm given a new job number, and we exchange unpleasantries.

All quickly forgotten, though, as it's off to kindergarten to read out loud about "beautiful baboon," "blowing bubbles," and "biking backwards." Then a stamping-dates-on-books interval before reading a story about a Gingerbread Boy who gets eaten by a fox. Should we really be reading these little kids stories in which the protagonist gets eaten at the end? Foxes don't even eat gingerbread, so far as I know, so this isn't even good science. Next some hand-holding – Andres is crying because he misses his brother in the first grade and he won't get to see him again until recess. But recess does eventually come and when it does, it's a riot of hula hoops.

Next up, I am performing the functions of the Assistant Principal – selling sodas through a double lunch period, breaking up a fight in the yard, freeing up the tangled-up tetherball, chasing away a couple of kids from somewheres else who some kids think came to beat some other kid up. The guy cleaning the cafeteria says, "Sometimes they crazy," with a circular motion to the head. He's from some country south of here; he says, "You know, in America it's a beautiful life, but it's working all the time."

The teacher I'm in for during seventh period returns and thanks me for riding such close herd on the kids. I explain to her my philosophy of subbing as a test of wills – the sub attempts to impose as much order as possible, while the kids impose as much disorder as possible.

In case you're wondering if maybe this constant switching gets disorienting, next month I get a job here and I'm not even sure I've ever been to the school before until I get the lunch monitoring schedule and I realize I've actually subbed for this same counselor before. And, by the way, I understand that on an average day, San Francisco uses 300-350 subs; some days go as high as 450. There were 300 Spartans at Thermopylae, as I recall.

Student misspelling of the day – earthquack.

OKAY, FOURTH GRADE – *Principal, William Dawes Elementary, September 11, 1998*

The sub machine explains that this principal's job will actually involve replacing a fourth grade teacher who has not yet been hired. But teacher or no, there's a set program here. First. they're supposed to read *Scholastic News* and do exercises based upon what they read. They are paying NO attention. Math, to my surprise, they do much better at. One of their problems shows a picture of something you buy at the store, along with its price and pictures of the coins you'd pay for it with. The kids are supposed to draw the coins they'd get back in change. There's a lot of these kids I wouldn't be sending to the store.

Before school starts, I'm warned about a kid named Deante, and there are multiple offers from other teachers to take him into their classes, which is much appreciated. A school that is all over what a sub will be walking into is a well-organized school, it seems to me, but then elementary schools are generally much closer operations than the older-grade schools. For the first few minutes it looks like I'll be taking up their offers, but Deante actually works out all right and I keep him.

TO THE DOGS? – *Principal, Clark Kerr Elementary, September 19, 1998*

I was not the first choice here. The principal is out for two weeks and the sub they really wanted was not available today, so I'll have to do. The secretary (male, pretty unusual) asks one teacher if she'd like me as a helper and it's off to the fourth grade bungalow. I'm sure glad they didn't give me these kids solo. I have to break up a couple of fights in class and have to use a surprising amount of force to separate the kids. Five of them will be sent out during the course of the day. Lisa, the regular teacher, tells me this is only a small taste of what greeted her the first week when one of the kids we sent out for fighting was throwing chairs at her. "This is what I borrowed $11,000 to go to grad school for.

I could make more money walking dogs." Says she'll quit by November if they don't give her an aide.

At one point I'm relieved to notice that there's only an hour to lunch, but where normally that's a much longer time for a small child than an adult, when there's twenty of them, this relationship can reverse and today an hour is eternity for this adult. At times I'm amazed that she gets them to shut up at all, because there are other times when there is simply no focus in the classroom whatsoever. I hope she makes it to November.

Elementary schools are not my first choice, but you sure get to see how the national consciousness is formed early. I listened to a dance teacher here once explain to the class that "There are socialist systems; there are communist systems; and there are democracies. We have a democracy." Much as I wanted to say a few things about socialist democracy, I watched in silence as the American way of seeing passes from one generation to the next. Later that day eight kids from University High, a private high school in the city, came in to teach my class about Islam. In general I figure the kids"ll probably finish the public school system with a better understanding of the religions of the world than of world politics, which does make sense when you think about it. They will learn to concentrate on the big, eternal matters like God, and good and evil, and the like and let the experts decide the transitory stuff like wealth, poverty, war and peace.

WORRIED – *Fifth Grade, Elaine L. Chao Elementary, September 21, 1998*

I haven't been subbing in South San Francisco because it pays substantially less, but after a day with no jobs that I was willing to take in the big city, I decided it was time to sign up for South City again. Unfortunately, their calling machine has developed a rejection complex. When I enter my PIN number (Personal Identification Number number – assigned by the District's Department of Redundancy Department), it should start to recite my options, e.g. Do I want to hear available jobs, cancel a job, etc. Instead, it immediately asks my reason for not taking the job it has not ever actually offered me. This makes it impossible for me to tell it that I will not be available today, so it calls at 6 AM to ask why I'm not taking another job it's not offering me. Thoughtful of it to see to it that I didn't get up late for this San Francisco job.

As I drive into the school yard, a large woman, who proves to be an unpleasant woman, asks if she can help me and then tells me I have to drive slowly because of the children. I tell her that I thought I was driving slowly. As the reader has probably already surmised, this is the principal, so we're off to a happy start. The office gives me an apple sticker to wear as an ID, my first ID sticker as a substitute teacher, I think. But we are in Chinatown and I subsequently hear that homeless people have been found in the halls, which does explain some of the behavior around here.

The school has two buildings connected upstairs, but not on the ground floor. I came in on the third floor, then upstairs to cross over to my classroom in the other building where there was no lesson plan, then back up and over to the office to see if I heard right that there is a para attached to this class (there is), and find out if I'm supposed to pick the kids up outside in the school yard (I am.) This was not mentioned, but probably they figure that every elementary school sub knows this.

The regular teacher, out all last week but expected back today, apparently injured herself exercising in the school yard the prior week – haven't run into that one before. P, the para, tells me most of the kids are Chinese, which I understand is meant to explain to me that they are an easy class – and they are.

I read them a story about an (American) Indian, very common elementary school fare. For journal writing, I tell them to write about what they did this weekend, which they claim they can't remember, so I suggest they write about how they came down with amnesia this weekend.

P has mentioned that the Chinese kids get worried if they've finished their assignment and don't have something to do, and at lunch time I have trouble getting a couple of them to line up because a boy wants to finish his math and a girl wants to know if she can come back up during lunch to finish hers. Unbelievable!

When the rudest person you encounter all day is the principal, that's a pretty good day at school.

GREEK TO ME – IF ONLY! – Skyline Elementary/Orozco Elementary/ Sun Yat Sen Center, September 22, 1998

A trifecta! I assume that I've at least tied some kind of substitute teacher record here. Got a call last night to replace the principal at Skyline, the school tucked below street level on Twin Peaks. But it turns out they had asked for a student teacher who was already at the school (the plan was actually for the substitute to teach third grade), and he had forgotten to change his availability listing on the machine, so the machine called me.

When this is reported to the sub office, they send me to a kindergarten job at Orozco, over in the Richmond, but by the time I get there they've already called a local sub because they didn't think anyone was coming, so I'm off and running again, this time to a K/1 class at the Sun Yat Sen Center in Chinatown.

I arrived at Skyline at 7:15. It's now 10. So there's a good bite out of the day already. The school secretary tells me I'm going to love it here. And don't I need to know Chinese? Not as a sub, she says. The further good news is that there are only nine kids in the class – and it comes with a para. The bad news is there's no sub plan, and the kids speak Chinese. The regular teacher's own lesson plan is there, and I wish I could say that it was Greek to me since I took Greek in high school, but unfortunately it's not – it's Chinese, at least part of it is. There is a daily schedule on the wall, so I've got to improvise from that, with the para's assistance. It calls for some instruction in Chinese, but we'll skip that today. The deal with this school is that kids come here for one year to learn English, so we go through a lot of basic words. What letter does it begin with? Can you spell it? We count to 100; we count to 100 by "2"s. They take recess on the padded roof of the building. The afternoon is tough since some of the kids flat-out don't understand me. I try math with them, but just can't do it. Yet although there are stretches when I lose them entirely, even at this age, Chinese kids know that when you're at school, you don't waste time, so when the math breaks down, they all start copying the words I'm writing on the board.

CERTIFICATED – *Special Education, Anza Elementary, September 23, 1998*

As I will learn, when the nature of a sub job isn't described on the recording, it's a good bet that it's a Special Ed class. There are only three kids here and there are two aides, but the kids are severely disabled. A teacher still hasn't been hired for this year. One Chinese-speaking para is assigned entirely to a Chinese boy who is apparently a big masturbator. The other para gives me the whole story. She's been with one of the other two kids, who has Down's Syndrome, for five years. (The other two are autistic.) Apparently no one stays in these classes after they get fully credentialed. She has done this job for twenty five years, in just two schools. If there is a heaven, this woman better be going there.

Then a third aide comes in and doesn't even introduce himself to me. It's now clear to me that absolutely nothing is really expected of me; I am just filling the requirement of a certificated person in the classroom. N, the talkative aide, says just find a comfortable chair. She would understand if I picked up my stuff and left but I tell her I just feel guilty not being able to do anything useful.

The kids are mostly tracing letters in stencils, or coloring or maybe a little assisted cutting and pasting. There is no plan and I cannot provide one. The silent aide asks me to take over with his kid while he goes and makes copies. I am absolutely unable to engage the kid. There are certainly times as a sub when I'm more than happy to do nothing at all, but this is not one of them.

Ultimately I settle in at my laptop. I never see another sub with one, which always surprises me a bit. One of the laptop's psychological virtues is that it is an active instrument. The book may look better than the newspaper for public reading, but when you're sitting in front of a computer, better still – you're working. Administrators and students alike will be impressed. And the students will, of course, assume I'm writing about them. And, a lot of the time, they're right, although the report's not going to the principal – it's going to you.

After lunch, N leaves, so I tend Armando who's a really lovable kid who throws blocks around the room. He takes his shoes off when it's time to go and has to be partially dragged down the hall. I tell the secretary that I don't think I really added anything to the mix, so they might as well see if they can find someone else who can.

SORRY – *Second Grade Spanish Bilingual, Barlett Elementary,*
September 24, 1998

Sub plans for early grades are usually quite detailed. So much new to learn. And so short an attention span. A lot of the start-of-day events in this teacher's lesson plan are in Spanish and I'm wondering if this school is entirely bilingual like Buenos Dias, but it appears that this is the bilingual second grade and there's also an all-English one. (This was something they didn't mention on the tape or in the office.)

The first grade teacher across the hall tells me this is a good class (she's right) and to send her anyone who's bad (I don't.) During recess yard duty she's talking about how cold it is, so I know she's a native Californian who doesn't know from cold. Yep. She's from the Peninsula, so this is even colder for her. The big action during recess is fetching the ball after it's kicked out of the yard and into the street – three times. And, oh yes, after recess a girl tells me, "She said there's poo poo on my paper." The accused says, "I'm sorry."

The sub sign-in book here has business cards stapled to the back cover. Never could quite adjust to this sub-with-a-business-card idea. The way I see it, lumpen proletarians don't have business cards, thank you.

NO POO POO – *Dance/Spanish, Appian Way High, September 28, 1998*

My wake-up call comes from the Edward R. Murrow Middle School. I have to listen to that whole crazy thing, just to say, "No" and it's not at its most enjoyable at 5:30 AM, which is when I hear it today. The job was on the machine last night at 10, and it doesn't sound any more appetizing before dawn. Past experience has demonstrated that Edward R. Murrow does not meet my "no reinforcements required" standard. The tape said the job was counseling, but you certainly can't trust that.

When the South San Francisco machine calls, I try punching my San Francisco sub ID number into the phone, in the dark. When I finally get my jurisdiction straight, I take a job at Appian Way High, my first South City job this year. Looking forward to no "poo poo on my paper" problems, actually.

The machine said this was a Spanish job, but there are only two periods of that. The rest are Dance class in the cafeteria. So, yes, I now have subbed for Dance class. Fortunately there is another teacher there and even a TA to take attendance. (TA's, or Teacher's Assistants, are students who've apparently performed well elsewhere and are therefore allowed to grade papers or do nothing in another class.)

I'M SURE YOUR CHILD'S HERE SOMEWHERE – *Bilingual Kindergarten, Tesla Academy, September 29, 1998*

Looking forward to seeing the inside of the infamous Tesla Academy, the charter school operated by the for-profit Tesla Corporation. The school had apparently been one of the most difficult in town and the School Board had voted to privatize it. This had been about the most controversial issue before the Board during the entire year and it became a litmus test for School Board candidates.

But first I've got to find it. The address I heard on the sub machine turns out to be the Salvation Army. Call in to check and get it again, so I go back home and look in the phone book – it's 22nd St., not 26th St. When I finally get to the right place, it turns out that the Resource Specialist I'm replacing is no longer at this school. Again a teacher who has not updated her recording. Now I've got to call the sub desk, which puts me on hold three times, after which the sub desk clerk and I listen to the tape together – upon my third listen through I could be persuaded it says 22nd St., but you'd have to know that first. Eventually I am assigned here after all – to kindergarten – bilingual.

I read to them in Spanish, during which they start singing the alphabet. The girls choo-choo in line after lunch. Lots of hugs from kids. And group hugs. And shoe tying. And the best part is the kids come with name tags. Bathroom conveniently located in the classroom, nonetheless is a major chore. And the lesson plan isn't up to snuff – might be if I were an everyday kindergarten teacher and had my own bag of tricks, I don't know. I do some addition and subtraction with blocks, but really have a difficult time keeping them occupied.

And there's a whole lot of "He hit me; she hit me," and kids putting the Legos in their mouths and their unwrapped sandwiches on the floor. My instructions say they get a snack after art; I ask the art teacher where the snack comes from; she asks the kids; they say in the cafeteria; we march to the cafeteria; there's no one there; we march back to the classroom. Now there's a lot of "Is it lunchtime; is it lunchtime?"

After lunch, but before dismissal time, a father comes and picks up his daughter and then a mother comes for her son. Then another mother comes for the daughter who's already been picked up, and soon there's a steady stream of parents picking up their kids. This is obviously part of the routine – it's only kindergarten, after all – but it's starting to make me nervous. How do I know who's supposed to be picking up whom? We've already had one parent come for a kid I couldn't provide. I could easily lose one of these. Didn't have this problem in high school yesterday.

By the way, I actually could not find much different here in the privatized Tesla, with one exception – my lunchtime duties included washing the tables.

OUTSPOKEN – *Benjamin Banneker Elementary/Osgood Conklin Elementary, September 30, 1998*

I'm in for a Resource teacher at Benjamin Banneker, which could mean anything. I'm guessing stamping books, but they assign me to a K-1 class for the morning to help a teacher who's just in her third week here. She taught Catholic school in the past and is obviously a bit shell shocked. She says she's noticed that the children "are a bit more outspoken here." She speaks quite proper English, so I'm a little surprised to hear her tell the kids, "Look at the person head in front of you."

She's been told that homework isn't corrected here, but feels that work she's specially asked kids to do must be acknowledged. So I'm drawing happy faces on homework, and later sorting papers and cleaning the paint stand. At one point there are four adults in the classroom. I'm not sure how the school gets its resources, but good for them, it's what's needed.

Before lunch, Winnie, the secretary with whom I always compare opera notes (on our wages, we're both standees), comes in to tell me to call the sub office at lunch. I'm thinking they're going to tell me I was expected to be back at Tesla even though I didn't have a job number, but, after sitting on hold for a long period, I'm told I can now go to the Osgood Conklin school or get paid for half a day. Seems they're taking the position that the job didn't actually exist although I have a number for it. I probably should have challenged that, and I wouldn't normally take a job at the Conklin , but ... God, I love the sub office!

Over to Conklin at about 12:20. No lesson plan here at all – big surprise. Since there was no sub here in the morning, the entire class has been dispersed and now they're sent back in dribs and drabs. The afternoon is fairly ragged. I taught them the days-in-the-month mnemonic – "Thirty days hath September, ... ," and the girl who learned it by heart hopes I'll come back as a teacher; but I don't hope that. A boy gives me a miniature pumpkin at the end of the day, a rare moment of pleasantness in this afternoon.

"BIN" – *Third Grade, Stokeley Elementary, October 1, 1998*

This school is right in the heart of Hunter's Point and as difficult as I feared it would be. I'm called as a Resource Specialist but wind up subbing for a third grade teacher who went to Hong Kong and hasn't yet been replaced permanently. The state government recently approved funding for smaller classes in the lower grades, so schools may now have more classes than rooms for them. This particular one has been squeezed out of a class room and forced to go mobile, dividing its time between the library and the teachers' lunch room.

For the morning I'm teaching reading and yelling phonics. We're going over the short vowel sounds and we have a real problem with "bin." They think I'm saying "been," which is pronounced "bin" in Black English. They repeat a wrong answer back to me about five times in a row: "I've bin in school." But we may actually be making some progress – the three kids who first refuse to write eventually do.

When kids are as badly behaved as they are at this school, I tend to forget how young they actually are. These kids are eight years old. One of them's got a beeper! He can't tell time from a clock with hands, but he can read the time off of his beeper. Ay, yay, yay! The morning ends with a boy lying on the ground and crying outside the door because somebody kicked him. Nothing to make you feel out of it as a sub like a kid wailing on the ground while the line (that is anything but a line) that you're supposed to be escorting has wandered off to God knows where. Since I'm tending to the kid I don't get word that the kids are supposed to go back to their classrooms after lunch instead of outside, so I have to hustle back to the library and wait for a while until someone comes with a TV to numb their minds.

A girl tells me that the substitute teachers never come back to this class. The office has told me that the teacher will be out again tomorrow, but it's Thursday already and I'd like to have some voice left for the weekend, which I won't if I come back tomorrow.

We do a math worksheet that involves adding two numbers, writing the sum and then subtracting a number from that, writing that answer down, and so forth. By the second step, there's no one with the right answer.

PHILOSOPHICAL JOKE – *English, Cappuccino High, October 2, 1998*

This is the other main high school in South San Francisco, a place that far more people have been to than realize it exists. "South City," a separate town of about sixty thousand, is where you actually are when you arrive at San Francisco International Airport – "the Industrial City," as it is painted in giant white letters on "Sign Hill" on your left on your way up from the airport on Route 101. It's San Francisco's Hollywood – but only in signage. Generally its schools are much calmer than up north. One look at Grand Avenue in "downtown" South San Francisco will tell you that people don't move here for the night life.

I spend my prep period in the teachers room where it unfortunately gets mostly eaten up by a not terribly interesting discussion with a sub whom I've met before who says he couldn't imagine subbing in San Francisco. We discuss *The Bell Curve* by Herrnstein and Murray and the question of what's genetic and what's socially determined. He sees black kids not being very good students and thinks that's nature's way. A student teacher comes for fourth period and she'd be happy to let me go elsewhere while she taught, but if I go back to the teachers' room I might wind up in another one of those conversations, so I'll just stick here.

One class has an open book exam and one kid says that somebody else has cheated. Since the test involves writing about a novel the students have read – any novel – the situation brings to mind Woody Allen's shtick about getting expelled from NYU for cheating on a philosophy exam by looking into the soul of the student next to him. I attempt to share my insight with the kids, but they don't appear to be familiar with Woody Allen or philosophy.

On the other hand, I once spotted a boy here reading *Marx for Beginners,* a translation of a Mexican book by a cartoonist named Rius that I've used in adult classes. To say the least, I am pleasantly surprised. I ask him how it is and he says it's kind of confusing. A girl asks why he would want to read that, and he tells her that Marx died penniless and that's his goal too. I hope for great things from this one.

WHAT'S THAT? – *Fourth Grade, Jose Marti Elementary, October 5, 1998*

This school's over in Merced Heights or Oceanside or one of those other southwest neighborhoods where the tour buses don't go and it's a bit of an adventure finding it. Class starts with a "sharing circle." On my second day here the kid I'm supposed to be sure is taking his medication (otherwise "he goes off the wall" after lunch) remembers that he just learned about sewer systems and has discovered that "we're drinking pee water." Unfortunately he didn't get to share that in the circle.

The regular teacher shows up on the second morning. She's on jury duty and heard that the kids weren't great for me, so she assigns them to write about how they acted yesterday and how they're going to act today and asks me to grade them in her star system. I give them a five out of ten for day one. Basically they're a nice bunch. Mostly Chinese and black and both the smart kids and the problem kids come from both groups.

Some of them are quite smart, but the norm – to the extent that you can even speak of a "norm" with a sub in the room – is pretty bone-headed. One of our readings discusses how the narrator's mind wanders. They don't know what that means, so I try to explain the concept, but they're not paying attention. In certain circumstances, this might provide what the professionals now like to call a "teachable moment," but irony doesn't take you very far in the fourth grade. The kids say "whatever" when they encounter words they don't recognize. When one of them gives me a "whatever" for "Mojave," in the course of figuring out the pronunciation I point out that it's the Spanish "j" just like in "Jose Marti," (the school name). One girl says, "What's that?"

The Chinese kids tell the class – and me – about moon cakes that they eat at harvest moon, which is now. I try explaining the concept of the harvest moon, but that harvesting doesn't have much meaning to these kids; maybe not moonlight either.

The regular teacher sent one girl to the office for recess and lunch because of all the bad behavior marks on the board next to her name from yesterday, and when she returns she tells me that she could hear me all the way down there. By the end of the second day my voice is getting pretty raggedy: this is not a three day job, that is to say it's not a job you'd want to do for three days.

At the end of the day, I ask them to tell me how many stars they think they deserve. Their answers range from zero to five. I'm generous and give them a four.

DON'T LOOK UP – *Math/Science, William Howard Taft Middle,*
October 7, 1998

I'm already driving to some other school before I properly recall which middle school is Taft. It's the one where you go out and move your car every two hours – which is likely why I preferred to remember it being somewheres else. A student teacher has first period and she'll be back during fourth and seventh to give them a questionnaire for her dissertation. I just have to oversee a math assignment for two periods, so this could be an opportunity for my vocal chords to heal.

A little firm talk actually goes a long way in this class. I have to shut one kid up while I go through the instructions for the assignment and another's working his comedy routine, but the whole thing is really quite civilized. Discipline problems don't run past someone writing "Free gum from the teacher" on the board and a certain amount of discussion of the ever popular middle school topic of farting. I even risk leaving my laptop out rather than packing and unpacking every two hours – I do check to see if the door is taped, though.

The kids ask if they can use calculators and the student teacher thinks it okay. So I say okay, but not without a cautionary tale on the danger of never learning how to multiply or divide on your own. They say the teacher will not let them use them for new stuff, and immediately I find an example of just what I'd warned them about – a girl can't tell me how many times four goes into nine. So I'm taking coins out of my pocket to work out this mathematical problem – with a seventh grader.

The student teacher comes back to explain the questionnaire to the fourth period kids and says she was glad I was there first period because I had good control. Watching these kids fill the things out after she goes, I think she's going to be disappointed with the answers she gets, but then that would be a finding in itself, I guess.

A 1934 mural of the arts as a woman with bared breasts looks down upon the school's main corridor.

CONSCIENTIOUS OBJECTION – *English, Cappuccino High, October 8, 1998*

The day starts with the guy who steals the returnable bottles on my street on recycling day calling me "fucking stupid" for driving up the street while he's pushing his shopping cart down it. But as soon as I pull my wits together to fire off a clever "Fuck you" riposte, I know that things will be just fine today. In fact, if I weren't pretty sure that this guy stole my collection of painted beer bottles from around the world off my deck so he could turn them in for four cents apiece, I might well have thanked him for getting me primed for the work day.

When I arrive, the school secretary is talking about how her son at USC just brought his car down to school and then heard that a student returning from the weekend had his car shot at in a drive-by shooting. Now, LA is what really scares them around here.

Sophomores today. Assembly-line writing. They have to produce outlines for upcoming essays. We also have a persistent, unidentifiable whistler, which I tell them is the sort of thing I expect from little kids in middle school trying to see what they can get away with. This is a feeble counterattack, I know, but I feel that I have to at least produce the appearance of opposition to unauthorized whistling. There are standards that must be maintained. And what else was I going to do? Call them sophomoric? Nothing here but the educational jousting that's gone on since Cain and Abel were in school. For the last minute or so, they all mass at the door waiting for the bell, like bees in a hive. At the end, a girl comes up and says, "I'm one of the quiet ones. That was really cool; you're the first substitute I ever saw with a computer. Okay, I'm done now."

During lunch time a request comes over the intercom for male teachers to go outside to prevent a potential riot or something. I'm not certain if substitutes are expected to participate in actual physical combat with students, or under what circumstances, but I contrived to fail to comprehend the message and remained in the teachers room in the company of women, reading about riots in Bosnia, until the crisis had apparently passed. Perhaps if they provided us with health insurance.

SOME CROWD! – *History, Millard Fillmore High, October 9, 1998*

Back here for Rich D and I'm supposed to be more insistent on the students working today, as they apparently told him that last time it looked like I was going to be a hardass but then I went to work on my computer and let them be. Say no more – today I am resolved to be a hardass, which determination, however, is dealt a serious blow by the girl who walks into class, sees me, and cheers – a member of the cheerleading squad, actually. It's always nice to be appreciated once in a while though, even if it is only for who I'm not. I tell the first student who asks where Mr. D is that "the bus was very large." Next period a student says he heard that Mr. D was hit by a bus. The little things can make your day.

I announce that today's assignment will be collected today – along with three other past assignments. A student then asks when the work will be collected. I repeat that today's assignment will be collected today – along with three other past assignments and explain this is why I try to insist on *everyone's* attention at the beginning of class. Another student then asks when the work will be collected. And so on. A girl has ECONIMICS written on her text book. Irony, or the decline of civilization? Often hard to say in high school.

By the way, word has pretty well gotten around that Mr. D is out and, whether it's due to the grief felt by students who have heard he is now roadkill, or some other reason, by the time the bell rings for last period, there's only twelve out of twenty-six students in their seats. Another two arrive late, though, so we do eventually capture a majority. The last guy in arrives real late, looks around, and says, "Wow, really some crowd here today!" I tell him he's lucky to get a seat. I notice in the attendance book that this is his third time late this week, so I suggest that he might want to see about getting a shorter fifth-to-sixth period commute. Obviously impressed with my level of concern, the student asks if I'm a counselor as well as a teacher. I tell him that I am not, but that I do try to look at the whole student. He wants to know do I get two salaries. I tell him that I do not, but that when I see a student in need ... And so forth. I miss urban high school repartee. Where did it go? Seemed like there was more in Boston. Of course, things were more rough and tumble back then and there since you couldn't always count on a lesson plan and often had to rely more upon your wits – a centerpiece of my M.O. was to get the rest of the class laughing at the guy who was giving me the most trouble. This was mostly a high school thing, of course, because the kids have got to be capable of understanding irony for it to work, which severely limits its use in middle school. But then I've never found the repartee as good since I moved out here.

FISHY – *Computer Lab, Castillo Elementary, October 14, 1998*

During lunch on my first of three days out here in the peaceful zone, I notice a female teacher picking up a glass in the teachers room, reading what's written on it, and showing it to another female teacher, who promptly throws it in the trash. They agree they've never noticed it before and wonder if anyone's going to come around and complain that their glass is missing. A male teacher who asks what it said is told that it's not for him to know. Well, I've got to know now, so I come back a few periods later when no one's around and root around in the trash until I find it. It reads, "If girls are made of sugar and spice and everything nice, how come they taste like anchovies?" I'll bet no one complained.

A fifth grade class is in the Computer Lab writing about Anne Frank and at one point their teacher says to me, "That was World War I that Hitler was in, right?" I tell her that it was WW II and she says, "Oh, no, World War II? World War I was the Korean War, right?" As she sees me looking askance, she says, "Oh, no, I'm all confused." I agree with her on that. At least she's only teaching elementary school.

One group is fourth and fifth graders composing biographies. Some are of famous people – Mark McGwire just broke Roger Maris' home run record, so he's a big item – but some kids write about other kids at school. One girl has chosen another girl whom she considers her sixth best friend. She writes that the friend, in turn, considers her as her fifth best friend. Will this inequality of affection lead to trouble down the line? Or will the fact that one of them is left-handed and the other right-handed bring problems? I'll never know. One biography reports that its subject's greatest achievement was reaching her tenth birthday.

An alarm rings and I don't know whether it's fire or earthquake. Duck and cover or flee? Unfortunately the teacher whose class is in the lab this period is a sub too. Of course, it could be the real thing and I don't want to be responsible for a classroom full of children found roasted under their desks, but ultimately the commotion in the hall convinces me that it's a fire drill and it all goes smoothly enough. The week finishes with a nice noisy crowd of fourth graders – "Help me. Help me. Can I print?" I turn off the lights in the lab leaving the screen savers glowing in the dark. One says, "I will not draw naked ladies in class."

Of course, I've got the usual PC-guy-in-Mac-World problem and on a later assignment here I have to go for help to the office where the receptionist has to call the sick teacher at home. She says don't touch the back, use the arrow key, and if they don't start, ask the kids. I'm sure she's quite comforted knowing that she has a sub who doesn't know how to turn the computers on.

Can't help but notice that there's stashes of chocolate all around this room. I check the staff photos again and see that the regular teacher is indeed on the large side.

BOSTON REVERIE – *Seventh Grade Language Arts/Social Science, Skyline Middle, October 20, 1998*

My car radio is tuned to the Sarah and Vinnie morning show which usually serves as a good warm-up for the juvenile mind. Today they're talking about how to prepare for a colonoscopy. What better preparation for a day at middle school?

The regular teacher has risen from her sickbed to come in and bring me the assignment which starts out with silent reading during which they're actually silent. Somehow this brings to mind a day subbing in an elementary school in Boston in the 70s when I was trying to figure out if I had just arrived in a class of deaf children. The Boston School Department provided subs a booklet of directions to the various schools, and when I consulted it one morning, I found that I'd just taken a job at what the booklet described as a school for the deaf. I hoped maybe there was a mistake here, and that they would not have assigned me to a class of deaf students, but I knew better than to assume it. After all, I hadn't really thought of myself as particularly qualified for auto shop, Spanish, typing, mechanics, or cooking before I took those classes either. So, when I got to the school I was very pleased to learn that there was a student teacher conducting the class at that very moment. He offered to turn things over to me as soon as I arrived in the classroom, but he seemed to be in the middle of something with them, so I said why didn't he continue until the recess that was scheduled in a few minutes. Mainly I wanted to figure out if the kids were actually deaf.

For the next several minutes, I watched a class of second-graders systematically pick the flesh off of this student teacher's psychic bones. Obviously this was no longer a school for the deaf – these kids could hear this teacher only too well. He seemed to have locked himself into arguing the practical importance of mathematics to a bunch of seven-year olds who were not taking him very seriously. He had even brought in a poster of an airplane cockpit and was asking them if they knew why he had done that. And they shouted out, "No! Tell us." And he explained to them that you had to know math to build and fly an airplane. And they didn't care about that. And one little girl was bouncing up and down the whole time, calling out, "What if you want to be a dancer? I want to be a dancer." And he says that he has seen this other poster illustrating the lines of stress on a ballet dancer as she's performing, and maybe he could get one of those and bring it in, too.

And he is wearing his heart on his sleeve. And he is telling them how he's bought these things for the class with his own money. And now the boy who was standing outside in the hall the whole time has stuck his head back into the room, and the student teacher says, "Johnny, get your head back in the hall." And he then turns to the class and says, "I sent Johnny out in the hall. Do you know why I sent him out in the hall?" And they say, "No! Tell us." And he says, "It was because of something he said to me." "What did he say? What did he say?" they cry. And the student teacher tells them: "He said, 'Shove it up your ass.'"

The class goes wild. They jump. They hoot. They turn around to me and say, "You teach! You teach!" Fortunately the recess bell rang right then before I had to step in and declare the match a TKO. When the kids were gone, the student teacher put his textbook down on my desk and said, "I can't teach!" After recess, I encountered a class that was undoubtedly much more cooperative than they would have been, absent that poor student teacher. They had seen the depths to which their own desire for disorder could actually take them and they collectively stepped back from the abyss when I took over. What is that poor guy now? Teacher? Principal? Cloistered monk? Serial killer? And those student teacher-destroying children? They walk among you.

I have digressed into a sub's reverie, simply because I've encountered silent reading that really is silent. Actually, I have always wondered whether silent reading was the best use of class time. For kids who would not read outside of class it may well be a good thing, while for those who will read on their own, it would seem to be a waste of instructional time, but in any case it was that unusual for it to be that silent.

The first class is scheduled to leave at 8:55, but the teacher on the other side of the large sliding door between this classroom and the next sends them back to me because she says that on a sub day they should stay until 9:15. With this change of plans, it's no longer clear what the kids are supposed to do and so that's exactly what they do. After second period another teacher comes in to write down the homework. She tells me she's the RSP person. I don't know what that means, so I give it the professional "aha." This place is very easygoing. The kids frequently work in the halls outside their classrooms; sometimes on the floor. At one point, I search for the men's room and leave my computer untended – in an unlocked room!

In the afternoon, a sub takes over in the adjoining class as well. The regular teacher has told me to pop my head in if I hear trouble and take names of problem students, so when the sub closes the door between the classes, I let her know that the regular teacher leaves it open, presumably for a better balance of terror. She tells me she's not into terror. Apparently she's new at this.

BRONX REVERIE – *Seventh Grade English, J.P. Morgan Middle, October 23, 1998*

As I'm pulling my car in, I find myself clenching up upon first sight of middle school kids, but an early class does a reading and writing assignment in reasonable quiet, which is the more impressive in that this is a class of thirty-seven – a very large number these days. Wasn't always. In the mid-fifties, the Hunts Point section of the South Bronx was a neighborhood in change, so kids came and went very fast at St. Athanasius School Elementary School, particularly in first grade. I think we must have had a weekly count off or something, because I have memories of knowing how many kids we had week by week. Probably this perversely amused Sister John then, as it does me now. And while I hesitate to say so because the number is so improbably large, I do believe that we peaked at 80 – first graders don't take up that much space – although we didn't finish the year with more than low fifties I think. (We graduated 42.) And Sister John handled them all. She did have the fear of God and corporal punishment on her side, of course.

But, back here in San Francisco in the nineties, as I read out today's school bulletin, it's so full of typographical errors that I frequently can't tell what its author was actually trying to say. Why Johnny can't write. A teachers' union flyer on the wall has pictures of the three school board candidates the union is endorsing; one kid asks if those people in the pictures are all missing. Someone sees my copy of *The Nation* and asks if it's *TV Guide*. What else would you need a magazine for?

During my prep period, I'm using the phone in the office when the assistant principal says, "Mr. Gallagher, Thank you for being here." Wow! A sub could go a long time in between hearing those words. Maybe he thinks I'm the phone repairman.

BOHEMIA – *Sixth Grade Science, Calvin Coolidge Middle, October 26, 1998*

Any doubts I may have had about whether I have truly lived the bohemian life are dispelled today. I spend the daylight hours of my fiftieth birthday (starting with a 4:38 AM phone call – the school department has not changed back from daylight savings time yet) at Calvin Coolidge Middle (which has an autographed picture of the President in the main office) and the evening at a performance of *Tristan and Isolde* at the San Francisco Opera – in standing room.

When I arrive at the school a woman is telling an administrator about her confrontation with two kids – two black kids, she then specifies (she's white) – who were sitting on her car and didn't want to get off and gave her attitude and then punched her car. And then I couldn't hear what she was saying, but she's clearly explaining that in her irritation she said something she wished she hadn't. I assume it was the "N" word and I think of the irony of the fact that I listen to black kids call each other, "nigger" all the time. But I must be off to my class and don't get to hear how it all came out.

At lunch I hear the lunch lady yelling at the kids to move on the lunchroom line. You can spend a lot of your life being yelled at at that age. Some regular teachers are discussing "bad subs" in the teachers' lunchroom. By this, they mean the ones the students run all over. Apparently they recently had a woman in who didn't speak much English and got assigned a chorus class of fifty-five students. A counselor had to come in and pull eight of them out.

I had one hauled out myself today – first one in a long time. Squirting water on the floor; wouldn't sit down; and then wouldn't tell me his name. A lot of kids pull this one because they know subs don't know their names, either because the seating charts are not accurate or because the kids are not sitting in their assigned seats. (And actually there's even some who have not yet figured out that seating charts contain that type of information.) So for me, not giving your name has become a guaranteed ejection. No changing your mind afterwards – you're gone, even if I have to call security to do it. Actually, a student not telling me his name can be very useful. If I want to get rid of a pain-in-the-ass kid quick, I just ask him his name, and as often as not he won't tell me and then the little tyke goes elsewhere. I see this as a variation of the Al Capone strategy – when the government couldn't get him for the big stuff, they got him on tax evasion. But I actually don't think of Capone, I think of Richie Biaggi.

Richie was a classmate during my first few years at St. Athanasius, before his family moved farther north in the Bronx, as most did – if they stayed in the Bronx at all. His father Mario was, at the time, said to be the most decorated cop in New York City history and went on to be elected to Congress where he gained fame as NORAID's best friend. Given that he was an Italo-American and NORAID

(Irish Northern Aid Committee) was widely viewed as a front for the Irish Republican Army (the Provisionals), you'd say the man covered his bases well.

I missed Richie when he moved because he had been the only other Dodger fan in our class; he's the one I remember commiserating with in fourth grade when word got out that the Dodgers were leaving. I followed him in a sense through his father's career, though. Mario went on to run for mayor but didn't make it and eventually things went south for him and in the eighties he got convicted of taking some kind of kickbacks. The stories I'd see leading up to the trial often mentioned that a son was also in the thick of things. I remembered Richie having at least one sister but I didn't know if there were any brothers and never saw a name until one day on the ferry from Newfoundland to Cape Breton I read in the *New York Times* that it was indeed Richie who was convicted under a wrinkle of the Al Capone approach – they got him for over-reporting his income, apparently listing his father's kickbacks as his own income. I've never seen or heard his name mentioned again, but I still think of him whenever some kid won't give me his name.

Anyhow, whether it's Al or Richie I should be thinking of, I call the counseling office on this one and ask to have him removed and while we await security, he's roaming around, shouting out, saying he'll sue me, throwing something across the room, and the like. He flicks off the lights as he's escorted out.

All of this is not particularly conducive to an educational environment. The counseling office calls me twice looking for a referral form on this kid. I understand why they need it, but giving them one does create a further problem. This guy's already disrupted the class and now I've got to divert more time from the task of restoring order to write up some paperwork. The kids tell me it was this guy's second referral of the day. I frequently wonder if I'm overreacting when I toss kids, but in most cases, like today, they prove my judgment right.

On my second day on this job, let's get serious here for a moment. Third period has seven black kids out of a class of thirty and I have to jump start four of them. One has no book because he forgot it. I give him a hall pass to go get it from his locker, but he comes back saying it wasn't there. Another is spending his time cleaning his binder; two girls are drawing. None of this is antagonistic today, as it was with the kids I kicked out yesterday, but these are the only kids that I have to push.

This is a sort of situation that is repeated all over the place and it's the kind of thing that almost no one knows how to talk about, so they don't. For instance, I haven't even really discussed it thus far. I usually don't even keep notes about how many of the kids I throw out are white and how many are black. But if I really get to talking to someone about what being in the schools is like, I invariably tell them it seriously heightens one's awareness of the plight of black America, a topic to which I shall return frequently.

There will be an anti-drug assembly in the auditorium during sixth. So drugs do have their use. Some pretty decent acting in one of the skits; the boy playing a father is pretty funny. Seventh period is honors and since they actually do the assignment, I find myself letting them get away with things in the last five minutes that I wouldn't have allowed in the other classes. One student announces he's going to suck the floor and assures everyone that it's clean. He somehow manages to get a "Tobacco is a drug" sticker in his hair and is looking for scissors to cut it out. I suggest that the whole head might have to be cut off, but they manage short of that. It is an unusual pleasure to actually be able to enjoy them being kids.

I'M MR. T – Math, Waterfront Middle, October 28, 1998

A teacher sticks her head in to say she's in the next room and I should send any problems to her; I'm the third different sub in three days. It's almost the end of grading period and she suspects maybe teachers are at home doing their grades. I tell her that I'm not really in this class but have been plugged in for the first block and that they always do this sort of thing here. She says she's not surprised, as their principal – whom I've certainly always considered strange – has no social skills. She's been here the same five years as he and he's improved maybe this much (she's holding her fingers about an inch apart). But she says he's equal opportunity – he yells at everyone. And everyone – parents, etc. – asks what's wrong with him.

The class is not bad. I've pretty much got them doing their assignment, but it's particularly striking today how virtually every black kid needs special attention to get them to work: they're talking out, wanting to go to the bathroom; don't have a pencil, etc.

During nutrition break I drop a referral form off at the counseling office and head to my regular class where I am greeted by someone who says he's Mr. T's sub. I respond, "I'm Mr. T's sub," and think of the episode in the TV series, *The Prisoner*, in which they drug Patrick McGoohan and change his number from the Nine which they first assigned him and give it to someone else, also played by McGoohan. If they can get him to assert that he REALLY IS Number Nine, they will have won, but McGoohan never falters. He always remembers that, "I am not a number, I am a free man." So, here we are, each asserting that "I'm Mr. T's sub. A machine called me up this morning and told me I was." When it's sorted out, I've got a free block after all, and by now I sure know better than to show up in the office, where they'll have me filing if I do.

In one class a black girl with serious vision problems and special large-print books complains about the Chinese kid coming up to another Chinese kid across the table from her and asking questions "in their stupid language." "At least we speak another language," the kid says. I tell them both to stifle themselves.

In sixth period the kids have to look up definitions. One of their words is "Martian," but it's not in the dictionary. I give one girl a hint that it has to do with a particular planet. She says, "Pluto?" The kid I gave a referral to is back. He's not disruptive – other than drinking a can of soda – which is not allowed in class, but he does no work. I wonder what you do with kids like this in the long run. I tell him he's going to spend the rest of his time in the counselor's office and learn nothing at this rate. He says, "What about when I graduate?" I don't say what's on my mind – that when he graduates there's unfortunately an excellent chance that a bench in a police station will replace the one in the counselor's office.

ADVANCED PAYNE – *Seventh Grade Math, J.P. Morgan Middle, October 29, 1998*

A nice 5:38 AM call for Morgan. Although this is usually my favorite middle school assignment in San Francisco, today I find the memories of unpleasant classes past wafting through my mind as I pass the rooms where they were created, on my way up to the third floor where unpleasant memories of the future await.

Today's job involves showing *Major Payne*, a movie perfectly pitched at middle school level idiocy. Damon Wayans plays a former military man who can't adjust to civilian life and gets a job with the ROTC program at a boarding school. In other words, the kids here have the day off. The teacher next door says he also uses the "hypnotic box" whenever he's absent. Says he used to leave assignments but the results were chaos – kind of like going away and the puppy chews up your shoes. I tell them they've got an easy assignment that I know they can handle – watching TV. No sooner said, than one of them proceeds to fall out of his chair, casting doubt upon even that proposition. But, in general, they rise to the occasion. One kid presents me with a "libary pass" that he wants me to sign, but I tell him I won't until he learns how to spell it. I know – how you going to learn to spell it if they won't let you go there?

My instructions say that one class has already seen *Major Payne* (must be an Honors class) so I'm supposed to get *Martian Chronicles* from downstairs, but it doesn't work a bit – bad tracking, and no student interest, so it's back to the Major for the rest of their double period. By eighth period the students definitely look like they could flunk even TV-watching.

CHEATING – *Fourth Grade, Benjamin Banneker Elementary, November 5, 1998*

My second day in an assignment that turns out to be assisting a fourth grade teacher. The class operates at an intermittent noise and disorganization level that I would not allow as a sub, yet the teacher seems to be in control.

The kids have to solve the problem of the farmer who has a wolf, a head of cabbage, and a goat and must get all three across the river without any of them getting eaten, in a boat that's only big enough to take one at a time. When I figure it out, I tell the mother of one of the kids who's visiting the class. She then apparently tells her daughter and her team wins, demonstrating that Little League is not the only competition that parents should be barred from.

It eventually turns out that my first instinct on this class may have been correct. By the end of this day the teacher's finally had it, loses her patience, cancels PE, and gives them six things for homework instead of the two that were planned.

Spend my lunch times talking to Winnie, the school secretary from Guyana who travels all over and stays in hostels with her thirteen year old daughter. She's done the Oregon Trail, and plans on going to the Metropolitan Opera this winter. I seldom meet teachers as interesting as she. And not that it's Secretaries Day or anything, but I'm thinking secretaries are the institutional glue of the education system. From grade school to university, they hear it from everybody: teachers, parents, students, and administrators. Come to think of it, I guess they're a lot like us subs.

I'm surprised when the machine calls me to come back to this job for the next day since I already had a job in San Francisco – at least I thought I did – and the machine won't call if you've already taken a job. But I hung up in the middle of the call, called the machine back, and found that the job I thought I had today is for December 6. So here I am back again with the same class as yesterday which has apparently driven the regular teacher to take a mental health day.

She's left a note on the board telling the class that she hopes things will improve. I have one of the kids read it out aloud before they do their daily affirmation. They want to play the Be Still game and I agree, but first I have someone read the class rules off the wall which includes the "no-blurting" clause that is violated so frequently that I cancel the game, send them to their seats, and lay down the law.

The lovely L, the teacher across the hall whom I've assisted in the past, has invited me to send problem kids over to the table at the back of her room any time. I send one before her class has even arrived. Not an auspicious start, but this proves to be the only ejection of the day. She says the boys are trouble and thinks they need more structure. I have noticed one who seems to roam freely during the day. After awhile I've got the class quieter than the regular teacher had it – I don't usually get to make this kind of comparison. At lunch the para tells me I'm doing a great job, and at the end of the day L tells me that the kids were the quietest she's ever seen them this morning. So I actually feel like I've accomplished something, and my self-doubt about maybe being too harsh after seeing how long a leash the regular teacher gave the kids has been dissipated.

And in addition to discipline, teaching even breaks out on occasion today. While the other kids are otherwise occupied, I am painstakingly trying to walk the girl who must be last in the class in math through the day's word problem. Mostly this involves getting her to pay attention and write down her partial answers as she goes along, so that she doesn't have to keep returning to step one. She's doing the same basic procedures anyone does – child or adult. She just has to be steered back on course about every ten seconds.

One of the main crises of the day is the scissors question – some of them want the good (sharp) ones to cut fabric. Eventually I let them use them, but only right next to me. I have to do some shouting about kids waving the sharpened ends of pencils in each other's faces and they've made me hoarse by pre-lunch cleanup time. Rogue (the girl whose mother spilled the beans yesterday) is having a bad day for some reason. The para tells me that she was crying because the story she's reading has a guy who wants to kill the kittens.

At one point I ask if anyone has seen the brown magic marker and a kid tells me it isn't magic. Sure enough, it says "Crayola." I suppose that the brand name "Magic Marker" disappeared years ago when I wasn't paying attention. (Likewise, I changed my original "xeroxes" to "photocopies" in yesterday's notes, so the contemporary reader could follow.) And, oh yes, there's a bird chirping in this classroom all day, along with a goldfish tank. A few years on in their school lives and you won't be able to trust the kids not to eat the fish.

PAPER CLIPS – *Seventh Grade Math/Science, Skyline Middle, November 9, 1998*

There's a piece of moldering bread on the teacher's desk with peanut butter on it and a fork stuck in the peanut butter. I ask a student about it. He says it's an experiment, it's been there for two weeks, and that the teacher probably doesn't want me to remove it. And have I mentioned that this teacher is on the cynical side? He was here at the beginning of the day because he has jury duty and told me, "Nothing personal, but when I have a sub, I usually have no paper clips left when I return." Big black market in those things, I hear. He types out the day's schedule for me and says that at 10:25 "unfortunately" I have prep time, something I wouldn't have if it were up to him. I recall that the last time I was here he was in the office saying that he wouldn't take a half day off because the sub wouldn't have to work enough to justify it. (Warms my heart to know I'm in the same union with this guy.) Maybe he'll get a murder trial, be sequestered for a month, and I can steal his post-it's – one every day. I love ya, man.

EVERY DAY – *Seventh Grade Math/Science, William Howard Taft Middle, November 13, 1998*

The regular teacher says on the recording that she has two tough seventh grades for double periods. Double periods are horrible things for subs. That's a whole lot of "He did it; she did it" time. A Chinese kid who finishes his work early sees my copy of *The Nation* with a cover article on bio-terrorism and wants to read it. Intellectual curiosity – now that's different. They'll probably put this kid on some kind of watch list. Otherwise, a pretty normal day, with an afternoon class that's mostly a collection of what My Friend the Evil Substitute Teacher would call "dopes and jerks." Myself, I consider them a group of sensible, intelligent young men and young women who are at the moment choosing to act like dopes and jerks. One class goes to the library where a student asks if he can go to his locker to get the book that he needs to read in the library. When I suggest that he should have thought of that earlier, he replies that he can't think. Another middle school student exhibiting self-awareness.

Back in the classroom for eighth period, an educational disaster area develops in the back of the room that I ignore as long as I can. My first consideration in these situations is always what's fair to the rest of the class, and I decide this one rude little girl has crossed the line by throwing things and the like and is interfering with other students who might, at least for the purpose of discussion, be interested in working. She makes a scene on her way out, won't get out of the door, etc. At the end of the day I mutter "This class is pathetic," to myself, but loudly enough so that it can be heard in the immediate vicinity. One girl responds: "I know, it's like this every day." But then the regular teacher never said it wouldn't be.

MARKET DOWN – *Sixth Grade Math, Calvin Coolidge Middle, November 16, 1998*

The regular teacher is here when I arrive. She has to take her son to a doctor in San Jose, and wishes me a pleasant day. Quite a change of pace from that guy at Skyline. I've had these kids before. One asks if he had annoyed me the last time I was here. I don't particularly remember, but explain that, as he is a middle school student, if I've had ever had him in class before, I assume that I've found him annoying. The class laughs. Another sign of self awareness – I wonder if this could be a trend.

To announce the need for quiet in first period, I do a mock-public address system voice. One of the kids says, "You sound like one of those space guys." I ask, "What makes you think I'm not?" Aha! Perhaps the slightest fear now in some little TV-addled brain that the sub might be a replicant, mutant, or android: advantage – sub. One kid who's been calling out and the like asks to go to the bathroom. I ask if he can tell me why it's always the nuisances that want to go to the bathroom, but he doesn't know what the word nuisance means – too busy living it to study it. As they say, those who can't do, learn.

As home room arrives, I'm thinking maybe I'm supposed to be out in the hall during passing period. No sane person would want to be there – imagine rush hour in the New York City subway, with smaller, less-socialized people. But who am I to speak about what the sane might want – I'm here subbing in middle school. And anyhow, in a lot of schools, watching the halls is one of your duties. In fact, I believe that My Friend the Evil Substitute Teacher first came into the business on some kind of Swineherd-to-Schools program in one of the more rural states, designed to utilize the abilities of people already trained to watch over sentient beings. Anyhow, my little bit of diligence at this moment allows the kids inside the room to knock the podium down when I'm out in the hall. The lesson plan is now somewhere in a pile of papers on the floor. Among other things, it contains the stock quotes I'm supposed to read out for fourth period stock class. Yes, stock class – where they will learn that "earning" has nothing to do with working. Corporate America needs good citizens and it's never too soon to start the obfuscation.

In seventh period I throw one out after numerous warnings to stop walking around, shouting out "faggot", "kiss my ass," etc. The counseling office sends him back because his counselor is at lunch – presumably to continue shouting out "faggot", "kiss my ass," etc. I have to call and ask them to take him back. This school is seriously deficient in backing you up. They get away with it because it's not too terrible here.

I find myself back here two days later with the same sixth grade booger-and-fart crowd, with a Language Arts/Social Science assignment and wind up throwing the same kid out as on Monday for the usual talking out, refusal to open book, feet on desk, etc. The absurdity of what I'm actually arguing about with these kids frequently occurs to me in the middle of it all, but I cannot give in to rationality and abrogate my responsibilities to civilization. After all, these children may one day be asked to go fight in a country whose name they cannot spell, for no reason at all and in order to do that they will need a strong foundation of doing what they're told, regardless of its intrinsic value.

The crusty little woman who controls the cafeteria line is working as a para in my first period class. We start the kids in a reading of a play based on *The Yearling*. It's in southern dialect and some of the kids get into doing it. It reminds me of an English class I had for two weeks in Brighton High in Boston that was scheduled to read some of the *Canterbury Tales* in the original Middle English. The regular teacher gave me the option of not doing it, but I relished the idea of trying to get them to hear the sound of what was written on the pages, which is the only way Middle English makes sense. Those kids were in the "Distributive Ed" program which meant part-time school and part-time work, so they were unlikely to ever meet Chaucer again and I've always ranked high among my educational achievements the one kid in that class concluding that "Chauncer was all right." Anyhow, back here in San Francisco, the dialogue in the play is similar to what a lot of the black kids speak. One of them, who had the biggest role, says it sounds like people in his family, which is from the south.

At lunch one of the teachers speaks about a teachers workshop on sexual minorities that he's attending. No such lunchroom discussions back in Boston.

Homework for last period is to write a sentence using each of the twenty spelling words the teacher has written on the board. He has spelled "disastrous" – "disasterous." I correct it, with a note to the teacher indicating that I have done so. I do wonder how this will be received by the regular, but figure my responsibility to the language comes first. When I collect the homework from yesterday, I notice that they had the option of defining yesterday's spelling words or using them in a sentence. One of the words was *substitute*. Only one kid took the usage option. His sentence read "I don't like substitute teachers." Hey, the feeling's mutual, kid.

CONFLICT – *Principal, Winter Hill Elementary, November 19, 1998*

Upon arrival, the secretary informs me that the bulk of my day's work as principal will be shelving books in the library, with some yard and lunch room coverage. I ask if the principal herself shelves books and the secretary says that yes she does, and that she and the principal sometimes sweep floors as well, a story backed up by another later in the day. Most significantly, I hope for a no-yelling day.

Kids walk around the cafeteria wearing *Winter Hill School Conflict Manager* wind breakers. Have a hunch there's lots of contracts in, and doctoral dissertations on "Conflict management in inner-city schools" these days. Mostly Chinese school; fried rice for lunch. They eat so fast, there are three shifts in one lunch period. They have to raise their hands to be excused. Not the normal lunchroom mayhem.

YOU DID IT – *Communication Handicapped, Whittier Elementary, November 20, 1998*

"Communication handicapped" class is a new one on me, but we're here to learn, right? The secretary is new and knows from nothing and the principal is out, so a teacher shows me to the room, but right away I've got to go outside and get the kids before I even have time to read the instructions. They don't even get to their seats before two are fighting while hanging up their coats. The pair will be trouble all day long. When I get a chance to read the instructions I see that the fracas was predictable in that I was only supposed to let two or three of them hang up their coats at a time. Oh, boy!

They settle down to some silent reading and the aide arrives at 9. At 9:15 they have "social language development" which involves visiting each other for over an hour. They're basically hanging out, which is apparently not a thing that all of them are easily able to do peacefully. I've quickly come to understand the distinction between "communication handicapped" and "speech impaired."

Shaneeka – one of the day-long-trouble kids – reads me Dr. Seuss' *Green Eggs and Ham*. She reads quite well, and if she had the teacher's attention to herself all day she'd probably be fine. I have to sharpen pencils for the kids here since they're not allowed to do it themselves, and one has an almost unsharpenable pencil. I admit I used to scoff at kids who said they couldn't sharpen their pencils until I worked the election in Bosnia last year and we were given a shipment of pencils from China that all the poll workers hated. Now I know there really is such a thing as a bad pencil.

Everyone gets a report for the day with eight categories, and may or may not get a star put up in the front of the room for the day. Shaneeka and Jason disqualify themselves by kicking chairs and Matthew who had the fight with Shaneeka to start the day disqualifies himself with almost everything he does. I'm liberal and give the rest stars.

I'm supposed to read a book to them after lunch. I try, but give up when I can't get them to pay attention. Then a spelling test. One group doesn't do it at all, presumably because they can't spell at all. The rest of the class is divided into two levels. They're allowed to study the words right before the test. Shaneeka's the only one who gets one wrong. She puts two "s"s in fresh. When I give the test back she says she didn't spell it wrong. I ask how the second "s" got there. She tells me that I put it there and throws her test down. The para and I have about had it with her by now. The para puts the test in her purse and says she'll speak to the teacher on Monday. At dismissal line Shaneeka attacks Matthew who has apparently taunted her. He's crying on the floor. I march Shaneeka into the principal's office and am told to leave a note for the regular teacher which I do. At the moment I consider her performance as bad as anything I've ever seen at that age level. This class is actually a shocker. What happens to these kids? Do they grow out of this? Or not?

THEY WANT ME – *Social Studies, Ralph Bunche High, November 30, 1998*

My first impressions are of grim corridors and sub handouts not reprinted clearly enough to be easily read. Gay and lesbian display in hallway on way in; flyer on the wall by the doorway in classroom: "Want Free Condoms?" Nothing like this at Regis High School. The first period class is already in before I get there, and looking quite settled. I look around for an adult presence to explain the lack of turmoil, but there is none. I'm to show a video on immigration. The teacher comes in after first period and he's one of the people from the union interview the other day. He asks how everything went and tells me that it will get rowdier, first period was the Honors class.

At lunchtime, I search all over for the teacher's lunch room because I can't read the room number on the fuzzy handout and when I finally find it there's almost no one there. Apparently this is another school where everyone eats in their own classroom. Mine turns out to be full of students during lunch. During class time it's another matter: two students absent from first period; eight from both fifth and sixth; and fifteen from seventh. Good news travels quickly among the student population.

All in all, not a bad gig. Nice to have a high school day. When I arrive home there's a message from a Skyline teacher I've replaced who wants to know if I'm available. Later a Waterfront teacher calls and says the secretary gave him my name. Ah, to be a substitute teacher at the peak of his powers, and in widespread demand!

WHY YOU LIE? – *Seventh Grade English/Social Studies, Waterfront Middle, December 2, 1998*

Yesterday's offerings were all for schools that would be nonstop scream fests. It was back in Boston that I developed my sub's credo: *If they call, you work. If they don't call, you've got the day off. Either way, No problem.* Of course, my rent was a lot cheaper then.

Anyhow, the keys they give me to the classroom today don't work and I'm on my third trip upstairs before the regular teacher arrives with the lesson plan and lets me in. He says the day will get better after first period; I sure hope so. Another regular teacher is in here for a few minutes and even she has quite a difficult time with the class. She calls two out in the hall to talk to her and they're refusing to go. I make an announcement that they should be respecting all the adults in the class and that I'll be sending people to the counselor if I have to. I've got a whole table of girls just mouthing off, interrupting other people when they're reading. And naturally, the kids who have been problems all morning start filing up asking to go to the bathroom while I'm trying to listen to the ones reading aloud. One kid asks if he should just throw up on the floor. I tell him, yes, he should. He doesn't.

My announcement that I'm taking down names for their teacher quiets them for about a minute. One of the girls the other teacher had asked to talk to her in the hall comes up to me and asks to go to the bathroom. I tell her no, that her table has been disruptive and I don't do favors for tables like that, and as a matter of fact I don't do favors for classes like this. She says "Man, you're stupid." I ask her name and she refuses to give it to me. The other students shout out various options, but whatever her name, I'm going to be rid of her now. I call the counselor to have her removed. He tells me to write a referral, but I don't have any forms, so he says he'll be up.

Meanwhile, I've seized one yo-yo and one paper plane and see another yo-yo, but the kid refuses to give it to me and so I have the counselor take it when he arrives, along with the one I took. The kid with the second yo-yo asks if it's true that I put him on the bad list. I tell him I did and point out that he did no work. He says he came late – which he did – very – and he didn't have the assignment sheet. A ridiculous discussion ensues as to whether an eighth grader is old enough to know to ask. I think subs were taking yo-yo's from kids in Babylon.

Sixth period proves to be what My Friend the Evil Substitute Teacher would call, "another bunch of assholes." This class is called *Academic Exploration*. I had asked the regular teacher what this meant before realizing that he had given me a Simpsons video to show in this period. When I said, "I see," he muttered something about how that was not really what the class was about. Of course there is an assignment preliminary to the Simpsons and we have to wait a long time for the class "fuck-ups" – as My Friend the Evil Substitute Teacher would call them – to finish it.

The counseling office has called up to let me know that they are sending a new girl to this class. She quietly sits through about the last half of it. What an introduction to school! On her way out I tell her I hope things will be better tomorrow.

After sixth, a girl I've thrown out earlier comes back to pick up her assignment. I tell her she can take her referral – which mentions her tearing up her assignment – or I'll just bring it to the counselor. She says, "Why you lie? Huh? Why you lie and say I rip it up?" I show her the assignment she had torn and ask what that is. After a few rounds of this elevated discussion, I tell her to get lost.

It's now the seventh and final round of today's bout. I tell the kids not to make a liar out of their teacher who told me they were the good class (while muttering under my breath that there's not much competition.) But they do, in fact, turn out to be much better and get quite a bit of work done. I almost feel guilty when I let some of them out to the bathroom when I wouldn't let the previous classes out, after all, jerks can have weak bladders just as well as nice kids. But eventually this class too degenerates because they have double periods here and they don't have enough to do.

HEY, KEEP IT DOWN – *First Grade, Benjamin Banneker Elementary, December 3, 1998*

Always a pleasant feeling going to the Banneker. The classes are often far from easy, but the atmosphere is supportive. It has the same open classroom layout as that elementary school in Hell – Ernest Everett Just, but the open structure here seems to facilitate communication with, and possible assistance from the other teachers. There it seemed only to provide a public forum for torture. Officially I'm replacing a resource room teacher, but I get a first grade class. It's a little rough at first as I don't know their start-of-the-day routine (posting the date, weather, and other variables on a board) and the kids are calling out from their morning circle with their various opinions as to what the routine actually is. One kid says, "Ooh, she called you an old man." To which the caller replies, "He is an old man." Dang! Everyone can hear in this open classroom structure, and I was hoping the young female teachers wouldn't notice.

Overall, they're difficult enough that I can't get through the morning song or poem, and I send them to their seats where they are supposed to start writing their journals. This improves them some immediately and when the para shows up at 9:30, that improves them some more. But the psychological problems of some of the kids are, as usual, obvious and immense. Two boys and one girl start crying when they get frustrated at getting something wrong.

We rhyme *r* words and think up *s* words. After recess it's off to the library. One girl wants a book without words; another wants me to find her a nature book; a boy wants an ABC book. More kids want to hold my hand than I've got hands, but the boy who's this week's "student of the week" asserts that his status means that he's entitled to hold my hand. Then it's math and then *Play and Do Review*, where, so far as I can see, my only duty is to make sure they don't kill themselves or one another. At one point I'm teaching a little girl, who reads very well, some standard English. She asks me, "What do this say?" and I tell her that it should be "What does this say?" which she dutifully repeats.

And the elementary school day goes by in its usual rush. As a substitute teacher, I'm so used to telling kids to keep quiet, that when I walk into a teachers room for lunch, I have to remind myself not to tell everyone there to shut up.

CLEAN RECORD – *Math, Nathaniel Hawthorne Middle, December 4, 1998*

The regular teacher is there when I arrive and we go over the day. She has a three-checks-and-you-get-detention system. When I remark on this, she says she's a first-year teacher and otherwise they would eat her alive. I tell her I'm a first-day teacher, every day.

(A bit more serious than the last time I was here for a music class when the day's educational presentation was the movie *Scrooge* – all day. Last period had some active yo-yoers and I told them I was willing to look the other way if they kept the yo-yo's to the back of the room – we couldn't have them distracting everyone else from watching *Scrooge*, could we?)

The kids are not bad in first period and then the assistant principal walks in and they get rather good, actually. Like a lot of math classes, they have a warm-up problem. Today's concerns area and perimeter and she notices that some of them don't seem to know how to do it, so she goes over it with them. She says they're a great class. I tell her that they're, of course, better in her presence. We agree that what we see has entirely to do with our respective titles. On the whole, a pleasant interaction with the school administration – unusual, unfortunately.

The later it gets on this Friday afternoon the crazier they get and by eighth period I've had about as much of these guys as I want to. The teacher's directions call for giving them the option of several activities but I'm not in the mood to give them anything, so it'll be silent reading – as if silence were actually a possibility. The only thing actually quiet at this point appears to be their brains. This class's main problem child asks if he can jump out the window. I tell him not until 3:30, because the paperwork would be onerous if he did something like that during class time. My Friend the Evil Substitute Teacher taught me that, and so far, it has worked – none have yet hurled themselves through the window on my watch. Who says you can't reason with them? And, I will proudly point out, I have yet to hurl any of them out the window myself. So, in order to keep that record intact, I eventually send this cute little fellow to the counselor, with apologies for giving her so much business. This is the sort of class where a stream of kids come up with some scam to leave the room, and if they can make their case at all plausible, I'm happy to let them go because there ain't nothing useful likely to happen here. Ah! It's 3:30, Friday afternoon! They leave. Nothing personal.

Two weeks later, I meet a woman at a School Committee campaign fundraiser who says she's the head of the Nathaniel Hawthorne Parents Association. When I tell her that I sub here sometimes, an alarmed look comes over her face. Apparently her son comes home with stories about the hard time he gives subs. Perhaps one of today's joys.

NO IDEA – *Resource Room, Waterfront Middle, December 9, 1998*

6:27 AM call for a 7:30 start. Breakfast in the car today. In third period, a kid walks in, gives me a dose of his charming pubescent attitude – and then apologizes! I search my memory for a precedent. This class writes about a tangerine and reads aloud the encyclopedia entries I have copied. Bad reading compounds bad reading – when a student reading aloud reads poorly, the rest of the class is going to lose interest. The regular teacher, who's actually in the building working on Union Building Committee business, comes in to read them the riot act – a major plus. The para in this class is also very good. She ejects kids on her own later in the day, which makes things go a lot more smoothly. She also tells me that the reason you don't find any teachers in the teachers room here is that they're all out on Chestnut St. for lunch. And teachers can afford to eat out nowadays. This is largely due to teachers unions, of course – something many of today's "reformers" would like to undo.

I am warned about the sixth period class. It's quieter than expected, but one hostile-looking girl isn't reading and tries to make eye contact with me, I expect so that she can say, "What are you looking at?" if she does. When the class has to write in their reading logs she says she doesn't have a pencil. I tell her the classroom rule that she can buy one for ten cents. She responds, "I ain't buying shit!" I write these proceedings down, at which point she comes up to see what I'm writing and ask why, although she assures me that she doesn't really care what I write. I ask her what she's worrying about then. She responds, "Racist!" When I describe this to the para who's been out of the room for all of this, she says that the girls in this class don't do well with men, and she wonders what might be behind that. You've got no idea what type of stories you might be in the middle of.

Seventh period is math bingo: I call out "four minus two," and "seven plus four" and the like, and the kids cover the resulting number on their cards. I catch one kid using a calculator – for two-plus-two! Twice! He steals it back off the desk the first time.

The para tells me I did well, that it was good that I was willing to raise my voice. I tell her I wouldn't know what else to do, other than to throw them out, and you can't throw them all out, much as you might like to. Always have to make an effort to remember that they may be totally different in a minute, particularly in a class of difficult kids like this. The para and I concur on just what a sorry part of the human voyage this age is.

IT BREAKS *– Ceramics, Appian Way High, December 10, 1998*
Ceramics is a class that probably no one really hates, except maybe today's ersatz instructor. I recognize full well the importance of ceramics in human history. 4,000 years ago there really weren't a lot of alternatives to ceramic bowls; and in a few primitive societies there still aren't. But remind me as to why we have public school classes in the making of heavy, fragile, generally unattractive objects. However, for most of the kids who are there, it beats things like, say, having to learn about the time when people actually used this stuff.

On my way in, the secretary tells me that they need me to cover a class during what should be my prep period because they're short of subs, and I understand her to say that I will be paid accordingly. We'll see.

At the beginning of class, I announce my superfluous presence to the students and explain that I assume my main role in their lives will be to verify their attendance. The day consists mostly of gentle prodding of kids who are studying other subjects instead of actually working on their ceramics project. A girl asks when Veterans Day is and I explain how the Armistice that stopped the war was signed at 11:00 on the eleventh day of the eleventh month. I ask if the kids know which war the Armistice ended and the girl next to her actually gets it right. This will be my educating for the day.

The teacher's note said to watch out for the boys on the side of the room by the kiln in third period, but it's all pretty mild stuff here. The main problem is the occasional kid who's not doing anything because she says her work has to dry; kinda like letting the pots soak when you're supposed to do dishes. One kid asks if I know anything about ceramics. I tell her I know that these things break if you drop them, which seems to satisfy her. I think this was about what she expected my knowledge to be.

Today I overhear a discussion on the subject of farting. But as this is high school, not middle school, it is a mature discussion in which both boys and girls participate.

NO SHOTS – *Assistant Principal, Waterfront Middle, December 12, 1998*
Philosophical ruminations:

By one theory, the perceived cuteness of infants and very young children is a characteristic evolved to enhance the likelihood of the child's nurture and survival at this most vulnerable stage of life. The cutest kids survived disproportionately to their numbers, thereby passing on their propensity for cuteness. So why do middle school students exist in their current form then? A strange silence shrouds this question and we are left to speculate. Could the extreme obnoxiousness displayed by so many of the species during the pubescent years be seen as some type of secondary weaning inducement? But from the perspective of the survival of the parent, wouldn't the simple, immediate elimination of the source of that behavior make as much, if not more evolutionary sense?

Could what we experience today be a form of species-level blowback? Logic would suggest wide-scale parental abandonment of what are now middle school-aged children should have occurred at some point in the history of the species. Perhaps certain traits were inadvertently magnified when the abandoned children discovered that the same behavior considered repugnant in human society also terrified beasts in the wild – and was therefore valuable?

Although no rational explanation for the creation of middle schools has yet to be articulated, their widespread development presumably came in response to an equally-widespread intuition. But what? A notion that the middle school age bracket is as useless to human society as the appendix is to the human body? And that middle school-age students, who in an earlier period might have been abandoned, as the appendix is surgically removed from the body, should be isolated from society in this milder form? (And could any of this be related to the reason for the persistence of ceramics in the school curriculum?)

Some see in human adolescence proof for the nonexistence of God, while others argue the opposite – that it demonstrates that there is, in fact, a God, but a malevolent one. Certain heretical Thomists, who infer the characteristics of the Creator from those of His creations, are particularly prone to this latter point of view – along with various others who find themselves exposed to middle schools for the first time. It is no accident that nowadays most Thomists inhabit cloistered monasteries, for just as they say that there are no atheists in a foxhole, you won't find many believers in a benevolent God within the walls of a middle school.

Ultimately it may be the philosophy known as "deep ecology" that offers the best hope for finding meaning in human adolescence. Deep ecology views all human activity from the perspective of its impact on Gaia – Mother Earth. From that point of view, the barnyard behavior one can observe on any middle school corridor may be seen as beneficial. For surely the human race would by now already have expanded to numbers well beyond the planet's capacity to support, absent this obvious disincentive to procreate.

I am aroused from my philosophical reverie by a student greeting me with a "Hello, Mr. Sub," to which I reply with a smart, "Hello, Ms. Student," and stride into the principal's office to find out what my exact role in the defense of Mother Earth will be today. I'm late, so I find I've missed the first part of my assignment – "Bring the eighth grade students into the building" after the morning bell. But, as if to assuage any doubt as to whether my assignment really means I am part of the management team for the day, my next task is collating photocopies of packets entitled "Management I and II."

There's a fire drill while I'm doing filing in the counseling office. Outside, I get to talking to an old-timer who had also been stationed in the counseling office for some reason. He's not pleased with what he's seeing in this drill, compared with how fire drills used to go when he was teaching. This was too slow-going for him – "We used to get out." He notices someone giving commands to students and asks me, "Is that a monitor?" When I inform him that that rather casually dressed person is actually a teacher, he says, "Well, at least they fit in, but they have to say something three times and they're not clearing anything!" I tell him I gather he hasn't been spending too much time around the schools lately.

During lunch we have a couple of fight false alarms in the yard. Each time, large numbers of kids stream in the direction the fight is thought to be in. The second time it happens, lunch is ended early. The scene reminds me of newspaper descriptions of fights in the yard at Corcoran State Prison. Of course, the guards there shoot the prisoners to break those up.

In the copy room I confer with Wednesday's teacher about my day subbing for her. At the end of the day she presents me with an apology note written by the pain-in-the-ass girl. An apology note to a substitute – another man bites dog story.

THAT ELIGIBILITY THING – Phys Ed, Appian Way High, December 14, 1998

On my instruction sheet, "absent" is consistently spelled "ascent" – it's the PE Department, you know. Two subs in the gym at the same time today: Advantage – kids. Neither of us knows them so they can easily disappear. One kid looks at my shoes and asks what size they are and I tell him 12, so he asks can we trade shoes so he can play basketball, as he has shown up without sneakers. I decline. A third period girl is curled up on the shopping cart used to transport the basketballs. She has cramps – "woman problems" – as her friends explain.

PE is a world unto itself. Today, the teachers are discussing the upcoming basketball season in the office. They're playing Alioto from San Francisco. "Bunch of brothers?" one of them asks. "Yeah, and they're not very good on that eligibility thing in the city." The basketball coach says, "If we go 2-8, I want a raise." One guy's got a sign over his desk that says: "Homework causes brain damage." One of my colleagues is reading Bobby Knight speeches on a web site. And the sub's job here may require different skills than in the classroom, like maybe holding things for the students while they play ball – key chains, maybe a stick earring.

At one point there is a coed basketball game and the boys actually pass to the girls! Of course, the girls look like they're probably on the varsity. But remarkably civilized, nonetheless; another reminder of why people move to the suburbs.

Back the next day for an English job. A first period student asks what room we are in. I start to ask how he got here if he doesn't know where he is, but I realize it can be cruel to ask a high school student such a penetrating question this early in the morning. Sixth period students ask why I'm so happy. I tell them because I'm not in middle school.

FROM PRIEDOR – *Computer Science, Calvin Coolidge Middle, January 10, 1999*

Frosty enough that I have to scrape the windshield this morning and I haven't owned a decent scraper since Boston – you throw those things out the window when you cross over the line from Nevada. I may have to send back to Boston for one. So this year, it would appear that it has to be a cold day in San Francisco before they call me to sub. This will turn out to be my coldest winter so far and Stephanie Salter says in her *Examiner* column that it's the coldest of her 23 here. Let's not lose perspective though. This is still winter in *San Francisco,* so some of those days when there's ice on the surface of the play area when I arrive turn out so warm that I have to return to school to retrieve the jacket I forgot in the closet.

Anyhow, today I cover some type of partial-semester elective second period. I am to choose from a list of assignments such as "Weather – what kind do you like?" or make up my own. I assign: "Iraq: What do you know? What do you think?" Some kids say they know nothing about it; some – mostly boys – say the bombing of Iraq probably had to be done; some – mostly girls – think war's too bad. (You didn't forget that Clinton Bombed Iraq in 1998, did you?)

A later class has a kid from Priedor in Bosnia who knows a lot of things that his classmates don't. Next month he's going back there for the first time in four years. He says his relatives are no longer in Priedor because the Serbs are; they're now in Sarajevo, Mostar and Bosanski Novi. Chances are that most of his classmates will grow up to be Americans who will never know very much about the sort of things he has experienced, which is nice for them, but maybe not so good for the world.

WHITE NIGGERS – *Industrial Arts, Appian Way High, January 12, 1999*

First three periods are photography where normally they learn to process film and make prints, but with a sub there will be no darkroom work. After all, we don't want the kids breaking the equipment, drinking the chemicals, and so forth. The TV in the room prompts the usual requests to watch Jerry Springer. I explain that watching Jerry Springer will lower their IQ's approximately a point for each minute they watch. I'm not sure if they follow that, though. It may be too late already. Next up is Electronics class and then Metal-working. Decidedly not an intellectual crowd here, although I think I see one kid actually doing the make-up bookwork that they are all officially supposed to be doing. I wonder what he's doing in this class. At this school, the Asian kids call white kids "nigger," etc. There are few black kids here, so the word has more or less gone over to the public domain. Always interesting to read of the campaigns to eliminate it from the language. I suspect those campaigners might be better off putting their energies elsewhere.

Back for the same program later in the week after being called in for something with an unintelligible three letter acronym that turns out to be Special Ed, which is what most unintelligible acronyms ultimately turn out to be. By the time I arrive, they'd already decided to switch me to Industrial Arts, but they still want me to cover the Special Ed class for first period – only for legal reasons, though; the para there will actually do the class. When I get there I find this really unpleasant para whom I've worked with before. In the past, her attitude seemed to be that I'm paid to be there to teach and so I should just figure it out. So, today I beat her to the punch at copping an attitude. I ask if she's got the scantrons – the attendance sheet you bubble for the absent and tardy. (Which reminds me: It is only the educational establishment that's keeping the word "tardy" in Websters', isn't it? And why? Who's making out on this? Am I the only one asking these questions these days?) Anyhow, she says no, yesterday the sub had them. I tell her I'm not the sub for this class. She says she guesses she'll have to get them. I mutter that I guess she will.

I wind up reading some civics chapter with the three (of four) kids here today. If someone was trying to make this stuff boring, they've done an excellent job. Of course, civics was ever so. Part of a plot to depress voter turnout?

Now on to Industrial Arts again. Three uneventful Photography periods, an Electronics and then Metal – only the page on the calendar has changed from the last time I was here. They're supposed to finish their book work, etc., etc. I don't get a very good feeling about all this, but then Industrial Arts has always been school for kids who don't want to or shouldn't be in school, hasn't it?

NOT CUT OUT? – *Third Grade, Bonanza Elementary, January 14, 1999*

There's no lesson plan because the teacher didn't expect to be out today, and I am late because I've never been here before (this is South San Francisco) and have read the map wrong. This all causes a bit of a panic until the principal comes in to the classroom and asks for helpers and I remember that I am not in the big city up north and things are all easier here. The kids want to read in pairs, and soon there's a peaceful sound of half of the class reading a *Boxcar Children* book to the other half. Yesterday's sub has left a business card on the desk. It says, "Educator 2nd-12th grades." Wonder what his problem is with first grade.

Another teacher shows me a paper folding-and-cutting trick to make an eight page book from a single sheet of paper. But as soon as I have the kids do it I can no longer remember how it works and have to look at one of the their books – I may not be cut out for this. The end of the day is spent outside sanding sticks for the totem poles they're making. Most of the kids are scraping with scissors instead of sanding. I suspect this is not part of the program; I don't think the Tlingits used scissors.

NON-EUCLIDIAN– *Second/Third Grade, Benjamin Banneker Elementary, January 27, 1999*

I have never claimed to be top of my class in getting down the morning details from the phone call in the dark. I'm just not that into taking notes in those circumstances. Name of school and starting time I'll get. Name of teacher? Not always. Job number? We can straighten that out later if necessary. But today Winnie, the regular secretary and opera friend, who would normally know all these things, is out and I don't know whom I'm replacing and there's more than one teacher out. So off to one class that turns out to already have a sub, then to the right one, where the regular teacher still is, enroute to a conference. She says the class responds well to positive reinforcement. Can be tough to get to that positive reinforcement level when you're subbing though.

At recess I've got a kid crying because he says a girl told him he couldn't play whatever because he was white (he's the only "white" kid in the class). She says that's not what she said. I'm going to let the final resolution of this matter carry over into tomorrow. I've thrown three kids out and it's something of a war of attrition. But the para seems to think I'm doing well and says he'll definitely ask to have me back the next time.

The geometry in this school is decidedly non-Euclidian, by the way – you can start out for somewhere and walk back into the other end of your classroom and never get where you've going. Open classroom; closed universe. Today I simply could not locate the geometric coordinates of the lunchroom, so I ate in the classroom.

IF THERE'S A HEAVEN– *First Grade, Grant Elementary, January 28, 1999*

I'm replacing a teacher who's replacing the principal. We say the Pledge of Allegiance. The kids immediately follow it up by singing "Yankee Doodle Dandy." Then they do aerobics. All with no prompting. Wow! Did I mention that the whole class is Chinese? I've died and gone to substitute teacher heaven (which I assume is somewhere in China).

The para here is very strict. Things that would be good behavior elsewhere are bad here. There are student papers draped over cords all around the room – it looks like laundry hung up to dry. Recess at 9:15, fire drill, another recess at 10:15. We climb stairs mostly; excellent physical fitness program here.

My Friend the Evil Substitute Teacher likes having all these fire drills. He sees them as a kind of taunt to the students, reminding them of how seldom their dreams of watching their school go up in flames actually come true.

TO THE PARK– *Eighth Grade Math/Science, Skyline Middle, January 29, 1999*

Skyline is considered a K-8 school, but it has two separate "campuses" for the elementary and middle schools that are connected by a steep path behind the buildings, but reached by different streets. And the meandering streets in Twin Peaks can make it pretty hard to figure how to get from one of them to the other if you haven't done it before. So after finding my way from the elementary to the middle school I ask the secretary if they can change the tape that gives the elementary school address. But she tells me the school department won't comply. The school's got one name; it gets one address on the machine. It's left to the middle school teachers to specify the other address on their own message – as Monday's teacher did, and today's didn't. Today's guy has been out all week and there's no lesson plan or attendance forms; not what I expect here.

The next-door teacher comes in and says that we can have the option of having half hour periods and then going to the park for two hours. The kids all like that; I like that. I've got one giving me some lip and saying he's got to go to the office. I ask his name and he say's it's Mr. Gallagher. Thank you, my child! Refusing to give his name makes him a multiple offender, so he's going to get his way and go to the office after all. But it seems these are not the terms he had in mind and now he won't go, so I call the office. The office asks is it so-and-so, and the others kids say that it is so-and-so, and the office tells me that so-and-so's supposed to go to some other room, anyhow. The teacher from there comes in to say she's supposed to have him for the nonce. I explain that after she's done with him, she should find somewhere else to send him other than back here. She says that's what she needed to know and thanks me. Hopefully he'll go on to better things for the day.

I pass around an attendance sheet and tell them that this is like in college and I'm willing to treat them that way to the degree that they're up to it. I've got three boys who all want to go to get the food for the class fish tank and we have a lengthy discussion before they grant that one of them will be sufficient for the task. First period thinks I look like Jack Nicholson as the "Joker." In second period, one kid wants to know if I'm an actor. I'm used to the Jack Nicholson stuff, so I'm starting to wonder if I can garner any real world benefit from it. Specifically, Jack is said to consort with Lara Flynn Boyle these days. Now I've greatly admired Ms. Flynn Boyle since she played Donna, my favorite member of the Twin Peaks High School senior class. I wonder if Donna would like a substitute teacher. If I remind the other students of Jack, why not her?

"Mandatory" is spelled "manditory" on the board – presumably by the regular teacher. I take the liberty of changing it. I assign the science classes to read the next couple of pages in their *Teen Health* books and give me a week's school lunch menus. The results include items like "Chinese Food," "Thai Food," peanut butter and jelly sandwiches, and water. The last two items comprise my own lunch, so we are pretty much on the same nutritional wavelength, but I wonder if I've done the right thing with this assignment. Will this encourage them to grow up to think that talking about food and wine constitutes intellectual discussion, as seems to be the norm in much of the Bay Area?

A couple of girls come up and ask me what a necrophiliac is. I tell them that someone will be reporting me to the principal if I tell them, so they can find it in a dictionary. They go next door to do so and return to class as grown-ups. Later one says that now that she knows will I tell her more? Not likely. Even in San Francisco, we don't discuss necrophilia with middle school girls in class – not yet, anyhow.

One girl asks to go to her locker. I ask what for. She says lip gloss. Request denied. It's all rather amiable and in fourth period they actually tell me what it is that they were supposed to be doing all along. The remains of a peanut butter and jelly sandwich lie on the floor in the front of the room – apparently it's a thing at this school. We go off to the park for the afternoon periods in a long, strung-out column. The other teacher gives me background. Skyline is pretty new. Most of the kids go on to Cabot, the top public school in the city; (St.) Ignatius (Loyola), which is Jesuit; Sacred Heart; Marin Catholic; University High, which is private; etc. What the parents dread most is their kids going to Alioto, the bottom-of-the-barrel public high school in the neighborhood. She finds it nice to be in a school where you can take the kids to the park and where even some of the boys are on the swings.

Why I don't have what it takes to be a real teacher: In the lunchroom a teacher says if she doesn't get to bed by 9:30 or 10, she can't sleep through the night.

SI, SE PUEDE – *Kindergarten/First Grade, Benjamin Cardozo Elementary, February 1, 1999*

I'm replacing Sister W. (Some of the black teachers call themselves Sister and Brother here) who has jury duty. She pops back into class every day, so I get a taste of the iron hand with which she rules. Great to see, because otherwise I probably would have gone easier on them at first and wasted time easing into being stricter. And I might have figured my inability to get better behavior out of them had a cultural component, that is to say that they would have performed better for a black teacher, and that I shouldn't be so harsh with a group of small, black children, who, after all, have things harder in the first place, and so forth. Susan, the white para, describes this as an African-American class and says that Nicole (Sister W) grew up in Hunter's Point in a stable household which many of these kids don't have.

Susan called me at home yesterday to tell me that they have just learned the school's principal has been removed. A new one will be in on Tuesday. Apparently there's some discrimination suit filed against the old one for telling one of the pre-K teachers that she was "too white." The *Examiner* later reports claims of anti-Semitism.

An assembly is held on the subject – in three languages. I take a Chinese bilingual class for first period, so the teacher can go explain the situation in Chinese to some kids in another class. A whole week of faculty actions will follow, all of which seem a bit strange to me in the degree to which they're trying to involve the kids. The class I have for the week certainly has no idea what's going on. There's a big "Si Se Puede" chant at the assembly and a banner hanging from the roof that says, "We need democracy in our school."

There's so much food thrown away at lunch that I ask a cafeteria woman if some of the stuff they haven't even opened can't be saved. She says no. Go to an American school cafeteria some time and then think about Africa.

The African-American, multicultural and hearing-impaired students all start the day off in a circle in the yard, reciting something called, "I stand tall" in which all of the role models are black. (People generally called "white" elsewhere are apparently "multicultural" here.) Susan has the kids write letters to Pilar, the principal who's been canned.

We've got a kindergartner named Frankie who can't tie his shoes, but wears a gold chain and carries a lot of money that he flashes around. I take to calling him the Tycoon. Maybe the plan is that he'll have enough cash that someone else will tie his shoes for him. Free time at the end of each day: I play my first Old Maid and Go Fish in some time

When the parents of a quiet kid named Donel introduce themselves before school one morning, I figure they must be here to complain about something. But no. They'd heard I was in for Sister W and just wanted to say hello. Lillian and Johnae both want to hold my hand on the way into class; The kids don't know evens from odds so one of the day's highlights is counting by twos – even and odd – all the way to 100. Quite raucous, but they like it and do seem to be learning something. I have a sore throat by the end of my four day week.

On Friday, the sub desk calls at 6:15 – live – to tell me not to come to Benjamin Cardozo because it's an in-service day, a fact not mentioned on the original school-year calendar. I already knew this and wasn't planning to come, but it's always nice to know that someone is thinking of you that early.
Student Names of the Day: Sinead Luong, Sir Denzel

N-N-N-NO – February 8, 1999

The machine calls for a Appian Way High job but on the tape the teacher requests her student teacher. South San Francisco's machine requires you to say why you're not taking a job, unlike San Francisco's. You punch in the number for the excuse describing your situation, but nothing on the list covers this, so I have to wait through them all and then recite the circumstances into the phone. Pretty annoying at six in the morning, but I do it because the one time I didn't Ms. K called me to find out my reason, so she'd know whether to have the machine keep calling me for other jobs. And while speaking to a machine may be annoying at this hour, it beats talking to a live human being. But the machine is having a bad day. It's stuttering, "in, in, in," trying to say, "invalid," meaning that it doesn't understand my reason. I've had it. Machines are not supposed to stutter. They're supposed to per-per-perfect. I hang up. Let Ms. K call.

Another day I learned that there's a point after which you don't want to answer the phone. On my way to a Morgan Phys Ed job, I was out of the shower and dressed, when the machine called to take away the job it gave me last night. And while the machine is telling me this, another call comes in on call waiting from a live person who tells me the same thing. I ask the human to tell the person I was scheduled to replace never to do this again, as I have probably missed out on other jobs. So if you call me early in the morning and I don't answer, nothing personal.

EXCUSE ME – *History/Social Science, Millard Fillmore High, February 10, 1999*

Rich D's class. His instructions invite me to provide commentary, as always. I give it a go in the second period class on the Great Depression, but, shockingly, the students evince no interest. I ask if there are any sentient beings out there. A lone voice responds: "What's that?" Almost none of the day's students seem to know anything about the plan currently being floated in Washington to invest Social Security funds in the stock market, but then I don't imagine their parents do either.

At lunch one of the most out-of-shape guys I've seen in awhile sits down near me. He appears to have trouble walking and even sitting down. At one point I hear him excuse himself and I look up and see that there's no one sitting closer than I – he's excused himself for having farted. He's wearing sneakers and has a whistle around his neck. This can't be a phys-ed teacher, can it?

A kid in last period tells a classmate that he asked a girl he knew from middle school to a Fillmore dance, but her father said he didn't want her going to another school's dance. (She goes to Cabot.) "He must think Fillmore is like Pizarro or Dolores."

Major cutting goes on here during some of my subbing stints. One student suggests I not write my name on the board and sit in the back of the room until class begins. That way the students won't realize there's a sub here until it's too late.

THE DEAD – *English, Cappuccino High, February 18, 1999*

Lately I've been holding off on South San Francisco jobs until 10PM to see if there's anything better coming from San Francisco, because South San Francisco pays so poorly (not that I didn't enjoy my day of showing crash-test dummy videos in Health class at Appian Way High last week.) But last night I broke down by 7:30 when all I'd found was something at Ghiradelli. The recent hire of a batch of new subs has been a big problem. Subs are like cab drivers: if you're the one looking for a cab at the airport on a rainy night you want as many as possible, but it's another matter if you're the cabdriver trying to make a living at it.

A first period kid asks me how I am and I say fine and him? Much better now he tells me. "Why?" I ask. He points to a girl who's just entered the room wearing a long skirt, slit up to here. She's sitting near my desk so I can hear her conversation. (Not a lot of work going on here. I ask one girl yelling something across the room about the beef jerky in her hand if she could be a little quieter so as not to interfere, if not with ongoing schoolwork, then at least with the quiet enjoyment of the breakfast that her classmates are consuming.) Anyhow, this girl who's just made this guy's day is going on about some other guy at work who's after her. He brings her lunch at school; he took her brother out to the Red Lobster to tell him how much he wants his sister in his life – after all, she's not a little girl now, he said. Meanwhile, her on-premises admirer demonstrates that he's likely only to be admiring her, and most girls, at arm's length for some time, as he presents her with his drawing of a penis with the wings of an airliner. She is unfazed by his artwork, though, and continues with her pencil and paint brush eye makeup that she's been working on throughout all of this. (And, yes, I did step in and confiscate the rendering of the winged member.)

By second period, breakfast is largely over and the kids settle into a bathroom pass mode. After a little calming action from me at the beginning, this freshman class becomes extraordinarily quiet. Later I notice a graveyard through the window of the classroom across the hall. Cappuccino is right on the border with Colma, a town estimated to have a thousand and a half live inhabitants and a million and a half dead ones. Back when San Francisco's real estate started getting expensive, they dug up all the people who were no longer paying rent and moved them there. So today Colma is mostly shopping malls, car dealerships and 17 cemeteries (15 for humans), one of which is right outside the classroom window. I hadn't realized we were so close. Perhaps the dead are having a calming effect upon the living.

The lunchroom here is in another building and it's raining so hard that I decide to stay put and eventually kids come in and ask if they can eat lunch here. I hear some speculation as to the nature of the ashes some kids received at church yesterday on Ash Wednesday. We're next to Colma, after all.

Back to the same classes the next day. Wasn't looking forward to it, but I'm sure not getting much from San Francisco lately. When a sub complained about the sub glut at the last union assembly meeting, the union's sub person said, "Well, you just have to get out to those schools and get yourself known." Now you've got to interview to be a sub?

At any rate, the kids do seem pretty glad not to have their regular teacher again. They don't seem too high on her, but I do suspect the feeling is mutual. Mostly breakfast and makeup. Yesterday's slit-up-to-the-waist girl is quite bitchy today. Now, that's a big surprise.

I was hoping to get something done on a presentation for my German class at the Goethe Institute, but I've forgotten my German dictionary. It occurs to me that there may be one at the school, but when I inquire a girl tells me that the only European language they teach here is French – not counting Spanish. She says she doesn't really know the difference between any of the languages that the ESL kids here speak, but she works at Denny's with a bunch of Germans, or maybe it's Austrians, or Russians – she's not sure.

In sixth period there's a bunch of boys talking about biting someone's dick off. I tell them to "Shut up," utilizing a phrase that has fallen out of favor in current education theory. But I figure if they're willing to complain to their guidance counselor that I traumatized them by telling them to shut up when they were discussing biting off someone's dick, well, more power to them.

AREN'T THEY CUTE? – *Principal, Goodhill Elementary, February 22, 1999*

Chaos in the office when I arrive, so I take a seat. Looks like they really could use me as principal here, but I'm guessing they won't. Preschool yard duty, late passes, answering phones, and then I start spelling teachers being called out for some kind of interviews throughout the day. When I arrive for my first stint, not only don't I know the name of the teacher I'm replacing, but I don't even know what grade I'm in. On top of that, I'm correcting work they're doing in Spanish – and I ain't bilingual. But if you can't do everything, you shouldn't be a sub. The hardest part is figuring out who they are when I'm supposed to pick them up after recess.

An article in today's *Chronicle* concerning the fallout surrounding the end of the city's desegregation plan quotes someone saying that these kids are not going to get good educations unless their teachers have courses in handling various cultures. Well, I'm sure the courses wouldn't hurt, but I chalk it up as yet another "educator" missing the point. The problem's a lot bigger than that. But then the story also cites Ernest Everett Just as a good school. What can that mean, I wonder. Seems unlikely that a place where a class of second graders can go through two subs in a single day, and no one seems surprised or lifts a finger to help, can be too "good" a school. This means there's worse out there?

The teacher I'm replacing after lunch describes her class as "extremely challenging." Fifth grade, I think. Lots of screaming and writing names on the board. I throw one kid out. The acting principal brings him back to say – under duress – that's he's ready to cooperate now, etc. He's good to his word for about five minutes and I throw him out again, but this time he refuses to go and his regular teacher has to leave her interview and come get him.

My last class looks like maybe it's first grade. I read them a story and then they read one back to me in unison, so they're a lot better than those presumed fifth graders, anyhow. At one point, a kid starts rolling around the floor, so I stop reading and look at him waiting for him to stop. Turns out it's an autistic kid whose one-on-one para has stepped out of the room for a few minutes. The other kids say it's okay, he's allowed to do that "because he doesn't know anything." A girl gives presents to all of her classmates, so things end on an up-note – until I leave, anyhow.

On a previous visit here, when my car was stopped at a light behind a school bus taking the Goodhill kids home, I recognized a bunch from my class waving at me from the back window. Seemed pleasant enough until just before the light changed I noticed they were only waving their middle fingers. And sure, enough, I'm stopped behind a school bus again today and look up and see all the kids in the back of the bus giving me the finger – my little fifth graders, presumably – what a cute bunch. I guess it's some kind of tradition at this school. It reminds me of how My Friend the Evil Substitute Teacher always says they shouldn't be so strict on school bus drivers – requiring clean driving and criminal records and all that.

METAL COVERS WOOD – *Industrial Arts, Appian Way High, February 23, 1999*

I pass up a day of screaming at Goat Hill Middle School before taking this late class which turns out to be the photography/electrical/metals gig. Two girls in second period ask for a joint pass to the bathroom and explain that the one with the notably tight pants needs the other one to help her with them because they don't fit right. I seek no further explanation and deliver the requested paper. A kid in metal shop asks if I know anything about the subject, at which point I correctly distinguish the metal from the wood parts of his desk.

Today's installment of the *Chronicle* education series says black kids are now getting shortchanged by missing out on Special Ed because of a recent effort to reduce what was seen as an inappropriately high number of blacks in Special Ed. There are infinite numbers of these blind alleys to run down when it comes to matters of race and education. Chances are that if a placement is going to result in a kid getting more adult attention, it's probably a good thing.

PARENTAL SUPPORT – *Second Grade, Yerba Buena Elementary, February 24, 1999*

Showed up for this job two weeks ago. The first bad sign was the secretary not thinking the teacher was planning to be absent. Another teacher was covering her morning yard duty for her, so that checked out, but when I got to the classroom she was there. Very disappointing, since you take the Bay Bridge to get to here (but get off in the middle), and I hadn't traveled that far in response to a phone call since I went to Sarajevo. I'd thought about packing a bag. But today I am wanted.

They give you a sub checklist to sign here, acknowledging your responsibilities. There are twelve of them – yard duty, etc. One of the things not listed, however, is picking up the kids in the yard, which is actually the first thing you are expected to do. The teacher's instructions, unfortunately, are not nearly so clear and I hope the kids know what they're supposed to do – which they pretty much do. After a while the teacher next door comes to tell them that she can hear them – and I don't even realize that they're being loud.

I've lost my checklist from this morning and get another in the office and check off the appropriate boxes until I notice that they expect me to provide a lesson plan for the next day. I tell the secretary that this makes no sense, as I don't know the class and soon I'm going at it with the principal in the front office, a sight perhaps not seen that often. When I finally leave, I find another sub I'd been chatting with in the office waiting outside to talk to me. She'd also gotten a second copy of the checklist, but in her case it was to send it to the union because of the part that requires you to correct all papers, presumably even after school hours. I had actually done the lion's share of that and told her that it was the lesson plan thing that made me crazy. But she tells me it's actually in the regs which pretty well floors me, as I've never been asked to leave a lesson plan before. But apparently I don't have a leg to stand on in regard to what I've been arguing.

Jose and Doris, my landlord and landlady, are getting out of their car as I arrive home. They've just been at some school because their nephew was being bad and had some problem with the school bus driver. Thinking of the kids in the back of the bus the other day, I reply that the bus drivers can't do anything to the kids because they won't let them carry small arms, to which Doris replies, "They should." I head inside encouraged by this all too rare display of parental understanding of the difficulties of the educational system. (Honest, this was a joke at the time it was written.)

JUST MISSED – *Sixth Grade Literature/Social Studies, Skyline Middle, February 25, 1999*

I have to interrupt the afternoon showing of *The Little Buddha* (after the class turns in their "Buddha's Path to Enlightenment" assignments) because some of the kids think we're having an earthquake. The stuff hanging from the classroom ceiling is undeniably moving, I grant, but it's been doing that long enough for this to be the longest earthquake on record. At least that's my position and I stick to it and eventually the para reports that it was the next door class jumping rope on the roof.

Five subs here today – major for a school this size with only two classes per grade. The students are bound to try to exploit this sort of mismatch and indeed it appears that one sub has been overrun. The principal says the guy called it the worst day of his career and the entire class got detention. You never like to hear of a colleague going down. And on my way out I see a kid sort of clipping an adult, whom I take to be a para, on top of the head and the next thing I know the principal is restraining him and suspending him for three days. The kid's breaking loose, saying he'll show him something to suspend him for. We're talking a wrestling match in the principal's chair. A nice flourish to end the day.

The talk at lunch is that Bill Clinton was scheduled to come to read to the Skyline students tomorrow, but today's paper says his California fundraising trip is canceled. With a couple of breaks, that kid in the principal's office might have been a national story.

Spelling test on my second day. Twenty questions; the most common score (the mode, in current mathematical parlance) was twenty, the median was eighteen, only eight (of fifty-something) score below fifteen, the only two black boys, who've been fairly steady problems these two days, score three and one. Numbers like this tell you these two guys probably dropped off the pace years ago. Otherwise, it's birthday cupcakes, Clinton calling in regrets, and chaperoning a dance after lunch. I recognize only one song, a retro-swing tune, and realize I've never seen rap danced to before.

Back here the next week for an eighth grade class where most of students are signed up to read to little kids in the lower grades up the hill during first period. The teacher in charge of the project thinks it makes the older kids feel and act more grown-up; kids known for acting out are remarkably transformed with little kids looking up to them. An elementary school teacher says it makes the older kids more gentle. So far as I am concerned, if some idiot hadn't invented middle school, they wouldn't have to be making these remarkable discoveries.

I'D HATE TO SEE A "10" – *Special Ed, Paradise Elementary, March 1, 1999*

The system's directions for this place are way off, so I ask a school bus driver who turns out to be going here. I'm subbing for the principal today, which is always a crap shoot and today – bingo! – it's Special Ed. The regular teacher is there when I arrive, but he's heading home to receive a delivery. Before he leaves he tells me, "They're terrible." This is not a good sign. The day starts with an assembly with a teacher performing a magic trick. One of the paras tells me to lock the door because some of the kids will steal stuff. This is also not a good sign. At least there's only eleven of them, and three of us.

The kids run from third to fifth grade. For their journal-writing assignment they are given something to copy because they will not write anything on their own. They start fighting during a fire drill. I throw one out, another goes off to a regular classroom for awhile, being "mainstreamed," as they say. Good luck, I say, since there ain't no one here close to mainstream. I read them a story about manatees but don't finish since they're paying absolutely no attention. Three kids try to bolt, so the para sends them to the guy who does discipline around here. He spends a lot of the day in here, actually.

There's no space in the teachers room at lunch so I return to the class room where I get to talking to the younger para who's pretty disgusted with all this and muttering about the private sector calling. She says this was actually a rather good day – a "2" on a 1-10 scale, with 1 the best. I'm impressed, since I'd just assumed that they were showing me their worst. Both paras and the regular teacher are black and all of the students, except for one Samoan girl, and I have the sense this para may be somewhat embarrassed that a white person should be seeing how these kids are behaving. We talk about where they'll be at by middle school and she says the kids who know how to do the work won't want to have anything to do with these kids and the only ones who will bother with them will be the ones up to no good. Those Skyline boys at the bottom of the class are fresh in my mind.

After lunch a girl is jumping around and hits me in the back. It's accidental, but I throw her out, nonetheless, as self control is one of the many things these kids are going to have to acquire. They send her back to apologize. One boy says he needs math help a couple of times, but will not listen when I try. Three of them have been assigned to write lines for recess. (I defer, as usual, to what the para tells me is the local practice.) By the afternoon we're reduced to coloring and when that wears thin a few of them just take to flat out insulting each other. I'm breaking up fights and waiting for the clock to run out. The disciplinarian is talking to one boy about how they shouldn't be calling each other "nigger" and tells the paras how one was an angel when he was put in one-on-one with a red-haired white woman.

The older para keeps good-naturedly asking me if I would return to this class and I'm not giving her a straight answer, which is – probably not. But I can honestly tell them I've seen worse, for whatever consolation that is.

COLORING – *Social Studies, Appian Way High, March 9, 1999*

There's a "Gene Mullin for City Council" sign in this classroom, a note on the wall thanking Mayor Mullin for reading to some kids, a United Farm Workers' "nickel-a-pint" strawberry workers organizing campaign poster, and something about how poorly funded education is in California. It appears that Mr. Mullin, the Social Studies teacher, was once Mayor Mullin. Today's assignment has the kids coloring maps which first strikes me as a little on the elementary side, but the point of the exercise is to distinguish the nature of various social institutions –

which are public, which are private, and so forth. And as I hear them asking each other if schools are public, I decide they may actually be getting a more useful dose of what they used to call "civics" than I'm used to seeing.

A LITTLE ZEN – Sixth Grade Science, Calvin Coolidge Middle, March 10, 1999

Three days in what's ranked as one of the city's top schools, but strikes me as just okay. The Science teacher I'm replacing consistently writes "cabnits" on his seating charts. (He's referring to the "cabinets," if you're still wondering.) At least he's not the English teacher.

Lunchroom topic today is the boys improperly touching the girls and the girls who seem to think that's just fine. One teacher has placed the remains of a stink bomb set off in a class on the lunch table. To my surprise, they come wrapped in aluminum foil with a trade mark. This was a *Simpsons* model. One of the subs I've seen around talks about what he does in the outer world – plays the stock market and does astrological charts. Two activities of approximately equal significance, in my book. Apparently Mercury is retrograde now, which he says explains a lot of things. Maybe there'll be a dot-com crash or something.

The afternoon classes are really rather good. When a couple of girls start kicking each other, I put a stop to it, to be sure, but I don't get on them in the way I would in a more out-of-control class because not only is this obviously being done in fun, but it doesn't seem to have the potential to ignite mayhem that an identical action might in another class. As a Zen substitute teaching master once said: "The class that tries to get away with less gets away with more."

Second period is awful and when a student of ambiguous gender (a boy, it will be later determined) leaves the room with a loud "Good-bye, asshole," I fly out of the classroom, down the hall, and into the stairwell where I grab him by his backpack and turn him over to the security guard. In the spirit of fair play, I will advise any student planning flagrant assholery not to wear a back pack, as it allows the pursuing teacher to apprehend you without actually touching your person and giving you the opportunity to make a scene yelling, "Get your hands off me!"

When this guy arrives the next day, I greet him with the bureaucratic salutation equivalent to his – a referral to send him packing. When two girls show up late and start disrupting the test; I send them out as well, although I can't be certain that any of these kids actually go to the counseling office when I send them, because at no time during my three days here am I ever able to reach it on the phone.

During home room, a kid comes up to me and apologizes for disrupting class yesterday and extends his hand. I shake it and thank him, all the while thinking this may just prove what the *X-Files* has been trying to tell us about the depth of alien infiltration of the planet – they've taken this kid over. I look for the black oil in the whites of his eyes, but I don't see anything. Likewise, the rumor you'll hear some subs whispering – about the government running some super hush-hush investigation on the DNA of an entire village somewhere in the Midwest where nice middle school students have been found – could just be an *X-Files*-related rumor.

Back to reality: Voice on the loudspeaker during fifth period: "Please excuse the interruption. Would whoever ordered the pizza, please contact 32B."

Two school-related stories in the news: A parent stabbing his daughter's teacher in the classroom in front of the students (went off his medication) and the San Francisco school board has taken its proposal prohibiting schools from calling the police, so as not to unnecessarily "criminalize" students, back to the drawing board. I think a few of these folks might benefit from a little face time in some of the rougher high schools.

MOTIVATION – *Eighth Grade Literature/Social Science, Skyline Middle, March 15, 1999*

I'm here for a teacher I've replaced before and I'm surprised to find there's no instructions for me, but I learn that she's actually here and track her down in the lunchroom. She asks whom I'm here for and is quite surprised to find out that it's she. But the job is verified and I spend the day as an extra wheel in her room. Her classes are very loosely run, particularly the GATE (Gifted and Talented Education) class. She says she doesn't think you could do this anywhere else in the city.

She actually gives them a lot longer time to settle down than I did. Today is flour child day. Every kid is supposed to cart around a five pound bag of flour as an ersatz baby. You see some strange stuff in the schools. Apparently it's a district-wide requirement to cart these sacks of flour about for a week to teach them responsibility or something. This probably comes from the same people who developed the "stamp out drugs" program that has kids physically stomping on ersatz drugs. The teacher warns them that if they don't get their children out of the way to do their class work, they'll be going to foster homes, perhaps become cupcakes.

A kid with "Motivation is the key to knowledge" on the back of his tee shirt is honoring the aphorism only in the breach, so I ask if he remembers what his shirt says. He does not. They start a "mandala" exercise involving writing four related essays around one topic written in the center of a page. One kid wants to write about basketball, but he can't spell it.

In fourth, they're supposed to watch a video on Mississippi Freedom Summer and take notes while the regular teacher does something else. The kids I have the most difficulty getting to pay attention are the black kids, so now I'm harassing black kids to get them to watch a movie on the Civil Rights movement. Ay, ay, ay! One girl simply will not pay attention until the very end and then can't write a coherent paragraph about the movie, so the regular teacher makes her write about how she needs to pay attention and take that home to have it signed. Apparently her father is a civil rights lawyer.

AUTO APPELATION – *English/Theater, Cappuccino High, March 16, 1999*

    Tomorrow I start working at the San Francisco teachers union office for the rest of the semester and I find myself reviewing the year. This was the place where I gave a girl a progress report that said "commendable effort," only to have her ask me if that was good. Also where I first had to deal with a kid talking on a cell phone in class. I imagine our ancestors felt the same wonder upon finding the first one listening to a radio in class. This was where a student told me he had to leave class for a moment to put his tennis racket back in his car. His car, naturally, was in the student parking lot, a concept that raised eyebrows when I mentioned it back east.

    My review stops with the sound of some fool student peeling out of said parking lot in his SUV. (It's a little known fact that SUV stands for Stupid Uman Vehicle, many SUV drivers being unfamiliar with the concept of silent letters.) When you see some of these kids driving you can understand how their parents would want them to have a vehicle at least as large as anyone else's – better to have a bigger SUV than the jerk in front of you because the jerk with the larger vehicle will likely have the lesser injuries when they crash. How we got into the arms race.

    But first period Honors English actually proves quite honorable and the biggest crisis here is that I'm not collecting the papers due today and the kids who did them on time wish they hadn't. The two afternoon classes are in the theater and in the first I've got a kid who will simply not stop talking when I'm trying to get the class's attention for the necessary two minutes and takes great offense to my raising my voice, so I tell him to leave and get a whole lot of "Why don't you come outside if you think you're so tight." The only black kid in the class; I think he thinks he's supposed to act that way. That notwithstanding, I imagine that if I were a black parent I'd want to get my kids out of the city to a place where such assumptions are less likely to be reinforced.

*****

RE-UPPING – September 14, 1999

I've just spent the summer in East Timor on the United Nations plebiscite where the Timorese voted to leave Indonesia, the country that invaded them twenty-four years earlier, after which the guys who lost the election burned the place down. Then ten days in Australia. I took an 11AM flight this morning and arrived in San Francisco before I left – at 7:20 AM, feeling somewhat better now about the day that simply disappeared from my life when I crossed the International Dateline in the other direction on the way over. By about an hour after I left Sydney, I am in the sub office getting papers to renew my certificate. My haste will not be reciprocated, though, to the point where I lower myself to distributing flyers advertising my services. Hustling to be a substitute teacher! For this I came back from the South Pacific? Or was that the Indian Ocean?

STILL THERE – *Literature/Social Studies, William Howard Taft Middle, October 12, 1999*

I finish out a week when the "regular" sub has come down seriously ill. The teacher she replaced broke two bones in her arm after becoming a last minute replacement for a guy who got some kind of grant. We're a lot of steps from normalcy. There'll be a new teacher on Monday – the fourth or fifth for this class, depending upon how you're counting. The principal sends word through the student teacher that she wants to see me; I wonder what this can be, but she wants to ask if it's okay to come into my classes and talk to them about the convoluted teacher situation. *Ask* me? I think about checking her ID – is this some fugitive from justice impersonating a principal? It's almost like when a cab driver lets you go ahead of him, so you know it must be a stolen cab.

We read an Anna Quindlen piece on homelessness that discusses mobility in contemporary America. I ask how many kids have a parent born in San Francisco. Two out of twenty-eight; only one has both.

On the blackboard in the teachers room: "Attention: The child found in the basement last week is still there. Please check your absentee student rosters." My Friend the Evil Substitute Teacher was here? I am joined in a few minutes by a teacher I take to be an older female until I hear him on the phone and realize is a transsexual or transgender when I get a good look. First I've seen subbing. I wonder how the kids react.

HOLLYWOOD STARS – *Math/Science, William Howard Taft Middle, October 29, 1999*

Just in case you've gotten to thinking this sub business is simple or anything, I wound up back here after a teacher called me direct at home for a Social Studies job at Cabot. The system now allows teachers to make direct arrangements with you without the machine having to call at all. But you don't know if the teacher has actually followed through unless you call into the machine and when I do so this morning, the job's not there. So I call the Cabot teacher who says she had difficulty with the machine. I explain that even though I was looking forward to Cabot, I won't go without a job number because they'll just send me somewhere else – at best. She says she'll call the school. The phone rings again – a live person at Taft wanting to know if I'm available. I tell them about Cabot. The phone rings again: the machine wants to know if I'll go to Ghiradelli. I call in again and still no Cabot job. Phone again – the machine now invites me to Taft and I go. Did I mention that flexibility is required in this line of work?

The regular teacher is here when I arrive and tells me it's baby-sitting today. A double period of watching *Shapeshifter*, some lame kids' movie about time travel and post-Cold War espionage. Last period is *My Favorite Martian*. Science, you know – astronomy, planetary geology, etc.

DIFFICULT CHILDREN – *Math/Science/Principal, William Howard Taft Middle, November 18, 1999*

Another day in for the principal, but they were short a Math/Science sub Someone at the last Teachers Union Executive Board meeting said that the system was short 80 subs one day last week.

The day deteriorates toward the sandbox level with each class. I have to quickly switch screens on my computer so a kid who comes up looking for help on her assignment won't see that I've described the class as "a bunch of assholes." That was, of course, only a draft written in the heat of the moment. In this final version, they are a bunch of difficult children who are acting out.

Lunchroom discussion is about Middle School Night, when elementary school parents can meet middle schools representatives. Apparently the Ghiradelli representative sat alone in a room waving for people to come in; the guy from Annunciation Gulch just left early.

Finally I do an actual day subbing for the principal (although for an hour I do fill in for the security guard and guide people to the parents meeting). My duties include opening the giant walk-in combination safe in the morning. They use it to store paper and the like, which My Friend the Evil Substitute Teacher considers near-criminal underutilization. He believes you could put a serious dent in student behavioral problems by locking a few in it overnight or, better still, for the weekend. I myself think that even a couple of hours spent locked in it during the school day might go a long way with a few of them.

SATURDAY? – *Social Studies, John Adams High, December 9, 1999*

Today a student asks the student teacher if World War I was America's first war since the Revolution and he says, "Yes." Perhaps one of the natural sciences would be a better placement. At home after school, I am in a nap so deep (how I avoid keeping school teacher's hours) that when the Citadel secretary calls at 4:00 PM, I assume it must be tomorrow already, which is to say Friday, even though it shouldn't be light out at four in the morning. My logical mind thinks I can't have slept that soundly and have it still be today and I hear myself ask the ridiculous question, "You mean Saturday?" to which she calmly and logically responds, "No Friday." Realizing that I must have been sleeping, she tells me to call back, which I do when I finally figure out what day it is and tell her that I'm

supposed to be at Cabot on Friday. Of course, the machine later calls to cancel that. Should have accepted that Saturday job.
Student Names Of The Day: Kit Ying and Ying-kit (sitting one behind the other)

MISDIRECTED – *Special Education, Goat Hill Middle, January 6, 2000*

Tina at the union office assured me the Cabot job had gone through, even though it's not on the machine, so I went after having sworn I'd never go to a job again without actually having a job number. Had to call three people to find out when it starts, too, something the machine will usually tell you. Well, she was wrong, and I'm already in class when they pull me out because the sub they actually gave the job to has arrived.

Tina eventually gets me sent to replace a teacher at Goat Hill, who's going to the same meeting as the Cabot teacher. I just turned down a day at this place on Tuesday, so I mutter my way across town. This teacher works with kids one on one, or one on two, or so; and most of them don't show up anyhow. I work with four kids the entire day; one's actually good, and two are okay. One of her students is working on translating Lewis Carroll's nonsense poem, *The Jabberwocky,* into regular English. I'm not sure I would assign something that's not even supposed to make sense to a "normal" kid to someone who's probably having trouble making sense of most of what he reads in the first place. But that's what they have professionals in these fields for, I guess.

The star of the day shows up about two thirds of the way through last period – although he had been by to drop off his coat earlier – turns the TV on twice when I tell him not to, spits on the floor, says, "Your mama smells bad, too," and splits. I write a referral on him and, I am happy to say, that's the last I see of him. And it'll be the last I see of Goat Hill Middle School for a while, as well.

Goat Hill Middle School closed at the end of the 2005-2006 academic year.

THE VALUE OF A CREDENTIAL – *Principal, William Howard Taft Middle, January 10, 2000*

During one of my two lunch-period yard duties subbing for the principal who's both sick and on jury duty, I witness a sort of pre-mating ritual display, as a physically developed girl wearing a tube top under her jacket continually picks up a pencil that a boy drops, fast enough that he would not be able to see anything down her top, but slow enough to keep him trying. On a rainy day lunch, I notice a "Muskie For President sticker" on the back of one of the seats. We know they haven't been varnished since 1972, anyhow.

When I am not out preventing misdemeanors, I'm in the corner of the front office at my laptop, apparently looking in charge. A teacher whom I've frequently chatted with tells me that he's going for an administrative credential and asks if I've found it worthwhile doing so. I have to break the news to him that I've actually reached this pinnacle of power without any such credential. I hope I haven't destroyed a career here. On my second day, a teacher tells me she's got a meeting at Goat Hill at 4 and I figure she's going to ask me to cover a class for her, but instead she asks if it's okay for her to leave at 3:15. I assure her that it's fine with me. Apparently the rules say she has to ask the principal. Probably good to leave before this aura of authority gets me to thinking about making some big moves around here.

ANNOYED – *Counseling, Waterfront Middle, January 13, 2000*

A lot of Waterfront lately. Had to show a Jackie Chan movie one day, with lots of "kick your ass" and "full of shit" in the dialogue. Just what these kids need to expand their horizons. Anyhow, I'm counselor today with my own office, not sitting outside the principal's office like at Taft. My duties include hall duty during passing periods, yard duty for lunch, issuing late passes, and apparently counseling as needed, which could include calling parents at home. My Friend the Evil Substitute Teacher says that when he gets a job like this he calls the parents of certain problem children and tells them to find a different school for their child. He believes the staff would actually love him for this if they knew, but he keeps it as his little secret. My most important task is calling the parents of kids who feel sick to see if it will be all right for them to go home. My Friend the Evil Substitute Teacher just sends them straight to the hospital, thinking it imperative to deal with the health crisis first. Says he doesn't always get around to letting the parents know.

While I am out in the hall for a passing period, a student comes up to the teacher I'm chatting with – for whom I've subbed in the past – and tells her she found yesterday's sub annoying because he wouldn't give her a pass to go to the bathroom. Must make note to curb my own annoying behavior.

The next day, comes the Memo from the Assistant Principal:
Immediate Security Measures:
This is only a precaution:
As you may know, there is police activity in the neighborhood regarding a search for two armed robbers. They are apparently still at large in the Pacific Heights area. In the event that we need to activate a lock-down of the school for safety reasons, I will announce over the PA system, <u>Alyse Danis, please come to the office.</u> That will be your signal to lock your doors, pull up the shades on the doors if possible, and keep all children in your classroom until further notice. Counseling staff, security, and administration will oversee locking the building and securing all staff and students. There will be one staff member at the main office phone; however, we will communicate with you by PA should this be necessary.

All day long, I keep expecting to hear the voice of My Friend the Evil Substitute Teacher come over the PA, asking Ms. Danis to come to the office.

Back in reality, a Chinese boy tells me, "Two blacks took my wallet yesterday" on the bus on the way home and he knows who one of them was. *This* I turn over to a real counselor.

As I'm checking out at the end of the day, I hear B, the secretary, on the phone with a "parent" who apparently can't remember his stepdaughter's last name. We discuss the possibility of a memo advising parents to have their children's last names at hand when calling the school. Another problem they didn't have so much back in St. Athanasius, I think.

The California state school rankings come out and this place scores an eight (out of ten), as did Taft Middle School. That seems high. I see that McClymonds, site of my one-day Oakland school system career, scored third lowest among all Bay Area high schools.

0.1, 0.11 – *Librarian, William Howard Taft Middle, February 8, 2000*

A para comes in during first period and dumps two kids on me, one of whom he tells to try not to get kicked out of Ms. V's class today. In a matter of minutes the kid takes a student aide's chair. I kick him out when he refuses to surrender it. I kicked him out a couple of weeks ago too and he goes off proclaiming that he won't pay his taxes because I don't teach him anything. At this point he looks like he'll be lucky if he gets to the point where he pays taxes. I don't think they withhold them when you make license plates.

When I ask the librarian if there's anything I should be doing, she says I could re-shelve the books, *if* I know the decimal system! When I come back here a couple days later, I will start the day off with work of the highest order – the maintenance of life – watering the plants. But then the librarian informs me that some kids got on a hard-core porn site ("no *Sports Illustrated* swimsuit stuff") during my watch on Tuesday, so I must step up my vigilance. While I'm checking for game playing during home room, I see a caption on a website that starts with "So fuck me with an 18 foot paddle ... ." I think maybe that's one they're not supposed to be at.

At the end of one class a girl tells me that she went to *girls.com* and it turned out to be naked women. She's got it covered with another window, but doesn't know how to make it go away. I can't figure out how to make it go away either. After I shoo her back to class at the bell, I hear someone coming into the library and hastily shut the computer down before I have to explain what I'm doing trying to get *girls.com* off of the screen.

SO LOUD – *Sixth Grade Math/Science, Yerba Buena Elementary, February 9, 2000*

I get the familiar "You remind me of the Joker, *The Shining*, Jack Nicholson" stuff; they want me to say, "Here's Johnny." But I also get "Are you a really old Arnold Schwarzenegger?" "Yeah, are you Arnold Schwarzenegger's father?" Now, this is a resemblance not noticed before – or since – and I figure some of these kids need their prescriptions checked. And as for being his father, I believe the man's a year older than I and just had a triple bypass or something, so I can't be too pleased about that. I also get, "Are you gay?" We are in the San Francisco school system, you will recall. They want to know why I talk so loud, so I try to explain the idea of speaking above background noise. I also show them how to solve the problem of the day using algebra. Both concepts are apparently lost on them. I also sell boxes of Pringles.

THIS IS SKYLINE – *Second Grade, Skyline Elementary, February 16, 2000*

School starts at 7:30 AM. A skunk crosses the driveway in front of my car. Parents arrive to take us off on a field trip to the Academy of Science. I'm in a van with a dad and four kids. Theoretically, I'm keeping tabs on nineteen kids I don't know in Golden Gate Park, which is entirely nuts, but we're in tandem with another teacher, so we don't lose any – so far as I know, anyhow – I won't be back tomorrow. At a Daly City school I used to sub at, they told me that the only teacher who they knew who'd ever lost a student on a field trip was a principal now. Besides, if I lost just one, that'd be like a 95% right? And that's an A, isn't it?

(They seemed to do a lot of field trips in Daly City. I suppose because they've got the Cow Palace right there. One time we packed it full of kids so they could listen to a couple of guys who apparently ride the role model circuit. One was a professional wrestler I'd never heard of; the other was Bo Jackson, who would have still been a baseball player if he hadn't more famously also played football and sustained an injury that required insertion of an artificial hip. I remember the wrestler telling the kids to hydrate. (Such advice does not seem to have fallen on deaf ears. Nowadays kids carry around water bottles like it was the Sahara. Back when we were kids we were much too busy to spend all that time drinking water.) But the day's shining memory is Bo telling the boys to wear a belt so that their pants won't hang down. Hopefully Bo changed some lives that day.)

Anyhow, today we're here to see a jazz drummer, along with two other musicians and a dancer, who tells the story of blacks in America along with the music. At one point he makes all the adults in the audience come up and do the *toyi toyi*, which a *New Yorker* article will later explain to me is "the historic dance of protest, in which (South African) demonstrators move forward military style."

The situation feels similar to the upper grades here: only three black kids in the class and two are continual problems, the only two in the class, actually. I have to separate them in the library, write their names on the board, etc. This class actually wants to do silent sustained reading after lunch, even though I hadn't planned on it. I mention my surprise at that to the principal when she sticks her head in the room. She replies, "This is Skyline."

OFF TO SEE THE WIZARD – *Resource Room, Waterfront Middle, February 18, 2000*

I've had this class before. The kids are difficult, but there aren't too many of them and there's only four periods. But then the para is out, the spelling test I'm supposed to give isn't here, I can't turn the TV on, and the video isn't here. At least the teacher next door shows me the power switch for the TV, which is apparently kept off because it also controls some giant blowers in the storeroom between the two classrooms, the purpose of which was known only to our predecessors. She also gives me a Mr. Wizard video. I can't believe I'm running into Mr. Wizard again. When I used to watch him on TV, the Big Bang hadn't even been thought up yet! The kids, naturally, have no use for it, but then they wouldn't even if it had up-to-date superstring theory, either, so I don't guess we can really blame Mr. Wizard.

BORING *– English, Cabot High, February 23, 2000*
Good high school – three days, no stories. Peace doesn't make good history; it's the wars we're made to memorize.

NEW MATH? *– Math, J.P. Morgan Middle, March 3, 2000*
My classroom is upstairs in what the secretary describes as the "shop wing." Immediate anxiety reaction – shop! As soon as I enter the classroom I remember a day spent up here baby-sitting some fuck-ups not allowed on a field trip. But then I see that today's work involves factoring polynomials, which I'm finding challenging looking at them. So I figure that at least the first class won't be crazy.

Music wafts in before class – a group of eight girls sitting in an oval in the hall playing things you shake that are like xylophone keys with a clapper that the kids later describe as handbells or chimes. A lot nicer sound than the usual in the halls.

The teacher has left geometrical problems for second period that are very unclear to me, with at least one I can't solve. Then he shows up briefly and a student asks him about it and, sure enough, he forgot to put a measurement in. For a while I was afraid that new geometrical laws had also been invented since I was in school.
Student Name of the Day: Jazz Banks

COLONIAL HISTORY *– Science, Cappuccino High, March 7, 2000*
First, third and sixth periods watch something called *Taste, Smell and Sex, and the Food Machine.* The sex is pretty disappointing, as I feel obligated to inform the hot little girl in sixth who has perked up at the title. Fourth and fifth are Biology classes which another teacher tells me are the school's best students. Their work consists of copying notes from three overhead projection sheets. One kid asks how can this be college prep when all they do is copy notes. Sounds like a reasonable question to me.

There's a photocopy on the door, apparently from the American Association of Retired Persons, making the point that one vote can matter, that is written ungrammatically, so as to suggest that Thomas Jefferson was elected Governor of Massachusetts. When I point this out, the kids seem to know he was actually from Virginia, something of a pleasant surprise to me. Someone then directs an apparently derogatory comment of "English major" toward one of the kids who knew. Has this become a standard insult in science class? I'd like to think it indicated someone picking up humor from *A Prairie Home Companion* but I honestly don't think there's a lot of public radio listening going on down here. I once had a junior honors class here doing a section on the Harlem Renaissance and there was only one student even vaguely aware of the Ken Burns Jazz documentary airing that week.

On the other hand, this is the school where I once sold lollipops during fourth period because it was something the regular teacher did. The kids thought this was pretty cool, because the last sub wouldn't do it. Maybe it was too hard for

him – it's not just a matter of red or green these days – I was filling orders for apple, watermelon and strawberry.
Student Name Of The Day: Wales But

BAD DAY– *Eighth Grade Math/Science, Skyline Middle, March 9, 2000*

Three day job and the secretary greets me with, "Oh boy, you've got the eighth grade!" as in, "I don't envy you," and the dour math teacher says send him the troublemakers. Not good. But the kids start out on autopilot. They knew the teacher would be out; the work is on the board; a kid takes attendance; we start with virtually no interaction. Kids ask permission to get up to get a book or a calculator. Then, with no signal from me, they up and leave about five minutes before the end of first period. I ask where they're going and a very mature girl tells me they'll be back at sixth.

Second period is more like it. Two girls want to work out in the hall and I let them until I see they're doing their hair and exchanging unpleasantries with passing students. Stereotypes hold up quite well here: the pain-in-the-ass black boys are "muthuh fuckuh" tough guys, and the pain-in-the-ass white boys are trench coat geeks. A final period kid says he's not coming tomorrow. I reply, "Excellent, that's the best thing I've heard all day." "That's cold," says a girl in the class. She's right there. At the end of the day, the secretary says she wants to keep my sub form to make sure I come back. The principal says it was a bad day all around the school. Seems I've heard that here before. A bad day at middle school! It was a cold day at the South Pole, too, I hear. The secretary starts me off with a "Go get em!" on my final day. This has really turned out to be one of my more unpleasant assignments in a while.

Lunchroom discussion on whether the beginning of a phone number was an "exchange," as we said in the east, or a prefix, as said out here. A younger teacher says, "So, is that why they have letters on the phone?"

BUT I KNOW WHAT I LIKE– *Art, Cappuccino High, March 23, 2000*

Third period is oil painting and we've got a boy with a painting titled "Slappa Hoe Tribe." There's also a poster entitled "Captian (sic) Wreckahoe." But some of the work in the back of the room is not bad – from a distance, anyhow, and that's the impressionist standard, right? I have to tell the babe of the class to stop wrestling with the boys; she's producing too much of a distraction. These classes are not so far removed from kindergarten finger painting.

SUBSTITUTE OLYMPICS– *Ceramics/English/Math, Cappuccino High, May 5, 2000*

I've been back from an election in Bosnia for about two weeks and I'm just now starting to take down notes about school, so I guess you could say I've been finding things pretty dull. But as if to shake me out of my doldrums, today we have something completely different every period.

1 – Shakespeare video.
2 – Kids are supposed to research the lives of the poets in library.

3 – Fill in for missing sub in a math class doing square roots of variables to odd powers. (The kid I threw out of class back in March shows up in this class and asks for a "time out"– something they hand out here as a sort of pre-referral – because he doesn't want to be in here with me. He did the same thing a few days after the referral, as well, and I am only too happy to oblige again. Does this mean I never have to have this guy in class again? I didn't know it got this good. This is like getting a ballplayer thrown out of the league.)

4 – Fill-in for unreplaced ceramics teacher where I show a Wallace and Gromit video – claymation, you know – and give them a question sheet. Now this movie I stop and watch – Wallace and Gromit build a rocket ship to go to the moon when they realize they're out of cheese (cause the moon is made of cheese).

5 – Reading chapter four of *The Catcher in the Rye,* which I don't think I've read any of since freshman year in high school. I explain its scandalous history and the author's life as a hermit and I think I notice one kid listening.

6 – Creative writing, completing academic hexathalon.

So, you still think anyone sees more of the school system than the sub?

CENTERPIECE– *History, Cabot High, May 9, 2000*
Bosnia slides today. The teacher told me that he was building me up as a guest speaker and asked what he should say. I told him to say that I'd been around a lot of violence in these electoral missions and there was always a possibility of my going off – a sub always wants to have the fear factor going for him, you know. I don't know whether he actually told them anything at all, but he didn't get around to providing them with any of the readings that I sent him. A lot of kids do homework while I'm showing the slides, but a few listen, and some even compliment me on their way out. One wants to know whether the UN would hire kids just out of high school for these things. I tell him I suspect not.

The oddest thing is this little wad of what appears to be dog shit in the center of the classroom.

STAGE PRESENCE– *Social Studies, John Adams High, May 12, 2000*
Second period senior assembly: Some student's got the mike and he's trying to get the kids to come into the auditorium and talking about kicking somebody in the balls. Needs to work on his presentation.

THAT'S SHAKESPEARE, RIGHT? – *English, Appian Way High, May 14, 2000*
I'm here twenty minutes early and the teacher I'm replacing is in the classroom preparing for me. This looks like pretty high-end stuff – all Joyce (*Portrait Of the Artist As a Young Man*) and Shakespeare (*Macbeth* and *Romeo and Juliet*). He asks me if I'm familiar with *Romeo and Juliet,* and I assure him that,

yes, I am a native born English speaker. Teachers discuss "jerk classes" in the lunch room (and they're convinced that the worst school administration there is is San Francisco's, although how they know that I'm not exactly sure).
Student Name of the Day: Whisperr Madrid

DUMBEST – *Sixth Grade Language Arts/Social Studies, Waterfront Middle, June 21, 2000*

My first summer school sub assignment. The regular teacher was supposed to return to town yesterday, but her plane was hit by lightning. That's her story and I'm sticking to it. This is day three of a four week program and the kids haven't met their teacher yet. They're supposed to be doing the *Iliad* and the *Odyssey*, but the appropriate video can't be found, so what's available? *Ace Ventura: When Nature Calls*. Yesterday it was *Dumb and Dumber*. We have a general discussion in which they say they want to watch Jerry Springer and when I rather unthinkingly give them my stock answer, not only can they point out that yesterday's viewing assignment proclaimed its idiocy, but in today's movie we see Jim Carrey shat out by a rhinoceros. (This sort of thing wasn't being shown in school when the country was worried about the Soviets beating us in the space race, you know.) All of this is too stupid for some of the kids – and they're not even seventh graders yet! Some ask if they can just go out and play in the yard. Their educational instincts are right on this one, but unfortunately I can't let them go.

*****

STRAIGHT, NO CHASER – *Eighth Grade Social Studies, Citadel Middle, September 1, 2000*

The non-ESL classes are supposed to report on what they saw on TV news. I resist quoting Garrison Keillor to the effect that you'll learn about as much about the world by watching TV news as you would drinking gin straight out of the bottle, as I don't want to be accused of encouraging drinking among middle schoolers.

Back a couple of days later for Mr. S, whom I know from the union Executive Board, who's on jury duty, I have to transcribe grades onto mini-report cards, so I tell the kids to come see me if they think I might have made an error. In one class, pretty much everyone with less than a straight A comes up to check; no errors found. No one with an A comes up; no self esteem problems here.

Of course they're learning the distributive property, which I don't believe I encountered until high school, even though I'm almost certain it had already been invented when I was in sixth grade.

BINGO! – *Ceramics/English Language Development, Cappuccino High, September 18, 2000*

Yes, I am replacing a Ceramics and English Language Development teacher. (English Language Development seems more or less the successor name to the old ESL.) First period is supposed to make pumpkins, but the other ceramics teacher (yes, Cappuccino has two ceramics teachers) drops by and says there's no clay. The plan calls for the three English Language Development classes to watch a movie, but the aide doesn't actually have it. She tells them to do homework or play bingo, bingo being considered good for their English Language Development.

A Korean girl in one class says – in a perfectly friendly manner – "Why are you here? You're not doing anything," clearly not yet grasping the fine points of her new country's educational system – I am fulfilling the educational mandate for a certificated person in the classroom. I would have to grant her point, though, that from an educational point of view, it was a notably superfluous day. Bingo was our educational high point and we couldn't even make clay pumpkins.

WHAT? ME WORRY? – *Special Education, Appian Way High, October 2, 2000*

First thing you do here is check in your skateboard at the front office, that is if you're a skateboarder. Today's "writing prompt" is: "If you could have one animal to accompany you to a desert island, what animal would you bring with you?" We get one whale, one camel, and five pit bulls. I can't help but thinking that the story with some of these kids is that they simply do nothing and that's been considered okay at home – they're just not "good" at school. For instance, the guy who says he wasn't told that there's an essay due today. When I point out that the assignment was written on the front board yesterday and that it is, in fact, still there, he says that he doesn't read the board. I ask if he plans to tell cops that he doesn't read Stop signs. He says he's not that stupid. Kids eat in this class all the time – Coke and chips. And guess what? There are a lot of fat kids in here.

SECRET LIFE – *English, Cappuccino High, October 25, 2000*

Three classes reading James Thurber's *The Secret Life of Walter Mitty*. Some days subbing is like home repair – by the time you're done, you might know what you're doing. By the end of the day, I know Walter Mitty pretty well. Their textbook mentions that the story originally appeared in *The New Yorker*, so I show them a current issue that I have with me. I ask for definitions of all the words I think they might not know – and most of them they don't – and go through lots of references that are pretty faint fifty-one years later and a continent away. They don't know where Waterbury is or what an A&P was. They have never heard of overshoes, and it isn't until the last reading that I realize that Mitty's fantasy of standing before the firing squad doesn't mean anything to most of them either, this being a lethal injection state these days. The next day Ms. K from the sub office leaves a message saying her daughter was in one of these classes and thought I was a great teacher – I explained all the words to them. All right, I'll take back everything I said about preferring the impersonal San Francisco machine to having to deal with a live human.

SEW WATT? – *English, Appian Way High, October 27, 2000*

Late call, I'm not there until second period and the teacher filling in informs me there's no lesson plan and one of the students has erased names off the section of the white board reserved for detention-related matters. At the end of this period, another one does the same. When I ask his name, he says, "Juan Corona." There's no seating chart, of course, and they've already picked up the scantron, so I figure he's probably giving me a fake name. I call the office to send security to find out his true identity. Security is here in a minute and Juan Corona turns out to be the real name. Problem for this kid is that when I hear Juan Corona, I think of the Southern California mass murderer. Only later will it hit me how long ago that was and that this kid would not likely have any idea about his infamous namesake.

Security obligingly takes the contemporary Juan Corona with them, nonetheless. As I point out to a kid who brings the matter up in the afternoon, he shouldn't have tried to pull something on me when I'd just walked in and the teacher had left me no plans. He, no doubt, saw it as precisely the time to do so, but it's my job is to impress upon the students the fact that they can never really know when they might be dealing with a sub who looks at one of them and sees a mass murderer – from decades ago.

In the afternoon we do a homonym exercise that the teacher who preceded me in second period copied for me. It's about homonyms as I knew them – words that sound alike but are spelled differently. Part of my eagerness to use the worksheet stems from the impressively large dictionary in the back of the room that I want an excuse to use. But a girl in the second class maintains that the worksheet defined not a homonym, but rather a homophone. So I look it up and, by golly, the Webster people are with her, not me. According to that dictionary, homonyms are words with the same sound *and* spelling, but different meanings, as in, "Pool your resources to play pool near the swimming pool."

I take this home and discover that my two dictionaries disagree with the one at school – and each other. All three agree on words spelled and pronounced alike, but both of my dictionaries also consider my old school, spelled-differently, sound-alike pairs to be homonyms, and one also includes spelled-alike, sound-differently pairs, as in "Sow the field, so that the sow may eat." I haven't been this excited about English grammar for decades.

Worked here Halloween, too. Not a great day: The only two black males in my fourth period class came dressed as pimps – one wears a tee shirt that says, "Pimpology 101," the other "Pimp Intern." Guys with an image to live down to. Plus there's a sub in the lunch room today advocating deporting immigrants, having the homeless pick vegetables, and more executions. Obviously they're letting just anyone sub these days. Seems to me there ought to be some kind of bohemianism test you have to pass. I was even at a San Francisco substitute teachers meeting once where subs were talking about Individual Retirement Accounts. IRA's!

On the up side, some kids think I look like Anthony Hopkins in *The Silence of the Lambs*. This is the first time I've heard that one, but I figure that if one kid says it there are others who registered it subliminally. I assure them I'm a vegetarian, but if they're worried that I might really be a cannibal, well that can't be a bad thing. Of course, My Friend the Evil Substitute Teacher always says that even if he were a cannibal, he wouldn't eat a middle school student.

FREAKY – *Computer Lab/Math, Citadel Middle, November 3, 2000*

A computer lab kid asks where I teach the most and I tell him that this year it's been South San Francisco. He asks if I mean down by the Cow Palace (which is in Daly City, on the San Francisco border) and says, "The schools are freaky down there. The teachers don't care about anyone. That's what my friends say." I suspect his friends are talking about maybe Gregor Mendel or Annunciation Gulch in the southern part of the city. For sure, things are different at those schools than here. Here I'm supposed to put the math answer sheets out on each table which assumes kids who will go past finding the correct answer and try to understand why it is correct. You'd be unlikely to find this in those schools, though not because the teachers don't care.

PLEASE HOLD – *English, Cappuccino High, November 14, 2000*

PA announcement for a "duck and cover" drill at 9, but I don't know what to duck or what to cover, so we do neither. Some second period kids claim they're supposed to be going to an assembly. I call the office. A student answers. The student gives me an adult. The adult transfers me to the attendance office. The attendance office says they'll transfer me to the main office which transferred me to them, at which point I decide we're not going. The students seem to do quite nicely without it.

Big run on Cappuccino lately. One class reads *A Separate Peace* which cites "Omnia Gallia in tres partes divisa est," the opening line of Caesar's *Gallic Wars*, so I get to use the high school Latin today. The others are reading a section in *To Kill a Mockingbird* that contains the phrase "nigger snowman." A white kid reads it aloud as "black snowman."

I pick up a period of PE one day when they're short a sub. It's tennis practice. By now you're surely wondering if there's anything these subs can't do, although I'll grant that this particular class does come with a teaching assistant who does everything. I'm given earnest instruction from the PE office to return all twenty of the tennis balls I'm given. At the end of the period we have twenty-three. Maybe I should do more PE after all – I seem to be pretty successful at it.

And then there was the day I took the ESL/Typing job. My principal responsibility in the Typing class is to dissuade kids from playing games rather than doing the assigned memo and to take down the names of those who persist. Get half a dozen in the first class – all boys, of course. One of them wants a bathroom pass, but I explain that he's not going to get it because he hasn't done any work. He asks how I know he hasn't already done it. I ask where it is. He says on his disk. I tell him to put it up on the screen. Wilting under this withering line of interrogation, he returns to game playing. A third period student remembers me from the Walter Mitty class when I apparently was wearing my green pants. The green pants horrify some of the young conformists – the sight of them can remain burned into their consciousnesses for years afterward.

And then there were the math classes. I'm subbing for a math teacher whom I sure can't fault for not leaving thorough instructions. They start with, "Stand in front of the class and announce yourself." First period is Record Keeping and is in a different classroom, where he keeps a pencil with his name on it and a chair with his name on it. That's Record Keeping, all right. He stops by in the morning and says sixth period is bad. We'll see what that means; first period has fourteen tardies.

He's still around well into third period, which is his prep. It appears that the high degree of organization of his instructions and classroom is an attempt to compensate for an underlying disorganization – he's changing his directions even now. Some of the fifth period kids tell me he's not a very good teacher and they actually don't generally offer opinions like that. Sixth period lives up to billing, though. Not only do they have me screaming at them to "shut up," a level to which I am often tempted, but rarely reduced, but I offer the opinion that they are the most juvenile, infantile class I've ever seen in this school, a distinction in which the morons among them will no doubt take pride. One kid who has given me a false name after shooting a rubber band at someone (unfortunately, Record Keeping does not extend to keeping accurate seating charts), then asks to go to the bathroom. He says he'll wet the seat if I don't let him, but I check after the bell and it's still dry.

(Now that I think about, I can remember losing it another time here with a guy putting on a kindergarten performance when I found the words, "shut up," "jerk," and "fool" passing my lips. Now, officially, *it is not done* to say such things these days, but, boy, was that class quiet afterwards.)

When I draw this class's number again in two weeks, I tell Ms. F in the office to expect a call looking for security. The regular teacher is here again in the morning, as his educational seminar does not begin until 11AM. We chat about last time and he allows that the sixth period students said some mean-spirited things about me as well. Says some of the students in that class don't respond well to yelling. I tell him that students who don't respond well to yelling shouldn't act out. This is the kind of educational theory they pay me the big bucks for. Always looking to help a rookie, you know.

He proceeds to tell his first period class that the recent monitoring of his teaching produced recommendations that he change certain things – as much as telling them he's been told he's an ineffective teacher. This guy can't be long for this business. He seems entirely at sixes and sevens, continually flustering about the things he needs to get done for me before he goes, but not actually getting them done. I help a lot of kids with the second period assignment and they say he never does this – not that I would take absolutely take them at their word, mind you, but I've seen what I've seen.

Sixth period proves somewhat anticlimactic. The Assistant Principal sticks his head in, as planned, and while no one would ever mistake this class for a mature bunch, neither is it ridiculously bad today. The teacher has gone to some trouble to make me a class list, so as I find kids not sitting by it, I move them accordingly, explaining that I'm not going to put up with getting phony names. But it soon becomes clear that the list is hopelessly off. Things really are out of this guy's control. At one point I hear a kid refer to me as Darth Vader. Now that's respect.

TAKE YOUR TIME – *Science, Calvin Coolidge Middle, November 22, 2000*
The assignment will be coloring and labeling drawings of the digestive system. In his instruction sheet, the teacher misspells the first name ("Carmon") of the student who's supposed to take first period "attendance." Can't draw too much either, I observe.

Every class has about thirty students, except for the difficult one. That one only has thirteen, but maybe two of them are actually working on the assignment so I'm not terribly upset when the fire alarm goes off and pretty much the whole class runs away as soon as we get outside. Real brush fire on land adjacent to the school, too. With all the school fire alarms that have (undoubtedly) damaged my brain over the years, I think this is the first time I've seen actual flame. So I'm not going to mind if it takes them, say, the rest of this period to get this thing under control, either. And if some enterprising student was behind the glow, at least he picked third period.

This place, by the way, is one of the spelling-challenged schools, of which there are far more than I'd think there ought to be. You can find a school bulletin here with all the plurals spelled with apostrophes. Finding this mistake in the city's signage was one of Herb Caen's old standbys and it looks like they could use a few "Herb Caen's" here. They might even rename the place Herb Caen Middle School since Calvin Coolidge doesn't seem to enjoy that much of a following these days.

MIDDLE SCHOOL UTOPIA – *Art/Social Studies, Waterfront Middle, November 27, 2000*

This teacher called me at home yesterday and asked if I could sub for her before saying either who she was or where she taught. Maybe she figured I might commit first and ask questions later. I ultimately agreed, of course, but not before prying loose the relevant information. After she called the job in, the sub machine said it was at Commodore Sloat Elementary, not Waterfront Middle as she had told me – apparently another one who didn't realize it was up to her to call in her location change. Said she'd wondered why no one showed up the one other time she called for a sub. Anyway, it's utopia when I get here, that is, the kids are supposed to write two page essays on their personal utopias. Unfortunately, they don't appear to actually be familiar with the word and seem to be largely ignoring the assignment. So this is definitely middle school and not utopia.

TOO EARLY – *Math, Appian Way High, November 28, 2000*

When I arrive early in my first period classroom, I find a teacher doing her make-up who asks if I would leave for a few minutes to allow her to continue. I'll say this for the students – they don't ask me to leave the room when they do theirs.

I'll be back for this teacher several times over the next couple of months. The next time there's no assignment when I arrive, so the principal calls the teacher at home and eventually it comes. I replace another subless teacher for third period. No assignment here either, so the kids get a free period during which I realize the Supreme Court is ruling on the presidential election and turn the TV on. The text of the decision making Bush president scrolls across the screen, so I have it on with no sound. Zero interest in class; they want me to turn on MTV, etc.

The math teacher with whom I'm sharing the room drops by and says he's noticed that I know math and that they need math teachers so maybe I could get a job. He himself was a physics major and had to test in, but when he hears I was a philosophy major he figures maybe it wouldn't be possible after all. I explain that we philosophers consider nothing human foreign to us and think that our degrees qualify us to teach anything, but he still doesn't seem to think it'd work out.

Back in January for a two-day for this same teacher. The last day there are once again no lesson plans and this thing is becoming a school-wide issue. An assistant principal hunts me down in the teachers room during prep to see what I've got that I can use with them. A couple of other teachers give me some stuff, and we wind up giving them practice exercises for their upcoming final. Word comes after lunch that she's quit. Guess those lesson plans won't be coming in today. Looks like she just felt in over her head.

A teacher comes by in fourth period to suggest that I do the chapter on the circumference of the circle because she'll be taking over the class and doesn't want them to fall any further behind. The teacher who had said, "I see you know math" also comes by to see if I want help, but I assure him that, as he knows, I know math and everything will be okay. It was like the whole math department was in on it – pretty impressive, actually.

The kids keep asking if the teacher's coming back and I just tell them they'll be told something tomorrow. One tells me that I'm a better teacher than she is. Always enjoy the compliment; always try to consider its source. I try explaining division to the algebra classes as multiplication by the reciprocal. Can I cut to the essence of a mathematical process in the brief time that I have?

And we've got a genuine Goth in class today – all in black, with these huge Dungeons and Dragons-type rings. These guys have been taking a lot of bad press lately. I'm guessing he's got the parents a bit tense. And a girl announces that there are condoms on her desk. I put my foot down and insist that there'll be no use of them during class time. During prep I get to talking to a teacher who's been huddled by the teachers room heater for warmth. I mention that I review books and she says she does too. I ask where and she looks around to see who might be listening and says that she does erotic stuff for Good Vibrations, the woman-owned sex shop in the Mission. I'm pretty sure none of my high school teachers did that sort of thing.

JUST SOME JERK – Literature/Social Studies, Waterfront Middle, November 30, 2000

I arrive late and the key doesn't work. Another teacher lets us in while we're all standing in the hall waiting for a kid to return from the office with another key – which is a good thing since the second key didn't work either. I think they just chuck all the keys in a drawer here. This sort of thing never helps – the wise sub will always want to be set in battle position before the enemy can array its forces. As it is, we experience a certain amount of restlessness, culminating in a girl whacking a boy in the face. This has the effect of setting the substitute teacher into a rage, which restores the system to equilibrium.

A fairly large sixth grade class at thirty-four, with five absent and I've got these kids for four periods which is, I think, without precedent in my middle school experience. Of course, Sister Rita did have us for the entire sixth grade day at St. Athanasius. She had God with her, though. Plus she was never absent, so no one ever subbed for her. The situation here is more one of a Petri dish of familiarity in which contempt grows by the hour. Apparently they've switched all the sixth grades over to single teachers in this school. We'll see how long that lasts.

I'm supposed to explain the underlined words in the Hammurabi assignment that they're supposed to copy in second period. One is "subpoenaed" and the sound drives 'em wild. When I ask if they can tell me what "oath" means, a girl suggests it's a kind of tree, you know – an oath tree. A black boy in the front of the room says that his school bag is full because he likes to read newspapers; his father says TV destroys your brain cells. There's a man I'd like to meet.

I talk to the regular guy at the end of the day and it turns out that he's got a detached retina and I'm going to replace him through Tuesday. One of the kids thinks I look like Mr. Rogers! Whew! That kid should be checked out by a professional. Another comes up with Jack Nicholson, which I hadn't heard in so long I was beginning to wonder if Lara Flynn Boyle would still be interested.

Kids rap on the classroom door as they pass by in the hall all day long and a somebody always wants to open it. At one point I tell a kid he can't open the door because it's just some jerk rapping. It turns out to be a teacher.

I'm back for a second day when the regular teacher has laser surgery. Understandably he didn't come in to make lesson plans as he said he would. Didn't call either, so I'm winging it, which is not what I want to be doing with a sixth grade class that I've got for four periods plus an eighth grade of thirty-six.

At one point I call counseling to say I want to send a kid down, but no one answers, so I call the front office where a substitute teacher answers. Eventually a security person comes up and talks to the guy and he says he'll be good. Right! Apart from the fact that I want this guy gone, the idea of taking everyone's class time to get this kid to say he'll be nice is not my idea of educational time well spent.

One of the many problems here is that the room is too small. Two kids work at the same front table that serves as the teacher's desk and kids have to walk behind me to get in and out of the room. This violates the basic rule of never allowing yourself to be surrounded by the enemy. By day's end, neither I nor the students can even get the VCR working, I've had security in twice, and ejected another kid for throwing things. I'm done. The sub who hopes to fight another day knows when to leave the field of combat. I understand full well why I've been left in the lurch, but in the lurch I've been left. Someone else can have the next two days. Maybe the teacher will be able to get lesson plans together over the weekend. At any rate, they'll have a fresh start.

Sign in the hall reads, "Math turtoring. 3:30-4:30 PM, T, W, Th, Rm 235." Spelling turtoring. M, F?

IF THE SHOE FITS – *English/Special Ed/Theater, Cappuccino High, December 4, 2000*

AP (Advanced Placement) English first. Half gone on a field trip to Stanford. I mention *And Still We Rise*, the book about an AP English class in an all-black high school in LA that I recently reviewed. One kid asks who the author is – a good sign. Another says he's been in honors for four years and there's never been a black kid in it.

Fill in at Special Education for third. Nine kids with an aide who throws one out early. I note that she handles it in a more easygoing manner than I would have, but ties up everyone's time processing the ejected.

A girl in fourth period theater says she had me in math and I called her class all morons. Apparently she's from that very special sixth period class. I believe I actually spoke of "the morons among you," but apparently they took that as applying to all of them and on that subject they would know better than I. I'm glad to see that somebody remembers something I said, though – at least some version of it.

GIRL PROBLEMS – *Seventh Grade Science, Nathaniel Hawthorne Middle, December 6, 2000*

A 7:30 AM call from payroll explains that they have just now received my green time sheet for the month, mail apparently taking two weeks to reach them. They've realized the last check they had sent me was a duplicate of the prior month's, so they'll deduct their overpayment from my next check. God, I love that office!

This tape says this job's for 8AM. Although memory says Nathaniel Hawthorne is 9:00, I shoot for 8 anyhow, but at 8:20 I'm just parking in a spot in sight of the school when I notice street cleaning posted for today, so I'm off looking again for the next half hour. When I finally arrive, the secretary says it is a 9 start, and then hands me a note from the teacher saying I should cover his 8 AM computer lab.

Maybe it's the science, but the kids' minds seem very much on bodily functions and they all have got to go to the bathroom. The girls tell me they have to change their pads. I don't recall them telling Sister Thomas that, but maybe they whispered.

PUBLISHING – *English, Appian Way High, December 12, 2000*

A beeping alarm goes off for a long time during class, but none of us knows what it means. No one leaves the other classes, so it's not a fire drill. Earthquake drill, maybe. Perhaps the students should be under their desks, but the ground holds anyway. Glad we're prepared.

The second and third period classes are seniors reading *Frankenstein* and have never heard of the movie! Now I know I've outlived my time. Guess they're not showing much Boris Karloff on TV these days. Maybe if they colorized it. One kid has seen *The Young Frankenstein*, though. (Now I'm wondering which Frankenstein that elementary school kid thought I looked like.)

Third period has a presentation from the Future Business Leaders of America club which does things like answering phones at KQED during pledge drive and wrapping Christmas books at Walden Books. The latter would appear to be charity work for a profit-making operation, but Business Leaders of America may not make such distinctions.

Fourth period is reading "Casey At the Bat," so I get to explain a few things about nineteenth century baseball which is rather fun and a girl asks if I'm a publisher. Apparently another teacher I've subbed for had told her that I review books and that that's why I always have my computer. Reviewer, publisher, what's the difference?

BLACK OUT – *Mathematics, Appian Way High, January 17, 2001*

Fifth period today brings one of those nationally-famous California rolling blackouts. We can't do much because we're in a portable classroom with no real windows, so we're really kind of blacked-out. And it looks like only the portables that have gone out. Thanks Enron – and thanks for giving us Governor Arnold Schwarzenegger.

Otherwise, I am surprised to hear a girl talking about going to her mother-in-law's, so I ask if she's married. She assures me that she's not. I break the news to her that she doesn't actually have a mother-in-law.

AID, PLEASE– *Resource Room, Waterfront Middle, January 22, 2001*
This is a 5 AM call, but I'm already up and working on a book review due for the *Moscow Times* last Friday. Here for Ms. G whom I've replaced before; I anticipate a small number of pretty difficult kids, which is what I get. One big change is with the aide. The prior one was quite good and is, in fact, now a teacher here herself. This new one is nice enough, but I'm not sure she's cut out for this. When I'm speaking to her before class she appears unable to maintain attention through an entire sentence. Later, as a kid with a very low voice is trying to read out loud, she starts talking with the kids who've come by to pick up the attendance strips in a voice much louder than the kid's reading. I call things to a halt until she finishes and I assume my annoyance was visible. She does take three loud ones off to the library during third period, though, and for this I am quite grateful.

Three days later I'm replacing that teacher who used to be the aide in Ms. G's class. She's really left no plans, but she now has an aide – who unfortunately really doesn't seem to know what they're up to. After I'm at it for a while, though, I start to see how you might lose track of what exactly you'd done here. We spend the entire second period reading one newspaper story. Three kids will read out loud, the rest won't. One guy is out hiding in the hall at the beginning of class. Another is brought in by the counselor midway through the period. Another aide comes in to confer with another kid midway. I've got them for another two periods and I must remind myself that we also serve who keep these kids from disrupting everyone else in the school.

Third period's nice though: a private office in the counseling department. The regular teacher calls as I'm leaving for the day. I'm scheduled to replace her tomorrow as well, but as it's been raining and she hasn't been able to get away for her ski trip, which is what this is all about, she wonders if I'd mind too much if she came in back tomorrow after all. I find it within myself to tear myself away and let her have them back.

FIVE, FOUR, ... – *Sixth Grade Mathematics/Science, Freeway Limits Middle, January 31, 2001*
Signed up for middle schools again since work has been short, so here I am back at Freeway for the first time in several years. Somehow this does not feel like progress in life. This is the most difficult of the three South City middle schools. They pleasantly surprise me by not being so bad at the start of class, but I'll be hoarse by the end of the day. A bunch of kids con me into letting them out to the food festival during third period, claiming they're supposed to be serving. Their story fails to past muster by those in the know and most are ultimately returned to me, but the smaller class is nice while it lasts. A reminder that pain-in-

the-ass students operate with the advantage that you'd always like to believe that their reason for asking to get out of your sight is legitimate.

It's a short period schedule today, which around here means that fifth period comes before fourth period – another example of the moral relativism eating at the fiber of the country's educational system, if you ask me. A fire drill is planned for last period and they use an alarm I've never heard before that's so loud that one student jumps out of his chair when it goes off. I suppose the idea's that if you make it loud enough no one can stand to stay in the building.

HYPNOTIZING – Eighth Grade Mathematics, Cucamonga Middle, February 1, 2001

First time back here since I started doing middle school in South City again. The usual skirmishing to get the kids to work ensues, but when I raise my voice and threaten to put one kid outside and the whole class becomes still, I know I'm not up in the big city.

I realize that I don't remember how to find the volume of pyramids that the kids are working on in second period and spend a lot of time trying to dope it out. Quite embarrassing, when the kids seem to be having no particular problem with this stuff, until I realize that all the necessary formulas are on their worksheets and all they have to do is the arithmetic. (It's one-third the volume of the corresponding cube, by the way.)

In fourth period, a girl I'm helping with Mathematics tells me I have pretty eyes – "They're like hypnotizing." Her follow-up question, "Are you married?" creates some amusement among the class, at which point she says, "I'm just trying to make conversation." Jeez, why didn't the girls say that when *I* was in eighth grade and it mattered? Anyhow, after class she says her father's a probation officer and has a program on his computer with people's criminal records on it, but he won't let her see. I let her know this buttresses my faith in the system.

INTERESTING – Eighth Grade, Wolfpack Middle, February 5, 2001

One of the options after the sub machine has made its job offer is pressing #3 to hear the job repeated. I pressed #3 several times last night because this is a middle school in South San Francisco that I had never heard of. This could only mean that it was in some way "special" – a place where they send the kids the authorities feel the need to send somewhere. Possibly entire classes full of kids who usually get thrown out of class. But subbing is not for the faint hearted or those lacking curiosity, so I took the job.

Immediately upon my arrival at an empty office, it's obvious that this is an "alternative" something. This proves to be a day care center, however, and I'm directed to a second location where I encounter a teacher who informs me that I want to be at a third place, saying, "You'll have quite an ..." before stopping himself, presumably deciding an excess of frankness might cause me never to arrive at that next location, perhaps wandering forever in some sort of limbo along with the kids I've sent off to various counseling offices who never did arrive.

"I'll have quite a what?" I inquire. "It'll be interesting," he replies. The substitute's curse: May you be condemned to have interesting classes.

The teacher turns out to be in the classroom when I finally get there, but is leaving for an appointment with an eye doctor. The kids are also there, working quietly. In the morning there will be two aides; one will stay the whole day. The day is all planned out and the teacher's notes say, "The kids need nothing from you." Now this ain't looking too bad at all. This turns out to be a class of kids who flunked their last semester of middle school, and as far as the teacher is concerned, they should go to regular high school when they're done here. Apparently that other teacher thought I had the behavioral problems who will probably go to Johnny Rotten High School.

These guys are somewhat antsy and no doubt not as well behaved as when the regular teacher is there, but on the whole they're rather good. One kid comes late and is sent home by the aide for acting up, but I don't even notice what it is he did. This situation is actually a pretty good deal for these kids: they need attention and they get it. That having been said, the class's after-lunch assignment is to watch a ridiculous slasher movie called *Candyman*. I simply cannot believe that anyone considers this sort of stuff a good use of school time.

NO BABYDOLLS? – Mathematics, William Howard Taft Middle, February 9, 2001

On my way in I notice a teacher walking by in red shiny pants. She turns out to be my student teacher for first and third periods who quickly explains that today is pajama day at school – lest I think her weird, presumably. I remind her that I live in San Francisco, so I'm hardly going to decide that someone is weird for a little matter of wearing pajamas to school. The daily bulletin prescribes: "No baby bottles, pacifiers, or thin clothing is appropriate." Of course, none of the students actually seem to have worn pajamas on this very rainy day, by the way. It seems more of a grown-up thing; perhaps the faculty's way of seeing what so-and-so is like in bed, you know.

A classroom poster invites the reader to "Find the sum of the first 100 odd numbers." So, did you know that the sum of the odd numbers at any point is the square of whatever rank odd number it is? Which is to say that 13 is the seventh odd number and the sum of the odd numbers up to 13 is 49, or seven squared, and so forth. So the answer for the poster will be 10,000. It's hard to beat substitute teaching for lifelong learning.

WHERE ARE MY PENCIL? – Industrial Arts, Waterfront Middle, February 13, 2001

To get into the parking lot here you have to drive through the school yard where hundreds of kids are playing. Maybe it was the lack of hot water this morning that got me thinking dark thoughts, but is this really a good idea? Am I the only one who can imagine the teacher who's gone over the edge not being able to resist the temptation to hang a right and put the pedal to the metal? My

Friend the Evil Substitute Teacher claims that he actually suggested this layout to the administration here a few years ago, but I never know when to believe him.

For all the times I've been in this school, I never knew that this Industrial Arts program existed — a family secret of sorts, I suspect. The room is decorated in sort of nineteenth century Dickensian, post-tornado mode — twenty foot ceilings, walls in two shades of green, tattered shades, broken machinery, cardboard boxes all over, and chilly. They're just not making classrooms that look like this anymore; haven't been since Grover Cleveland was president. You might be able to find spare parts for your Packard around here somewhere. I haven't seen anything like this since my days at the now happily demolished Boston Trade High School.

(I have gone far too long saying too little about that school which still holds its place at the bottom of my memory pile. As was the case in all the other shop classes I subbed in in Boston, there was always another teacher with me in the classes I had at Trade. Subs were apparently not to be left alone with students and industrial equipment, a policy for which I was grateful. Another teacher in machine shop once told me about how a kid had told him that his family was going to Walpole for Christmas, which sounded like a nice rural holiday experience to the teacher until he realized that the kid was talking about visiting his father in the State Penitentiary, where, once he started asking questions, he learned that half the class had family. (The prison has been since renamed Cedar Junction in order to eliminate future confusion with the 400 year-old town itself.) When I did sheet-metal shop another time, my assignment was strictly to guard the door and not let anybody in or out without a pass, while the other regular teacher attempted to conduct class. Well into one class period, a couple of kids come bopping in and one of them has paperwork that indicates that this is his first day in school — and it's maybe November. The new guy picks up one of the shop products that happens to be lying in the vicinity of the door — a dust pan. He tosses it away and says to the other guy, "See what they make here? Fucking garbage cans." An effective rebuttal did not immediately come to mind. There probably were a lot of guys making license plates in Walpole who did their first sheet metal work in this very shop. Public schools are training kids for real world work in a lot of ways that are not always obvious.)

Meanwhile, back here I'm supposed to start them off with a "word of the day" that's defined and used in a sentence on a transparency for them to copy down. The subject and verb are not in agreement, though. I wonder — A simple mistake on the part of the instructor? After all, this ain't English class or nothing. But maybe not. Industrial Arts has been on something of a down slide since the days when the Univac ruled the computer market and it seems highly unlikely that the Brotherhood of Industrial Arts Instructors wouldn't have noticed the trend. Could this, then, be part of a plan to build a workforce with a more picaresque affect? You know, strapping young craftsmen declaiming, "Yes, ma'am, I are, indeed, quite skilled with the use of my tools" to suburban housewives who might then be more willing to pay prices they might otherwise consider exorbitant in order to help the children of the lower classes to grow up to be less colorful than their parents.

You have the time to think about this sort of thing when you're subbing, but whatever the deeper meaning of this lack of agreement between subject and predicate might really be, one of the kids says they've already done this word, and I do now notice that the transparency is dated February 2.

First period is pretty good on the whole, but there are three boys who disappear, so I take attendance for a second time and mark them absent. When they return, I tell them to go to counseling to get a pass. One knocks over a desk and refuses to pick it up, so I call the office on them. But then, if you can't find thuggish behavior in shop class, where can you find it? And sixth period was entirely what I was expecting. I throw out the kid who announces he's a pimp and had to call security to get him to go. This was an eighth grade class, so perhaps the little feller will have to be out supporting himself on the streets next year. By the end of the day I appear to have depleted this teacher's entire stock of pencils and only then notice that he uses sign-out lists for them. I just hope I don't see some of these guys wearing sunglasses and selling these pencils out of tin cups on my way home.

Before I leave I've accepted another job here for the remainder of the week. Susan G tells me that the teacher I'll be in for doesn't teach and is basically waiting to trip and fall and go out on workers comp. There are no lesson plans, so the assistant principal works out one for tomorrow. Two of these classes will be pretty big – one has thirty-three kids. I am not optimistic.

Sure enough, the next day the principal comes in during first period to tell the kids that their regular teacher won't be coming back. Apparently she fell down that flight of stairs or something – at least she didn't take the right turn through the schoolyard option, anyhow. This class only has 19 in it, but it's awful. The window side of the classroom is more or less Chinese and they more or less work. The door side is more or less black and they more or less scream, eat, and look at stuff. A few kids actually do the essays on high school that I've assigned and I go over them with them, but if all of the classes are like this, I'm out of here after today. Too familiar and depressing.

Second is better, though. They're not doing a great deal, but they are civil. This is a sixth grade and sixth graders sometimes have not developed their true, fully-evil middle school essence yet, as is the case here. A girl asks if she can take attendance for me. I ask if it will come out right. She assures me it will, but I have to give it back to her twice for corrections before finally doing it myself. Why do I even let them ever try?

A teacher down the hall who had introduced himself earlier comes back and asks me about buying a laptop, as he has noticed mine. We compare computer-stolen-at-school stories. His was stolen by an adult!

The day ends like it started: seventh period also sucks. This one big guy I've seen before comes in late, immediately wants to go to his locker, and then starts to argue with me that he wasn't late. I throw him out before he even sits down, which I think may be some kind of record – like an eleven second knockout in a boxing match. A girl soon follows him out and there's only seven left, but still I'm separating them to try to keep them quiet. A girl says they never do anything in this class, that the teacher just talked about books. She remembers once she brought in a book about pizza.

There is a natural ebb and flow in the endless war between sub and student, and the second day I start out MEAN, so even though my call to the counseling office for assistance goes unanswered, I am eventually able to achieve something approaching order. Those who did nothing yesterday actually write something today. Part of our problem is that what we're doing is make-work. Today's assignment is writing about the prospect of learning a foreign language in high school. Only an already motivated student is going to rise to the occasion of having something to say about high school, but I actually get some interesting answers and even discuss the difference between Cantonese and Mandarin with one kid.

During second period I return a lot of essays with "unacceptable" written on them, but one girl who wrote squat yesterday today effuses on yesterday's question, as well as today's, and actually writes something half decent. Progress, although things are sort of evening out in that today I'm doing more yelling in third period which wasn't so bad yesterday. There's a Russian kid in fourth period who doesn't speak English. I don't understand what he's doing here, actually. I'm running ragged today, trying to correct one class's papers while kids are asking for help on their reading work. This, I suppose, must be reckoned a good thing, though, considering where these classes have apparently been.

The sixth grade classes use readers with questions. I don't have an answer key and, in one case, none of the three available answers is really correct, so far as I'm concerned. Two answers are obviously wrong, so using the SAT method of test-taking, the remaining one, that is not clearly wrong, must be right. But this one says that we know that bricks are hard to come by in Tahiti, when the story has only told us how and why people build with thatch there. It could well be the case that bricks are actually are readily available there but people simply choose not to use them. A mildly interesting discussion ensues.

Seventh period is improved today, if for no other reason than that yesterday's main offender is absent today – poor attendance does have its upside. At the end of the period, a girl who's been a pain knocks over some books on her way out, apparently unintentional, but when I tell her to stop and pick them up, she runs away – something you figure you can get away with a sub. I yell after her that she better not come tomorrow. I have already written up a referral and will eject her upon entry – if she comes. But if she doesn't show up, that won't be the worst thing either.

This has been a day to make you swear off of Mr. Nice Guy – there's no doubt that raging at these kids provides results. In a one-day assignment anything goes, but I figure that if I do come back for two, I know what I've gotten myself into and I've got some responsibility to try to make something happen.

Third day I step in a pile of trash when I open the rear door. Broom's still here, too, so I'm guessing the janitor was interrupted. One thing these kids do well is produce litter. And you can be sure that some of the biggest slobs will arrive in last period and complain about what a mess the other classes have made.

A teacher comes in before first period and asks how it's going and I tell her yesterday was better than the day before. She says it seems quiet, and, in the life of a sub, that will have to do as a compliment. Yet I am determined to get them quieter still and tell them so in first period. When one of the pains-in-the-ass walks in late, making noise and won't give me his name, I tell him to leave and he refuses. I call security, after which a kid starts telling me there is no security at this school, after which security arrives. I mean it's one thing not knowing how to read or add, but you ought to know if there's security at your school — at least that's how it seems to me. Meanwhile I can't do anything with the class because I'm writing a referral. The head counselor arrives to tell the class they're shorthanded down there today and anyone with a referral will be sent home. Home schooling sounds like a good option for some of these guys.

I'm asking grammar questions about errors in their writing in second period and one girl is actually engaged until the phone rings and someone tells me to send her somewhere else. With this girl gone I can't pull anything out of the rest of the class. But maybe I've stumbled onto something here — just ask them grammar questions all day and they'd be absolutely quiet.

By fourth, I've thrown two kids out and am planning on making the girl who ran away yesterday the third, if she shows up. All three are black. A few years ago one of the School Board members started asking for a racial breakdown of kids who were suspended, presumably on the assumption that a disproportionate number of suspensions of blacks would indicate racism of some sort on the part of the faculty and/or administration. But as Y, the sub I did the week with in the Citadel Middle book room way back, once said, if suspensions were actually done totally evenhandedly, the ratio would be even heavier. His point, I think, was that as teachers or administrators see how many black kids they're throwing out, many probably pull back, out of the desire not to feel or seem to be prejudiced. I know I think about it, as I am doing today.

On days like this, I find myself running through the logic of discipline de novo. If I don't get strict, it's not fair to the kids inclined to work. And many of the kids who aren't so inclined will start to perform a little when you come down on the class. But to get strict, you have to get some kids in trouble. And you have to be fair in that — you can't have separate standards. And the kids who get in trouble will be way disproportionately black. All this runs through my mind as I'm on the verge of throwing out another kid, also black. But since he was simply refusing to cooperate, rather than being disruptive, I decide to let it slide and I don't know if I would have let it go were he not black.

When yesterday's runaway girl arrives for seventh period, I have her walking papers at the ready. Then the guy from day one reappears and starts his usual riff, so out he goes. Then I've got another kid acting up and I'm once again thinking I'd throw him out if he weren't black and he essentially decides to leave on his own; says he wants to see his counselor. So counting him, I'm five for five. But then the girl I threw out yesterday is just doodling and refuses to give up her doodle sheet to me, so I send her packing again. And she's white, so I can go home for the weekend at ease. But boy, I think I'd have to go back a long time for a day when I ejected six students. On the plus side, though, I was actually teaching some of these kids about the subjunctive and the proper usage of apostrophes, things a whole lot of adults don't have down.

The principal did come into the classroom on my first day here, and the head counselor came in on the last. Still I feel that there might have been a bit more attention paid by the administration to a fairly difficult situation of which they were aware. And words of gratitude at the end of the week? Come on, I'm just a sub.

Nonetheless, I'm back next week because I had already signed on for that horror of a Special Ed class I recently had. I've only got three kids present in first period when another teacher arrives and informs me that he and the teacher I'm replacing switch rooms for first. And indeed, her notes do say that, although the schedule I was given did not. Off to the next room for what will be my only non-Special Ed class of the day. They start with Silent Sustained Reading and my instructions say that no pencils or pens are to be out. I have to ride a couple of kids on that, and there's this one Chinese boy who won't put his pencil away; he doesn't say anything, just won't put it away. I take it from him and ask him to get his book out. No response. I try a few times and tell him to get up. No nothing. He's basically gone catatonic on me. This is freaky. I'm about to call the counselor on him, but see he's crying by now and figure I'll just back off and give it a rest. But in a few minutes there's no change and I figure I've got a problem, so I call counseling after all, but while I'm out in the hall talking on the phone I hear a fight start back in the room. I have to drop the phone on the floor and rush in to break that up. It was that kid and the kid next to him.

He's got a bloody nose now, and he's still not responsive. I tell counseling they've got to send someone up. I have to call them again and then call the office because no one shows. Finally, I look out in the hall, and I see they're looking for me at this teacher's regular classroom. I had noticed last week that this school distributes out-of-date schedules, so they don't know where she actually is this period. Finally security comes in and takes the kids away, along with one witness I've identified for them. I think that other kid taunted the catatonic guy, but I can't be sure. And I actually have to compliment the other kids for being good after this, although I'd sure be happy to leave right about now, this being my one *non-Special Ed* class.

The rest of the day is pretty much as I expect. The girls are okay and the boys are amazingly immature, as is often the case. They demand virtually one-on-one attention the entire day. I believe the regular teacher to be off on the prolonged ski weekend that was scheduled the other time I replaced her when she returned early because the skiing prospects weren't great. I generally find the idea of taking off skiing on a school day troubling, but after another day in her horrible surreal classroom, I find myself feeling less judgmental.

SO YOUNG – *Sixth Grade RSP (Resource Specialist Program), Cucamonga Middle, February 21, 2001*

Well, I'm in middle school again and Special Ed even, but compared to yesterday, this job is like giving Sisyphus wheels for that rock he's pushing. It comes with an aide who seems on the cranky side – she's telling the kids to pick up their feet while they're walking. Me, I'm just happy they're not kicking anybody with them. She also checks under the boys' shirts to make sure they're not practicing the current fashion of wearing pants below the crotch. I suppose there's a public safety factor here – if this gravity-defying style is left unchecked, some of these guys are going to just topple over and may be reduced to pulling themselves along the ground with their arms.

I read them an article on the controversy over removing the Confederate Stars and Bars from the Georgia state flag. The kids don't know what the opposing sides in the US Civil War were; in fact, they didn't know what a civil war is. But this is what we have school for, isn't it? Later they get a question sheet about Washington and Lincoln. This school has book covers with the names, pictures and terms of office of all the presidents, which years the kids write down as the answers to the question of when Washington and Lincoln lived. But when I point out that the presidents all look like they lived longer than the four or eight year spans listed on the covers, they decide that this question may bear further research.

YOU CAN TELL A BOOK BY ITS COVER – *Resource Room, Waterfront Middle, April 16, 2001*

At one point, kids who've been doing nothing but talk say they want to work in the hall, but when the aide indicates this is not done, I shoo them back in the classroom. One says, "We'll do our work." I tell him I doubt it, to which he replies, "You say that because I'm black." The aide upbraids him on that and he sits down and continues to noisily do nothing until the aide tells him to go to his proper seat which he refuses to do, and I send him to the counselor who seems not at all surprised to hear from me. I've already sent another back-talking girl.

Does this guy actually thinks he's discriminated against because he's black, or does he just say it because it gets a reaction? Actually, although I think he's wrong, I don't know that his analysis – if it really is that – is any more wrong than most of what goes around on the topic these days. Certainly there are people who think he won't or can't do school work because he's black, although not too many of them will say that publicly these days. And there's others who'll say that his work is poor because his school or his teachers are failing him. And I don't think they're actually on the mark either, to the extent that they think that the primary cause of black students' difficulties lies in unequal treatment or unequal expectations within the educational system. He's not being sent out because he is black, and he's not not doing his work because he's black, and yet insofar as he thinks that his race has everything to do with his relationship with the educational system, he's right. And that delicately worded statement is about as far as the public discussion on race and education goes these days.

Technology update: One difference between high school and middle school used to be that the middle school kids didn't have cell phones. But today a girl asks if she can make a phone call in class and as I start to indicate that I'm not going to let her use the classroom phone, she assures me that she only wants to make a call on her own phone. It's still a negative.

For two periods I take kids to the library to do book reports. It turns out they are not required to read the books. They're allowed to write their report from the dust jacket descriptions. Well, I suppose it's a step.

GETTING LUCKY – *Sixth Grade ESL, Freeway Limits Middle, May 9, 2001*

Fourth period is a continuation of a puberty video; a female teacher gets the girls. The video immediately starts into a discussion of how masturbation is okay. And while we've got a tape rolling that's discussing sexual intercourse, I'm busy confiscating the kids' little paper-fold things on which you pick a number and get a message – quintessential middle school moment. At least they're not being unduly influenced by sex education, any way.

CLEAVAGE – *Roving, Worcester Middle, May 10, 2001*

The sub I often see at Appian Way High is here today; tells me this is the only middle school he goes to. It's the high-end one in South San Francisco. We're rovers today, relieving teachers who have parent conferences. I've got a couple of big nose blowers in my first class. Nose-blowing can be a very popular bodily function in the middle school environment. It's gross, and you can do it publicly. It gives the kids an opportunity to get out of their seats, get a tissue, maybe step outside to do the deed – an important avenue of self-expression at this age. One of the nose-blowers, whom I've had to instruct to open his book several times, now announces his need to spit. Here we move into areas of expression not as clearly protected by the Constitution, so I send him to the office to discuss his medical condition.

Another group runs me through the usual stuff about whether I'm related to the comedian named Gallagher, primarily known for smashing watermelons, or if I'm married to the Mary Frances Gallagher from Saturday Night Live. Then one of them asks what middle school I went to and I tell them I didn't go to middle school. Well, that sets them off – that I went to school back before they had middle schools – in the middle ages. And we've got an eighth grade girl showing a lot of cleavage here, something I don't remember girls having when I was back in Sister Acquin's class.

The teachers room lunchtime discussion revolves around liposuction and cellulite. My first afternoon stint is sixth graders reading aloud from *Child of the Owl*, a novel set in San Francisco's Chinatown, at which they do well. I ask them a lot of definitions – pompous, fastidious, et al, and act out a few of them. The class smart boy (Chinese) says, "You're eccentric. You're like the other sub who made us change the words of the national anthem." I like that other sub already. The day's final act is computer lab where the kids are working on web pages. The boys have stuff on frogs, dogs, rats and insects; the girls on recipes, why you shouldn't smoke, etc.

And speaking of cleavage, today's *Examiner* – the pathetic ersatz replacement *Examiner* – has a blurb on one Dana Gibson, who says, "It didn't seem like a big deal, but maybe something's totally wrong with me." Ms. Gibson, of "Morro Bay, was fired as a substitute teacher at St. Joseph High after she responded to student complaints that her class was boring by removing her shirt and teaching Spanish in her sports bra." That'll teach them to allow substitute teachers in Catholic school. No nun wearing the habit would do that sort of thing.

I proctor a spelling test here that has "hassle" spelled "hassel." Perhaps this teacher would be better placed outside of language arts.

ACCOMPLISHMENT – *History/Social Studies, Cappuccino High, May 14, 2001*

The day starts out very quiet, with kids mostly doing their worksheets from their economics textbooks and seeming totally unfazed that the teacher is not there. The TA has nothing to do and asks if he can read my sports page. When he's finished it, I suggest he read some of Howard Zinn's *The People's History of the United States* that's sitting on the teacher's desk. He giggles, then asks for a pass to the bathroom, so at least this period isn't a total loss for him. Later he asks what I'm doing on this machine. I tell him I might write part of a book review. He asks what a book review is.

By fourth period there are fifteen absences, as word has gotten around. Sixth period history is watching the opening scene of *Saving Private Ryan*, the Normandy invasion, actually the only really noteworthy part of the movie, if you ask me.

This was the sort of day that keeps me in the subbing business. I reviewed the interminable report I'm writing for the State AFL-CIO, made some editorial changes, did up an alternative section dealing with some new contradictory data I encountered, wrote two memos on it and a letter requesting more information, and made some preliminary notes for a book review. Suspect I wouldn't have gotten that much done at home. How you gonna beat that in a job?

THE PROGRAM – *Reading, Freeway Limits Middle, May 16, 2001*

The sub machine called me for an art job, neglecting to mention that it was also part PE. But I don't get to check out the combo because they switch me to Reading as soon as I arrive. Not a job for the inflexible. I am led to a strange room with painted-over windows where I am introduced to the SRA reading program. But first there is a pair of very foul-mouthed girls to be dealt with. There's about eight girls outside my room before class and a couple of them are screaming at each other. I go out and speak to them three times before finally telling them they have to disperse because I'm not going to listen to them any longer. Fortunately, they don't seem to be in my class, apparently they just gather here to scream their "Fuck you"s at each other before school starts.

This reading program feels like some sort of cult activity. The way it goes is that I'm supposed to read a script out of a book and do something like rap a pencil on the desk as a signal for them to perform various actions. Too Pavlovian for my educational theories and I drop the rapping part, figuring they can probably respond to words just as well as to sharp sounds. I also depart from the script by explaining the origin of some words. Somewhere out there, there's probably some researcher planning to sue me now that he's realized who screwed up that project.

And so the day goes forward, machinelike, interrupted only by constant messages over the PA system about cars that need to be moved and the like.

DRAMA AND REALITY – English, Appian Way High, May 18, 2001

At sign-in this morning I run into the Math teacher I replaced last week and tell him of my problems with the box and whisker plots his class was supposed to be doing. He says he never learned it in school either, didn't find it very helpful, and actually hadn't gone over the sheet he'd left for me, so couldn't enlighten me on its mysteries. I feel better about my math now. I didn't remember it from school and, sure enough, it hadn't been invented then. 1977, actually. And while I'm sure that John Tukey, the man who made it up, is a very nice man, I think they should take it and store it alongside binary math.

First period is reading *The Crucible*, which actually goes pretty well. When one kid stumbles over the pronunciation of Pontius Pilate, a name he's clearly unfamiliar with, I tell them it's a famous name from the New Testament. A girl says that no one here knows the Bible, so I do a little fill-in. The next three periods are reading *A Raisin In the Sun*, which is a lot more animated. Surprisingly, boys are not reluctant to take women's roles and in third, a boy asks for the role of Mama and does a bang-up job.

I happen to be reviewing a book about over-reliance on standardized testing and what do we have right here in this classroom but a videotape entitled *Six Steps to SAT Success* and a book called *Test-Taking Strategies: Reading, Language and Vocabulary for California High School Students*.

I notice a class picture on a teacher's desk here – that has me in it! I can't tell if it's from this year or last. This is what can happen when you hang around too long.

Today's lunchroom discussion is about how they have some of the saddest bunches of students they've ever had. Absolutely no curiosity they say. Some think the kids need to go to bed earlier; some say they need to get up later. The teachers' lunchroom here is something of a throwback to what I remember in Boston in that there really is group discussion here, although the real crowd – and camaraderie – is in the next room where the paras eat, but, not being a para, I don't go in there.

"A FOOL" – Study Skills, Freeway Limits Middle, May 22, 2001

Sixth grade Study Skills – that would be something like the null set. This will be a job for Mr. Hard Ass Substitute Teacher – Good morning, class. First task – get them in their seats; second is to locate an assignment. The standard sub form in this school has a spot for teachers to note students who might be helpful and there are actually two names listed for first period. Unfortunately, these kids are not actually in this class. Last year's form? Students the teacher wished she had? I don't know. I ask the students who are there what they're doing in class, but they say they don't know. A call to the office does produce results – hands immediately rise out of the cloud of unknowing that follows substitutes about, as a few of the sharper minds recall that they were working on filling out job description forms for their career folders. The secretary has meanwhile called the teacher who has reported same and says she will fax assignments for later in the day. So they start on their forms and I answer a few individual questions about what salary means and what someone's interests and abilities are. Four or five don't have pencils; one needs an ice pack; one discovers he has pinkeye. This is a class of nonnative English speakers who have learned the ways of students of their new country unusually quickly. Today, I go so far as to write the word "nuisance" on the board and ask them to define it. One kid says, "a fool." Not bad.

In the teachers room a regular teacher gets to talking to me about subbing. Asks if I'm retired. (Oh my!) I say, no it's just an odd thing that I do. He says, "You must be a writer." When I tell him I sub in San Francisco too, he thinks I'm brave. There's a lunchtime discussion among teachers of last night's episode of *Boston Public* in which a female teacher was dating a student. So, yes, they do watch it.

AT LEAST IT'S NOT 8 – Seventh Grade Science, Calvin Coolidge Middle, May 25, 2001

This place doesn't start until 9 – evidence of intelligent design somewhere. Pretty stark racial divide in this school. On the way back from lunch, I hear a black boy call a Chinese girl a slut. She just looks at him like he's from another world, which he pretty much is, even within this one school. Today only two black kids will set foot in my classroom the entire day, that during the break following third period when a boy runs in one door and out the other, followed by a girl yelling, "Bitch, I'm going to get you." All in fun, mind you.

OLE ONE NOT TALKING – Social Studies, Citadel Middle, June 1, 2001

Yesterday's mail brought a package of apology letters from the first period Freeway class that couldn't remember what they were supposed to do. The secretary had told me that day that the regular teacher was really disappointed with the class for acting that way, but since all the teacher would have had to do to prevent that was leave me a note or call in instructions, I took her disappointment with a grain of salt. But I guess she was serious. I've saved the letters for reading in school. Let's see what we have here.

The kids were nonnative English speakers, so their spelling combines that background with the usual alphabetical creativity of sixth graders (many of whom, as you've seen, have teachers who can't spell so gud themselves.) The first letter tells me that it's from the one kid who did tell me what they were doing. Another writer explains that he didn't tell me what they were doing because "I'm just not one to raise my hand." Geraldine writes that, "even though I did not do nothing

bad I am very sorry that they were acting like that." She was "the girl that was asking you what does words mean." She hopes that I "no ho I'am and you no who is writing to you." Karla tells me that some of them wanted to tell me what they were supposed to be doing, "but the other screamed at us." However, I am "the greatest substitute." Jocene lets me know that she was the "ole one not talking." Even Shivnal who wasn't there that day had to write an apology letter. And Ivan, who "was in the office the whole time because when I was playing basketball and then when I wasn't looking at the basketball, a kid passed to me and when I turned around the basketball hit my lip." Jonathan allows that "we acted like first graders," but is certain that "we'll change in the future," and, at any rate, he "didn't do anything." And Tyler "had little or nothing to do with it," when "no one said anything but lies until after Mr. Gallager called the office." Robert is so sorry that he writes, "If I do this agany sane my to the office," but if you "don't come agane I will unrstand."
Student name of the day: Moonlit Li

YOUR FRIEND – *Sixth Grade Social Studies/Language Arts, Worcester Middle, June 4, 2001*

After home room and before first period, a few kids gather around to look at my computer. One asks how much it costs and I just tell him more than I'll see today. So another kid asks if I get paid to be here. Hey, he doesn't, so maybe I don't either – you don't ask, you don't learn. A girl brings up a box of tissues to donate to the class. Glad to see the teachers are not expected to provide everything.

Today a *Jason and the Argonauts* video will be playing and the kids tell me I'm supposed to stop it every few minutes and write notes on the board. A very good day for the one-time high school Greek student always dying to use his Greek. I get to write a lot of it on the board, explain the origin of the word "alphabet," the whole works. Of course, I also realize I don't properly know the Jason story. I do see that Jason and the A's have fished Medea out of the water and her hair is perfect.

Then a map exercise locating a few states, mountains, and neighboring countries. I ask the kids who's been to the places they find on the map and they're certainly better traveled than my sixth grade class was. A surprising number have been to Toronto. I notice a class with a "Wall Street" sign above the door, a newspaper headline, "Bush Wins It," on the door, and class posters proclaiming, "Your friend, corporate America." Maybe that kid donating the Kleenex in first period should have tipped me off that the neighborhood was going bourgie.

BE MEAN – *Second/Third Grade, Benjamin Banneker Elementary, June 7, 2001*

The secretary says that since school ends tomorrow, I should just try to get through the day – show them videos or whatever. Paula, the para, has a bit more ambitious plan at first, but eventually the two plans converge. The regular teacher had only started with this class after Christmas and left at the end of last week, by which time, "She was going crazy," according to Paula who's got to submit the kids' final grades today. She says, "Be mean from the start." Things are okay when she's in the room, which is most of the day, but when she's not, there's not a whole lot I can do. She's suggested I read to them at the start of class when she won't be there. I do, and a couple of them ostentatiously jam their fingers in and out of their ears to demonstrate that they have other ideas on how to spend this time.

When Paula returns at 9 she takes the nine girls and I take the five boys and read out of their reader. Some serious chaos develops after recess, at which point another teacher appears and quiets them remarkably effectively, for which I am quite grateful. She says she'll be back shortly and she's so convincing that it's a few minutes before even I realize that she just said that to keep the kids quiet. Like the kids, I'm still waiting.

I'm showing them *Aladdin* to general complaint that they want to see *The Emperor's New Groove* instead, but still it's working okay. When a woman in the cartoon snuggles up to a tiger, I warn one of the boys watching it in the back with me that he wouldn't want to do that with a real tiger, but he tells me that it is a real tiger. But then, when the carpet starts flying, he says, "Mr. G, that's fiction isn't it?" I tell him he's right and he tells another boy that he knew that because carpets can't fly.

When I pick the kids up in the school yard after lunch, only four follow me in. I don't know them and they won't listen to me, so I just head in with what I've got and eventually the rest mostly trickle in, but Paula notices that Mustafa isn't there and goes looking for him. When she brings him back, she says he was "helping the janitors." A few minutes later he asks if he can go drink water and disappears again. This time Paula finds him in the office and decides to just leave him there. He's a regular wanderer. Apparently he'll just walk out the front door if no one stops him, but he's in his second foster home this week, so what would you expect?

This place is a lot rougher since the departure of that principal that everyone seems to have considered extraordinary. It was always challenging here, but back then it felt like a sort of racial equivalent of Buenos Dias – a black/white magnet school where whites voluntarily sent their kids.

Benjamin Banneker doesn't seem to have that kind of appeal any more, though and the problems of difficult schools just compound themselves. A class is a lot less likely to change hands in December in a west side school, and it's certainly less likely to have a teacher walk with only a week to go. Unfortunately, however, most discussions of so-called "failing schools" seldom get past symptoms such as the turnover in classes like this. Certainly the fact that a class like this gets a less experienced teacher is a legitimate issue, but it's really more a symptom of the problems these kids have – and bring with them, than it is the cause.

REJECTION– *Economics/History, Appian Way High, June 8, 2001*

Third period is a small ESL class of some type, where one kid is eating a rather elaborate breakfast at his desk. This appears to be of no concern to the regular teacher who has stayed around for the first few minutes, so it is therefore of no concern to me, although I must admit that seeing this fellow actually put Doritos in his ham-and-cream-cheese-on-a-bagel sandwich does trouble me from a gustatory point of view. After he's done he asks if he can go to the bathroom to wash his hands. I say sure, but ask if third period isn't a little late for breakfast and doesn't he think it might be better to eat a good breakfast during first period. He's noncommittal in his response.

On my way out the secretary tells me that Ms. B, the head counselor, wants to see me. I'm figuring that she's maybe going to question me about throwing a student out of class, but it turns out that she's just gotten the Summer school application that I returned very late, in a sort of what-the-heck, nothing to lose mode. I actually applied for only one subject – high school Government – but she proceeds to interview me about teaching eighth grade English – grammar specifically. She decides to keep looking, so, in other words, she's just interviewed and rejected me for a job I didn't apply for – I tell you, they go out of their way. That's another plus about being a sub, though – I get to reject their jobs more often than they can reject me.

At the UESF Executive Board meeting this afternoon, Ken T distributes a flyer that some Cabot teachers have distributed to their colleagues asking them to contribute all or part of the bonus they received as a result of the school's rise in state test scores into a scholarship fund for graduating seniors. A great idea. Arguably these guys have the best high school jobs in the city, where most of the challenges they face are actually educational rather than disciplinary in nature. A lot of teachers at Pizarro would die to be in a school with the best students. And Cabot teachers get a bonus for being there? A prime example of the foolishness of the testing mania.

TWO, ONE, ZERO, ZERO ... – *Sixth Grade, Cucamonga Middle, June 14, 2001*
Last school day in South San Francisco. My arrival is greeted with jubilation in the office where I am told, "They're watching videos, it's a half day, it's a no-brainer." My class is watching *Wayne's World,* along with another class, their teacher, and an aide. Now *Wayne's World* doesn't strike me as an educational travesty on the last day of school, but I do have to wonder if every parent actually wants school time to include Wayne flashing a sign that says, "He's got no penis," and announcing, "I'm being shat on," and Garth saying, "If he were an ice cream flavor, it'd be Pralines and Dick." On the other hand, the movie does feature Alice Cooper telling the boys that Milwaukee is the only American city to have thrice elected a socialist mayor, so it does have some educational merits beyond the norm. (And there is the fact that I actually think it's really funny.)

Third period is gardening class, but they're watching movies today as well. A few of them prefer to continue a water balloon toss outside and I have to chase them inside. I require one boy to place his water balloon in the sink to keep him from tossing it up in the air during class and perhaps breaking the concentration of his classmates who are watching *Dumb and Dumber.* But I have soon settled them to the point where the movie can take over and dumb them right down.

The school is full of kids with last-day-of-school messages written all over their white uniform shirts. A huge soft football starts getting tossed around during fifth so I confiscate it, setting off quite a racket which prompts me to turn on the light, which in turn starts a discussion as to why they can't just do anything they want. Given that the day's educational program consists of a movie featuring lines like "That John Denver's full of shit, man," I am at something of a disadvantage in this debate and am forced back upon that eternally reliable argument – "Because." Actually, a lot of the kids clearly do want to watch the movie, so it turns out that "Because" is the right answer once again.

With less than fifteen minutes left on the school year I'm turning on the lights on and telling kids to stop throwing stuff; with ten minutes to go I throw a guy out for throwing stuff; with three minutes to go I see him out the back door and run him off again. A substitute's job is not done until the final bell. The students count down the final seconds, but they don't actually manage to get the timing down exactly right. Hey, they've been watching *Dumb and Dumber* all afternoon, so whaddya want?

****

PERIPATETIC – *Sixth/Eighth Grade PE/Science, William Howard Taft Middle, August 30, 2001*

Back for more. I was back east until Tuesday and then the San Francisco machine invented an expiration date that did not allow me to be assigned. Calling the Sub Office doesn't get it straightened out, as they are not so diligent at following up their answering machine as they expect us to be and I have to go down there.

So anyway, this is a PE/Science assignment and I think they only mention the Science so's you'll take the job. I passed up a couple of other jobs last night, thinking that if the *Examiner* had decided to run my Sub column I would be a lot more adventurous in search of new material. And as long as we're on the topic, this book would likely have reached your hands a lot earlier, were it not for the paper's rejection of my column proposal. At that point the *Examiner* was a serious but failing afternoon broadsheet published within a joint operating agreement with the larger, more successful morning *Chronicle*. It should not be confused with subsequent tabloids of the same name, the first of which read like it was edited maybe in Talinn, Estonia. It once ran a front page with the tagline "Keeping San Francico (sic) a two-newspaper town." The next one devoted more space to attempting to convert San Francisco to Republicanism than to news.

The "original" *Examiner* was then running a column by an anonymous cabbie, so I proposed the anonymous sub, arguing that people will find what actually goes on in schools at least as strange – and interesting – as what a cabbie hears. My journalism industry veteran friend Mary's take on editors is that they figure out "What can I *not* get away with rejecting?" It took a while, but the editor in this case decided that the need to give the schools fictitious names – to prevent them from quickly knowing that *Anonymous Sub* had just entered the building – was the deal stopper. (The paper's precipitous decline followed soon after this decision.)

Back here in Taft, I think this teacher's going to get pretty tired of this job this year. The kids are all right, but she has to move after every class. First period is science, on the third floor, where I can't even use the teacher's desk because the *real* teacher in this room is here on her prep period, using *her* desk while the teacher I'm replacing – and today me – sits at some little table.

Then PE in the upper gym, where my class is one of three. No uniforms yet, so it's free whatever – basketball, girls jumping Double Dutch (do they still call it that?) Some of the longest minutes of my life will be spent looking at my watch over these four periods these two days.

Fourth period is in one of the two bungalows I'd never noticed out back; fifth – lunch; sixth PE again, now solo, trying to keep kids from kicking balls around; seventh back to the bungalow. No keys, including for the bathroom. Maybe this teacher doesn't have bathroom privileges either.

9/11 – *English, Appian Way High, September 11, 2001*
   The day the World Trade Center is attacked. All San Francisco schools closed, but not here. Sign on 101 says all flights canceled at the airport; radio says for seven hours. The plane that crashed outside Pittsburgh was apparently heading here from Newark. All subs asked to speak with the principal before class. He tells us the teachers we're subbing for are actually in an onsite meeting and will come by at the beginning of each class and release any students who appear to be having any emotional problems, and that we should do so as well.
   Turned on the TV this morning for the first time since I don't know when after hearing the news on the radio. Saw the first tower collapse and I'm now in a classroom watching footage of the Pentagon burning. Two weeks ago yesterday, I spent the entire day walking around lower Manhattan and was actually in the Trade Center for the first time in years. This was supposed to be primary day in New York.
   First period honors class is supposed to be taking a test, but that's canceled. A memo from the principal advises against watching the news all day. I ignore it, but an administrator comes and asks that I turn it off. The kids think this is ridiculous, and so do I, but I don't feel that I can ignore a direct request.
   The second period teacher comes in and says that Bush has declared this an act of war and that therefore eighteen year olds might be getting called up for military service. Seems a foolish thing to say; I downplay Bush's remark as rhetoric after the teacher leaves. Class actually goes on as normal, watching *Lord of the Flies*, which seems eerier than ever for today. Third period also as normal, watching *Dead Poets Society*. One kid asks isn't this Bush's fault? If Clinton was president they never would have done this, he thinks.

SUB INSIDE – *Auto Shop/Health, Cappuccino High, September 19, 2001*
   Today I'm issued a substitute teacher badge to wear; a post-World Trade Center precaution I guess. This strikes me pretty much like wearing a "Kick Me" sign, so I attach it to my pants pocket where my sweatshirt covers it and no one ever mentions it. There's also a new two-sided yellow/red card that I'm supposed to display in the window in case of a security alert, an eventuality that I'm supposed to recognize by a British police siren-like bell that presumably has been in the movies. My signs indicate that a "substitute teacher" will be found within. Seems like a foolish idea. I mean do you really want to tip the terrorists off as to what rooms they should avoid? (On second thought, maybe the authorities fear we'd join forces with them.)
   These'll be the first grease monkeys I've had since Brighton High. But first I've got to find them in a part of the campus I've never seen before, where every room has two different numbers, apparently because no one has gotten around to removing the old numbers after the new ones were painted on. I was never sent into the garage solo at Brighton High and I'm not here either. The difference is that the Brighton garage was considerably larger, as it was the one automotive program for the entire city of Boston, so I sometimes was in there with

other teachers. Today we'll be in the small classroom next door with no tools or weapons in hand.

NATURE– *Seventh/Eighth Science, Cucamonga Middle, September 21, 2001*
Mr. O who used to be the union building rep at Taft Middle School in San Francisco last year, is now the assistant principal here. Says he's "gone over to the dark side."

My classroom has a cage with a snake; a tropical fish tank; and one with frogs and fish. And there's a tarantula. At St. Athanasius all we had was the roaches. During fifth and sixth periods I grade science tests until I'm bleary-eyed. It's a multiple choice biology test and I must continually refer to the answer key because my Catholic grammar school offered no science whatsoever and my Jesuit high school did not offer biology, apparently at that time not yet considering it a valid means of apprehending reality. Or perhaps it was the danger of flirting too closely with God's work. They've since relented, I understand. At any rate, since I never had to dissect a frog, I've always felt that I made out pretty well on that deal.

During fourth period the aide gets into a thing with one of the girls and tells her to go read outside of the classroom; the kid keeps sticking her head in, and so forth, and the aide's yelling at her. I've seen the girl before and remember her as being a bit odd, but don't really know what's going on. She really has this aide's goat and the aide starts muttering about how this makes her doubt that she wants to complete the course to get her teaching certificate.

The home room kids are supposed to either do homework or read, but one girl tells me that she has no homework and has finished her book. I offer her the *New York Times;* she decides she'll start reading her book for a second time instead. A fifth period kid asks if his textbook isn't incorrect in using "a" rather than "an" before the word "unifying." Good question, in that I can't really remember having actually learned a formulated rule for using an "a" before a long "u."

NEW MATH– *Roving, Appian Way High, September 24, 2001*
I'm here to replace teachers who have to go to IEP (Independent Education Program) meetings. First period is a Special Day Class with a test on *The Old Man and the Sea*, which the aide reviews with the students beforehand. One has spelled the capital of Cuba "Habana," and she tells him that it's with a "v." For better or worse, I butt in and back up the "b." Afterwards, as some work on a styrofoam jigsaw puzzle one kid says, "Does this mean that three-year olds are smarter than us?" because he's seen "For ages three and up" on the box.

In second period Geometry I find that various rectangular sorts of solids have become prisms since I took the subject in the last century. Prisms have parallelogram sides and regular polygon ends, the dictionary will later inform me.

BUTCHERY– *English, William Howard Taft Middle, September 25, 2001*
The teachers room here has been moved to its third location in the last three years. Last year's was a kitchen, but that's a classroom now. This year's is

mostly full of sewing machines – and no teachers. Today we read Poe's *The Tell-tale Heart*. With all of the scrutinizing of literary material for objectionable elements that has gone on in America over the years, it's comforting to see that this tale of a madman killing and dismembering an old man and carefully catching all the blood in a tub has survived as material appropriate for eighth graders.

A ONE, A TWO, ... – *Music, Cucamonga Middle, September 28, 2001*

I'm used to being superfluous in music class, but in this second period Advanced Band class there are students issuing detention slips to their peers, seriously encroaching upon my area of expertise. They were, in fact, such a confident little bunch that I let the designated student helper take attendance, after which I count fewer heads than she counted present. The students generally take a more metaphysical sort of roll – someone's *here* if they've seen em somewhere. I take it from a more empiricist perspective.

Fourth period Intermediate Band marks my debut as a band leader after the designated student bandleaders are unable to control the class and to my amazement soon I've got em playing together in 2/4 time. I think maybe I'll put this on my resume. How hard could it be to conduct an orchestra, I wonder, when you figure that those people actually know how to play. And I'd work a lot cheaper than those maestros they're hiring now.

By the way, the other night I heard the best argument for restoring music education that I've heard in some time: A speaker at Johnny Otis's black music history class theorized that the rise in rap music had to do with a generation unable to learn to play instruments in school after the elimination of music programs. I had always figured it for a form of blowback for the all the years that sixties music held sway: My generation's children heard a lot more Beatles and Supremes on the radio than we did Glen Miller or the Mills Brothers. It was unnatural. Finally something had to be done to throw off the chains of the past and alienate the older generation that had been hegemonic for far too long and thus heavy metal and rap were born. But just think, it could be as easy as putting music back in the schools.

Student Name of the Day (if not the Year): Czar Nicholas

AFFECT – *English, Citadel Middle, October 1, 2001*

For part of the way here I'm driving behind a truck carrying a porta-potty with the door swinging open. Not the way you like to start the day. The sub machine called this job English and the schedule they give me says it's Language Arts, but I've had it before and so far as I knew it was computer lab. Don't ever think modern education is a simple matter.

Fourth period produces a rare educational controversy. It's Newspaper class and I'm supposed to correct the students' work. The first piece I get contains the sentence, "Did you type the correct words and not substitute or change words that effect the meaning of the paragraph?" So I mark the kid wrong because he should have used "affect," but he shows me that the original said "effect." The dictionary seems to back me up, so I tell the kids that while I won't mark them wrong, I believe that affect is correct and that they should raise it with their regular teacher tomorrow. My dictionaries at home also support me, so it seems to have been a worthwhile linguistic intervention.

LETHAL INJECTION NEXT? – Health/History, Cappuccino High, October 3, 2001

The second period health class features a police officer telling the kids about their rights and what to do when they're stopped by the police – how not to get arrested, pepper sprayed, hit or shot, etc. Tomorrow's speaker will be a probation officer, moving them right along the criminal justice system.

MOTIVATED LEARNING – Science, Appian Way High, October 8, 2001

I pull into the parking lot as both sides are unloading for the day's combat. Some of the enemy drive themselves; many more are dropped off. We are badly outnumbered and their logistical support is vastly superior, but with God's help, we will once again prevail. God bless America!

This is Columbus/Indigenous Peoples Day, but it's not a holiday down here. Second period Physics features one loud kid who is something of a wit. He says he's trying to get into Skyline and the concept of "trying to get into Skyline," which is the local junior college, amuses a lot of the others. A review of higher education ensues. He says maybe he'll go to UC Davis and learn to drive a tractor, or maybe he'll go to UC Kansas. UC Santa Cruz enters the discussion and one girl says the students all looked wasted down there – they were wearing dreadlocks and that sort of thing. One guy says he hears that the UC Santa Barbara kids have a lot of Sexually Transmitted Diseases.

One girl asks, "When did we go to war?" She's told, "Yesterday." "Oh, I just heard we were dropping bombs and stuff." They mention some teacher who they figure will talk about it in his class. (The new war referred to here is the one in Afghanistan, still going on as of this writing.) A third period girl asks if I was "around for World War II and stuff." At least she's got the right century.

Fifth period is freshmen. In October, freshmen are at a sort of polliwog stage, only barely past middle school. A bunch of girls are doing their make-up. I'm impressed with their level of intentness and as I'm staring down one of them using the eyelash gizmo, another says, "You're starting to make me nervous." Then a guy asks if I've seen *Silence of the Lambs* and says I remind him of Hannibal Lector a little bit. "Good," I reply. This causes a little bit of a stir. When I express my amazement at the level of cosmetology going on here, someone asks for a dictionary to look up cosmetology. Now this is what I call education. One guy asks if I get paid, and I tell him that I only do it for the love of working with freshmen. I will give out a referral with only four minutes left in the school day – subbing beyond the call of duty.

On my second day, a girl expresses surprise that I've brought a laptop with me. I ask why and she says something about this being a ghetto school. Apparently she thinks this is a tough place. Third period is reading an article about the moon out loud. I ask them questions about the words and phrases that most of them don't know but would otherwise just pass right over. There's a Sea of Putrefaction on the moon. I find this a pretty funny name, but you've got to know what putrefaction means. None of these guys do and no one seems in a hurry to learn.

I write the words Tycho, Brahe and Gdansk on the board, the first two being the name of the guy whom the crater Tycho was named after, and the last being the current Polish name of Danzig, the then German hometown of one of the scientists the reading mentioned. This board is also used for question of the day, which has not been updated today. A guy in sixth wants to know if Tycho, Brahe, and Gdansk are the answer to yesterday's question: Name three flightless birds.

Fourth period I fill in for World History which simply has to review for a test. One girl tells me she can't find a certain name in her book, so I introduce her to her index where the name stands in alphabetical order. I hope she'll remember that.

COOL MILLION– *Computer Lab, Citadel Middle, October 12, 2001*

The kid who came in to check out the computers during lunch says he's very good with them, although he's taking shop rather than computer lab for his elective. He rattles off a whole lot of computer stuff and says he wants to open a cyber café – now. Says he's got a million dollars to work with, or at least he will when his mother liquidates her thirty-nine diamonds. Who knows? This is the school known for having all the lawyer, law student, paralegal parents who want to take things to court and have hearings, and so forth. One girl looks at my computer and says, "I thought teachers didn't have any money. They're always complaining about how they don't make any money."

VATICAN MORMONS– *Social Studies, Cucamonga Middle, October 15, 2001*

Four periods of a video on the Vatican. I'm off to the side of the room when the video's on, so I can't see, but I hear a "yeooh, that's not for children." Must have been David's genitalia. A girl asks if some people in the video are Mormons. I tell her there are no Mormons in the Vatican. She says, "Oh, I mean Jews." I tell her there are no Jews in the Vatican. "But who wears those pointed hats?" I explain that it must be the bishops – they do have bishops in the Vatican and they're all Catholics.

SCOOL DAZE– *Seventh Grade Science, Calvin Coolidge Middle, October 25, 2001*

I have to tell two boys wrestling during second period multiple times to sit down and be quiet. One starts muttering something about a lawsuit – not Citadel, but still this is the west side of town. I throw him out. The instructions here say you're supposed to call the counselor and fill out a referral when you do that. Of course, they don't answer the phone and there are no referral forms. I've done what I could.

I lecture a girl about walking on a chair and she apologizes. This brings to mind the time I was at a Dylan concert and did the same thing to a grown-up who walked over the seat next to me to get to the row above. A substitute teacher is never really off the job.

A seventh period kid hands me a flyer left over from sixth that reads:

SCOOL AGE Student Looking for Job By Doing ...
Lawing grass ...
Racking up leave
Sweep in front of the House

Perhaps to earn money for tutoring in English.

My second day I show all classes an animal film: *Trials of Life: Fighting*. They are to take fifteen notes and turn them in. It's got a good share of "Ooh, gross!" stuff, like peculiar mating practices, and most spectacularly, a gorilla apparently pissing during a fight. Second period is ESL; the only difference is that I write a number of animal names on the board. In the afternoon we have a request for a rewind on the spewing gorilla.

CONSISTENCY — *ESL, Freeway Limits Middle, November 1, 2001*

When I arrive at Cucamonga, the administration building door is locked. And with good reason – they don't start there until 8:30 and it's actually Freeway where I'm due at 8:00. So it's right off to class and we're into our first assignment – grammar – and I ask which of them originally spoke another language and find out it's ESL. Not a particularly well-behaved bunch – worse than the average San Francisco ESL class even, I'd say.

For fifth period, we're supposed to read a handout on Hindu symbols before doing some Halloween drawing, but I only get three-quarters of the way through it because it contains words like "concentric" and "auspiciousness" that I know they don't know, so there doesn't seem much point in reading it without explaining it to them. Getting their attention is not easy, but at least I know that it's not just me they don't listen to when five of them in a row answer a question incorrectly – with the identical wrong answer.

PRESENT ARMS — *Language Arts/Social Studies, Cucamonga Middle, November 2, 2001*

They're covering it all here. I once had to give kids here an assignment to describe how hunter-gatherers might live in their neighborhoods. (Up my way, the hunter gatherers live in a shopping cart encampment under the freeway.) Today over the intercom: "All of you who were in Mr. Black's armor-making class can pick up your helmets and shields after school." It's Medieval Faire Assembly day. And they teach English Language Development classes in the Home Economics classroom, so I accepted delivery of a couple of washing machines during one ELD class. All these piles of clean clothes lying around, but I always forget to bring my laundry!

Kids start asking how long I've been a sub and why I don't become a real teacher. I blow by this impertinence. Big fart episode during last period – screaming, shouting, the whole thing. Probably pretty much the same thing as in the Middle Ages, I imagine.

NON-VOTERS – *Music, Ralph Bunche High, November 5, 2001*

The call for this one comes after 9 and as I'm arriving, a woman on the other side of the street asks if I'm Mr. Gallagher and walkie-talkies that I'm on my way. The doors are locked. I bang and a teacher good naturedly asks if I'm legit, not an anthrax weirdo or anything. The office is staffed by an aide who takes my demand sheet and directs me downstairs where I find some other class with another sub. No keys, no schedule – normal here. Back upstairs; back downstairs, guided by an administrator this time.

I find an all-Chinese group of fourteen in the classroom and a few black guys in the hall. I think they're probably in this class but never enter. There are twenty-five electric pianos, but none are in use. A few girls are playing on one of the three acoustics. The attendance strips I find contain no third period which is what the clock says we're in. The girls explain that we're on a Tuesday schedule even though it's Monday, so not only don't I have a schedule, as is usually the case here, but today it's not even clear what day it is. I pass around a sign-in sheet and try to coax the students to pianos. A card-playing boy says the power's off but I find the power strips. But as they say, you can lead a student to a piano, but you cannot make him play.

The teacher's recording alerts me to a couple of anticipated problem kids for the afternoon, one of whom is named Rigoberto. During lunch I hear his name frequently on the security guard's walkie talkie which prompts a regular teacher to mention Rigoberto's recent hurling about of chunks of asphalt on the street. And, oh yeah, for one class I am to give them a choice of *Lethal Weapon II* and *George of the Jungle*. *Lethal Weapon II* – what a great idea! However, when I ask which they prefer, no one can muster the effort to raise a hand for either. I put them both back in the drawer, but they protest they want to watch something so I hold a re-vote and *George* wins, four votes to one (out of a potential electorate of 20.)

NO HANDS? – *Sixth Grade Art/PE, Freeway Limits Middle, November 6, 2001*

By the time I arrive they have switched me into this Art/PE job from whatever it was that I actually accepted because the teacher who showed up for it was female and couldn't properly replace the absent male teacher, as they saw it, because she couldn't cover the boys locker room. I tell them I've done girls gym before many times – you just don't do the locker room coverage part of the job. But what is done is done.

These sixth graders seem quite young and shy. Antsy, but not yet defiant – mostly. At one point we do encounter a situation of boy crawling on the floor. As I said, they're really young. For fifth period, the other PE teacher takes both classes under his wing and runs a soccer drill with two groups lining up along opposite sides of the field. For seventh I'm doing it myself. I'm running a soccer drill and I've never played soccer. And we wonder why the U.S. doesn't figure in the World Cup?

BELL GAME RALLY – *Biology/Chemistry, Appian Way High, November 9, 2001*
  Teacher's notes say: "Their is a rally after sixth period." (Not a liberal arts guy.) It's for the Bell Game, the annual football game with Cappuccino, of which the student newspaper informs me Appian Way has won 32 of 40, including the last seven – with 16 shutouts. The rally starts with two sets of boys and girls cross dressed as Appian Way and Cappuccino students. The Polynesian Club comes out and dances. Then it's Twister, with teams from each of the four years. Then the duct tape game in which a member of each class is taped up to the wall, the class whose captive remains on the wall last winning. (I think the fix could be in here. In any case, I gotta call My Friend the Evil Substitute Teacher to let him know this sort of thing is allowed.) And just as the volleyball team is introduced, the sound goes off. The whole event is one of those things where the student activities/student government/athlete kids are up front and everyone else in the stands is supposed to be enthusiastic. The sophomores actually win the cheering competition, but the senior emcee calls it for the seniors. Afterwards, the kids mutter about how lame it all was.

ACTUAL ACADEMIC ACTIVITY – *English, Appian Way High, November 14, 2001*
  On my way to first period, an aide I've seen around says, "Nice pants." A girl in first period repeats the sentiment. I've got the green ones on. Appreciation finally! First period is senior AP English. I ask the first kid in if that means that they actually read books on their own, for fun. Says not him, but mentions some girl who might.
  There's a poster for Godard's *Band of Outsiders* on the wall, so I ask if anyone's seen it. "Yes," in unison, "Let's have a discussion." They went up to the Castro to see it on a weekend. That's nice to see. During third period silent reading I notice one kid reading Che Guevara's *Motorcycle Diaries*, and ask him where he got it. Says the regular teacher gave it to him – this guy does good work. I have to wait fifteen minutes after sixth period for five students to finish their essays comparing and contrasting *Frankenstein* and *The Elephant Man*. The only really troublesome thing about the day is some really scary mold in a coffee pot in the classroom. Nowadays that could be anthrax or something.
  A couple of days later I have to make a very early decision on whether to take a job at Alioto, where I've never been. I play the tape over a couple of times but I don't know my own mind. What are my criteria? I'm thinking if the *Examiner* had run that sub column I'd take the job for copy. Certainly there would be a story. But I don't have the column and I decide to wait. This was a 7:40 start and it's Friday. Calls could come for hours.
  Fifteen minutes later it's math at Appian Way High, which – like some kind of subatomic particle – has transmuted to ESL by the time I arrive. The day will consist of showing two movies: *Ghost Story* and *Independence Day*. A giggle from the girls makes me look up and I realize I've missed the famous hands-in-the-

clay scene in *Ghost Story*. And then there's *Independence Day,* and the President's evocation of the Gulf War when "We knew what we had to do," which now is to "Nuke em. Let's nuke the bastards." After watching what I have to watch, I feel obligated to tell the kids I'm with the aliens in this one.

And this in the newspaper:

Subs Accused Of Sex In School *Student Reportedly Discovered Pair WETHERSFIELD – A high school student stumbled on two substitute teachers having sex last week in the back of a locked classroom, according to school documents released Wednesday ... In a memo to Assistant Superintendent Robert Buganski ... high school Principal Thomas Moore wrote that the student had intended to visit another teacher in the classroom on Nov. 5 when she discovered 22-year-old Martha Czernicki and the other substitute, whose name was not disclosed.*

"When [the student] went to open the door it was locked ... there was some yellow paper covering the window of the classroom ...the paper did not cover the entire window and when [the student] peeked through the window to see if [the teacher] was available, [the student] observed the two substitute teachers, in the back of the room having sexual relations."

Even substitute teachers need heroes.
Student Names of the Day: Rajan Engineer and Billy General

LIKE THE ZOO – *Mathematics, Cucamonga Middle, November 19, 2001*
I'm already on the road to Cucamonga before I realize I'm on Freeway time, which means I'm a half hour early. I'd think about a nap in the car but the image of a sub living out of his car is not what I'm shooting for. I've got this job for this entire three-day Thanksgiving week, so I have hall duty from 8:30-8:40. Rocio comes by and asks, "Do you remember me from summer school?" and tells me, "I'm getting good grades now." This is a small pleasure.

From the teacher's calendar, I see that he flew home last Friday – teachers don't have enough time off, you know. I'll be giving a test to all classes today and his notes say "Collect All Test," and "Student who do not finish can finish on Tuesday." On the board in cutout letters it says, "Mr. Cristians seventh and Eighth." At least he's not an English teacher. The student aides have nothing to do while I'm here. I ask if they have books with them or would like to go get books, but they prefer to stare.

The home room TA tells me they usually watch movies. One kid says they're watching *Dumb and Dumber*. This does not seems plausible. I mean it's not the last day of school or anything – why would middle school students have any need to watch *Dumb and Dumber*? They've got all that down already. They settle on *Toy Story II*.

A girl comes up during fifth period, test in hand, to tell me she got the wrong one because it started with number 57. Turning it over to the front page immediately solved her problem. By the end of the day the classroom doesn't smell very good. I may not have mentioned that middle school kids sometimes don't smell great in large numbers. Just developing their adult hygiene habits, you know.

My third and final day on this job it's all movies; the tests have been mailed to the teacher. First period asks to see *The Wedding Singer*. The song lyrics include "fucking kill me," "she's got a hot ass," and "he's gonna get laid." I hide it after this period. When I'm showing another class a video about Wishbone, a talking dog, a girl comes to the front of the class to ask if she can go to the bathroom and announces to the class that it has something to do with her bra. Some of them can be rather proud of that sort of thing at that age.

And I get to provide guidance to a substitute aide who tells me he's working towards being a substitute teacher. Just think – working towards being a sub! But at the end of the day he says that watching kids with subs has given him a good idea of what to expect: "They try to sink the sub."

BIRDS AND BEER – *RSP Secondary, Cucamonga Middle, November 28, 2001*

On my way up the hill to my car this morning, I pass a twentyish woman with a black can in her hand – Miller Genuine Draft. I guess I was too obviously staring, or maybe she was just very self-conscious, but she feels the need to explain: "I've got a bit of a hangover. You've got a coffee (I have a travel mug in my hand), I've got a beer."

I learn that the regular teacher is in Paris – someone gave her frequent flyer miles they couldn't use. The aide tells me she's been to Europe twice herself – chaperoning her kids' trips with Worcester Middle! South San Francisco may not be a particularly wealthy suburb, but the U.S.A. sure is a very wealthy country.

After an easy day like this, I find myself starting to feel somewhat mellow and charitable about middle schoolers. Of course this is flu season – maybe I'm starting to come down with something.

Fabulous home room announcement over the PA system: "For those of you who have been complaining about birds poohing on your head, there wouldn't be any birds there, if you'd use the garbage cans." My Friend the Evil Substitute Teacher claims he brings trash from home and leaves it in middle school yards to prime the birds.

DREAMING – *Computer Lab, Citadel Middle, November 29, 2001*

One girl catches me falling asleep during the assembly when kids from Alamo Elementary School are singing "In America" from *West Side Story*. My kids are sitting in the front row of the balcony, and there is some complaint from downstairs about things going over the edge. No entire students, though.

FUCKING TEACHERS – *Science/Spanish, Cucamonga Middle, December 3, 2001*

Two TAs come in to feed the corn snake and water the toad during third period. They tell me the snake eats baby mice, and that once when their teacher fed it in front of the class, one of the mice peed before it was eaten – just in case

I'd forgotten why I don't have a snake for a pet. I mention this to My Friend the Evil Substitute Teacher and he says he figures if you want to teach kids a lesson about the law of the jungle, it'd be less messy and more memorable to show them videos of boa constrictors eating middle-school-age children.

These guys have apparently distinguished themselves by stealing things from the classroom when they had a sub for the three days before Thanksgiving. And just to prove that this wasn't out of character, one of the two boys getting into some kind of thing during first period is wearing a "Conflict Manager" shirt. Manager, manage thyself! After the last period, a girl apologizes for her classmates; she says they're not all evil.

After finishing this as a two-day job, a wake-up call offers it to me for another day. A note from the teacher says that since it's their third day of sub, they can watch a movie. A reward for their good behavior, I guess. (This is sarcasm.)

At one point, Rory, the security woman, comes in while I'm reading the class the riot act, and finds their behavior not up to snuff as I'm giving them their choices of which of the *Star Wars* movies they want and suggests that we just scrap it for today. She returns with the principal who wants to know what movie they've been seeing. I show him the *Star Wars* Trilogy and he says, "Well, that's not appropriate, anyhow – that's not your fault." Glad to see someone finally paying attention to the stuff being passed off as educational.

My little buddy Jaguar, the worst kid I've ever dealt with in this school, starts acting up in front of the principal, who tells him to come with him, but then thinks the better of it and leaves him with me. Gee thanks. But the boy really wants to go and soon he's leaving with his referral muttering about "fucking teachers." I call Mr. O to make sure that the referral didn't get lost in transit and he asks, "Do we have a suspension here?" After a little conversation on the question, he decides he'll send him home for a few days. Now, that was satisfying. Man, these last couple of days were like being in the city!

The principal comes by as I'm leaving because he's got some meeting in the room. He wants me to write down stuff on my report form that he can use, e.g., that the movie was inappropriate, that they didn't have enough work. I don't really like doing this, but I can't argue on the facts.
Student Name of the Day: Jon Jovi Bodestyne

IS THAT NICE? – *Seventh Grade Mathematics/Science, Waterfront Middle, December 14, 2001*
Today I have to erase a "Jennifer sucks cock" from the black board and administer a stern warning to my students against commenting on the sexual practices of their peers.

CUT-UP – *Principal, William Howard Taft Middle, December 19, 2001*
After my usual riff soliciting opinion as to what I ought to decree during my stint as principal, I get to work rousting kids out of the halls and into class during passing period. Then stand in for the seventh grade counselor while the counselor meets with the AP. A sub calls to say that one of his students has up and

left and that he sent another down with a referral that he told her to write out herself. The regular counselor in the next office whom I consult on this says she has never heard of such a thing. However, she says this in front of other kids which, to my mind, doesn't speak well for the solidarity here.

Then a double lunch security duty, order being the part of the principal's job in which I specialize. Toward the end of the second, I notice a boy cutting up (literally true, it turns out) among a bunch of girls at the other side of the school yard. He's darting after them and some appear to be enjoying this, others clearly not. I see he's got a pair of scissors. He's not really brandishing them as a pointed weapon, and I think they're not sharply-pointed, but he probably shouldn't be waving them about, which I walk over and tell him.

He puts them in his backpack – with typical bad little boy trash talk – but stuff still goes on between him and the girls and he's not listening to me telling him to get away from them, so I take it to the head counselor and the security guy who are standing together on the other side of the school yard and suggest that one of them separate the boy from the girls. The counselor goes to do so. After lunch, the seventh grade counselor asks me into her office to write a statement about what I saw, as apparently he'd cut some of the girls' hair and told them he'd get them tomorrow, and they're planning to suspend him. I'd learned that they'd had the police in on his account already, but still I was surprised to notice the form I'm filling out says "under penalty of perjury." I'll be keeping a photocopy of this.

There is talk at the end of the day of bringing me in for a mathematics/science teacher who has just now announced the extension of her sick leave to February. Don't know that the system will hire me for a month, but I go up to the fourth floor, which I didn't know existed, to observe the class. Not too bad, considering that they've apparently had three teachers already this school year.

Recent newspaper story, "Adolescence a fairly recent phenomenon," would appear to refute the commonly held belief that evolution is an ever upward process.

LEAVE THIS MOTHERFUCKER OPEN – Mathematics, Copernicus High, December 21, 2001

Off to a March Hare start today: I'm late! I'm late! And I have no gas! Quick pit stop for about $5 worth and on my way. The parking situation here is prohibitive. I find a two hour spot that's good until 10 and ask the secretary what the solution is. She says, "Well, you can erase the chalk mark on your tire," so I'll be hopping out every two hours.

First time here. A first time in a school is always somewhat foreboding, particularly when it's high school, which does present the possibility of actual danger. The look of the place doesn't help. The halls are pretty battered, with ugly red-orange carpeting, supplemented by broad swaths of duct tape. And it's as hot as a New York City apartment building.

The first two classes are just fine. The next, smaller ones are not. One kid asks me how many pennies are in $7.26 (this was a question on the puzzle I distributed). He turns out not to know how many cents there are in a dollar, or even in a nickel. (I'll save you the trouble of looking back up at the heading – yes, this is high school.) I'm keeping the door locked because the teacher's instructions say he's concerned that students not in his class not get into the room. I let one girl go to the bathroom and when she comes back she says, "You got to leave this motherfucker open." Later the same charmer yells, "Miss Lee, you bitch," out the window, so the windows get closed. She really starts acting up right before the end, tells me to shut up, etc. Since it's too close to the end to be able to call down and nail her, I just let it slide and leave the teacher a note. She takes her worksheet from class with her, realizing that I'd get her name off it.

My last class has only four kids, one of whom comes with a Special Ed aide, and halts the day's downward trend. One of the kids remembers me from Waterfront Middle last year. He doesn't like this school; me neither. He wants to transfer to School of the Arts. Remembering that girl from the morning, I probably just won't come back.

SETTLING IN – *Seventh Grade Math/Science, William Howard Taft Middle, January 7, 2002*

I'm scheduled here for the week, maybe the month. The principal comes in during home room, and chases the kids back to their proper seats. First period is remedial math with only nine students and an aide and the assistant principal actually does the whole thing. Presumably they want to start me off on the right foot. She gives a quiz on times tables and there are kids getting things wrong from the three and four times tables.

She reappears for the back-to-back math and science periods with a class of thirty-two and again teaches the entire thing herself. She comes for the afternoon periods as well, but she's late and by the time she arrives, I have already thrown a girl out for refusing to give me the lipstick, or other lip product, that she was using. I see I have a much quicker trigger than the AP does, probably because I am always having to assert myself.

One girl here just doesn't talk. I had assumed that it was because she didn't speak English, but apparently not, she just won't talk when called on. Ms. F is working on that, so I'll just let that pass. (We should have more such problems!) And then there is a Russian girl named Yekaterina, who wants to be called Catherine, or actually Kathy. I actually love the name Yekaterina because it brings Russian ice skaters to mind. How long does an immigrant group have to be in the country, I wonder, before their original names become fashionable, like the Irish with their Siobhans and Seamus's?

One day my third and fourth period nuisance boy will start repeatedly saying, "sphincter" out loud. I inform him that if he doesn't stop, he can take his sphincter down to the counselor. I attend my first parent conference ever with a nice Russian immigrant Russian couple whose daughter, also very nice and best buddy of the above-mentioned Yekaterina, is not paying any attention to school. She sucks her thumb in class, by the way. (And yes, this is middle school.) I saw her start thinking about going for the thumb during the meeting in a moment of stress brought on by the presence of her teachers, guidance counselor, and assistant principal, but her mother also spotted it and headed her off. The girl pledges total academic reform, but by sixth period her resolve has already demonstrably weakened.

Then we have Richard. I used to have him in the first period remedial math class, but the class was dissolved, so now I have him in home room only. Today he's wearing a fishing hat that he calls his pimp hat. The story is that he actually lives in Richmond (the city, not the San Francisco neighborhood) and he's here on some kind of courtesy exchange program which the AP's thinking of discontinuing as he's generally late and disruptive – he ain't courteous. When we had the remedial class, he would ask for help, not pay attention when I came over, and then blame me for it. What is the responsibility of a school or any institution is in regard to a kid like this, I wonder. So far as things around here go, this school'd probably be better off sending him back to Richmond. There's another kid in the class, Roki, whom I tell not to hang around with Richard. Roki's just a sort of mischievous kid; Richard's going to jail.

In my third week they start muttering about keeping me for more . It seems that previous to me they had two core subs – the subs with guaranteed work every day who must take any assignment given them – in this class and they failed miserably. And this experience is starting to bear fruit in the rest of my life: Last week at our Democratic Club meeting there appeared to be some surprise at how quickly I cleared the room of the Central Committee candidates we'd invited to a pre-meeting reception when it came time to start the actual meeting. I explained that I'd been in middle school for twelve straight days and could talk just as loud as I had to.

By the fourth week there's still no sign of the regular teacher; apparently she doesn't return phone calls. The administration wants me to stay, but the teachers union wants to send me to work on Harry Britt and Dan Kelly's Assembly campaigns. That's certainly where I'd rather be, and it's where I would already be if I had not previously committed to this for four weeks. I hate to leave the kids in the lurch again, but I think I've got to do this.

Polly, the cute little girl from Macau tells me today about another sub they had who insisted that the class was not going to leave at dismissal time until Bettie (a girl I eject about every other day) apologized for something. She wouldn't do it, so the entire rest of the class was apologizing, but not her. Eventually she did, but it was halfhearted, so the sub still wouldn't let them go and blocked them at the door when they tried to get out. Some of them wound up on the floor in midst of the shoving. The next day there was a new sub.

They revolted in third period Tuesday of my final week. Ms. F had already been there, but after she left, three of the girls started singing, one guy started his usual mouthing off and wouldn't get off the couch that's in the room, so I called for reinforcements. A counselor came up and stayed the whole time. She threw two guys out; I had already thrown another out for refusing to work; and another gets himself a referral in the last minute by standing up and giving someone the finger. Three more days!

I totally go wild at the afternoon class after the din had been building up and I see a couple of kids shoving each other. It works; they go totally silent. And all of this does have the benefit of making my decision to leave easier. There's something quite humbling about getting near the point of talking to yourself over the carrying-ons of twelve-year-olds.

When I toss one of my regular thorns on my next-to-last day, he comes back saying that Ms. W, the counselor, sent him back. Well, I don't know if that's true or not, but I don't care. He's not staying here and I have security come take him out. I'm not sure what they think of my methods here, but if they send them back to me after I throw them out, I walk. I'm about to tell another guy that he has to leave, when he says, "One outburst and I go, okay?" I say, "Okay," and he doesn't give me any more real trouble, so I think that something worked. And even one of my regular problem girls actually seems to be coming around. All of this does make me curious about what might happen if I were around for a long time, but I gotta go. I think of telling the administration that if they don't have something worked out in a month, they can call me to come back.

In one stretch I think I threw Bettie out of class five out of nine days. On my last day, I turn around and see her hitting Victor. Now, Victor is a boy who definitely deserves to be whacked upside the head a few times, but if there's one person in the world who doesn't have the right to do it, it's Bettie. I tell her to get out as usual – today with only ten or fifteen minutes left – which unleashes a torrent of obscenity and other verbal abuse.

At the end of the day, I tell Ms. F that I had been thinking of saying that they should call me if they find themselves in the lurch, but upon further consideration, I wouldn't take the morning class again as currently constituted, which is to say with Bettie in it. She says I should have called the parents and probably I should have, but given my tentative standing here I guess that I thought it was incumbent upon the administration to do it.

At the end of fourth period, which I knew would be my last with them (although they don't know that because Ms. F preferred that I not say anything), following my shouting match with Bettie, I told the rest of the class that they might want to speak with their classmates about their continual disruption of class and that no parents would want to send their children to a class like this. Unlike Victor, Bettie has a following – two or three other black girls, a group that should have been broken up.

It's an odd realization, when I am trying to rally the class – something that I am unsure can be done in any case – that I am in essence organizing against four black girls. This certainly feels like an odd thing to be doing, yet I have little doubt that it was the right thing to do, as the four of them are in no way benefiting from the chaos they create either. They all did extremely poorly on the last test. They probably all fell within the bottom eight of the two classes combined. At the same time we have Eugene, for example, who needs the help and will gladly accept it, but gets little of it while I battle with that spoiled, self-righteous monster Bettie.

At the end of the day I tell Ms. M, the school secretary, that something needs to be done about that girl. She tells me everyone does know that (and apparently they also know the new replacement and think she can't handle a class). They are tremendously grateful to me and Ms. F thinks I did well to even keep Bettie in class as much as I did.

This class would certainly have been easier had there been a regular teacher before me, and it would likely have gotten easier for me had I stayed longer, but there are plenty of teachers facing classrooms like this all the time. This is no way one of the most difficult middle schools in the city. The mere fact that I still come here is proof of that.

ALL POWER TO THE SOVIETS! – *RSP, Appian Way High, March 8, 2002*
The month spent on Harry Britt's (unsuccessful) campaign for the California Assembly was quite a pleasure after that month in Taft – an upside of not having a real job. And I haven't lost my knack for microeconomics – this morning when I looked behind the hamper to see if my socks had fallen there, I found my most recent paycheck. I was, however, up to date in my reading for last night's Kafka class at the Goethe Institute. There are priorities.

I'd hoped my first day back would be here. Maybe I wouldn't have asked for Special Ed, but this is not half bad – six kids in first period, and no one's nasty. There are answers to various questions on the board, including, "Lenin did not have the right to close down the democratically elected constituent assembly in January, 1918. By closing down the assembly, Lenin turned the Russian government into a dictatorship." This being a question I have devoted considerable time to mulling over the years, I am disappointed to find that the class doesn't do things as a group. They're here to get extra time and help with work from other classes, so this must have been just been one kid's project and I don't get to introduce the "soviets" into the mix.

The afternoon assignment is watching "*Jurassic Park III.*" IIII! Special Education, indeed.

YOU ARE ABOUT TO ENTER ... – *Language Arts, Cucamonga Middle,*
March 12, 2002
My schedule, which turns out to be one period of Social Studies and four of PE is not what I remember from the tape. Social Studies and Language Arts I might confuse, but I would know if they said PE. I'm being a little insistent about this, I guess, because Mrs. P, the school secretary, offers to give me a schedule to take home so that I can check what any teacher actually does before accepting the job. I don't take her up on her offer because I just don't see myself turning on the light to fact check a middle school assignment at 5:30 AM. I'm just settling in at the gym when the phone rings and Mrs. P tells me she's sent me to the wrong class. When I go back and get the English assignment that I was expecting, there's a big PE-looking guy who apparently came for looking for his job.

My job will be a little something on compound nouns followed by a teleplay of *The Twilight Zone* episode, "The Monsters Are Due On Main Street," which the kids follow along in their books. One class has a real Twilight Zone fan who describes his favorite show about the guy who's stuck in the bank vault when the atom bomb hits and decides that he now has all the time in the world to read – and then steps on his glasses. Lively discussion follows as to whether he couldn't have found other glasses. During the last period, another kid goes on about the episode with the gremlin tearing the wing off of the plane and no one believing the only guy who sees him. My hope in the future of humanity is restored, however briefly.

NOT CRAZY, YET – March 19, 2002

There's no sub packet on the desk when I show up at Cucamonga and Mrs. P is asking what I'm doing there. Oh no, not this again. The same thing happened just last Wednesday when it turned out that neither of the jobs I had taken the prior afternoon when the phone woke me out of a nap had been for that day. After spending a great deal of time on the phone with Ms. K, it turns out that I'm not mistaken today – she gave my job away to someone else. They pay me for half a day, which is a pain in the ass, but at least I know I'm not crazy. I'm sure there are subs out there who keep showing up at schools long after they've actually stopped calling them – and I don't want to be one of those – at least not yet.

IT SUCKS IN HERE – Science, Ralph Bunche High, March 21, 2002

In the competition for least helpful office in the San Francisco school system, this one is right up there. Never any keys, despite this being required by the union contract. Today the secretary tells me the classroom door will be open. It's not, so I stand around in the hall waiting for a kid to fetch someone.

Schedule's not bad, though – this teacher's got only one hour-and-a-half long period today, plus a half hour "Advisory." So meanwhile I'm deployed to tend the students left behind from a class trip to Muir Woods on this drizzly day. Six kids: four black kids hanging around and two Chinese kids working.

For "Advisory," which is apparently what they call home room here, I'm supposed to be in Room 210. It's not open. Downstairs looking for keys again. No, I'm actually supposed to be in 210B, where I find an additional sub, but no assignment for the next period. The teacher I'm replacing is in Thailand, by the way. At the next period starts, another teacher appears and shows me the regular teacher's desk in the adjacent room, with a well-laid out plan for today, the week she will be gone following the break, and even an attendance strip for last period, which I was not aware was even a class.

Two girls start a ragtime conversation across the classroom and I tell them to stop. One says, "It sucks in here." I tell her to leave. She doesn't go. I call the office. She leaves. Eventually the office calls and asks if she can come back.

After lunch, the secretary tells me to wait in the teachers room to see if there's anything they need me to do. They don't. At the end of the day, she has no green demand sheet (this is the first day of the pay period and the school generally provides them), which means I'll have to come back here another day to get one signed. You know, that girl was right: "It sucks in here."

TRIPLE PLAY— *Special Ed Para, Alioto High /Ralph Bunche High / Nelson Mandela Middle, April 5, 2002*

Today I have a music class at Cucamonga that I picked up off the machine last night. Wrong. The phone rings a little after 6 AM. This can only be trouble. Sure enough, the job's canceled. There's nothing on either machine now but after 9 comes a science class at Alioto. Alioto ranks as a "one" on the state's "one-to-ten" academic ranking (that's the bottom), so this won't be a choice assignment. But I've never been there and the school is slated to close down, and I figure I want to see it before it does.

Wrong, again. When I arrive at 10:20 for an 8 AM start, the secretary tells me that the guy I'm to replace has only two classes before he goes to work at another location and she'd told them not to send anyone after 10. She calls the sub office and puts me on the phone. They say I can have a one-on-one para sub job for which I will be paid as a teacher and offered a choice of three high schools: Bunche, Fillmore and Schindler. I pick Schindler because I've never been there. Wrong, yet again. They were just fooling – the sub lady looks again and sees that the Schindler job doesn't actually exist and neither does the one at Fillmore. My three choices are now Bunche, Bunche, and Bunche.

So I pick Bunche where I arrive around 11 and the secretary tells me that the para I've been sent to replace doesn't really work at Bunche, he actually works at Nelson Mandela Middle School. At least that's in the neighborhood, but before I go anywhere, I'm calling the sub office again to get their opinion on this latest development, which is, "Oh yeah, sorry, it's Nelson Mandela." Back in the car. It's nearly 11:30, I'm heading to my fourth assignment of the day – in two cities – and I haven't been in a classroom yet. Fortunately, we subs are made of some pretty stern stuff.

At Nelson Mandela, I am steered to a classroom with a teacher, twelve special-ed kids, and two other paras. The teacher points out the kid I'm there for, but just tells me to take a seat and relax while he proceeds with math. In about fifteen minutes, it's lunchtime. And then after lunch, there's – lunch. The regular para has brought in several trays to feed the kids, as well as half the faculty, it seems. The teacher asks for my ID number, but I tell him I'm not a para. Teacher? Even better. You don't mind taking a Special Day Class, do you   I don't answer, which he takes as affirmation. Another inclusion teacher wants me for three days next week, but I already have a job for next Thursday – fortunately.

Apparently the kids are now getting a reward for some past good behavior, which is to watch some movie about slavery. It does keep them pretty quiet, and since they keep some of the lights on, I make it through a back issue of the *New Yorker* brought for just such an eventuality. It's got a short story about an American second wife of an older upper class Italian who hires him two hookers for his birthday, maintaining the magazine's commitment to exploring the lives of everyday people. And then it's 2 o'clock and the day is over.

KEEPING THE SKILLS UP – *Health, Cucamonga Middle, April 26, 2002*

The first question of an assignment written on the board concerns rape, another subject not covered back at St. Athanasius. Sixth period is difficult – last period on a Friday afternoon in spring, after all. Three guys ultimately get excessed in this class, including young Jaguar, who has achieved preeminence in his field at his school, his field being pain-in-the-ass. Shame to see his talent wasted on the suburbs – this fellow could play in the big city. Other students are quite surprised to see me calling him by name without having to ask, but I'm a keen judge of talent and today is the third time I've thrown him out. One problem with spending too much time in the suburbs is that your combat skills can deteriorate, so today was a good brush-up.

NATIONAL EMERGENCY IN THE MAKING? – *April 27, 2002*

The *San Francisco Chronicle* reports: *"A house fire ignited by a model rocket fired as part of a school science project has sparked debate in the East Bay town of Orinda over whether the missiles are valuable physics lessons – or dangerous projectiles.*

"The rocket had been fired by students at nearby Orinda Intermediate School, which holds the event at its softball field each year for about 300 eight-grade science students. The rocket's engine struck the wood-shake roof of John and Linda Minamoto's home at 3:40 p.m. on Thursday, probably causing the $200,000 blaze, fire officials said."

Middle schoolers armed with missiles? Is anyone paying attention? What happens when they get nuclear weapons? I think the Bush Doctrine would allow for preemptive strikes.

THE PIT, AT LAST – *English, Alioto High, Wednesday, May 1, 2002*

Last night I saw a TV clip of Gilda Radner doing her Emily Litella character substitute teaching in Bedford Stuyvesant. She's replacing a teacher who's absent because of a "stubbing," and Emily figures he must have stubbed his toe pretty badly because he had to go the hospital and she's heard that it was the third stubbing of the month at this school. And then this morning a call for Computer Lab at Alioto. Last Saturday night my friend Brian N told me he'd met a cop who claimed there had been six rapes at Alioto last year that had not been reported to the police. So I certainly don't think this will be pleasant day, but I figure I should know for myself. It's another shot (hmm – bad word choice, maybe) at experiencing the soon-to-be defunct worst high school in the city, and it could be my last.

The whole place is about security. Guard at the door; walkie-talkies squawking in the office. By the time I arrive, my assignment has already been changed from Computers to Literature. Today's schedule has three two-hour periods and since there's only half an hour to go on the first, the secretary says to just sit tight, since it's already covered. No problem with that here. Meanwhile, an administrator of some sort sits down to assure me of the full support and back-up of the administration. Could there be some kind of problem keeping subs here?

When I head down to the class I meet the first period sub who appears to know the regular teacher's classes and says they're tough. I've got twenty-one on my list; twelve show up. There are two second period assemblies to inform kids about the trips scheduled for visiting the schools they will be transferring to next year. One starts at the beginning of second period, a little after 10:00, the other at 11:30. My class goes to the first, which unfortunately lasts only half an hour. Still, four students fail to make it back from the assembly, so that's a help.

When I and my eight remaining students do return, it becomes absolutely clear that there will be no order whatsoever in this class. The assignment on the board seems like it must be some kind of mistake, maybe something written for night school which no one erased. Supposedly these kids are going to answer questions on "The Lorelei," by Heinrich Heine; a Victor Hugo poem about Napoleon's campaign in Russia; and Leo Tolstoy's essay, "How Much Land Does A Peasant Need?" Looking around this room, I've never seen a more incongruous assignment in my life. Not a single student touches it. Instead, we get a little coed wrestling and as I'm moving to phone security, the police officer stationed next door appears. That's right, stationed next door – they do take security seriously here.

Unfortunately, several more students also appear, assembly stragglers as well as some making their first appearances. And as the song from *West Side Story* goes, "The minutes go like hours; the hours go so slowly." I smell something burning and realize that someone has lit a matchbook on the floor, which I stamp out. Why that could set the school on fire. My Friend the Evil Substitute Teacher would say ... well, by now you know what he would say. On the bright side, the attrition rate is high and by lunch time there's only four students – using a broad definition of "student" – remaining. The others have drifted off, presumably mulling over the meaning of Heine, Hugo, and Tolstoy elsewhere. After the class, the female police officer says I was doing better than most. After all, she only had to come in here once, right?

The sub handout says that the teachers room is downstairs, but I can't find it, so I return to eat in my windowless classroom. The first girl who arrives for the next period is actually a student in the traditional sense of the word. When everyone else is in – at least everyone I'm going to get – I tell them what the assignment is and that I'm happy to help anyone who wants help. And this girl does want help, so I work on several questions about Hugo's poem with her when I'm not screaming at someone else. They're all freshmen, except for her. She's a senior. She uses an electronic Chinese translator. In September she'll have been here from Taiwan for two years and is going to the Conservatory to study piano in the fall. Now that's going to be some kind of a change. Probably a bit more of what the family had in mind when they came to this country than Alioto was.

My strategy for what I anticipate will be two of the longest hours of my life – no assembly this period – is to leave the door open, the better to attract outside attention. Two of our boys have brought their scooters back with them

147

from lunch and are now riding them around the classroom which causes me to raise my voice frequently, eventually drawing the attention of a Ms. B who comes in to sit on the class. After she's been there for awhile, I say, "So, are you a para?" She tells me she's the Dean. I tell her she's a pretty hands-on Dean for me to be mistaking her for a para. She asks isn't this normal? Not at every school, I tell her. She spends the better part of the period there, during which the students are quiet – for real. And various students are extracted, so it all goes much better than expected.

It does get a little noisy later when a teacher comes by to chat and starts talking about how much he enjoyed throwing students out of summer school last year – you can do that in summer school because summer school is not an entitlement like regular school. It turns out that this guy ran for union president last year, although he says he told everyone to vote for someone else, as he himself did. When I mention that it's my first time here, he says, "The question is, will you come again?" I explain my general rule of thumb that if I have to call outside assistance in to get order, I don't return. Ms. B says, "Sounds like a pretty reasonable standard." She suggests that I bring a movie with me in the future, but I explain it's not usually like this. She has previously been a Severely Emotionally Disturbed teacher at Copernicus, so she's always been in tough class rooms. Luisa, an Alioto teacher I know through the union, later tells me that Ms. B came to teaching after a career as an airline stewardess. Luisa also confirmed that the classes I had were considered tough, even for this place. She says the way the regular teacher attempts to keep his sanity is by staying home.

Late in the period, a girl wants to go to the bathroom and Ms. B says she'll find someone to walk her. A note in my sub instructions said bathroom passes should not be issued, but in case they were, it provided a couple of numbers to call. Looks like no girl goes to the bathroom alone here. Nothing I see today contradicts the story I heard over the weekend.

At the end of the day, a kid who is a bit of a wit returns from taking a make-up STAR test and starts talking about how he wants to go to the office to report one of the other students because he thinks "There's a school law against smelling like that."

So long, Alioto.

Today's education story-of-the-day comes from an entirely other world. The *Chronicle* reports that a Southern California high school conducted a prom thong check in which a female administrator apparently made the girls wearing short skirts show her their underwear in the presence of male administrators and police. Perhaps one pre-chaperoning cocktail too many for that administrator.

Joseph Alioto High School closed at the end of the 2001-2002 academic year.

HE WHO HESITATES IS NOT ALWAYS LOST – Math, Worcester Middle, May 6, 2002

I get a late call for Girls PE at Freeway and when the machine says, "Press One to accept the assignment; Press Five to hear the assignment repeated; Press Nine to decline the assignment." I do nothing. I am paralyzed. Do I want this? Not really. Do I need the money? Well, yes. The machine repeats the question and I press Five. We repeat the entire process before I finally press One, at which point the machine says that the job is no longer available.

A PE job at Alioto comes in later, but I don't have a gun permit which pretty much rules that out as a viable prospect. Then comes what the machine says is a sixth grade job at Worcester and an hour later, I've got my sunglasses on, driving down 280, "Layla" on the radio, it's a warm and sunny California day. The only thing missing is that I don't have the top down, because I don't have a convertible.

The regular teacher is in the room starting second period by the time I arrive. He felt ill when he got to school in the morning, hence the late call. I recently had a class at Taft dealing with interest problems and thought I couldn't remember anything in math less interesting than calculating interest (which may account for my financial successes), but today we've got discount and markup, so I stand corrected.

A boy comes up during fifth period and asks if he can go to the bathroom. When I ask what the regular teacher, would say, he tells me that Mr. P would say, "Take the terrorist." The terrorist is a little Osama-bin-Laden doll with pins stuck in it that they use as the classroom pass. Hmm. For all I know the Department of Homeland Security is issuing these things.

Student Name of The Day: Oceanic Latu

A DAY FOR SUPER SUB – Math – sort of, Cucamonga Middle, May 7, 2002

Officially I'm replacing a math teacher, but really I'm rotating, replacing four teachers who have to go to Student Success Team meetings, or something like that. The first one seems surprised to see me, but manages to throw together an assignment for first period and hustles off. The next is showing the movie *Sandlot*.

After that I step in for a math teacher who's teaching "box and whisker" charts. Today I have to learn the danged things. We order a series of numbers from lowest to highest; we find and mark the median, the lower and upper quartiles – which are the medians of the lower and upper halves, and the lowest and highest numbers. We then draw a box around the portion of the line between the quarries, and draw "whiskers" from the box to the extreme numbers at either end.

Why do we do this? What does this show? I have no idea. The regular teacher, who is roughly my age, which means he grew up before boxes and whiskers, appears to have no opinion as to the actual value of doing this, but he does explain why it is being taught – it will be on the statewide exam.

The next day I encounter a teacher dressed like a Latina Heidi in the office when I arrive, so I ask what day today is and she tells me it's Diversity Day. Diversity Day starts with an assembly dedicated to Japanese Daikon drumming which is explained to the kids in Spanish and English.

And the home room girls will be quite creative today, citing various female problems in their pleas for bathroom passes. One tells me "a girl could get cancer down there" if she's not allowed to go to the bathroom.

I DON'T KNOW ART ... – *English, Worcester Middle, May 14, 2002*

Last period is drama class which is supposed to be preparing two minute skits. A couple of girls are playing patty-cake in the back. *Are they working? Is this drama?* A sub can have to make some pretty tough calls in some of these classes. *Do they know art? Or do they just know what they like?*

And lest you think the issues a sub may face are limited to the human realm, I'm back here a couple of days later for a Social Studies job when I have to take a period for the Girl's PE teacher toward the end of which an apparently scared gopher appears on the field. I have to shoo the children away to protect it. In a conflict between a rodent and a bunch of middle school students, my choice is clear.

FORGOT HER PENIS – *Science, Cucamonga Middle, May 15, 2002*

One of my eighth grades is supposed to have a lecturer on sex who's been here all week but hasn't arrived when class begins, although her notes are all over the board: female condom, male condom, cervical cap, diaphragm, IUD, vasectomy, abstinence and so forth. A replacement appears and the kids are quite looking forward to putting condoms on today, but unfortunately, Shelley didn't bring her styrofoam penis. And then the regular speaker shows up – mix-up with the short periods on an early release day. Meanwhile, the replacement is demonstrating how to take a condom out of a package and the regular speaker has them doing a birth control worksheet determining which form would be best for couples in various situations.

If they have heart attacks in heaven, Sister Acquin just had one. For all I know, she may have had a plastic penis back at the convent, but if she did she wasn't about to share it with us kids.

I also discover a most alarming document this week – *The Middle Level News: The Newsletter of the California League of Middle Schools*. I generally am quite liberal on matters of freedom of speech and association, but this publication really should be suppressed, along with the organization that publishes it, the institutions it serves, and its parent organization, the Association of Persons of Middling Intelligence.

CARLOS ES UN GRANDE ... – *English Language Development, Cucamonga Middle, June 4, 2002*

The regular teacher has sent an e-mail to the principal explaining that she's going to be out for a second day because over the weekend she mistook a bug bomb for bug spray and failed to leave the room when she used it. My question is whether the brain damage came before or after the bug bomb incident.

Home room announcement over the PA system: No grabbing of any part of the anatomy is acceptable on this campus. Greek Day today and I'm quite impressed to see a poster on a stick in the classroom that says Sparta, spelled correctly – in Greek. The last period class ask if they can play Hangman on the board, which seems like a pretty good idea for an ESL class, but at one point I look up and see that the phrase they've filled out is "Carlos is a big dick." Good grasp of the vernacular, I suppose. And you can hear some pretty creative stuff in these classes. I once asked what "muddle" meant and someone said a puddle made of mud. You could probably copyright that.

I'm back in a couple of days showing *Shrek,* cause it's the end of the year and all. No one watches it, though, so from an educational point of view I'd call it a draw.

*****

THE FACTS OF LIFE – *Eighth Grade Math, Cucamonga Middle, November 15, 2002*

Just back from managing Barry Hermanson's long-shot Green Party campaign for Supervisor from the west side of San Francisco. He finished sixth, which was disappointing, since we had fifth place potential.

I have an aide today who asks me if I sub with this age group very often. She says it's her first year back in school after twenty years and she's still adjusting to the fact that with this age group "it's all penis and vagina." I was going to ask her at what age that changes, but I suspected she was a married woman and might take the question amiss.

And new ground is broken in this school with the girl who says she needs to call home because the ball has fallen off the bar in her tongue piercing. Another one Sister Thomas never had to deal with.

LIFE'S RICH TAPESTRY – *English, Cappuccino High, November 20, 2002*

Very civilized. Small, polite classes. Three of them are reading the Cyclops episode from the *Odyssey*. After the first class, I write the first four lines of it in Greek, to the best of my memory, to see if anyone asks. It works like a charm. Eventually the kids want to know what it is and then they want me to write their names in Greek. At the end of class one of them says, "Bye substitute. You were great." A lesser man would have fainted away then and there, but I knew I had three more classes to go.

These are all freshmen. First and last are Honors, fourth is Reading, which is more of a *Welcome Back Kotter*, Sweat Hog sort of experience. They're reading a novel – individually, but they start asking me what page they're on. Apparently the teacher keeps track of this for them. I tell them they'll just have to make do on their own for today, since the teacher has not left me a list of where they're each at. One of them tells me, "We have bad memories. That's why we're in this class." I wonder if the teacher has tried bookmarks.

A group of teachers gets to talking at lunch about what titillates their students. Things that sound like "See me pee;" "sex;" and "pussy." The ceramics teacher describes the stages of clay as "wet, leather-hard, and bone-dry," and the kids apparently love that. The dance teacher says she tells her kids to imagine they have flashlights in their crotches. You can see how some parents might not be all that up in arms when funding cuts are made in the arts programs. I wonder if some Education Ph.D. student is doing a dissertation on this somewhere.

Which reminds me that I noticed a copy of *Understanding Power: The Indispensable Noam Chomsky* on a teacher's desk here the other day. I'm always surprised to see stuff like this, since I never feel like I'm surrounded by a bunch of radicals when I'm in teachers' lunch rooms.

GUTE REISE! – *Seventh Grade English, Cucamonga Middle, November 22, 2002*

This will be my last day in front of a classroom for the year. Next week I'll be sitting in one – a German class in Berlin that I won in a lottery at the Goethe

Institute. Ah yes, the upside of subbing – saying, "Auf Wiedersehen" mid-semester.

Saw a notice in the paper about a Buenos Dias Elementary School benefit featuring Dr. Loco and His Rockin' Jalapeno Band. A sort of sticky matter for urban public schools where everyone'd like to raise more money, but schools with parents with connections generally have more ways to get the money. The new superintendent has tried to do something about that situation with a "weighted student formula" that steers somewhat more funding to schools with students with greater needs. Unfortunately, the pot is just too small, the money transfer too minor, and there's also the complaint that it funds bilingual students more heavily than blacks.

WE ALL EASE BACK – Special Education, Cucamonga Middle, January 3, 2003

I'm up until 2:30 AM and I think, "They could call you in three hours." They do. Way too much Cucamonga this year. First two periods today involve helping kids in the class of another teacher who tells me the one I'm replacing is still on vacation – the two weeks off not enough, apparently. The aide suggests that fifth period watch a movie of their choice. They pick *Ten Things I Hate About You*, featuring the line "What does she have, beer-flavored nipples?"

Another day here, a girl tells me, "You look like that actress." Ignoring the gender confusion the experts tells us is common at this age, I ask which?" She can't remember the name, but says *he* was in a movie with a dog that he had to take care of, but didn't like. I ask if he threw the dog down the garbage disposal. She says yes. *As Good As It Gets.* Jack, I'm back!

And another day here I will find intimations of eternity washing over me while giving my cooperation rap to eighth graders wanting to go the bathroom after they've been nuisances. Individual children may eventually grow up and out of this stage, but the eighth grade endures.

FROM SCRATCH – Kindergarten, Benjamin Banneker Elementary, January 27, 2003

My December in Berlin was great prep for this – surrounded by things I didn't know with names I didn't know. So are these kids. We do the calendar; we spell "January"; we count to 100 by ones, two, fives, and tens; we identify "I" words from pictures on a piece of paper ("iguana" and "iris" are hard.)

Bob F, the union VP for subs, later expressed surprise to learn that I had subbed (and taught summer school second grade math) here, apparently not seeing me as temperamentally so inclined. I explained that I'd come to embrace the attitude of Terentius (Terence): "Homo sum: humani nil a me alienum puto" (I am a man; I consider nothing human foreign to me) as that of the true substitute teacher – although I acknowledge that the Roman philosopher might hot have felt that way had he ever encountered middle school students.

OUT OF MY FIELD – *ESL Math/Science, William Howard Taft Middle, February 13, 2003*

The teacher's notes show that she does not spell or write very well. But then she's not an English teacher, is she? I'm supposed to show them two video programs for science. I let the kids put them on and only after the first set do I realize that there were three programs on the tape and one of the ones they've seen is the wrong one. But then I'm not a science teacher, am I?

A Taft day is always punctuated by every-two-hour car-moves, during one of which I see the "new teacher" I'd noticed in the schoolyard on my way in this morning heading into the girls room rather than the faculty women's bathroom. Honest, she looked twenty-five.

ANOTHER ONE DOWN – *English, Cappuccino High, February 24, 2003*

Someone has been poking around the cemetery visible out the classroom window most of the morning, and during fourth period a man in flowing white robes arrives with a coffin and about twenty darkly clad mourners. The kids don't seem to think anything of it. "The Effect of Continual Burial Services on Learning Among High School Students in a Working Class Suburb" – another dissertation waiting to be written.

Classroom bulletin board heading: "Safe Schools for Transgender Youth." A number of appropriate clippings. Next to it is a piece of butcher paper with the heading, "Abusive Relationships," with characteristics of such listed below. A small rainbow flag on the wall behind me; a big one furled up in a nook. A poster for "questioning" youth and an anti-war poster. Scotch taped to the top of the podium a small news story: "Same-sex marriage bill passes in Belgium." Not your mother's classroom.

REAL LIFE – *Health/Science, Cucamonga Middle, March 24, 2003*

Four periods of a video on dissecting frogs. Lots of "eeeuuuu-ing" over the innards, but I ain't watching myself. I think would have been a conscientious objector, had I ever personally been confronted with dissection. (Of course not having ever taken biology has left me still fuzzy on where babies come from to this day.) The video ends with an advertisement for a variety of corpses the video company sells for dissection purposes – including cats! This is really a savage situation here.

The one non-video class is an eighth grade health class that's been doing a sex section for two weeks. Today there's a panel with three teenage mothers. One says her mother tells her she's just about ruined the whole world and everyone back in the Philippines would be upset and wouldn't be seen with her in public, but her father was okay. At her all-girls high school they called her a slut and a ho. She now finds it pretty strange living with her husband. "I mean like he's always there. When you go home your boyfriend isn't there, is he? Sometimes I want to watch Lifetime and he wants to watch wrestling. And it's hard being with my friends now. I talk about my baby and they talk about boys at the clubs."

Fourth period we're back to the slicer movie. This is probably about as close to torturing middle schoolers as the law will allow me, so perhaps I should at least enjoy it. When I tell My Friend the Evil Substitute Teacher about this, he wants the video company's name so he can get a copy of his own to show when the teachers don't leave assignments.

A girl sitting in front of me who's not watching the video picks up on my "No war on Iraq" button and asks, "Why no war on Iraq?" and runs through just about every line that's been fed to the American people: "They attacked us on September 11. Well, they supported the terrorists. Are we supposed to wait for proof before we attack them? They have nuclear weapons. They threatened to use them on us. We told Saddam Hussein to leave and he didn't." I suspect that she fairly represents the mush that her elders believe. Eventually I decide that I should not be complicit in her distraction from the actual class topic, even though she clearly has no intention of watching.

The AP stops by during sixth and asks how they've been today. I tell him not too bad; I only sent one student out. Turns out he never arrived, though. So we've caught that little sweetheart. I'd say about six hours of dissection video'd be a good idea for him.

BORING STUFF – *English, Cucamonga Middle, March 31, 2003*

A significant part of each of today's classes is devoted to commas, taken from a book called *Teaching students to use commas correctly without bringing them to tears,* from the *Teaching the Boring Stuff* Series. (I'm not making this up, you know.) To illustrate the meaning of compound sentences, it uses the example of a compound fracture, which it describes as a bone break in two places. During first period, I check the dictionary to make sure that the definition has not changed, but apparently it still means a broken bone protruding through the flesh, and not a double break as people often assume. But the guys who wrote the book aren't biology teachers, are they? Their real failure, though, is in not following up on the analogy, i.e., learning about commas is a pleasant as breaking a bone and looking at it sticking out of your leg. I inform the students of this error in the later classes. I may hesitate in correcting a teacher, but never a textbook.

There's a lunch room discussion about the Iraq War that includes the Principal, the AP, and a few others – it's pretty dismal stuff. I saw German TV footage of injured American soldiers speaking of how surprised they were that they weren't being viewed as liberators. These guys here are about as well informed.

The next day I have the girl who wanted to argue the war with me last week and since I'm wearing my antiwar button again today, so she wants to have another go. She says Iraq should have let the weapons inspectors in. I point out that they were there and had to leave when the US was about to attack. She says, no, that can't be. So I talk about the idea of one country attacking another because it doesn't like it. She gives me the address of a website she says is full of pro and con about the war. I tell her that I think the fact that she wants to argue this is great. She thanks me.

Another class is full of questions about my button: "Where did you get it? Did you go to the protest? Were you at the violent one or the non-violent one? Do you support our troops?" They're much more curious than they would be in San Francisco, I think. Protest seems a lot more exotic in the burbs. I'm pleased with the curiosity. A girl in sixth period says her uncle who is in the Army just called from Iraq. Says he was scared, and you could hear explosions in the background. This all sure beats the teachers lunch room crowd, anyhow.

Today, one of the twins I've seen around here for a couple of years is sitting in front of me. I tell her she's not as quiet as she used to be and she asks if I'm sure it's not her sister I'm thinking of. I am anything but sure. She then tells me that she and her sister went to two different summer schools last summer and switched places maybe eight times. Their friends all knew but the teachers only caught them once. Oh young men of South San Francisco, marry at your own peril!

NOT FOR EVERYONE – *English, Appian Way High, April 4, 2003*
Today's first two classes are Reading – for freshman who are slow readers. The room has terrible lighting which is probably not going to help them become fast readers, either.

The other night my friend J told me that his substitute teacher career has come to an end after four days. He couldn't take the constant need to deal with discipline. No, this is not a calling for everyone.

I'M SORRY – *Health, Cucamonga Middle, April 7, 2003*
The seventh grade classes work on a health triangle: physical, social, mental/emotional, etc. The one eighth grade class gets an article entitled, "I had sex with him – now I'm sorry." Sister Acquin never gave out stuff like that. "Sorry" wouldn't have begun to describe …

Major fart incident third period – their little noses are growing in size and sensitivity at this age. I also confiscate $21 in cash being flashed around the room. I could work for tips here. Of course, I do have to return it.

A couple of days later I find myself driving down here on a beautiful sunny morning thinking about how I've been liking these kids lately. This worries me. Could it finally be time to find something else?

During a break I notice a spontaneous outbreak of a hand clapping game mostly played by girls that I recognize from my elementary school days. It's now called slide. I'll bet they were playing it in Shakespeare's time.

ARE YOU A PROTESTOR? – *Sixth Grade, Freeway Limits Middle, April 10, 2003*
The Cucamonga secretary called me yesterday after school. She had forgotten to give me the message that Ms. K had called and given me a job at Freeway for tomorrow, and accepted for me. Ms. L, the teacher I'm replacing, calls before class; says the first period class will be polite and groggy, but that the day will deteriorate as they become "friskier," as she puts it.

My button draws attention at the beginning of fourth: "Are you a protestor? So's my father. I went to one protest once." "Can we protest? No more school!" This is the lower class middle school in South City, so no doubt it will have the highest percentage of alumni winding up in the military.

LUFTMENSCH – *Counseling, Waterfront Middle, April 21, 2003*
    A friend recently declared (in a bar) "Gallagher's my ideal. He lives on air. He doesn't even apply for real jobs." Well, both districts had spring break last week and tax day came and the air that I live on is feeling a bit rarefied right about now.
    Counseling: Private office. Issue "permit to leave school" and ice packs. Watch the pizza line; monitor basketball courts. Repeat.

COMPLEMENTS – *English, Appian Way High, April 23, 2003*
    Junior English. Twenty minutes silent reading of *The Grapes of Wrath*, followed by some grammar – objects, direct and indirect; and complements, subject and objective, which I believe we used to call nouns in apposition. The instructions say I should "feel free to discuss and go over the subject material" if I "feel familiar enough with the topic." Well, the Sisters of Charity didn't learn me grammar for nothing – of course I'll go over it.
    Freshman English is, well, a bit pre-sophomoric. Even a bit of crayon throwing. Third period is yearbook, which is assumed to be a self-motivating group. At one point I smell food and see that students are microwaving in class. When I was in school we were never allowed to use the fireplaces to cook in the classroom. Which reminds me, as I'm writing out hall passes, I sometimes wonder if kids in some of these open-air California suburban schools even realize that hall passes were once meant literally, that there were once halls on the way to the bathroom.
Student Name of the Day: Sincerely Anselmo.

COME IN OUT OF THE RAIN? – *Health, Cucamonga Middle, May 2, 2003*
    Since the last time I worked, a junior high student in Red Lion, Pennsylvania has killed the principal and himself in the school cafeteria. The newspaper story notes that "The same school district was the site of a machete attack on a kindergarten class that injured a principal, two teachers and 11 of the 23 pupils in 2001." And still they won't let us carry guns. *(Ed note: Delete – no longer a joke.)*
    They're doing STAR testing here, which I assume is part of the reason I haven't been around lately. The schedule had to be changed around for this, so the day starts with fifth period. The assignment is to read the *Teen Health* textbook chapter on mental health, including "Notes on Suicide." My Friend the Evil Substitute Teacher says he has his students write suicide notes – as a literary exercise like writing haikus. That way if anything happens he's covered. And when they cover the question, "What do you do if a friend talks about suicide?" he

would remind the kids that good friends are always supportive of friends' decisions.

It's raining during the break after testing. A lot of kids just stand out in it until it gets real heavy. They could probably save a lot of money from their testing budget by just timing the point when they come in out of the rain. But next time I come there's more testing and sixth period comes first. I fear that some kids may never recover from this disorientation.

DREAM TIME– *Special Education, Nelson Mandela Middle, May 9, 2003*

There are two aides in this classroom. One, an older black woman, is reading the newspaper and doesn't even acknowledge me when I come in. She sort of acts like a tough grandmother with these kids. My instructions for the day are simply to distribute work packages and help as needed. I assume that I am pretty much going to be a placeholder.

The packages are eleven pages long, cover language arts, math, social studies and science and are meant to cover the entire day until it's movie watching time. They include things like "Make up a story about Mr. X (the teacher uses his own actual name but misspells it) as Principal of this school? (sic) How would he help students to learn better?" and "Draw and color a picture of Mr. X as a super hero saving the planet form (sic) an alien invasion." and "Make up a story about going to a strange planets (sic) where people were the size of insaects (sic) and insects were the size of humans? (sic)" Mr. X (whom I know) also has left me a couple of pieces of his campaign literature for union office.

The second aide turns out to be assigned exclusively to an autistic kid but says the other kids often ask why he's only helping one of them, so he helps in general where he can. The class is pretty loud and his kid has a great deal of difficulty with that and eventually they withdraw to the library. But before he goes he tells me that most of these kids are emotionally disturbed and he finds the whole situation in the class pretty crazy: "What's going to happen to these kids – they get a job and they're not going to be able to handle it. They start squabbling with each other all the time."

THE PLEASURE OF READING – *Drama/English, Cappuccino High, May 14, 2003*

This was the place where I once mentioned *And Still We Rise*, the book about the all-black AP English class in LA and some kid said that he had never seen a black kid in an AP class here. There are none in these two classes either – not that there are that many black kids in the entire school – but I observe one kid reading Maya Angelou and another group discussing Langston Hughes and other black poets. Easier to find a black author in an AP English class than a black student.

Fourth and sixth period drama have been moved to the dance studio, a room I've never been to before. This is a class of 32 and it's pretty nuts. They're supposed to "work with their partners or in groups." The "partners or in groups" part is okay, but exactly what "work" they're doing is pretty obscure. I ask the guys who are wrestling if they are rehearsing a wrestling scene and they assure me they are. Then I ask the guys shooting dice if they are rehearsing a gambling scene. They say it's not gambling, they're practicing their algebra. This is the wrong answer.

Today I notice for the first time the portion of the substitute teacher material that explains the 18 minute school-wide reading period that follows the announcements in third period. It says, "You are invited to read during this period as well, as all adults are asked to participate and model the pleasure of reading." "Model the pleasure of reading" – yes, I must do that.

WHO I'M NOT – Science, Appian Way High, May 20, 2003

Before my first class a girl announces, "I love this day." It's summer – for real, which you can come to forget about sometimes around here. It's visions of Southern California high school today, though, with one girl even wearing a tiny Hawaiian-style skirt and a plastic flower in her hair. My presence elicits a few "yea"s from the students arriving for General Science but I get one girl to concede that she's happy for who I am not rather than for who I am. She says she's sorry, but I assure her that I understand. A kid arriving for third period physics, says, "Okay, now we'll learn something." This does seem a stretch, but I do get the point that this teacher is not highly regarded.

KISS ASS UNION – Language Arts/Phys Ed, Cucamonga Middle, May 21, 2003

Rich D called late last night to tell me the UESF election results. I've been re-elected to the Executive Board, but not elected to the Labor Council (on which I was not incumbent) – pretty much what I expected. But what I did not expect is that my slate lost and I was only re-elected on a fluke. The other incumbent E-Board Sub Rep, who had gone with the insurgent slate, won reelection handily. But her slate mate had been disqualified for not having renewed his membership (he was a retired member) when he started subbing. One of the seats was therefore guaranteed to go to one of the two of us on the losing slate.

The fellow I beat out was V, who had previously sought the incumbent slate's backing and finally gotten it due to my E-Board colleague's defection. V had showed up at the pre-election union assembly meeting with the single most unfortunate piece of campaign literature I've ever seen – a flyer stating that for a vote for V was a vote for a "kiss ass union." To be fair, when someone pointed out to him that the flyer did not actually say "kick-ass union," as he had presumably intended, he nimbly snatched back as many as he could, as quickly as he could. (Mixing gin with proof reading was the only plausible explanation offered for the confusion over what exact approach toward the posterior he advocated for the union.) And I didn't beat him by all that many votes. I don't think I'll put this win on the resume.

Today, this one rather large, brooding sort of kid whom other kids make fun of and who is not himself very pleasant walks by in first period and says, "Mr. Gallagher." I say, "Yes." He says, "You sub here too often." I respond, "You're right." So, apparently everyone knows.

The kids are supposed to do some silent reading and complete a "Strategic Reading Sheet." The teacher's note suggests that her classes will be well behaved, but also says, "SHOW THEM NO MERCY." So, I throw one out at the beginning of fifth period and am taking down another name for her, when the AP sends the kid back. This breaks my cardinal rule of discipline and now I've got a revolt on my hands – kids applauding this guy's return, a girl gives him a high five, and we have a coughing outbreak. I send the kid out to get a pass to return, which the AP gives to him. I've taken down three more names by now and decide if the administration is going to cause this problem for me, they can damn well clean it up, so I call the office and have them send someone down. They do send a suitably stern woman who does put the fear of the lord into the kids and stays for a bit into sixth. I leave notes both for the teacher and the administration regarding my displeasure.

WHAT THEY SAID – *Health/Social Studies, Skyline Middle, May 23, 2003*

I toss a kid in sixth, but I can't rouse anyone in the office to tell them he should be arriving, so I guess that it's just going to have to be out of sight, out of mind. As this guy was one of the few black kids in this school, it brings to mind the columns Joan Ryan wrote in this week's *Chronicle,* as well as a typically uncomfortable discussion at last week's union meeting.

Ryan wrote about a new book by a black author named John Ogbu who had been invited to study the Shaker Heights, Ohio school system by a group of black parents concerned about the difficulties their kids were experiencing in school despite the families' relative affluence. The book doesn't make the usual arguments about unqualified teachers, etc. and apparently says a lot of things that many might prefer not to discuss in front of whites. (For more on John Ogbu, see my essay, "The Anti-Suspension Movement," at the end of the book.)

In the union meeting, on the other hand, people pretty much said what they were expected to say. The discussion started with a proposed resolution calling on the School Board to end a police-in-the-schools program in order to keep from criminalizing students, an issue that resurfaces from time to time. Rich B was giving a basically right-headed speech about a generally wrong-headed resolution until he went off talking about how Latino students don't have a great deal of respect for female administrators. Well, thirty seconds of stereotype will outweigh thirty minutes of common sense any day, and you can be sure that some people in the room heard nothing of what he said after that.

One of the teachers says that as a Latina she's very concerned about the negative aspects of the cops in the schools. Another Latina tells me afterwards that she's worked with the Latino community plenty and she was always concerned with having adequate security on campus, rather than being worried about having too much. The one who supports the resolution is from Buenos Dias Elementary, a bilingual school that parents fight to get their kids into. The one against is retired; she used to be at Alioto, the worst high school in the system until it closed. Seems like elementary school teachers might find it easier to oppose cops on campus than high school teachers, anyhow – there's a lot more dangerous high schoolers than first graders out there, ya know.

CAREERS AND MEETINGS – *Roving, Freeway Limits Middle, May 28, 2003*

This is one dumb day at school. I'm here to replace a succession of teachers attending half-hour meetings with parents of students in danger of being held back. During my first stint, a trombonist for the San Francisco Ballet Orchestra and a guy who does multi-media work walk in and inform me that it's Student Career Day. The fact that the regular teacher has left and I'm just now hearing about this can't be too encouraging for them. And, indeed, the musician is fairly terse and rather disappointed that there aren't actually any kids interested in music in this class. This, it turns out, will take up the first four periods for eighth-graders.

As for me, I'm off to my next class, which doesn't turn out to be my next class because the teacher I'm sent to replace isn't actually teaching this period. She team teaches and sends me to her partner's classroom where a woman from Marine World is talking about being an animal trainer and the importance of doing blood work on animals. And while I'm there, could I go back to the office and get the teacher a copy of the meeting schedule?

Next up is a real estate agent. He has a teaching background and currently coaches teachers, so he's in his element. After a few introductory remarks he asks if there are any questions. A girl raises her hand, "Can I go to the bathroom?" Welcome back to school. Oh, and could I make twenty-five copies of his handout for him? Thanks. In the copy room I run into my co-teacher from two summers ago (she had them for English, I had math) who's a regular here now. She says she's teaching kindergarten this summer. Kindergarten in summer school!

Next it's back to the trombonist and Career Day is over and it's on to a couple of periods of drawing box and whisker charts in math to make sure our students are absolutely prepared for the real world.

After lunchtime on the meeting schedule, which is different from the class schedule, I go to replace another teacher who doesn't show up until fifteen minutes later, which is the end of lunch on the class schedule. And, oh, she's not actually doing that meeting, so back to the lunchroom and then back to the first room to replace the other roving sub who goes to the room where I was supposed to have spent the last half hour, which is also where he spent the block before lunch – got that? Then one last one down at the other end of the school – the schedule actually says that it's in the room where I've spent most of the day, but I checked on that early, since I suspected it must be an error like most of the rest of this ill-conceived day. One teacher tells me that they had these parent meetings sprung on them just yesterday, after they'd been planning the Career Day for some time. Clearly not an organizational mastermind running this place.

Last period there's an outbreak of fluid-exchange compulsion: "Can I drink water?" "Can I go to the bathroom?" I promulgate a general fluid-hold-fast decree and this ridiculous day is over.

TELL ME THAT AGAIN – *Math, Cucamonga Middle, June 10, 2003*

At eighth grade graduation practice the AP tells the kids, who have been writing messages all over each others' uniform white shirts and khaki pants all day, that it's time for them to get sophisticated. Now telling middle school students to get sophisticated is about the most ridiculous statement I've heard in a long time and it sets me to wondering if this guy actually has the credential for this job or whether perhaps he has actually killed the real credential-holder and has assumed his identity.

Today is "Day On the Green," which appears to mean three hours playing games on the back field. My assignment is supervising the Water Balloon Toss. Don't like the sound of that, but my instructions say that the kids in the leadership program are in charge and I'm dutifully referring all student inquiry there, until the assistant principal comes by and shuts the whole thing down. Apparently I have been unable to distinguish chaos from an orderly water balloon toss.

There's another teacher scheduled to work this with me, but she's late because she's a PE teacher and they have lunch after everyone else. So with no event to supervise, we chat. She wants to know if I'm trying to get a regular job and I explain the credential situation. She says she thinks education classes are probably better nowadays and points out the advantage of getting paid while you're in school, but admits that she did attend one recently when she'd thought about getting a counseling credential and mostly remembers shifting from one hip to the other in her first class.

I also explain the freedom of movement about the world that not having a regular job has given me. She asks a couple of questions about whom I worked for when I did foreign elections, and after I answer them she asks them again. I'm not sure what the information transmission problem is here. PE teacher – multiple concussions, possibly?

*****

THE WONGS – *Physics, Cabot High, August 27, 2003*
>Over the course of my five physics periods, I have 18 students named Wong, plus one more in home room. None will be absent in my three days here. Advanced Physics is 27 girls and five boys. Are the demographers aware of this trend, I wonder. Kids here discuss summer vacations in France and Australia.

SUBURB? – *English, Cucamonga Middle, September 15, 2003*
>I ask a girl reading a Nancy Drew book if she knows there was no *real* Caroline Keene. She doesn't. I tell her I knew one of the women who wrote one of the books under the pseudonym and she doesn't seem impressed. But then what could I expect, telling a middle school student that I'd met someone who I just told her didn't exist?

>I ask if anyone has seen *Spellbound,* the movie about the National Spelling Bee kids, to maybe make a point about just how unphonetic and therefore difficult to spell English really is. They've never heard of it, however, and I say that's understandable because a movie like that probably didn't play in the suburbs. Then they ask what a suburb is.

SUPER REGULARS – *English, Cappuccino High, September 18, 2003*
>Classes that used to be called General are now College Prep here. I once had a job that involved driving from one gas station to another, scraping Super Regular stickers off of gas pumps and replacing them with Shell of the Future, so I recognize the marketing concept here – these are Super Regular students. My TA grades today's thirty-question quizzes – the Honors kids all get twenty-eight or better; in College Prep she gets tens.

SHOULD I WRITE IT DOWN? – *Sixth Grade Language Arts/Reading/ Social Studies, Cucamonga Middle, September 26, 2003*
>Weekly spelling test with five bonus words; twenty-five chances to make twenty. A couple of twenty-fives and the lowest I see is about fifteen until I notice a two and it turns out to be one of the two black girls in this class. I note things like this because keeping a handle on the situation of black kids that I encounter is always of interest. At the same time, I feel queasy about even writing it down – or passing it along. I think of Nicole Hollander's Sylvia cartoon with *The Woman Who Lies in Her Journal* and feel like the guy who doesn't know if he should tell his journal everything.

BABY SHOWER – *Spanish, Appian Way High, September 30, 2003*
>Overheard one cafeteria worker telling the other she's got to buy a baby shower present for her daughter's girlfriend. I don't remember any high school cafeteria workers' discussions, but I don't think they had that one.

NO ONE'S LATE HERE – *RSP/Science, Appian Way High, October 1, 2003*
>The regular teacher, who's out sick, drops by to tell me they get to watch a video because they've worked hard. They can pick from *Austin Powers,*

Braveheart, Twister, The Lost World and *Twilight Zone*. I'm having my usual private doubts when along comes my aide who looks at the videos and pulls *Austin Powers* from the options; says she thinks it's vulgar and that they ought to see one of the science videos that's available instead of these. Glad to see someone paying attention here. Of course, when I ask which kids haven't arrived at the beginning of second, I learn they don't register tardies on the attendance sheet in special ed.

The aide's got an elementary ed degree, but hurt her back and works as a para. Sent her kids to Catholic schools and says she's glad she did that every time she looks around here. Thinks these kids with us should be challenged more, but she's not the teacher. She'll get no argument from me on that.

WHERE AM I?– *Newcomer, Freeway Limits Middle, October 3, 2003*

I'm just arrived in my classroom and the new AP comes to ask me to cover a first period math class missing a sub during this teacher's prep period. The AP just came over from Oakland and says the kids seem pretty good here. Coming over from Oakland will do that to you. Anyhow, I'm no sooner in the new room than someone calls and asks if this is so-and-so's room, but I don't honestly know whose room I'm in. Not a job for the easily disoriented – or those too proud to admit that not only don't they know what they're doing, they don't even know where they're doing it.

"Newcomer" is an ESL class for brand new immigrants. Ten Latinos, one Russian, one Chinese, and an aide. After lunch it's computer lab where they're supposed to find out what dolphins eat. One kid winds up at the Miami Dolphins website and not because he's trying to read about American football.

Sixth period drama class with a different group – eighth graders who are actually doing debate preparation. Topics are lowering the driving age, condom distribution at school, and abortion. What did I know about abortion in the eighth grade?

BUT I'M RIGHT IN 1998– *Wood Shop, Freeway Limits Middle, October 9, 2003*

Ms. K left a message on my machine telling me she had taken the liberty of signing me up for this class. (Think maybe they have trouble getting subs here?) They watch *Spy Kids*. When the kids start moving their chairs back, toward the end of second period, I tell them to relax cause there's still four minutes to go and then the bell rings in two. Then I notice that schedule I'm reading on the wall only has six periods while the teacher has left instructions for a seven period day. It turns out to be five years old.

NO SUBSTITUTE– *Phys Ed, Citadel Middle, October 14, 2003*

A sign in the hall here says, "There is no substitute for knowledge." But the experienced substitute can sub for anything; he doesn't need no stinking knowledge. I *am* the substitute for knowledge.

This four-day gig includes a couple of middle school assemblies, events that can sometimes be a little hard on the prefrontal lobes. Here, a former 49ers football player pitches a magazine-and-cd-selling campaign to raise money for the school. The sellers' prizes include battery-operated blinking lights you can stick in your ear, sun glasses you can drink beer through (soda is what they tell the kids); a gizmo you can empty a two liter bottle into and then it's a tapper keg – and if you sell a whole lot, free lunch with a ride in a twenty-seater Hummer limo.

The best is last: They roll out a transparent plastic booth with air hose attached, into which they insert a kid and paper money blown about by the hose. The kid keeps anything snatched out of the air in her allotted time – $46 today.

I gave a boy the key to the locker room before the end of one class so he could open it up before the kids got there. When he returns I ask, "Was it locked?" "Yes," he says. "Did you open it?" "No." I guess middle school is the place for learning the things one takes for granted. PE's different here in that a lot of times you have to roust a lot of the girls and make them do something other than leaning on the walls or sitting on the floor, but not here. I've been watching a coed basketball game for two days. They've obviously done this before and the girls are all real players. I noticed a very good girl ball handler yesterday and today there's a better one.

I run into Y. I know no one else in this town with whom I can have a better conversation about the sociological aspects of education. He's read my *Bay Guardian* review of education books, even, and we're quickly off to discussing how wrong-headed we consider most of the current public discussion. He thinks the idea that schools are underfunded in matters of new textbooks and the like is misguided, and I agree. The problems of the kids we see are not all about inadequate textbooks. I push my educational reparations idea and have to remind myself that it is rather exotic and I should be prepared to not find acceptance.

SECURITY? SECURITY? – Social Studies, Pizarro High, October 20, 2003

Given the recent newspaper coverage of gun battles between Pizarro and Bono students, taking this job is a questionable decision, but off I go, zipping quickly upstairs to take over from another teacher, noticing four security guards talking together on my way. They seem prepared, but appearances can be deceiving.

First period is an Advanced Placement History class taking a test in perfect silence – absolutely not what I expected. Next period is more like it, starting with the first arrival declaring, "We've got a fucking substitute." We've also got a San Francisco State undergraduate in here doing the forty hours of community service required for his degree. He says this second period class will be the worst I'll see today. He comes from twelve years of private school in the Sacramento area, so this scene at Pizarro is all pretty foreign for him.

If fourth period is actually any better than second, the difference is too subtle for me. Perhaps if I were here for a while I'd see it, but I won't be. Then comes a pleasant surprise in the form of a teacher who says she's taking the class to a play next period and will come back in fifteen minutes to get half of them. Unfortunately, shortly after she does, a girl throws something at a boy – perhaps a stapler. The boy throws something back – definitely a stapler. Now the substitute code of conduct may allow for many departures from the norm of the well-behaved class, but flying heavy objects is not one of them, so I call the office for security, at which point three boys flee. Security does not arrive in what seems a reasonable amount of time, so I call again. The girl leaves. The office says security was busy dealing with another kid. Security does arrive some time later, however, but this is by coincidence – during an earthquake drill later in the day someone checks that the kids are ducking and covering under their desks. Half are not, so whoever this guy is shoos them under.

Well, the chances of my coming back here were already pretty slim by this point, but if worrying about things that might fly during an earthquake takes precedence over things that actually are flying from students' hands, they're going to have to carry on without me. When the "all clear" is given after the earthquake drill, some students prefer to stay under their desks, which seems like a pretty good idea to me. How much damage can they do there?

PIMP DADDY– *Special Education, Cucamonga Middle, October 23, 2003*
The three computers here have all have name tags on them. There's Sponge Bob Squarepants, Billy Bob, and Pimp Daddy. A computer named Pimp Daddy in a middle school classroom – Are you shitting me?

SHOELESS– *Math, Freeway Limits Middle, October 28, 2003*
I had a small party on Saturday night which fell within the octaves of both my birthday and Halloween which meant that I wore a bit of a costume and no one else did – the San Francisco Police Department shirt I got at a thrift shop when I first lived in San Francisco thirty years ago. When asked, my story was that I was in a pilot police department substitute teacher training program, established in response to recent difficulty in recruiting officers and based upon the principle that subs were doing a good part of the job already. (I apparently laid down a line of bullshit on the topic sufficiently good to convince my friend C.) So today, I feel ready.

And when a kid takes off his shoe for some other kid to check out in third period, I remove said shoe from the other kid's desk and place it in the front of the room. When the period ends he asks for his shoe, to general merriment, and I tell him I will be turning it in to the office where he can get it after school. So he hops off to his next class. The AP comes by later to pick it up.

Announcement on PA: "Friday (Halloween) is Costume Day, but you have to wear a real costume – you can't come as a Worcester student. And no bare bellies."

Student Name of the Day: Einstein Gutierrez. (You're no Einstein, Gutierrez. Matter of fact, I am.)

I'LL TAKE THOSE– *Language Arts/Math, Cucamonga Middle, October 31, 2003*
My one Math period involves graphing (x,y) coordinate points to make a picture that they're then supposed to color, so we have to do some remedial work about which way is vertical and horizontal. Then when the usual non-participants

start asking to go to the bathroom I tell one, "That's a negative." "What's a negative?" "That means no." So now they're brushed up on multiple meanings of negative and they know which way is up. They can't pay you enough for that kind of teaching.

Halloween in middle school – now that's scary. A lot of witches walking around as I drive in. During home room I confiscate a guy's boobs when they fall out of his Halloween costume. Teachers in the lunchroom are talking about kids dressed up as pimps and hookers. At Saint Athanasius the pimps and hookers stayed outside.

QUICK VISIT – *History, Sonny and Cher Bono High, November 3, 2003*

Half day job starting at 11:30 – probably the ideal way to introduce myself to Pizarro's rival in the recent shooting wars. There's a police car parked outside when I arrive. Is this a good sign or a bad one? Then I have to identify myself for security sitting at a table outside, which is probably good. The secretary says it's now lunchtime and they've been trying to get someone all morning. Guess that shows where I am on the list these days.

Another teacher also appears in my class, a 51 year old disability retiree working on a mentoring program. His disability appears related to having been hit in the neck from behind with a computer by a student at Juvenile Hall, a place that he had said he enjoyed working at earlier in our conversation. He gives me his card when we leave – he sells insurance to teachers. Disability insurance, perhaps. On my way out, I see a new person sitting at the outdoor security table – and she's asleep.

There's a message from the principal of Pizarro High School on my answering machine when I get home: "It would have been nice had you come to me and told me that this happened in your room and that no one sent security. Then I could have done something about it … I could have done something immediately had you let me know immediately. … So, wherever you go, I hope that you will talk to the principal prior to writing letters and cc-ing them to the Superintendent" (which is what has gotten her attention, leading to this call).

I call her and we do manage to keep things from degenerating into a mutual whining session, but the fact remains that anything she could have done to correct the situation on the afternoon of the incident, she could do two or three days later when my letter arrived. And there sure wasn't anything that she said that would make me want to go back there again.

A few days later I will read that the bystander kid from Pizarro, who was shot in the head on a bus when some Bono kid was trying to shoot another Pizarro kid – or maybe it was the other way around – has died.

GLENN GOULD? – *English, Cappuccino High, November 4, 2003*

I read out the teacher's instructions to continue taking notes about the character of Glenn Gould as they continue watching the movie *Thirty Two Short Films About Glenn Gould*, whereupon I am asked, "Who's Glenn Gould?" Looks like it may take all thirty two of the films to get through to some of them. I don't think these guys are likely to be buying a lot of art house movie tickets throughout the rest of their lives – or Glenn Gould recordings.

OUT OF THIS WORLD – Roving Special Education, Appian Way High, November 13, 2003

I'm filling in for teachers for five different IEP meetings, which means these will be Special Education classes. First stint is for a long-term sub, who's himself replacing a teacher having a baby. A kid coming in says, "Who is you?" The teacher tells him I'm a sub, to which he says, "We don't need no substitute." Same to you buddy – I've thrown him out well before the end of the period. As the teacher, who is really a brother-sub, says upon his return, "A sub doesn't have to take (silent pause here) from anyone."

The day ends on an up note. Last period is reading about Venus and I see my chance to put twenty-five years of subscribing to *Astronomy* magazine to use, and we get *into* the solar system. One guy is really excited when I tell him that he could go outside and see Mars tonight and Venus soon. I've got the globe out and I'm spinning it backwards to show how Venus' day goes in the opposite direction and I'm on the board showing them what a year means in astronomical terms and why you always see Venus near the sun. The nicest bit of teaching I've gotten to do in a while.

NO PUDDLES – Special Education, Cucamonga Middle, November 14, 2003

Today's main accomplishment will be defending the integrity of the teacher's bathroom policy, not during the five periods of special education, but during the one non-special ed class – home room. The instructions are precise: they're limited to once a week and she's left me a printed record of the week ending today, so that if they are marked as having gone on any prior day they can't go today. But what do these guys have to lose? They might as well try to wear me down by coming at me in waves, and besides, just asking or whining is in itself a break from the twenty minutes of reading that home room is supposed to entail.

Two cleared the paper check, but maybe five didn't and how they howled. Oh, it was an emergency! It was a female emergency! The first special emergency rejected carried on to the extent that when she asked if she could go to the corner, I said yes and she squirmed there for the rest of the period, part of the time on the floor. Another girls tells her, "Pee on his foot," in response to which I invite her to take the fresh air. But when the bell rings, all students leave Toilet Training 7 under their own power, none obviously dripping, with no puddles in evidence. The system prevails. The substitute has done his job.

GOOD DAY ON THE MOUND – Everything, Johnny Rotten High, November 17, 2003

Haven't been to South City's high school-for-kids-who-don't-like-school for a long time. The regular teacher's got two periods of Industrial Arts, one English and two PE's, so he's sort of a permanent sub himself. The guy covering in Industrial Arts when I arrive says the main thing is to get back all the exacto knife blades you give out. They're quite sharp so this seems quite a sensible priority. I hear one girl tell her friends, "It was like a ghetto-ass baptism." Another is singing "nigger" this and "nigger" that along to the rap she's listening to on her headphones. There are not actually any black students in the class.

Second period gets a little rowdier and we have some boy-girl fooling-around pushing that goes out the back door and won't come back in, so I call the office on the phone that the principal has pointed out for me. The call itself does the trick of getting the kids back in, but the principal comes down anyhow. Some kids have their heads down on their desks for the entire period, even when he's in the room. Did I mention that this is not the place for the motivated?

English class is in a different room and the principal shows me where the phone is there too. This place is quite spread out for the small number of people in it, but they certainly try not to leave you isolated. The kids in this class are supposed to write a three paragraph essay on *Cool Running*, the movie about the Jamaican bobsled team. I don't know what to expect but they all buckle right down to it – the only time this happens all day, which also happens to the only time they have a clear academic assignment. There seems to be a message there, but I will reserve judgment

PE's supposed to play whiffleball. One class tells me I've got to be permanent pitcher and I say fine. I strike the first batter out, get the next to hit me a popup, and throw the third one out at first, and they tell me they'll have someone else pitch. After about twenty minutes the game is declared over and they hang around, shoot a little pool and listen to a boombox, which plays a song with the refrain:

If you don't give a damn, we don't give a fuck. Hey!
If you don't give a damn, we don't give a fuck. Hey!
If you don't give a damn, we don't give a fuck. Hey!

Easy to remember the lyrics, I suppose.

When it's all over, I pick up the children's toys, something they showed no sign of thinking to do for themselves, an assessment the principal seconds. He asks if I'll come back tomorrow if the teacher is still out. I tell him that I will if the machine gets me, but it doesn't.

NOT MY HANGOVER, THOUGH – Music, Worcester Middle,
November 24, 2003

A teacher called into the KFOG morning show to report on a concert at the Fillmore last night. The DJs noted that she sounded a little rough from her night out and she said she was and as a result she'd be showing videos in class today. For the last three periods here my assignment is to show *Sister Act* – just like a hung over teacher.

UNPAID? – *Art/English, Oskar Schindler High, November 25, 2003*

The English class is supposed to finish some written work before they continue watching *Shrek*. *Shrek!* This is high school! I will grant that there is a good line in *Shrek*, though, when the king tells his subjects, "Some of you may die, but it's a sacrifice I'm willing to make" – reminiscent of Madeline Albright's saying that she found the number of Iraqi children who would die as a result of sanctions a price that was "worth it."

The teacher comes in to drop off grades with her three or four-year-old daughter, who she says is "very contagious" with a lung infection. The kids want their grades and before she relents and gives them to them, she says, "I'm not working; I'm on my time; I'm not getting paid." Not exactly accurate, I suspect, as I assume this is a sick day.

Student Name of the Day: Unique Oliver

JUST KIDDING – BANG – *Math, William Howard Taft Middle, November 26, 2003*

A double period class at the end of the day gets to watch a movie. Guess which? *Shrek*! Just what could it be that makes this movie central to Bay Area educational curricula, particularly when it appears that every kid in America has already seen it by now? Is it maybe our *Iliad*? Our communal experience?

Heard on the radio this morning that a high school kid got off five shots at a MUNI bus yesterday, apparently because another student teased him. Teased him! Whoa, guess these kids can't take a joke these days.

TEN DAYS IN HELL – *Eighth Grade Math, Mateo Middle, December 1, 2003*

Be careful what you wish for. When my check from South San Francisco arrived last Wednesday and I was fretting about how little they paid, in comes a call from the San Francisco machine inviting me to teach math for two weeks at Mateo Middle School, the only middle school in the city I haven't been to. Since I avoid more than half of the city's other middle schools, I realize that the chance that I've making a big mistake taking this job is better than fifty-fifty, but a full week in San Francisco is worth more than six days in South San Francisco.

Ms. J, the teacher I'm replacing, shows up with everything in hand. She'll be out taking care of her mother who recently had a stroke. She's got three eighth grade basic math classes and two Algebra. The Algebra she tells me will be no problem. The basic math, on the other hand, are really basic. Everything has been very slow with them she says. And oh, by the way, the sixth period class is the worst she's ever had in thirty-eight years. And I just took it for ten days!

She stays and does the first class herself. It's small and, therefore, reasonably manageable. Her material is quite well organized and hopefully also manageable. The next basic math class is somewhat more challenging and the Algebra class is as advertised. Then comes sixth period. She's starred the names of potential problem students on the seating chart. Nine students have stars; five are double-starred; one is a triple. Well, the class is so bad that I can't even properly introduce myself. It's chaos from the get-go and I have to make my stand quickly and tell a girl who will not sit down and be quiet to leave. She refuses, so I call downstairs to have her removed. The counselor comes up and takes her as she issues a stream of "this fucking teacher, blah, blah, blah." This should get her suspended in my book, but we'll see. I eject two more before the period is over; both decide they'll go on their own. And the office calls up to request another starred student before I get to asking ask him to leave. By the end of the period I can no longer get anyone to answer the phone in the counseling office.

Seldom have I been so glad to see a class as seventh period Algebra, and seldom has the academic racial divide been starker. This school draws from Chinatown and the North Beach projects that are in the process of being rebuilt. There are no black students in either Algebra class; mostly Chinese. I warn the seventh period kids that my voice may be a little ragged from the last period and I'm very short with the student aides who are all over me at the beginning of the period, wanting to know what to do as I'm trying to figure out which end is up. Meanwhile, one of my useless sixth period students returns to drop his pants and dance outside the door. I'll eject him tomorrow as soon as he sits down and I get his name.

The second day, Ms. J stops by just before lunch to see how things are going. I thank her, but she says she's probably coming for her own benefit as much as mine. She's concerned that I might not last and then she'd have to deal with multiple subs which would be a total disaster. I tell her sixth period lived up to billing and that my voice may be giving out. She says do anything necessary, don't take it personally and she's not surprised by whom I threw out of class.

And more – a kid wanders into the room at lunch time, asking a million questions and not particularly listening to the answers, but why should that surprise me in a middle school kid? I slowly realize that this kid is a bit off: *Do you get paid? Do teachers get paid? Are you white?* (He's Chinese.) *The other teachers said no when I asked them; they lied to me. Did you wear a red sweater?* Finally I ask him to leave when my patience runs out and I start getting sarcasm from him. There's no end to the aggravating permutations of this age group.

Today I have written on the board that anyone not in their assigned seat will be marked absent, which causes a great deal of scurrying in sixth period and I then eject yesterday's dancing boy as soon as he takes his seat and I can identify him from the seating chart. He asks why and I explain that it's for dancing outside my door with his pants on the ground during seventh period yesterday. He says that he doesn't know how I dance, but that wasn't dancing he was doing. I actually hadn't thought that much of it either, but in any case, he's out. He returns, though, saying there was no one in the counseling office. I send him back out again. The phone rings. It's the principal who says that if I don't want the guy in the class, I need to send some work down for him. Eventually a kid goes down with a book, which is actually not supposed to leave the classroom. The way this class is going, this guy sitting in the counseling office could be the only one who gets anything done.

Meanwhile, yesterday's really nasty little bitch is back. I told Ms. J that I thought her performance warranted a suspension, but she says this girl curses out the principal like that and if cursing out the principal doesn't get you sent home, she doesn't know what will. But she's not as bad today, and when she gets to the brink as I tell her to take her seat, she says, "If I don't, you gonna send me downstairs?" and I say yes, she takes her seat. A couple more of her peers get their walking papers, including the big guy in the back of the room – who Ms. J says will usually just sleep for her – when he makes a mock-threatening hand gesture, as if to hit me. Second student ousted for this in two days. Another guy insists on his right to keep changing seats because his glasses are broken. I let it go once; the second time I tell him that if he doesn't stick in a seat, he'll have to leave. He ups and leaves. You like a student who takes initiative.

On the one hand, I certainly have better order. Ms. J had told me that the utterly charming girl I'd ejected yesterday had a virtue often found in the extremely obnoxious student – she was absent a lot. Frequently it is the only virtue that such students will display for the substitute teacher and although this particular girl is here today, there are a few more who aren't. This, plus a few quick ejections leads one student to exclaim, "Man, there ain't many people here." On the other hand, educationally speaking, this is a farce. Homework correction is part of the everyday routine. I read out the answers and I might as well be reading them out on Van Ness Avenue – none of them are paying attention. But overall, progress has been made, believe it or not. I expect a setback tomorrow.

Meanwhile, I think I've more or less mastered the idea of what kind of notes to write on the overhead for the Algebra kids and I'm even helping a few of them with problems. They can start on their homework as soon as we're finished with the notes, which are based on the problems in the assigned section and these guys take full advantage of that.

Third day – to my battle station. First open the windows; the room is so hot it's got five fans. Then take today's Basic Math Warm-up from the big artist's pad on which Ms. J has written them and post it. Next, take down the transparencies from the hall windows where the student aides put them to dry after they've washed them. Finally review both math texts to see what notes I will write for the class.

My current take is that this school is right on the cusp, about at the level of Nathaniel Hawthorne. Maybe, I'd come back, maybe not. Long time to go and, as they always reminded you back in the Massachusetts House, there are no permanent friends and no permanent enemies in middle school. Yesterday's monster can be perfectly fine today, while yesterday's angel snarls. And never forget just how nasty kids can be.

Today is Progress Report day and the Counselor tells me he'll be coming around to fill in Ms. J's grades, but apparently she has only reported the failing grades, so he won't be coming to either of the Algebra classes, since nobody fails there. Before he arrives for sixth, Little Ms. Foul Mouth from Day One has yelled "Fuck ____ (something or other)" across the room, and I've told her to leave, and she's refused. I apprise him of the situation and ultimately we work out an agreement that she can stay if she doesn't do it again, which she doesn't. Meanwhile, he's here for a long time, which is that much less time I have them to myself. I've got one guy who's been just this side of getting thrown out each day who yells out "What the hell is something or other," which he repeats upon my request and the counselor takes him with. Our best day so far. At the end I tell them they're almost at the level they need to be.

And I finish the day in a tranquil island of Algebra Class where a girl who asks me for help is apologetic for asking for the second time. Wow, is that a change! But the throat grows raw and I fear that I may be but a germ away from silence.

Ms. J is black, and I really wonder how she feels about the fact that her two best classes – the Algebra classes – have not a single black student in them, but I'm sure I'll never speak with her about it. At least I can report a measure of equality on the racial front, though – the list of students I have ejected from class already includes black, white, Asian, and Latino.

So what shall today's tack be? For the small class second period, I think I need to learn to roll with these guys a little more. They're annoying, but that's to be expected – they're in middle school. They are ill-mannered, but, hey, this ain't the suburbs. I need to keep their habit of constantly interrupting from getting under my skin. Sixth period is a tougher question. I'll be lucky to have as good a day as yesterday and the kids are muttering that I should lay off the ones who are doing nothing but not being particularly disruptive because they say Ms. J lets them just put their heads down. I am certainly not going to second-guess her triage strategy, yet I do always come back to the idea that parents expect their children to be prodded. Meanwhile, the kids are muttering about anger management as I rage at them. The perennial subbing question: What's to be accepted, and what can be changed? I think that's the alcoholic's question, too, isn't it?

Third period has four ejections, including the TA. The first guy wouldn't sit in his seat because he said someone spit on it. Told him to clean it off; wouldn't; bye. The aide was grabbing something back and forth with another student. Aides are expected to be part of the solution, not part of the problem. Two down. Next two kids fighting over items of clothing – "He took mine first, etc." I told them to surrender said items; they wouldn't.

Sixth period, on the other hand, is almost reasonable – for here. Yesterday's little sweetheart appears to be getting a much needed rest at home and another walks out on his own, after I won't accede to his daily request to get an ice pack. About six of our boys confine their activities to continually interrupting to ask if they can go to the bathroom, soak their heads, or whatever – an activity I keep at bay only by continual threats to send them to the counselor. The rest of the students could actually be construed as a math class.

The day ends, as always, with the Silence of the Algebra Students. The only sound we hear is the whirring of the fans.

A ten day job is much like a ten round fight. As I start round five, I'm feeling pretty good about the bout, but I gotta remember that I'm in there with an opponent who could take me out at any time. There's now something of an equilibrium in sixth period. We've got about six guys who do nothing and the trick is keeping them quiet enough so that the ones who want to do something can. A recent Bob Herbert column in the *New York Times* mentioned how many people remember high school classes with the bunch of kids in the back who did nothing and what a disgrace it was that teachers let that happen. Like most people who discuss education with good intent, Herbert could use a little face time with the kids in the back of the room. What he remembers probably happened because the teachers felt the best they could get out of the situation was to neutralize these kids and work with the ones who didn't have to have their arms twisted. If you've got another teacher or aide to throw at these guys to twist their arms, you might be in business with them, but otherwise you've got to teach the readily teachable first. It took me a few days, but I've come to comprehend the equilibrium the regular teacher has settled at, not that I can necessarily achieve it, mind you. Herbert is right in the sense that this ought not to be happening, but wrong if he thinks the fault is the teacher's.

There's a kid in third period who comes with a full-time adult shadow and is quite a productive student, actually, when his shadow's there. Apparently he's been living in foster homes. He observes the Algebra class coming in today: "There's not a black man in this class."

In Algebra, I give the kids a wrong interpretation of how to determine the degree of a polynomial. Luckily, the kids are doing problems that have answers in the back of the book and they find answers that don't jive with what I've said, so I can correct it before too much damage is done. The notes I gave them were correct, it was only my interpretation of them that was wrong. But this is not the first time I have found myself being retaught a lesson – that I learned in high school, I think – in eighth grade math. I am impressed.

My car hasn't run since Saturday, so for my second Monday I am on the bus. The one I want to transfer to doesn't seem to stop at the Caltrans station any more, so I take a chance on another heading toward Fisherman's Wharf and I know it's the right one when I recognize and am recognized by some of my students. The horror! The bus is chock full of students shouting and smacking each other. My Friend the Evil Substitute Teacher used to say that middle school students fighting was like watching the Iran-Iraq War – you hoped they'd both lose. Will search for a middle school student-free route.

The next day Ms. J conveniently appears, in the company of a security woman, just as one girl is acting out so they just take her away. Ms. J wants to know how I'm holding up under the onslaught. I show her my ejection list, now up to fourteen ejections of thirteen different students, but I tell her I assume I'll compete the two weeks. She says this eighth grade has been this way since it was sixth grade and the elementary school principals told them that they were problems when they were coming in. I think of what My Friend the Evil Substitute Teacher always says: "There's no middle school problem that an outbreak of bubonic plague couldn't improve."

But wait, the counselor happens by during sixth period and is shocked by the silence, as am I, and I don't want to say anything to jinx it. Of course, Bob Herbert would not be happy to see the five boys who are doing absolutely nothing of any redeeming social value. Two of them are doing their nothing silently and the other three I try to tamp down before eventually ejecting one, a fairly charming kid, actually, who does mimicry and dancing – in class, unfortunately.

My second Wednesday will provide the definitive answer of whether Mateo will be a go or a no-go school in the future. The guy I threw out of second period yesterday comes in muttering things I assume to be generally uncomplimentary toward me that seem to have the thrust that he doesn't want to be here. We are able to come to a quick meeting of the minds on this and he won't be here. And then the counseling office calls and requests the presence of another one of God's little angels and so this period isn't so bad. However, there is the matter of the assembly that is announced over the loudspeaker during my first period prep and is entirely news to me. Apparently the eighth graders are supposed to go during third period – now this could be a challenge.

The period actually starts out all right. They're reasonably quiet and I get them lined up out in the hall and then I see Joey kick Katrina and tell him to go to the counselor. He refuses. I then tell all the kids to get back in the classroom. Half do and half run away, so I call the office and ask them to tell the counselor that I cannot bring this class to the assembly. The runaway half of the class filters back in and then the counselor and a security aide arrive and take Joey. He tells them, "But Katrina did such and such to me," so they take Katrina, too, which is all right. At the end of sixth period, a nice girl says, "You hate this class, don't you?" I respond with a "No comment," but she continues, "Ms. G say she hate this class. Mr. B say he hate this class. I hate this class, so you can hate this class."

The kids in seventh period Algebra start telling me that some of them won't be here tomorrow. I ask why and they tell me the school dance will be happening during sixth and seventh periods. Now I see I'm hoist on the petard of the bad-behavior/can't-go-to-the-dance list I've just given Mr. A, the guidance counselor – the sixth period guys will have to stay with me.

To answer my question: When will I come back to Mateo? After all the other subs working in San Francisco have completed their ten days here.

I see Mr. A on my way in on the day of the dance and tell him I've realized what a terrible mistake I've made in trying to exclude some of my little sixth period charges from the dance. He said that the same consideration had occurred to him and we agree that some of them were probably better at dancing than they are at math – they'd have to be. He told me he'd had to deal with five different kids from the basketball team yesterday and thought about calling the coach and telling him they shouldn't play, but that would make him the most unpopular man around here. (I think that perhaps he should have chosen to be that, but I'm not here full time and I know better than to second guess such things.) He did decide not to go to the game, because he just couldn't support them. He did go to the school concert last night though, because he did want to support those kids. Fortunate is the school without considerations such as these.

When I arrive in the classroom, I find a note from Ms. J who's been by to finish off the warm ups for the week. It says, in part, "Thanks for your commitment to this sub job. My hat is off to you." Someone knows, anyhow.

I eject a kid for the third day in a row in second period. It's the kid who pushed me two days ago, and I call security when he won't go. He convinces the security guy he'll be good, but I tell the guard that the kid's got to say it to me. He does and lives up to it. No third period ejections today, following yesterday's insanity.

The dance doesn't begin at the beginning of sixth period, so they're all sitting there in their seats for awhile and a girl from another class comes in and I tell her to leave and go back to her room, to which she replies, "No, motherfucker." I follow her down to her classroom and get her name from the sub who's there and start trying to reach Mr. A, who's naturally tied up with the dance. Eventually I write a note and have the only girl (out of four total) remaining in the class bring it to him. I've told him that as far as I'm concerned there should be immediate consequences and I've decided that if they're not to my satisfaction, I'm not finishing the job tomorrow.

After school, I hunt down Mr. A and ask if something's going to happen to that girl, because if not ... He says he prefers witnesses. I tell him there will be none and keep pushing the point that SOMETHING must happen, even if it is only a call to her mother. He says you should hear how the mother talks, so I tell him to give me her number and we'll curse at each other. He assures me something will happen. I keep pressing for "for instance"s before deciding I've done what I could.

The mutual contempt that has simmered these last two weeks in the basic math classes is bound to boil over on the last day. In second period I tell Tommy P to stop arm wrestling, or whatever he'll claim it is he's doing, and am greeted with, "You're an asshole." He leaves. I call Mr. A and a student picks up and says, "Mr. Asshole." I reach Mr. A via other means and he gets back to me to let me know that it was not little Tommy I spoke with, but some other mother's darling also sent to his office who decided to make himself useful by answering the phone. This will be hammer and tongs today.

I get a slight assistance from the gods when a fire drill materializes five minutes after I've called the office for ejection assistance, so I get to march said ejectee to the counselor. Plus we're down two pains because they started fighting in PE class the prior period. Still, we have young Seamus starts acting up and I tell him to leave and he won't go and gives me a "Suck my dick" for my troubles. So it's to the phone to Mr. A again – he's going to be as glad that Ms. J's back on Monday as I am – to have someone pick the boy up. I cannot, of course, repeat the boy's invitation within potential earshot of the class, so, sotto voce, with the phone extended into the hall I explain that the lad has extended an invitation to fellatio. After repeating the last word for him for clarification, he says, "You mean, 'Suck my dick'?" Affirmative.

Fourth period Algebra is, of course, another matter entirely. The class requires a tenth the psychic energy of the prior period and ten times as much learning occurs. For the tenth straight day I execute the plan Ms. J has left me, without a hitch. At the end of class, a girl even gives me a Christmas card that says it was fun to have me in class for two weeks. That girl received about two percent of the attention from me that some of the others did.

Much of sixth period is lost in the fog of combat. The foul-mouthed girl from day one decides to bookend her opening day performance and soon she and another nasty one whom I ejected before – but happily also has a bad attendance record – take off on their own. I report them gone and they return, at which point I call downstairs again. Up comes a party of three, the counselor, another guy, and a woman dressed like a gym teacher whom I assumed to be a security person I hadn't seen before but turns out to be the principal. She says she wants to talk to the class without me in the room, so I step out into the hall with the other guy who says he used to teach here but is now a nutritionist and a coach. He ruminates about the horrible level of behavior around us and mentions that he went to Catholic schools himself which I say we shouldn't even try to compare with the situation here.

The principal comes out and says the two girls will stay and that they'll be all right now. I don't like this. It's time for me to go. But there's less than two periods left and there's really nothing to be done at this point And who knows? Maybe she's even right.

She's not. On my best days in this class, I've ejected as many as need be and laid on a heavy enough hand to get everyone in their seats and quiet. On a good day, a majority of the those remaining were actually putting their pencils to paper. Today was not going to be one of those days and my little friend knows it and is up out of her seat, refusing to return and refusing to leave. I call downstairs again and get a return call from the principal, who asks me to put the girl on, which I do. When she gets off the phone, she starts up again. I call one more time and tell the secretary – with the phone extended out to the hall out of student earshot – that if someone doesn't get up here to get this kid I'm leaving. I give it another five minutes and when no one comes, I start packing up my bag. Half the class is up walking around at this point and I've decided that all I'm going to do for the remaining ten minutes is try to make sure that no blood is shed, so when a kid starts to put a pen in one of the fans, I stop that, but otherwise we simply wait out the bell, at which point I leave.

Two seventh period Algebra kids have come in the room before all the sixth period guys are out, so I shoo them back out into the hall, tell the other kids not to come in, lock the door and tell the secretary there's a class waiting in the hall, while I'm boiling over to her about not being backed up and simultaneously apologizing for my agitation which has nothing to do with her. And then, as I'm only inching my way out due to my reluctance to leave under these circumstances, I look back and see the person I'm really looking for – the principal.

We immediately enter into high-level hostility and she quickly moves us into her office where we can even turn it up a notch. She tells me that we don't do things like that here. I tell her she that when she left that kid in the classroom she let her know that she could get away with anything. She tells me I told the kids to shut up, which only inflames them. Teachers told her they heard me. I tell her that, yes, I lost my temper – I told them to shut up once when there were four kids in the room and it was after a girl had given me a "No, motherfucker." She tells me that she told the girl to come down when she spoke to her on the phone and was on her way up until she got caught up in another situation. And if I leave I'll never get another assignment in the district. I tell her I don't care.

Suddenly we understand that we've both spent our anger and I say, all right, I'll do the last class, it's a nice class. And we actually smile for a moment. Since it's Algebra class, they're still standing there in the hall and we head inside and conduct a class as if everything was normal, although they obviously know it isn't. There's one last call from Mr. A, seeking clarification on just who the "No, motherfucker" girl was. Apparently the principal had called him on it and thought I was speaking of the girl she failed to eject. I take this opportunity to thank him for his support.

So as the final bell rings the tenth round to a close, I am on my feet, heading to my corner, waiting for the referee to announce the decision.

I walk out with the long-term sub in the room next door whom I've talked to occasionally. He figured I was making an emergency bathroom run after sixth period. My actual departure is not so quick. I have to make two trips back to the office to page the owner of the car that's blocking me and another teacher in. When I see the principal now, we're not smiling any more, just nodding.

A couple of hours later, the landlord's son starts on his electronic keyboard in the laundry room next to my apartment. It's fairly loud, but not really a big deal and I've never complained. Then he starts doing a little rapping, as he and his friends usually do and soon there's a drone of "the mother-fucking" this and the "the mother-fucking" that, and I go next door and explain that I've been dealing with a bunch of rude children for the past two weeks and I just can't take any more "mother fuckers" today. By the morning, my voice will be gone.

But I sure got a thorough refresher course on life in a tough school. The problems just feed on themselves. Everything is harder. There's just more tension between everyone. You could see it reflected in the fact that the teachers union core of activists was disproportionately made up of teachers from the "better" schools, where everyday education was not so difficult. Nothing was fun at Mateo. I didn't even note any students with unusual names, as I usually do. But it was a record-setting experience, as well. Since I'd kept a list of kids who shouldn't be allowed to go to the dance for the counselor, I know that my two weeks at Mateo set the following new personal records:

Ejections in a Single Period – 7
Individual Students Ejected Over an Extended Period – 16
Total Ejections Over an Extended Period – Exact number unknown, but without any doubt a new record.

A DREAM? – *Science, Cappuccino High, December 15, 2003*

When I arrive in the office the teacher is there with fully typed out plans that include two or three student assistants per class. He offers me a cookie on our way to his classroom and then gives me a tangerine. Students introduce themselves; some shake my hand; they offer to take attendance. I'm now wondering if maybe I actually expired in an apoplectic fit set off by the Motherfucking Mantra in the laundry room Friday afternoon and I'm now in the place where good substitute teachers go.

A couple of education articles I read over the weekend stuck with me. A Richmond public school teacher described teaching in the Bay Area's poorest system where kids' lives are such that many of them have never seen the ocean and you spend most of your time simply trying to get them to the point of being able to teach them. That article should get more circulation. Bob Herbert, for one, should see it.

Unfortunately, he's more likely to see the one in *The Nation*, by a journalist who didn't appear to have spent much time in classrooms like the ones the Richmond teacher wrote about. Citing education professors who didn't appear to have spent much time in such classrooms either, the author bemoaned the increased number of school suspensions and the disproportionate number going to black students, all of which he generally attributed to the pressures of teaching to increasingly standardized tests. Now I'm sure it's ultimately a good thing that Ed School professors are paying attention to the problems of maintaining order in the classroom, and there's certainly a lot to be said about over-reliance on standardized testing, and there should be other options for the kids removed from classrooms, but the writer seemed pretty well unfamiliar with the difficulty of teaching anything at all in a disrupted classroom.

Instead, he wrote of studies showing kids suspended from school were more likely to wind up getting arrested and going to jail than other kids, which would draw a "Well, duh!" from anyone who's spent any time in city schools. The professors seemed to think that capping the number of suspensions and meting them out proportionally to a school's racial make-up would improve things. The basic fact that kids are removed from classrooms primarily to improve the odds of a teacher reaching the remaining students did not seem to occur to the *Nation* writer.

I will admit to a personal edge in this: When I sent *The Nation* an article on John Ogbu, they declined to run it, saying they had a number of education pieces already coming – and this is what they print!

But back here in South City the kids are just fine today in all classes. My main problem, actually, is remembering that I can, and am expected to enforce a much higher standard of behavior here. The guy the teacher pointed out as my potential problem of the day is so benign that he would have been a model student in the three basic math classes I had last week. Of course, he is four years older – a senior in a class of freshman, I'm told. I don't raise my voice once today.
Student Name of the Day: Robydoll Wolfert

***CAKE**– First Grade, Woody Guthrie Elementary, December 19, 2003*
Toughest part of my day was cutting the cake for the class holiday party. Read a book called *Santa Claus Gets the Sniffles* (or something like that) while the

class listened on the rug. My demand sheet shows thirteen days working in San Francisco this pay period and this was the first enjoyable one. And during this period various friends of mine have been treated to rants about *The Nation's* lame article on education.

GOODBYE, NIGGER – Health/Science, Cucamonga Middle, January 13, 2004

When a girl asks, "Do you like teaching." I attempt some clever reply about the tenuous relationship between subbing and teaching, but she's already no longer listening by the time I get to the end – the attention span of mayflies. If you want to do one-liner stand-up comedy in middle school, you've got to be *really* quick. One guy asks if I graduated from high school. I tell him he can pretty much assume that anyone who comes into the classroom has graduated from high school, but he says there might be phoney teachers – maybe he figured he might catch me off guard. Only the last period is any real problem. It's got lovely Dianne, whom I've thrown out before. She starts again and she's gone in about ten minutes, with a "Goodbye, nigger" on her way out. She's Latina, so you figure it out.

THINK YOU'VE GOT IT BAD? – Math/Science, Citadel Middle, January 20, 2004

A couple of kids tell me that their teacher can't teach. I speak with him on the phone a number of times during the day and I'd say that the jury is out on the question. The board says, "A negative exponent means the number is in the wrong part of the equation." What does that mean? At one point I hear a kid say, "He scares me," referring to me. Music to a sub's ears.

At the end of the day, I run into Mr. S and Y and impassioned discussion ensues. Y is still going to all of the SF middle schools that I no longer go to, so he is somewhat crazed. He thinks the current district administration is a sham that plays the race card while making little or no improvement in the actual education of black kids. Thinks money is misspent on various consultants, advisors, and computers rather than classroom personnel. Says the principals are rated upon the number of suspensions they mete out – the fewer, the better – so some of them do it off the books. Must find out more about this. Mr. S tells a passing teacher, "I'm just hearing how lucky we are here."
Student Name of the Day: Max Bizarro

BASICS – Social Studies, Cucamonga Middle, January 22, 2004

A kid tells me he thinks there's a typo in their worksheet because it asks what African country Cairo is the capital of and he knows Cairo's the capital of Egypt which, of course, is certainly not in Africa. Just Monday night, my friend J told me that, prompted by the fact that his wife is planning a trip to Ireland and Scotland, he was moved to look at a map and discovered for the first time that Scotland and England were connected. As they say, "War is God's way of teaching Americans geography" and we have not been at war with Egypt or Scotland for a while.

The demand for bathroom passes runs high in fourth period, so I have the kids fill out their own. One girl say's "It's 11:33, right?" I look. It's 11:38. "A little trouble telling time?" I ask. She says, "I don't like those clocks," which means clocks with hands.
Student Name of the Day: Cherish Meredith

RACE, GENDER, CLASS– *Special Ed, Appian Way High, January 27, 2004*
I am a rover today, replacing a bunch of Special Day Program teachers (and one Resource Room) while they go to IEP meetings. The first period Economics text (Globe-Fearon, Pearson Learning Group) adds to the usual three forces of production – labor, capital, and natural resources – entrepreneurs, who get three paragraphs to one for each of the others. "During the twentieth century, entrepreneurs changed the way most Americans lived." We read of Walt Disney, Steve Jobs, and Steve Wozniak. I give the (young) teacher my opinion on the book. She says she's never taught economics before and she's one chapter ahead of them, but she does know about the history books and they're the history of what white males did. (I'd say her combination of perceptions – critical on race and gender and neutral on class is pretty common out there, in fact it's pretty much like reading the *San Francisco Chronicle*.) I say that they probably gave the system these books for free and she says, no they actually spent a lot of money, which of course is actually what I would assume.

A LEGEND– *Math/Science, Freeway Limits Middle, January 30, 2004*
Note from teacher: "Please make a list of absent students, my roosters are being updated." And who's looking after the hens, I wonder? After lunch, a kid comes in and says, "Did you take a student's shoe, once?" Hey, better than not being remembered at all, I figure.

WITH PRACTICE– *Math, Cucamonga Middle, February 2, 2004*
Students are claiming they're allowed to use their notes for quizzes but I explain that unless the teacher leaves specific instructions I feel I have no choice but to say no. But during third period, the regular teacher in that room (I'm in three over the course of the day) calls the one I'm replacing who says the kids were right. She hadn't mentioned letting them use their notes because she wasn't used to leaving instructions – apparently her first absence of the year. So it seems that, as with most things, a teacher gets better at being absent with practice. I guess you really want to sub for the ones who do it a lot.

MAN BITES DOG STORY– *Math/Science, Freeway Limits Middle, February 9, 2004*
A note on the board from the teacher says students must sit in their assigned seats and behave. The kids say she only wrote that because the last sub just looked at papers in the front of the room and let them run around and they got into trouble. In other words, they think the last sub wasn't strict enough!

A FIGHT *– Science, Citadel Middle, February 12, 2004*
A couple of boys complain that another one is annoying. I try explaining that if we were to get rid of all the middle school kids who were annoying, they'd have no friends. And then we have a fight! In class! But as My Friend the Evil Substitute Teacher always says, the up side of kids fighting is that it's the one time that you may actually get to lay hands on them.

SCHOOL FOR ME *– English Language Development, Cucamonga Middle, February 18, 2004*
I myself went to Beer School last night at the Twenty-first Amendment brewery pub. Class was good, but for some reason the teachers stopped making sense after about half an hour – it was a strong ale class. As I was doing some tossing and turning this morning after the first calls started coming in, it hit me that what I imagined getting an education degree would be like was going to traffic school – for an entire year! One course on signage, a semester of lane usage, etc. Of course, California has comedy traffic schools (really!) Now if someone would open up a comedy education school ...

THE WAY *– Economics/History, Ralph Bunche High, February 24, 2004*

>Poster found all over the school:
>**The Ralph Bunche Way**
>I am responsible.
>I am safe.
>I am prepared.

This is never a good sign. When you have to continually assert that such things are true, it's obviously because they're not and as I'm checking the mail box in the teachers' room I hear one informing another about the fights she missed yesterday when she was absent. All of the wall clocks are wrong here. My room has a second clock for real time. Last period has 16 out of 30 absent; for the last twenty minutes a loud, very unpleasant girl tells whomever's listening about the fight she had with some boy and what her mother said to his mother and "fucking with that bitch," and so forth. A small wraith-like white woman comes in and asks to talk with her. She refuses; the woman leaves and that's the end of that. The class turns in no work.
Student Name of the Day: Aloha Galimba

AMO, AMAS, AMAT *– Spanish, Appian Way High, March 2, 2004*
The first day I'm here the teacher's grandfather has died suddenly. Understandably there's not a lesson plan, so it's a video day. But when I return three days later, there's still nothing but a note from a sub from one of the intervening days saying he continued showing the video of *Finding Nemo* (chosen because it had Spanish available). I call the office and the secretary confirms that he has never sent anything in. I tell her that I consider this a recipe for chaos and

that I probably wouldn't have taken the job had I known it would be more of this. She says that she also doesn't think this is right and will contact the department chairman and see if anyone can come up with anything.

Eventually a French teacher brings two-sided pictures with an exercise of making up a profile of the person depicted. So we'll have them write for half the period and present for the second half. I make up my own assignment the following day, asking them to describe their school, its students, each of their classes; the last book they read (?), and the last movie they saw. The best I can say is that many of them work at it – and it's better than cartoons, anyhow.

These kids don't seem to know much, though. The first day a girl comes in and writes, "I love myself" on the board. I ask, "Shouldn't you write that in Spanish?" So she writes "Yo me amor." Another asks how to say "they are" and I have to find her the conjugation of the verb "ser" in the book. This is March! Somehow I suspect a connection between how little they know and the fact that they were assigned to watch cartoons in the teacher's absence. According to the students, they can listen to the radio, check their email, eat, and cook on the microwave in class. And I don't doubt them. After all, they must be doing something when they're not learning Spanish. After seeing these classes for the better part of a week, I'd say we're safe from any sudden outburst of bilingualism in America.

Embarrassing Substitute Teacher Moment of the Day: R, a sub I've seen around South City for years – who has never claimed to be particularly smart – asks at lunch, "Are somosas those things with graham crackers and marshmallows?" Someone kindly explains to him that those are s'mores.

Student Names of the Day – Lace Alvarez, Diploma Faleta

ZIPPED UP TIGHT – Health/History, Appian Way High, March 19, 2004

The final period of the day has a guest speaker on abstinence – a woman in her seventies talking about natural family planning. The teacher's notes tell me: "This freshman class very immature with a few smart mouths ... Do Not Hesitate to Boot Out Any Problems," which directions I announce to them.

The speaker sets up an array of posters on the whiteboard ledge:

"Sex is like driving. You need a license for both."
"Do the right thing. Wait for the ring."
"Sex Tips for a safe date. Keep all of your clothes all of the way on all of the time. Don't let any part of anyone else's body get between you and your clothes. Avoid arousal."
"The safest birth control is self control."

And so on.

Next a video with abstinence speakers combined with warnings about STD's and the like. *Two virgins are like two pieces of virgin scotch tape; they stick together much better than used tape* – and on and on.

Finishes with a flourish, reciting a poem starting with "Keep those zippers zipped up tight."

Oooee! Through it all I defend to the death her right to say it, do my part to enforce discipline and generally perform my police duties.
Student Name of the Day: Babyleen Saballa

6 AM I *– RSP, Appian Way High, March 24, 2004*

I'm looking for instructions when a para I've worked with several times in the past arrives with them. She says the teacher called her at 6:00 this morning and she's bent out of shape about being called then – in the friendliest of ways, mind you – seemingly oblivious to the fact that she's bemoaning this to one who sleeps with his phone and dials (pushes buttons, actually) in the dark.

Our instructions here are pretty unclear, so the para calls the teacher and puts me on. The third period, she explains, had a test on *Macbeth* yesterday and they have the option of retaking it as a group, if everyone wishes to do so. I can't say that I understand this, but this is special ed. Also another teacher should be in to talk about senior exit project essays.

The aide and I go looking for said teacher but can't find her and the aide goes off to print out the answers from the midterms. She returns saying she just saw the other teacher in question, but somehow didn't find out if she's actually coming here. But anyhow, right now she's hungry and wants to know if I'd like half her bagel. Then she finds out her bagel hasn't been cut! So she's off to get her bagel cut and go look in the teacher's box for more essays, which she also didn't manage to do the last time she was out.

After the third period announcements – during which the aide talks to students continuously – I attempt to carry out the planned group test operation, but it rapidly falls of its own weight, as questions reveal it makes no sense to the students or the aide – and it certainly never made any sense to me.

So then it's on to reading *Macbeth*, following along to a tape. The aide mentions that she's never read it. After class I suggest she should but she says she probably wouldn't understand it. I point out that the edition we've been reading has a modern language translation on facing pages. She hadn't noticed that. Did I mention she was woken at 6? Not everyone is cut out for this work, you know.

Last night I saw a black woman on TV talking about the poor state of health care in the black community, the lack of black doctors, blacks not being as well educated, etc. She says, "We've got kids with shoes that light up when they walk and minds that shut down when they talk." Today I've got a guy lacing up a humongous pair of new Nikes that he tells another guy cost $100. Later he tells a story having something to do with his shoes being stolen: "They can take the money, but not my shoes." He's supposed to finish a midterm exam from yesterday but says he doesn't have a pencil. A $100 pair of shoes and no pencil.
Student Name of the Day: Czarina Maliwat

SEVEN INTO SIX *– Basic Math, Cucamonga Middle, March 31, 2004*

Basic Math generally means the math will be easy and the students won't. The first class is barely in as a girl is telling me, "You're going to hate this class," and the fire alarm goes off. Well that cuts down the time for enmity to build, anyhow. In a later class a student says, "He (the regular teacher) doesn't teach us very well." I would greet that remark with skepticism if the teacher hadn't left me seating charts – that he specifically told me to use – showing seven rows when the classroom is set up with only six. You worry when the math teacher displays difficulty with the single digit numbers.

COOL DUDS– *Social Studies, Cucamonga Middle, April 2, 2004*
        School wide assemblies today, watching a production called "Quest for Success," on three screens:
Don't – do drugs.
Do – play sports, even if you only have one leg.
Remember – Dr. Martin Luther King.
        I gotta think there's a better use for the money spent on this. Afterwards, a girl comes in with worksheets on the presentation that I'm supposed to go over with the classes. Seventh graders are called upon to rate the technicians' grooming and such.

JUST OKAY– *ESL Language Arts/Science/(Regular) Language Arts/Social Studies, Waterfront Middle, April 6, 2004*
        A teacher grabbed me on my way out of here yesterday and asked if I'd take her classes today. She said subs didn't seem to hate them, she has a couple of pains, but she'll pre-write the referrals, etc., so I took the job. However, when I checked the machine after midnight it wasn't there. The standard rules of engagement say that I shouldn't come without a job number, but there being no South San Francisco option today, I figured I'd go for it anyhow.
        As expected, my name is not on the sub list at the school and after a few minutes of waiting for the harried secretary's attention, the regular teacher is on the phone. She is apparently also on the phone with the sub office and starts talking to them as I listen: she hadn't realized that she needed to ... and that she couldn't ... and so forth. But the secretary promises that I'll get paid, a kid gives me a key for the wrong room, after which the secretary gives me the key for the right room and off I go.
        This teacher has left five specific categories in which to grade her classes which I reprint below to give the reader a reference point on the day of a sub:
1. *Excellent: Everyone was really quiet and worked really hard without even needing to be reminded.*
2. *Good: Most of the class was quiet and worked hard with only one or two reminders.*
3. *Just Okay: The class had to be reminded several times to be quiet and work. Once reminded, they were quiet.*
4. *Poor: The class had to be reminded many times to be quiet and work, even then they weren't all working.*
5. *No matter how many times I asked, the class wouldn't quiet down and work.*

        I give first period a 4; second – 3.5; third – 3; sixth – 5; seventh – 5. In other words, "Just Okay" was the highlight of the day. And this wasn't all that bad a day. I leave a note for the teacher explaining that I would not necessarily have rated the students that low in the context of what a sub sees on a daily basis – but she asked.

BON VOYAGE – *Resource Specialist, Pamplona Elementary, April 7, 2004*
Perhaps the most frightening task a sub can be assigned is after school bus duty. Don't let them run under a bus, or let some guy who looks like he's out of an R. Crumb cartoon give them candy or anything, sure – but after that I'm shaky. How do I really know if they all got on the right bus? But generally I'm not around the next day to hear if one of them turned up missing.

My Friend the Evil Substitute Teacher loves bus duty, but then you knew that.

THE OTHER SIDE OF TOWN – *Kindergarten, Benjamin Banneker Elementary, April 8, 2004*
Quite the different neighborhood here than up at Pamplona yesterday. A sign on the wall says: *Dr. Benjamin Banneker Elementary School Celebrates Days of NON-DESTRUCTIVE Language* and Janet, the teacher I partnered with when I taught second grade math in summer school, says that she caught a guy who had broken into her car and was putting her CDs into his pack and just kept on doing it and everyone in the neighborhood seemed to know the guy, who was apparently not a kid. Another guy comes in later and says that guy had dug up his rosebushes and sold them. Junkie, I assume.

BEYOND BRUTAL – *Language Arts/Social Studies, William Howard Taft Middle, April 9, 2004*
The regular teacher's note is quite frank: "These guys will abuse you if they can – Call x3103 and ask Mr. L [the head counselor] for help."

A girl tells the boy who's taking first period attendance, "I'll knock your teeth out," so she's ejected before we've even got a count. But when I call counseling to tell them she's enroute, the counselor who answers says the student isn't hers – although the sheet the teacher left says she is – and gives the name of another counselor who's name isn't even on my list. At least there are clear instructions written on the wall here regarding bathroom and water fountain passes, though – none. The ejected returns for second period, but by the end I've thrown her out again, this time for standing up and mouthing off.

At the end of this two-period block, a teacher who'd sent a student to borrow a cd player returns it herself after class and says, "Wait until you see your next class." "Brutal?" "Beyond." Oh boy. Suffice it to say that we have multiple ejections, unauthorized returns of ejectees to class, and a personal visit from the counselor.

I run into Nancy M and notice a mark by her nose. She explains that a student literally ran into her and broke her nose, but the principal won't allow as how the kid could have been running, presumably because that would look bad. I congratulate her on the return of her student newspaper which I'd read about in the *Chronicle*. She said that (School Superintendent) Ackerman had to call the principal up and tell her to do it.

KILLER VIDEO – *Metal Shop, Freeway Limits Middle, April 14, 2004*

The shop teacher is in the library for some kind of meeting all day. When I ask him if second period has to take notes on the safety video they have to watch, he says, no, we'll just bore them to death. Pops in after class and says, "That video's a killer, ain't it?"

STUPID – *Social Studies/Computers, Cucamonga Middle, April 19, 2004*

I'll be here a lot the next month – too much? I ask the girl I discussed the war with last year what she thinks of the President's war now. She says, "It's stupid. Everyone knows it's stupid." I thank her.

A math teacher I cover for offers a five percent upgrade in math grade for a purchase at the school's Roundtable Pizza Night this Thursday (receipt required).

When the biggest pain-in-the-ass of one particular class asks if he can go to the bathroom and then asks why not, I tell him it's because he's a pain. He seems to understand – as opposed to when I tell them they're nuisances. Enough with the vocabulary-building in middle school, I guess. But then I find that very word "nuisance" on a spelling/vocabulary test I am to give to a couple of classes, so now many students previously unable to name their essential characteristic should now be able to do so. Of course, they'd have to be paying attention.

And I confiscate a whoopee cushion. Kind of surprised to see they're still around. Makes me want to run out and buy a copy of *Mad Magazine* for old time's sake. Anyhow, this one says it produces a Bronx cheer so I tell them I should get to keep it seeing as how I'm from the Bronx. Well, they don't want to believe that because they don't expect me to be coming from "the ghetto." I assure them I am.

Examples of "Personal Timelines" assignments are posted on the bulletin board in one classroom. One girl tells us that in 1990, she was born; she was "bathized" later that year; in 1996, Selena died; and on September 11, 2001, "terrisom" happened in New York.

OUTMATCHED – *Unknown Grade, Harriet Tubman Elementary, May 5, 2004*

This is a Fillmore District school I've never been to before. It was supposed to be a resource room job, but apparently the teacher hadn't changed her sub tape when she left that job. Anyhow, in the office they tell me this class is so difficult they usually assign two subs to it and one was already in there.

We're supposed to read a book to the kids and then have them write about what they heard. The other sub is southeast Asian, I would say, and he asks if I will read the book because of his accent. This I gladly do, as animated reading is one of my (few) talents relevant to this age group. They choose *I Have a Hippopotamus*. During the reading they're not so bad; during the writing they're not so good. There's a regular aide here and also a one-on-one aide. And for a while, we've got another substitute in as well – five adults and there are moments when we can't manage eighteen kids. And after lunch, the first aide tells me that two of the kids are in the principal's office, so I shouldn't worry about missing two of the twenty. I wasn't worrying, actually; I didn't realize I was supposed to have twenty. Another thing I didn't know was what grade these kids were. First, second – I never did find out.

At one point when the five of us were outmatched, the principal dropped in for a look-see. Afterwards a woman who called herself a counselor, something I did not think existed in elementary school, came by for a couple of stints. Well, she was from another planet. She could start Simon Says-ing them and getting them to do things the other guy and I never could. She was way better than the five of us put together and I told her, "I wish I could do that." She explained that her father was a counselor at Pizarro High School for thirty years and just had this look that could go right through you, so she learned it from him.

The noteworthy thing is that this was actually a nice bunch of kids, on the whole. They just had a lot of problems learning.

MORE HOOPS – *Drama/Math/Science, Citadel Middle, May 13, 2004*
When I see a girl in home room reading *Trainspotting*, I think of the South San Francisco teacher/coach saying that South San Francisco was basically a conservative community and how he got flak for assigning *Catcher in the Rye* years ago. I ask this girl if her parents knew she was reading it and she said they did. A science class has to read a couple of sections from their Teen Health book about nutrition, so I ask if anyone's heard of *Super Size Me*, the documentary about the guy who ate nothing but McDonalds food for thirty days. One boy is able to give an excellent summation. I wonder if any of the kids in South City could.

Have I mentioned (recently enough) how annoying it is to have phone calls come in during class? I time it today and I've received five phone calls in the first twenty-four minutes of second period.

I meet a student teacher who's my age, or something like that, hurrying to get her credential before the No Child Left Behind law adds more requirements. Speaking of the overall experience, she uses the standard phrase, "They make you jump through a lot of hoops." (I wonder if maybe they even have to take a course rationalizing why education courses are so pointless – the Contemporary Relevance of Irrelevance in Urban Education, or something like that – where they learn the "jumping through hoops" concept.) She mentions the acquaintance in ed school who made her living as a webmaster but nevertheless had to take the website design class, and such. I engage in these conversations to confirm the wisdom of my remaining permanent-credential-free, I guess.

CHEWING GUM! – *Math/Science, Citadel Middle, May 17, 2004*
Back for an entire week replacing a teacher who's with the class trip to Yosemite. Middle school kids, 24/7. Can't say I envy him that. But as I'm making 99 copies of a few handouts during my first period prep, another copyroom teacher grimaces when I tell her whom I'm in for. "You're going to earn your money." Indeed, in fourth period we have chewing gum on my chair! Right out of

Katzenjammer Kids or something. Don't know that I've actually seen it before. Fifth period is supposed to be the prize. Enough arrive late that I halt them by the door until I can get their names down. Waving a stack of referrals, I explain the no-pass and conference-with-your-parents-if-you-get-thrown-out policies. The two kids indicated as the top problems immediately back up the scouting report. I fill out advance referrals on them as time allows and let them know it. When one walks over the edge, I call for an escort to counseling, as per teacher's instruction. The head counselor arrives himself and decides he'll stay and we have good order.

The next day, the two stars from yesterday are okay for awhile, but one eventually starts to blurting out and I call the office when it gets to outbursts like, "Your nipples are erect." Meanwhile the other guy's now on the floor. The head counselor returns and takes these lovely children away; says he'll be calling home. Amazing how pleasant the class feels after they're gone. There are kids actually interested.

The third day, a girl comes in during lunch to ask if she can put her backpack down and says, "I'm so sorry I was mean. Today I'm going to be an excellent student." Wow! Of course I have to move her within the first five minutes after the bell. A seventh grader's resolve can be a fragile thing.

Later one of our stars from the previous days starts making noises that he probably thinks are within the bounds of what he's going to get away with. But I call the bullpen real quick today, at which point we get: "You suck. You suck big. I masturbate. I masturbate seven times a day. Sometimes it bleeds." And so forth. I suggest suspension when the counselor arrives.

The regular teacher calls in and we're discussing how yesterday went and whether I've been able to locate a book I need until I realize I'm talking to myself. Cell phone coverage not that good in Yosemite. Guess I'm on my own here.

I run into Y on my way out and he tells me he thinks my class is an example of the problems with tenure. He knows the teacher and thinks the guy thinks he's better than teaching. The following day, the principal is very solicitous as to whether there were instructions for me. Seems to me he thinks there might be an issue here too. Our disturbed child returns for fifth period and gets ejected again – a perfect four for four and a walk – when you count the period the counselor spent in class. I think this guy may have the highest average yet recorded – the Ty Cobb of my subbing career. Spitting paper, chewing gum, throwing work on floor, shouting out curses in English and Spanish – he does it all. It'll be good to be out of here.

When I get to the office to turn in my key at the end of the day, he's there with the AP who had come to get him today. The AP shows me what he has written under continual prodding as he sat on the bench outside the counselor's office. It goes on in basically literate fashion about how he wouldn't want to be the teacher who had him in class during fifth period today.

This whole subbing business can be quite another thing when you get an assignment of more than a couple of days. So tonight I can't help but think seriously about the week. I have tried to maintain the maximum educational edge I could, simultaneously silencing the unruly and prodding the silent to speak;

throwing out kids and writing referrals in class; giving the kids who were into it a chance to shine; demanding the attention of the dawdling; getting the kids who don't raise their hands to answer; and looking for any chance to bring the recalcitrant back. In short, I have tried to make the good fight.

Over the weekend, I gave my friend Rebecca B, who hasn't lived in the country for a quite a while, a long description of the schools as I've seen them. To give her a sense of the racial situation, I estimated that if ten percent of the other kids at Cucamonga, where I've been so much lately, are behavior problems, fifty percent of the black kids are.

***RETARTED**– Science, Freeway Limits Middle, May 25, 2004*

Here for one science class yesterday and a different one today. The secretary says yesterday's sub called in for help during sixth period and is not back today. Sure enough, here's a note from her explaining that "the students were just out of control. They were loud, unruly, etc. ... How do you do it? 2 of 3 experiences (at Freeway) have been unfavorable."

Two light bulbs out in this classroom. This school is always like this. I realize I don't even know who the principal is. No seating chart and no class schedule – not even on the wall. And they announce that there will be an assembly, a fire drill, and an earthquake drill. They say bring your roll book. Well, I don't have a roll book. Then there's a fire alarm during break, but it turns out to be a false false alarm, which is to say a student did it, which fact is announced over the loudspeaker. And it appears that I'm supposed to take the kids to a third period assembly for a band concert, which I couldn't hear when it was announced because I was yelling at them to be quiet.

During the assembly, an aide introduces herself and says she's with me for sixth period — which is when the drills will be. An RSP teacher also stops by and says she'll come in for sixth too and that I can send any acter-outers to her, for which I am grateful. In the time remaining in this period we go back and continue watching *Pay It Forward* and the girls debate whether Helen Hunt's character is a waitress or a hooker.

Both other adults show up for sixth period. I tell the aide of my impressions of disorganization around here and she says, "Yeah, it is kind of like a ghetto school here." But I appear to impress them with the ferocity of my approach: Kids are coming in saying, "Oh good, we've got a sub" and starting in to screaming and I start threatening ejections even before the bell has rung. The other teacher says, "Good job;" the aide said the new AP was going to come down (I learned that the assistant principal who thought this was a good school has been replaced by a stricter one, by mutual agreement – he wasn't tough enough on the students) but she'd tell him he wouldn't need to. And with all the adults, cramming the students under desks and running them out to the yard for the emergency drills really isn't so hard as it might have been. The only problem now is that they may want me to come back.

And indeed, I do return the next day, when the secretary gives me a schedule, which she allows is old and therefore has lunch at the wrong time, and sends me to an empty classroom. Apparently she has given me the wrong out-of-date schedule – I'm supposed to be in the room next door.

Fifth period is sufficiently loud and annoying that I keep them into lunchtime. If I were to tell them that this hurts me more than it does them, it would be without trace of even venial sin-level lying. (Of course, I wouldn't say something like that to them for fear it would encourage them.) And speaking of food, I see the same pies and cookies have been sitting out in the faculty room all week.

Question on today's health worksheet: "What problems might a teen who uses alcohol or drugs face at school?" One student's answer: "might look retarded."

Student Names of the Day – Trucker S. Gopez, Queen Mulipola

*****

GOD'S WILL BE DONE – *Art, Audre Lorde Liberty Academy, September 20, 2004*
  Fourth week of school, but first day for me. Was working on a political campaign, but eased out by mutual agreement and now am once again what God intended – a full time substitute teacher.
  Time and location are wrong on the recording, so when I arrive there's someone else covering. It's Matt, whom I know from the union Executive Board, who's the "head teacher" here. The school has only freshman and sophomores because it's in the first month of its second year (and first at this ominous location – the Gregor Mendel Middle School building. Last year it was at San Francisco State, where the machine tried to send me) and they've put everything into classroom teaching, e.g., no principal.
  By my second day of this assignment, I hate to say it but this school looks like it could use a principal. This teacher has left me crap. I'm scrambling around to find rulers and paper for their project. According to the class – which seems credible on this question – the teacher lets them listen to the radio, so I get to hear a girl rapping a song called *Cameltoe*.
  Today's work involves using a ruler to make one inch borders and marking off eighths of an inch. The teacher's instructions say she's pretty sure they won't know how to use rulers. And in fact there aren't many who can figure out eighths of an inch and there is one guy who really can't use it at all. (Yes, if you're checking the heading, this is high school.)
  They also need to draw twenty or more circles using a dime. One of the black kids *tells* me to give him a dime and I won't. The Chinese kid next to him *asks* for one and I give it to him. So the first guy asks why won't I give it to him and I tell him that when he's polite I will. His response is: "Give me a freaking dime," and I refuse again. He says, "It's because I'm black," with a smile. I reply, "It's because you're rude."
  On my way out, I tell Matt the school's location and starting time need to be changed on the tape and that the teacher I replaced perhaps got stuck in the middle of her plans for setting me up. I do want this place to succeed. He appears genuinely appreciative.

COULD YOU PLEASE STEP OUT ON THE BLACKTOP – *English, Ralph Bunche High, September 23, 2004*
  Never my favorite place to go, but somehow never bad enough to not return. I arrive at 7:40. The office clock says 9:05. The newspaper has a story about a recent riot at this school that was being reviewed at last night's Police Commission hearing. Eventually I'm sent to a Reading Class from which it appears the teacher has been absent all week. At 8:00, the clock here reads 7:20. Everything here is wrong in its separate way.
  First period only has eight kids who already know what to do and seven of them are doing it and all of them are quiet. So far, so good. There are student-made posters on reading topics in the back of the room, including one that reads, "Choose a book by its cover" with an illustration of a book whose cover reads, *Let's Get It Crackin Pimpin'*.

And, oh, these are double periods which will make it much tougher. Second is not starting out promising – more roaming around, more sitting on the window sill and talking out the window, etc. By the end of advisory, when I've now had the same kids for more than two hours, one kid is coming in and out of the classroom, so I decide I'll call one of the numbers that my instruction sheet says to call. The first turns out to be the nurse; the second gets a recording of a secretary who says she'll be back in August.

The note on the third and fourth period group says they will be rowdy. One guy comes in and knocks over a chair and starts singing a song about "fucking" something. I invite him to leave; he does. And, oh no, I've got another kid from those horror classes at Mateo Middle School. (I had one at Audre Lorde, too, but as My Friend the Evil Substitute Teacher always says, they've got to go somewhere for a few years before jail.) This one is an extremely immature pain-in-the-ass named Joey.

So in a few minutes the class settles into a pattern: eight Asian kids all of whom are all working, with the exception of Joey; one black girl, who is working; and six black boys in the back who are not (plus the one ejected). The story of urban education. One of the guys starts on the gotta-go-to-the bathroom stuff (she left specific instructions against bathroom passes) and just walks out saying he'll get a pass. I follow him to the door and say within earshot of two adults that he's out without permission and will need a pass to get back. He comes back without one and says the dean told him to return. I tell him to leave and call the office. The dean comes and tells him to stay in class. I tell the dean the kid's been mouthing off since he came back in and he's going to get away with that? He takes him away. Another two guys then bop in. There are two adults in the hall outside: a female security aide who doesn't look like she's planning to do a lot of anything on her own and the maintenance man who's been in before to deliver a couple of tables and acts like the guy who's actually in charge. He rousts the kids.

Much of fourth period is spent picking up the phone in order to get kids to sit down or get unauthorized newcomers to leave. Throw one guy out for throwing stuff. Two guys start fighting, more play than anything, but fighting nonetheless, so I call the office and they skip out. We are right down the hall from the office, though, so there are people who see them. This is an extremely long hour and I just hope bloodshed will be avoided. The teacher asked me to leave a list of students who were engaged in "unruly behavior." I note that in third and fourth periods there were many and that it's very difficult to get names as a sub. I could have left her a perfectly accurate list by saying "every black male present," but that sort of thing is not done. I'm not even sure that it's done to be writing it here, yet I do want to describe what it's like out there.

At lunchtime, I hear a clamor out the window and I see a cop has grabbed one girl to separate her from another. Almost at the end of lunch, there's an announcement: "To all teachers. Could you please step out on the blacktop and assist administration in breaking up some fights. Thank you." I pass on this request (we don't get health insurance, you know) and the bell rings a minute later, followed by an announcement that lunch has been shortened.

Sixth period is Drama. This supposed to be a "good" class. Wrong. The only way that I can get the reading about Chekhov done over the noise of the room is by reading it myself and I can't say that that's working all that well. I think I'll take some time off from this place.

ADVANCED TOPOLOGY– *Basic Math, Cucamonga Middle, September 28, 2004*
This math teacher writes her seating charts with the names written upside down, no doubt based upon a mathematical principle with which I am not familiar. When, on my second day of having to direct undue attention to a non-cooperator, I direct him to leave, he says, "It's because I'm black, isn't it?" followed by "All right, I'm calling Doctor King." Sense of history; sense of humor – the suburbs do have their virtues. A last period movie on The Human Machine creates some commotion among the sixth graders over the skimpiness of the bikinis they're seeing during the skin portion and some excellent groans during the leeches section. I find that when the zoot suit phenomenon happens to come up, there's an easy explanation: You know how guys wear their pants falling down because their parents think it looks idiotic?
Student Name of the Day: Gethsemane Pita

GRANDFATHER– *History/Leadership, Appian Way High, October 5, 2004*
A student asks, "Do you have a grandson named Jeremy Gallagher?" and I think, "cruel but fair," until I read one student's Leadership class paper on personal and professional goals and realize the league I'm in here. This guy plans to be a grandfather by the time he's 45. (His professional goal is playing basketball for the Lakers, first step toward which is practicing every *other* day. Wisely, he has a backup goal of attending an actual Lakers game, which he figures will cost $300 for game and plane tickets, (seeing them play Golden State in Oakland apparently not being an option).

JUST KEEP GOING– *October 7, 2004*
After maybe twenty minutes circling Connolly High School looking for parking, I put the flashers on out front and run in to announce my presence in the neighborhood. The secretary says I "might have to park a block away." "A block, away? I've been five blocks away" I exaggerate a block or two maybe. While I'm there, a woman, presumably the principal, announces over the PA that classroom doors are to be locked and students who have not made it to class should head to the cafeteria for late classes. A security guard arrives reporting a couple of students seen making their way over the fence. I push on with my search, but at 10 AM, I just decide to head off home. I think the image of the inmates scaling the fence may have had something to do with it.

BELTOLOGY– *Special Education Para, Hanna Elementary, October 14, 2004*
Four kids in the classroom (where "Wensday," is written on the board in an adult hand, left over from yesterday) and I make the fourth adult – there's some

mix-up, as I appear to be actually filling a Special Ed para job and there's another substitute teacher as well. All is calm, but the real sub says there have been two fights already before I arrived. And one kid's temporarily in another room, so it won't be even sides – they'll outnumber us after all. Judging from the posted schedule, the day revolves around food: breakfast at 8:00; snack at 10:00; lunch at 11:45; snack at 12:45.

What we have is five boys – four black, one white – who can't get along. They scream, shut off the lights, throw chairs, overturn desks, and run out of the room. The other sub's view is: "Too much psychology here. They need beltology. I guarantee that if they knew that the strap was coming across their behind they wouldn't be acting like this. "

The other para is somewhat more, shall we say, "sensitive." She considers the kids very afraid and insecure due to their home situations. She describes a call to one kid's mother who said she'd come in and beat him right in class. So they try to minimize the calls there.

HEY, MY CART! – *Sixth Grade Math/Science, Worcester Middle, October 29, 2004*

On my way through the halls full of Halloween masqueraders, I witness a girl who has come as a homeless person having her shopping cart confiscated by school officials because it belongs to a supermarket. Talk about verisimilitude! I tell my class that I am actually their real teacher, Ms. T, wearing the best costume they're going to see all day. A home room duty is choosing the scariest, silliest, and most unique costumes to represent the class in a lunchtime competition. The kids vote and most unique is won by one who isn't actually wearing a costume.
Student Names of the Day: Proud Benyasri, Xenophon Collins

AIR STRIKES – *Special Ed, Cucamonga Middle, November 5, 2004*

Today's *New York Times* reports an F-16 strafed a New Jersey elementary school with cannon fire, I know I speak for every American substitute teacher when I say I found it most edifying to see this kind of support, particularly at a time when many feared the wars in Afghanistan and Iraq might have drawn the nation's defenses too thin. Of course, it's true that, as My Friend the Evil Substitute Teacher says, it'll take more than just a few air strikes on middle schools to return this country to greatness.

ASK NICE – *Vocal Music, Cabot High, November 15, 2004*

The principal wants to know if I'll take this job for eight days while the regular teacher attends an International Children's Culture and Art Festival in Shenzhen, China with eight of his Chamber Choir students. That I am not a vocal music teacher appears not to faze them at all. *Eight days at Cabot? Well, maybe if you ask me nice.* One piano class, three choral music, and Leadership, which is to say, a course where students get credit for doing student government.

The corridors here are full of kids sitting in front of lockers comparing algebra answers at 7:30 AM and I find walking down the corridors of friendly, motivated kids at the start of the day actually brings a smile to my face. I'm struck, however, by the clarity of this example of an immigrant group passing America's native blacks. The Chinese kids here sound totally mainstream American; black kids famously do not. And let's not forget that while the whole Ebonics thing in Oakland may have been a fiasco, it stemmed from a serious issue – Spanish-speaking Latino kids could get special language assistance, but black kids could not, even though they too were held back in life if they didn't master the mainstream argot that was different from what they spoke at home.

Since the downside of this shocking early morning cheer is a 5:30 AM wake-up, I head off to the deadly dull Cabot faculty room for a few winks during my prep, bringing along a copy of the *New Yorker* to prompt sleep. (I figure I can turn to the humor.) The para who comes in with the autistic kids in the afternoon is doing the same, but when a grounds crew guy passes through I try to snap to attention. Don't want to let the grounds crew catch you napping. After all, they're in the *Chronicle* if they're caught doing that.

In piano class I have interaction with virtually no one except the TA who takes attendance after I open the room. On the fourth day, I realize that I'm only hearing soft thumping. Apparently someone has finally gotten into the closet in which the headsets have been locked for the last three days, so all of the kids are now playing silently. Rather eerie.

So far as vocal music goes, when the Advanced Choir kids start on "Zigeunerleben," a Lied by Schumann, I let the very self-possessed girl who's actually been running the class know that I speak German and she says maybe I could help them with their pronunciation. I'm on. I've been in training for this all my life, pronunciation having always been the strongest part of my German game. My useful ten minutes out of eight days.

One day's Leadership class is a full student government meeting and the president wants me to introduce myself as a former legislator. One of the students knows all about Massachusetts politics and I don't mean just Kerry and Kennedy – this guy wants to know about Jane Swift, who became Governor when my B.C. classmate Paul Cellucci (he was in the Business School, so we didn't even know of each other's existence until meeting in the Legislature, btw) resigned to become Ambassador to Canada. He even knew about her running mate (that is, before Swift dropped out of the race for reelection in the face of Mitt Romney's 50 point poll lead) who was a gay Republican. The kid turns out to be a Republican himself. *Student Name of the Day: May Yu*

BACK TO REALITY– *Special Ed, Cucamonga Middle, November 29, 2004*
Man, I ain't at Cabot any more – after a brief warm-up, most of first period math is devoted to watching *Doctor Doolittle* with Eddie Murphy. We're in the middle, when the dog is worrying about getting fixed at the vet's and then "swallows" the rectal thermometer. I don't make up these assignments up.

A LITTLE LENIN *– Principal, Benjamin Cardozo Elementary, December 1, 2004*
Spend part of the day shadowing a kid the secretary describes as autistic and brilliant. When his first grade class has some kind of group reading, the teacher says it's not at his level and asks me to work with him on comprehension. There's a bunch of the little kids' books on the rug with him and I get him to zip through one of them and then we turn to a large world history book that he's able to read. By the end of class, the other kids are on the little red hen or something and this guy's reading about Lenin.

WELCOME, AS USUAL *– Career Ed, Sonny and Cher Bono High, December 2, 2004*
I'm not dying to be here, but the alternative is a multiple day assignment at Nations of the World and I am still too chastened by my Mateo experience to sign on for more than a single day at a place I haven't been before.

The usual tough school syndrome. I'm not particularly well received by the secretary, who's wearing a santa hat and wants to know if I've written everything on my demand sheet, which would generally be something she'd fill in – not that I feel in any position to throw stones about not doing much work today, as it is already about 11 when I arrive. She sends me on up to the classroom – with no key – where I can't find anything necessary. A teacher from across the hall who's in her first year (and therefore not yet ground down) takes me around in search of help from people who are too busy or stressed out to give it until we locate the building sub who covered in the morning.

I've got two afternoon periods of drama. The class is supposed to finish watching *The Titanic* and I'm to give them an assignment to write up a four character scene on their own. And actually, after a certain amount of shouting them down, they are absolutely fine watching it – even in the dark.

At the end of the day, I've got attendance strips and no directions as to what to do with them. I did notice a box outside a counselor's office during my futile trek in search of assistance earlier, so I head there. This school might want to consider supplying subs with an instruction sheet, but then I suppose that'd run the risk of subs getting the idea that they're welcome here. The secretary is reading an advertising flyer as I leave, so I can see why she might be too busy to fill out sub forms. But, again, those who live in glass houses ...

THUGSITTING *– Math, Ralph Bunche High, December 6, 2004*
Late call and they send me right up to relieve another sub, who turns out to be Erwin, the German guy from South City summer school. The first two periods are a double period intervention. About a dozen of them; as Erwin says, they're very talkative. Very talkative and pretty damn unpleasant. We have a girl saying she's going to bring her BB gun tomorrow and shoot a guy. Seems to be in jest, although she claims she was shooting people with it from a bus yesterday – "And did the boy piss on himself!" Another girl talks about how you need to wash your ass. So I figure I won't be denying bathroom passes this period – I hand them out to about half the class.

I've got a prep and lunch back to back, and I'd like to talk to Erwin, but much as I disapprove of the bowling alone syndrome, I stay in the classroom because this place doesn't give you keys. Presumably I shouldn't leave the door open in a place where kids come by in the middle of class to pick up cd's from other students. So if I left I'd have to go around begging to get let in again.

Last period I'm sent to cover a class in a empty room. Back upstairs, then back down to the right room where a security guy is sitting in. My job will be thug sitting for a group watching *Roger Rabbit.* After a pencil-type object is thrown in my direction, I turn on the lights, then decide to turn them back off, but stand by the door where I can watch over them but not actually be among them. On my way upstairs after class, another object lands. If I'm a woman, I don't even want to be down in this corridor.

YOU'RE ALL CAPITALISTS NOW — Economics, Cappuccino High, January 10, 2005

The regular teacher has broken her shoulder and pelvis and is coming in now, but with help. She's a very self-confident woman, probably in her fifties, who tells her classes that they are all capitalists because they live in a capitalist society. If they want to be something else they could move to Cuba which is communist or to Scandinavia which is socialist. And, by the way, in Norway they called in the friend of a friend of hers to ask her if maybe she really wasn't living in too large an apartment. And what is capital? Capital is wealth. And wealth is determined by scarcity, so she plays a video of the *Antique Road Show* for them to explain it all. I want to scream. And we wonder why the nation is so confused. The cause of Third World poverty revealed – insufficient antiques.

NO COMMENT — Social Studies, William Howard Taft Middle, February 4, 2005

These are the weeks that try subs' souls. My fourth different middle school of the week. There's a note from a prior sub to the effect that the morning classes were okay, but for the afternoon, he had to have the counselor or someone else in. Fair warning.

And like the man said, the morning was okay. On her way in for the afternoon double period sixth grade, a Chinese girl says, "You wouldn't like it in here; it's a jungle." I assume she's using the subjunctive more out of uncertainty about the language than about the likelihood of my not liking it. Sure enough, as soon as I look up, somebody's throwing something, so I tell him to leave. He appears to be lurking in the halls, but he's out of here and that'll have to do for the moment. Later I'm calling the counseling office to let them know that I will be sending kids down – first to the wrong counselor, though, because that's the one the sub form said to call. Then I'm calling the front office for security to come remove another guy who's throwing stuff and won't leave. No one's arriving and I'm calling counseling again and the front office again.

On one of my many calls for reinforcements, I am distracted sufficiently so as to actually turn my back upon the enemy – at which point I am hit with a wad of paper – at which point I turn on them in a rage and explain my intent to bring as much trouble upon their heads as need be to get them to shape up; I will have as many of them thrown out as I need to – and so forth. And when I think I've probably raged enough, I rage some more. At which point I immediately shift to gentle voice and say, "Where were we?"

We have some release-of-tension laughter and back-up arrives. The security guy, whom I recognize for years, eventually comes to get the thrower and while he's there, one of the talker-outers starts, so she goes with, saving him a trip. The counselor then arrives and tells them if he has to come back again, they'll be there until 4:30, which threat I remind them of over and over. I eject another one or two and keep the level of disruption within reasonable bounds, but what we do get ain't all that great – even the kids I'd expect to be keeping up don't know where we are when asked to read.

At the end of the day, I tell Ms. M, the secretary who called to ask me to take the job, that I don't need that class again. She says, "Sorry." The principal, who's standing right next to her, does not comment.

And in cultural news, the *Chronicle* reports a number of San Francisco parents are expected to tell the School Board they don't want school opening before Labor Day because they want to take their kids to the Burning Man Festival. Meanwhile. I've read that they're proposing to take away a sub's option to turn down an assignment. If they think they're going to eliminate any sub who turns a job down, they may have to start flying them in from Kazakhstan.

SWEET TOOTH – Language Arts/Social Science, Cucamonga Middle, February 9, 2005

Mrs. P, the secretary, has ashes on her forehead. Must be Ash Wednesday. They live more by the traditional ways down here. On my second day, I see the Tooth Wagon in the parking lot. My Friend the Evil Substitute Teacher loves to see that. Claims he volunteers there on his off days. Threatens pain-in-the-ass students with root canals and so forth.

Watching *Never Cry Wolf* has the kids "ew"ing over the skinny dipping and other such scenes to the point where the teacher next door comes in to ask them to keep quiet. At various points the TA attempts to cover the flashes with a piece of paper. I attempt a discussion when it's over. One kid refers to one of the indigenous American characters (Inuit/Eskimo) as "the Filipino." I try to situate the Philippines in relation to the arctic zone. But we haven't been bombing either of these areas recently, so you really couldn't blame an American kid for not being able to tell them apart..

Sixth grade has what they call "large group" during home room – every sixth grader in one big room where they get the pitch to sell Otis Spunkmayer cookie dough to raise money for the school. Four out of every ten cookies sold in these parts are Otis Spunkmayers, they tell us. There's Reese's Pieces, Double Chocolate Brownie, and Triple Chocolate Chip available. I think the Tooth Wagon's gone by now.

HARRY POTTER – *Economics/History, Millard Fillmore High, February 17, 2005*

Late call, so there's a sub-to-the-second-degree is in the room when I arrive. Kids playing cards, which I figure he'd have stopped, but he explains he's yet to find the Harry Potter video, the watching of which constitutes the assignment for all classes today. I actually find it, but reckon that card playing is likely to teach the kids as much about History and Economics as Harry Potter, so I let them play out first period. When Rich D calls to see if I can sub for him next week I chide him for interrupting a very important part of the Harry Potter movie. But I have not had to yell once and it would be churlish of me to bemoan the day.

The teacher's desk has a pile of issues of a *New York Times* student magazine I've never seen before. One cover story asks, "Should the Death Penalty Apply to Teen Offenders?" My Friend the Evil Substitute Teacher of course believes the death penalty should *only* apply to offensive teenagers.

Student Names Of The Day: Yoyo Chan, Moe Moe Ko, Bossini Nguyen, Finesse Wong

AH, NOW I REMEMBER – *Assistant Principal, William Howard Taft Middle, February 22, 2005*

Scratch a substitute teacher and find a writer. I spend a fair amount of supervision time chatting with Eugene L. The principal's at some meeting and Eugene's her sub, so in one interpretation of reality we are the powers that be out here in the schoolyard. He's somewhere in my age range, maybe older. Asks do I have the substitute teacher book – which he's also got, of course. He's also got a book of 600 biographies of people born in San Francisco, books of poems, and thirty year-old novels. Comes in by bus from Mill Valley. I tell him I review books. The "Washington Consensus" comes up and I don't have to explain what it is!

Dinner with David C tonight and I'm filling his head with subbing stories for some time before something finally uncorks deeply buried school-age memories deep within him and he remembers what school was like when you had a substitute teacher and realizes what I've been talking about all this time. I wonder how many others really don't know what I'm talking about because they've also suppressed their memories.

When I return for this same assignment on a later date, after a morning of hall and lunch monitoring and car moving, I am deployed as second sub in the class I've previously objected to. I propose to the other sub that I serve the function of enforcing discipline swiftly – writing referrals and making calls to the office. He accepts. When we toss two in first period, I have their assignments written out for them to take down to the counselor's office. They are sent back for the final period and I eject one again, this time with a referral completed with four counts. Very satisfying to be able to write them up thoroughly and not worry about the rest of the class getting away from you while you do. And the fact is that this is about what is required.

We concur that this teacher's frequent absences are turning this class into a farce. There are no consequences for bad behavior and even the good students are deteriorating. Were we able to keep to a higher standard, I would have ejected at least an additional two rude students. Turns out this other sub used to teach at Mateo. As I recount my experience there he concurs with my sense of the principal. He wouldn't work there under her.

THEY ALL HATE US ANYHOW – *English, Appian Way High, March 4, 2005*

Pretty depressing lunch room banter today: The right-wing teacher who's usually here, the half bright sub I see around, and another teacher chipping in on the military necessity of bombing the Japanese cities in World War II. And, oh yes, the French hate us. This lunch room sometimes brings to mind Garrison Keillor's description of our parents: "Those poorly informed but well intentioned people who brought us into the world."

Fly-on-the-wall in the afternoon: Girls theorizing about certain types of girl's shirts designed by guys that are "just an excuse to stare at girls' chests." But the one guy in the class, who seems likely gay, asks, "What about those girls who wear those tight little shirts that say 'Honey Baby, Daddy's Girl'?"

The school newspaper has the stats on the racial composition of the school: 38.3% Latino; 20.7% Filipino; 20.6% white; 11.1% Asian, and 3.7% black.

TCCH! – *Science, Worcester Middle, March 10, 2005*

In just about every other school I go to in South San Francisco, and most of San Francisco as well, there's no need to write down your assignment, as they're going to know why you're there when you get there. Not here, though, where the most-put-upon-secretary–in-the-world works. I have forgotten this today. I offer to call in and get it, but she does it herself, with the customary *Tcch*. Then asks if I've got a demand sheet. Now I assume she remembers that yesterday was the last day of the pay period, the day when you turn them in, so it's unlikely that I'd already have one, but why pass up an opportunity to act put-upon. Gives me a key without mentioning what room it's for. Etc. If only they'd just tear down the school around her and let her sit here in an open field and let her do her job!

I'm in one of those classrooms with wild animals – rodents, serpents, etc. – that are not to be touched except by designated students. The room smells a little something, so I open a few windows. During fourth period feeding and cleaning we have a mouse running about the room with two little boys in pursuit. I just hope they haven't let any pythons loose or anything.

WAY OUT? – *Biology/Chemistry, Appian Way High, March 21, 2005*

Just when you least expect it, a conceptual breakthrough! I can't find any passes here, so I've been telling the kids to write their name on a piece of paper. One kid spots a paper towel on the desk and uses that. Bathroom passes made out of paper towels? No waste. Environmentally sound. I see a patent here. This could be my ticket out of subbing!

VARIETY SHOW – *Literacy, Nations of the World Institute, March 25, 2005*

With a 8:30 AM call, my NOWI moment has finally arrived. The office doesn't appear to know whom I'm here for and when a school still doesn't know which of its classes are uncovered this far into the day, well that can't be a good sign. They send me to the room next door but it's locked, so I have to go back for a key. Obviously there are no students there, although my reading of a schedule on the wall (they have given me nothing) says they should be there. Back to office where a second secretary, or such, says that there's a special schedule, which she now gives me. I mean, why would you give me the schedule the first time? And she says the teacher I'm replacing has a prep. I ask about a lesson plan but she flits off and, seeing no signs of her imminent return, I return to the classroom. According to this schedule, I'm looking at one 70 minute class followed by a rally. Well, how bad can that be? Really, I've been around too long to ask such naive questions but I still do. Long term effects of sleep deprivation, I think.

No chalk in evidence, so I can't even write my name on the board. Eventually I locate the Teacher's Binder that appears to indicate that she's been out all this week and most of last and I will later learn that she's in Mali with two of the students, building hospitals. And the building sub is out, so there are no lesson plans.

The half of the class who show up say they've been told they can watch a movie today, but after two students return from the library with *Homeward Bound* and a movie about Selena, no one actually wants to watch. Thirteen students eventually show; not one of them will tell me what they did in their last class. So we do absolutely nothing, other than breathing and a bit of verbal jousting. So I figure 70 minutes of NOWI classroom time will be about enough for today and forever. One student says the assembly will have something to do with gay marriage but he "ain't going to watch that faggot-ass shit."

No lack of variety at the gathering, though. We have:
* An event involving students pushing the faces of other students into cream pies. None of the other teachers at the back of the hall can tell me exactly what is going on.
* A speech by Assemblyman Mark Leno.
* A presentation by the Gay/Straight Student Alliance, which explains the earlier classroom remark.
* A break dancing demonstration.
* YMAC (Youth Making A Change) explains its district-wide clean bathrooms program.
* A presentation by some guy who repeats the line, "We shall overcome, from being dumb."

Sign on wall: *"Abstinence is the best choice you can make. Condoms available in Room 1, Tuesday and Thursday."*

URANUS – *Math/Science, Waterfront Middle, April 5, 2005*

Passed up the chance to visit my new little friends at Nations of the World Institute and took this job for a teacher whose recording said that her classes were easy. Memories of Waterfront made me skeptical but she was right – honors classes, mostly Chinese. They're reading about the planets and I ask the teacher – who's met me in the morning before going to a doctor's appointment –

if telling them about the planets in the evening sky would be useful. She says definitely, so I give them a spiel about Jupiter in opposition tonight, and which planets had specific discoverers and I actually think some of them were interested. I ask the afternoon class if anyone had ever seen a planet. One guy claims to have seen Uranus and I caught myself asking if "Have you ever seen Uranus with your naked eye?" Excluding that dubious claim, not a single one has ever seen a planet, or realized that they were seeing one, anyhow.

The teacher says that for the last 25 minutes of their double periods, I can let them go into their science groups, unless I can't stand the noise. I tell her that as a sub, I've heard some horrendous noise, but she says you never know – she had a sub once who said he couldn't take it and the kids had to read silently the whole time because their din was disturbing his video game playing. Now that sub should get some kind of award.

SOUL SEARCHING – *Roving, Cucamonga Middle, April 28, 2005*

This is the fourth straight day of roving assignments here and the one that will bring about the end of my relationship with this school. I replace a long term sub who's here for Ms. G and the para here confirms that Ms. G has some type of blood cancer and is permanently gone and will presumably be gone from the planet in a couple of years. Also says it was her fourth period class that made her decide to leave before the year was out.

Anyhow, at lunch, I am approached by Ms. K, for whom I have just subbed, and Ms. H, for whom I subbed earlier. Ms. K proceeds to ask me if it's true that I told a student, "Don't ask me again" in response to a question during her class, and then goes on about how she trusts her TA who said that I said that and how the kids said I was on my computer and didn't help them and the like. And Ms. H doesn't like my computer either and the kids tell her I don't help them. I am quite taken aback and tell them that as a sub, I get gamed every day, and go off and mull this for the rest of the afternoon.

I decide I'll visit Ms. K after school and when I get to her room, I once again get the two of them for the price of one. I tell her that what burns me is that she has come bearing tales of twelve year olds about how they couldn't get help, and that as I thought about it, I could specifically recall five or six kids I helped after making the statement in question and that I was pretty sure that the class understood that I meant that when I answered a question before the entire class they were expected to listen and shouldn't ask me the same question over and over again. And if the computer was an issue for these teachers, I wouldn't use it if I had to cover their classes, and otherwise, I just wouldn't take any jobs replacing them, and waved good bye.

So what do I think? A kid once told me I subbed here too much and it's been true lately. My position has always been that I do what's asked: when I am actually asked to instruct, I instruct; should I be asked to correct papers, I correct papers; if students ask for help, I give it to them – always. But in what you might call baby-sitting situations, I do nothing but what teachers do all the time – when the situation allows it from a discipline point of view, I watch them with one eye and do something else with the other.

Naturally, my first assignment the next day is several hours in Ms. H's class. As she explains the work and tells me what pages they're on, I find myself recalling that she was wrong on that for both classes on one of my recent stints. She also doesn't leave me any seating charts, and I can recall recently leaving her a note that her seating charts were inaccurate.

Anyhow, I throw one guy out for having other stuff on his desk and refusing to give it to me and I am generally as hard on them as I usually am, despite her bs about my not giving them sufficient attention. I think I should have maybe told her the kids would probably tell her I was mean to them if they thought that would play with her; instead they say they don't get help from me. Of course, I am burned by everything about her at this point. Nonetheless, I make my usual effort of trying to bring any kind of outside info to bear that I can and leave the board covered with the names of the cities we're reading about, written in Greek letters. Somehow, I suspect that this will be lost on her – Greek to her, maybe.

There is one amusing moment here, though – when I ask if anyone knows where Troy is in today's world, the student teacher raises his hand. Anyhow, this is the last time I'll be in one of Ms. H's classes – she can go bleep herself.
Student Name of the Day: Jay Guevara

CONSERVATIVE? – *Second Grade Bilingual, Aldo Leopold Elementary, May 2, 2005*

A poster on the bulletin board asks you to pick the gay parents out of a crowd and explains that it doesn't matter. Can there possibly be any social conservative with kids in public schools left in San Francisco? Or at least one fluent in English?

HEMMING – *History/Sewing, Worcester Middle, May 5, 2005*

The tape calls this a History/Social Science job, but the second part should have said Home Economics, specifically Sewing. The teacher's notes say, "You may have to show students how to do an END KNOT and hemming stitch as well." Unfortunately, my hemming has never been all that good.

Really, the worst thing about this place, which is the best of the three South City middle schools, is that unlike the other two, it has indoor corridors and the kids are allowed in them before class. Nothing can bring your spirits down before a day of subbing at middle school like a walk amongst the clientele.

ODD STUDENTS – *Computer Lab/PE, Freeway Limits Middle, Friday, May 6, 2005*

Another daily double that might surprise the general public. I took this as a computer job, only to be told upon arrival that it was half PE. First and third periods are not too bad, but second is: I've got kids throwing stuff at each other and I'm seizing basketballs back before I've even gotten to hand them out.

Computer lab is a lot better, though – the computers are plugged in so they're harder to throw at each other. After lunch, I see one boy turn over a trash can in the rush and another boy stop to turn it back upright! I follow the second boy into his class to thank him – he's probably an extraterrestrial or something. A girl in Computer Lab says we had you for PE. I ask what period; she says third and adds, "We agree that second period is a terrible class." So I'm meeting some reasonable students today. How odd.

Sign in PE Office:
> **Whether you think you can**
> **or think you can't**
> **YOUR RIGHT**

Even if your spelling isn't.

NASTY BITCH – *Math/Science, William Howard Taft Middle, May 9, 2005*

The regular teacher is here when I arrive; she's got medical tests today. She tells me I look brave. I ask if I'm going to need to be. She's got two periods of sixth grade honors that presumably won't be a problem, but she's quite concerned about an eighth grade math class. She tells me to read them instructions about how they can win raffle tickets and I can show them a *Sponge Bob Square Pants* video if they're good. I'm expecting guards to bring them in in chains after all this, but they're really not that bad. Science class gets a geology movie, and boy, is that not exciting. Tough to keep things interesting when you're moving on a geological time scale.

The sixth and seventh period sixth graders are another matter, however. One girl is continually testing me and won't even feint toward work until I head toward her. When I finally write up her assignment, give it to her and tell her to go to the counselor's office, she crumples it up and throws it on her desk. I head to the phone to have her removed and she leaves yelling, "you ugly piece of shit." This after an episode of her screaming, "If you don't let me pee, I'll pee all over myself and make you clean it up." There are no referral forms in evidence, which seems strange given the low opinion in which the teacher held her students. But I write my own note, stating that it is my opinion that she should be suspended. And just in case you think it's just me she took a dislike to, there's the notes Friday's sub left: "Arianna is awful" and "Arianna C is a <u>nasty</u> bitch." And I'm sure Mrs. C thinks she has a very nice little daughter.

On days like this I long for a more traditional type of society where children like little Arianna would be tied up and left outside the village at night for the lions, tigers, bears, army ants, or other local carnivores to snack on while the horrendous child's shrieks rent the air and served as warning to the other children in the village (and as a source of satisfaction to the adults.)

Sweet Arianna was white, but the five black kids in the class are also putting on an educational clinic that would make the writer of the *Boondocks,* the too short-lived comic strip about black kids, cringe. Eventually I eighty-six two of them for shouting at each other across the room.

Later at night, recalling that one of the main pains-in-the-ass acted like he'd had me in class before and another had remarked about remembering my wristwatch which has no numbers on the face, I realize that this is the same bunch I'd had as a Language Arts/Social Science class and had determined not to go back to. So at least there's only one class like this, not two. Today's extremely nasty little bitch wasn't there then, though. Maybe she was suspended or maybe she'd just peed all over herself on the way to school.

"THAT MOTHERFUCKER"– *English, Cappuccino High, May 10, 2005*

Regina Spektor, the Russian singer from the Bronx, has a song that asks what summer makes her think of. The answer is "cleavage." And there's a girl here first period with the same thing on her mind. The amazing thing is that I think that I never actually ran into the phenomenon anywhere in my own educational career – not in the Bronx, not in my all-boys high school, not even in college – it too being Catholic and all. But anyhow, it's nice to be back in high school. After lunch, I hear a student say, "Look at that motherfucker's briefcase," and I realize that I am "that motherfucker" and when I look at how weathered my computer case actually is, I figure it's traveled more miles than many of these kids will in their entire lives – excepting, of course, the ones the nation recruits to fight its wars.
Student Name of the Day: Tianna Jingles

PUNK ASS NIGGER– *Math, Appian Way High, May 11, 2005*

One guy arrives deep into second period, takes the attendance sheet from the folder on the wall in the back of the room, erases the absent bubble next to his name, and sits down. I advise him against that procedure, and he proceeds to loudly discuss his opinions on the NBA playoffs, which I shush several times, culminating in my saying that he should go home if he can't be quiet and do the class work. He leaves, declaring "He told me to go home," with a "punk-ass nigger" verbal chaser. He forgets to take his referral, though, which I bring to the office since I don't have class third period. They seem unsurprised there.

I tell a fourth period kid reading the newspaper that he needs to do his math before reading something else, but the rest of the class quite convincingly assure me that he never works in class, he just warms the seat. I've noticed an already filled-out referral and, sure enough, it's for him. And guess what he wants to do? Yes, he wants to go to the bathroom. I am torn, in that going to the bathroom would at least represent some kind of accomplishment, but ultimately I decide against.

I will later take a class to an assembly previewing an upcoming dance show. It's quite dark and some time after taking my seat, a student wakes me up to ask if she can go to the bathroom. Just glad it wasn't the principal.

Quote on classroom wall: "As I have said before, the ever more sophisticated weapons piling up in the arsenals of the wealthiest and the mightiest can kill the illiterate, the ill, the poor and the hungry, but they cannot kill ignorance, illness, poverty or hunger." Fidel Castro. Seen some Che Guevara, but this may be the Fidel Castro quote I've seen in a classroom.

EDUCATION? – *Sixth Grade, Freeway Limits Middle, June 13, 2005*
Last week of school. I've got two classes for three periods each. The first one has to watch an educational video on ancient Egypt and they are not happy – education in school? The next guys watch *The Sandlot* and then the first guys come back for *Angels in the Outfield*. Now that's more like it.

*****

THE LEAST YOU CAN DO – *Math, Sonny and Cher Bono High, September 2, 2005*

Back at Bono. The teacher's schedule is all you get. No keys: you have to find someone to let you into the men's room and then someone to let you back into the classroom. I go to the office. They call for security to let me back in. No one shows. They tell me I can find the deans down in the cafeteria. I have to ask where the cafeteria is because they don't give you a layout map. At the beginning of last period, as I'm wondering if I'll need outside help quieting this class down, I notice the phone list on the wall includes no counselors or deans. And, no, there were no written instructions on handling difficult situations. I exchange unpleasantries with the secretary on some of this on my way out at the end of the day.

CALL-UPS, REVOLUTIONARIES, DICTATORS – *American History/Economics, Millard Fillmore High, September 23, 2005*

Last day of a two weeks here for Rich D as he replaced a union staffer on maternity leave, the highlight of which period was a substitute teacher getting called up to the majors: Doug Clark, who was back to his off-season job subbing in a history class at Central High in Springfield, MA when the San Francisco Giants called him up. This could be the highest achievement ever recorded by one of our number.

A couple of for-profit college representatives spoke to classes. One from Heald College talked about how much money you need to make to pay the cable bill, cell phone, etc. Another one says some of the students here are idealists and that's okay. He's an idealist himself, he says. He thought he'd go back to the Philippines and be a revolutionary, or a dictator. He went to Jesuit schools, where they train presidents and dictators. Dictators and having enough money to have a good looking girl friend are very big in his world view. He represents DeVry University.

And there was politics. The home room class is supposed to hold an election for class officers. There are only two nominations and they decide they won't need a treasurer because they won't have any funds. On election day, one of the candidates offers to be VP, after which a girl asks if she can go to the bathroom. Not knowing the players, I ask how the other candidate feels about this proposed election arrangement at which point I realize that the bathroom request had been the president-elect's acceptance speech.

Rich D emails: "The students under your tutelage whine about you as 'mean,' 'worse than you, Mr. D,' but all in all I (and they...somehow) appreciate your 2 week role in my stead." And this after I mostly looked the other way when they were using iPods, with the notable exception of the girl listening to one while the DeVry guy was talking. Probably just as well if she hadn't heard what he actually had to say, but ...

PATHETIC AS YOU ARE – *Auto/Career/Health, Cappuccino High,*
September 29, 2005

When I came here three days ago, there was an awful lot of room in the parking lot and when I reached the office Ms. F asked me what I was doing there, as it was a staff development day. Ms. K apologized profusely – the call came in and without thinking she put a sub request into the system. An argument for keeping the humans out of the process.

Today, I am off to the far corner of the campus, where they keep the wrecked cars, to a class is full of kids I used to throw out in middle school. They tell me they haven't been allowed in the shop yet – a good thing, no doubt. No bathroom passes in evidence, so I write one on a post-it which I recommend the bearer attach to his forehead to allow for easier verification by the authorities. He complies.

A call at lunch informs me that the Air Force guy expected for the two afternoon Career/Health classes just canceled because he's now got to go to the ski jump they've installed on Fillmore Street for the day. Projected invasion of North Korea? Instead I am to go to the library and see if the librarian will take them a day early to work on their career papers. Fifth period generally embarrasses itself and the librarian, who's been doing this all day, tells sixth "you're the best of the six classes, pathetic as you are." He probably made the right choice deciding against classroom teaching.

Student Name of the Day: Hustler Mataverde

NOT A GREAT FIT – *Seventh/Eighth Grades, Skyline Middle,*
September 30, 2005

Parking prohibitive; steep hike; hustled right up to the classroom by Maria, a young assistant principal I worked with last week when I was shuffled off to the elementary school. Within a few minutes, I've got a kid out of his chair chesting up to me – you know, like a couple of inches away – a new level of boldness really. He goes. (Maria brings him back to apologize at the end of the period.) Another guy goes after getting caught cheating on a test and subsequent mouthing off.

Maria will tell me the kid who had gone chest to chest with me is really a good kid and I will tell her they're all someone's little darling. But she thinks maybe my tone wasn't right and maybe this wasn't a great fit and how much better I seemed to get along with the second graders, etc. – in the most polite way possible saying maybe they don't want me for this job again. Well, I can live with that. She's new to middle school, I'm guessing.

Student Names of the Day: Elektra Ditto, Quetzal Maucci

ANOTHER ONE DOWN – *ESL/Language Arts, Nathaniel Hawthorne Middle,*
October 3, 2005

First two periods are ESL with another teacher. A bit noisy, but pretty good, as ESL kids generally are. Not so with the next. They're supposed to read a section in their text from "Joy Luck Club" and they tell me that the teacher reads to them. I'm willing to buy that, so I start, but since my reading gives them a chance to throw things, I eventually stop and tell them to do the written assignment. I have no seating chart or attendance list, so I don't even have the pleasure of being introduced to the kids I eject. I call counseling. No answer. I call the secretary. She says the counselor has lunch this period; she will call security. Security never arrives. After class, I notice someone has stolen the cord from the phone receiver. You see something new every day – that's why we stay in the business.

The first period teacher suggests a movie. After a long process of deciding on a film, shutting off the lights, and pulling the shades, unauthorized flying objects again appear in the air, so lights on, back to a written assignment. Then a couple of boys insulting each other across the room. I throw a couple of more out, but can't really get order, so head across the hall to call downstairs since my phone isn't connected. The teacher there calls for me and a security guy comes and sits on them for the remainder of the period. Yesterday, Nathaniel Hawthorne was the worst San Francisco middle school I was still willing to go to; today, it's the best of the ones I won't go to.

DREAM/NIGHTMARE*– Fifth Grade, Alcatraz Elementary, October 5, 2005*

Like playing the lottery every day, this sub's life. Some days I can't believe they pay me for doing this (those are the days you don't read about); on others they couldn't give me enough money to repeat what I've just experienced. This will be a four hour day – not counting lunch – but I wouldn't willingly repeat those four hours. I do recall Alcatraz being surprisingly difficult in the past – maybe it's just the setting in the middle of San Francisco Bay that makes me expect something idyllic – but the call doesn't come until 9:20, so I figure maybe the place is worth another shot.

The secretary, very happy to see me, asks, "Are you tough?" and is somewhat disappointed to hear that I'm only here for today – the tape had originally listed this as a two-week assignment. The Instructional Reform Facilitator is in the classroom with fourteen badly behaved children to whom I am to start out teaching math. Chaos ensues. Two kids appear to be listening. The rest are continually up and about, throwing things, whacking each other with books, and the like, as various parents and such wander in to shut them up.

Half of them eventually demonstrate that they can do something but we have a closing flourish before lunch, when a boy starts stomping on a girls' backpack, throws over a chair, and hits my hand when I point – not so that you would say that he was trying to hurt me, but he certainly did hit me and he repeats it. So I'm hoping he gets a trip home to his mother, but she turns out to already be at the school and wants to know what happened and assures me it won't happen again. During lunch, the kids run the halls and pound on the door until I roust them.

At the end of the day, I learn this is one of the "Dream Schools," the brainchild of Superintendent Arlene Ackerman who has announced her departure, effective the end of the school year. While I've never been particularly fond of her administration, I can't argue with the concept, which is somehow to amass extra resources to provide a prolonged school day for kids who would likely benefit the most. Of course, the reality of Dream Schools is pretty much that they are currently nightmares and any extra resources the School District can muster to the kids' support will not likely to match up to the challenge of their lives. Anyhow, good luck on finding a regular teacher for this class. On my way out, the secretary asks if I'm coming back tomorrow." I tell her that I have another job, which is true. The other secretary says, "The real question is if you were free would you ever come back here?" I laugh. She laughs. I don't answer. I leave.

A story in the *Examiner* later in the year reports a "recent incident in which one of the older students at the K-5 public school assaulted a teacher" and goes on to say that the school could be closed in December, as it "has dropped to 95 students, with only four full-time teachers and one classroom position filled by substitutes [I imagine that's where I was] – most of them new since the school went through a reform process during the summer that required existing teachers to reapply for their jobs or transfer to another school. [That worked out pretty good, eh?]

"Many of the children were from families that were previously homeless, and this contributed to the struggles within the classroom, [Superintendent] Ackerman said. When discipline issues surfaced, there was no way to divide students and send them to different classrooms, because each grade only had one classroom and teacher."

Alcatraz School closed mid-term, December 16, 2005.

STILL THE SAME– *Science, Appian Way High, October 7, 2005*

I have a kid from Greece first period, so I take the opportunity to find out from him if the Greek alphabet remains unchanged since Homer. It does. He says he hasn't seen it written on a classroom board in ten years. We have a quite pleasant interchange on the permeability of language. My next time here we have a video on Ecuador that shows a colonial era painting with Jesus and the boys eating guinea pig at the last supper. Most people have to pay for experience like this.

TOO MUCH MONEY – *Testing, Benjamin Cardozo Elementary, October 18, 2005*

Mix-up today. Too many subs so I am assigned to help in testing a kid. I study the materials for a while and then start to administering more than a dozen tests to this boy. He's quite nice and seems pretty smart. I gather he's been in bilingual and his English is perfectly fine. There's one section where they ask that you point out the cow jumping over the moon after the cat running away with the spoon, but only if the earth is rotating counter-clockwise – or something like that. It was all I could do to keep from laughing about how hard some of these tests were.

At lunch, I ask what's he being tested for. The woman in charge says, "special ed." Well this kid ain't no special ed student and she doesn't think his tests look that way either, but since he was referred, he's got to go through all these tests and be interviewed by a psychologist. "They've got too much money, I think," she says. In some areas, maybe so.

THAT'S NOT FUNNY– *Special Ed, Worcester Middle, October 31, 2005*
One teacher has arrived for Halloween as a substitute teacher – "Kick me" sign on her back, eraser marks on her black skirt, and a paper plane in her hair. An announcement concerning Halloween costumes at Dolores High on Friday had a somewhat different tone: "You may not wear masks. You may not bring weapons. And you may not be a criminal." Very urban.
Student Name of the Day: Maverick Concepcion

ECHT "FREEWAY"– *Math, Freeway Limits Middle, November 15, 2005*
The secretary's out, so the place is coming off the hinges. First the wrong key, then none at all. Off to cover a class that's already covered. And I see the principal covering the secretary's desk, so good luck if you're calling here today.

Sixth period is *echt* Freeway. I'm ostensibly giving them a quiz but they talk continuously, ask each other for answers, and are exceedingly rude and annoying specimens of their most rude and annoying age group. As I'm throwing a student out at the end of the period – to make an example of him (which move produces no discernible effect) – the regular teacher returns. His presence makes no difference, so as I suspected, this guy has no particular control over them either.

The entire class will eventually leave before the bell. There would be no way to stop them and no reason to want to, really. A minute more of these guys? No thanks. The principal checks me out at the end of the day as the secretary is absent and I'm waiting for her to ask how things went, but she doesn't. Maybe she doesn't want to know; or maybe she already does. The machine later offers another job here tomorrow but I decline. Cancel my job here Thursday as well.

NO THANKS– *English, Appian Way High, November 16, 2005*
Another sub who was at Freeway yesterday is also checking in as I arrive and we compare notes. Says his last couple of periods were horrors too. On the other hand, my first class today is AP and it's a pleasure to turn on the TV and show them the final scene of *Hamlet* and see a volume of Pinter plays lying around the classroom. Second period is quite other. They're supposed to do their homework for the first thirty minutes. Class begins with a guy who wants a pass to go to the office to complain that the school didn't do anything to a kid who just got caught with pot when this guy got suspended for getting caught with even less last year.

I am a tad under the weather and tell the kids that I don't have much voice and will appreciate it if they don't make me use it. One kid is noticeably struck by the concept of a substitute teacher being sick.

Overheard conversation in class: "Girls make noise. Guys just lie there." (Giggles when she notices I've heard.)

I arrive home to find a message from Ms. K saying she's given me a job at Freeway tomorrow. The same job I canceled, I think. I cancel it again.

Student Name of the Day: Shtiv Valenica (that's pronounced "Steve," not ssh - tiv, as I did)

QUIET, I'M READING – Biology/Chemistry, Dolores High, November 21, 2005

What you can say about Dolores these days is it's maybe not as bad as you'd expect. The teacher advises that the classes are not great, particularly fifth period where we've got one table of four that will start throwing stuff at each other and such, unless I intervene. Another table has only a cellphone to occupy them. Others are looking at photos. I'm showing a cyborg video today. (A sticker on the TV set says it was donated by Carlos and Deborah Santana. His alma mater, I believe.) By ten minutes in, no one is watching any more. A girl reading *The Diary of Anne Frank* asks me to lower the volume arguing, logically, that no one is watching. And so, figuring that something is preferable to nothing, I lower the sound of the assigned movie so that it will not disturb the girl trying to read.

Student Names of the Day – Claudeen Nacnac, Amber and Jade Solomon apparent twins), Chloe Underdue.

LIFE IS A BOWL OF – Math/Science, Ishi Middle, November 29, 2005

Got called for an ESL job, but the school says there is no ESL program here. During lunch a teacher comes by with a couple of turtles in a bowl that she wants me to give to a last period student. Try to remember – things could always be worse. You could be a middle school student's turtle.

DOWN WITH UP – English, Appian Way High, November 30, 2005

A senior class is watching *Pirates of the Carribean* when I arrive. When I ask how that came to be, a girl says the teacher has two movies in the room and this was one of them. In the course of the day here, I discover the full collection of all six *Up* movies, the British series that started with *Seven Up!* which interviewed fourteen seven-year-olds of dramatically different backgrounds in 1964 and has returned to film those still interested every seven years thereafter. So they were watching a movie based on a Disneyland ride with one of the great achievements in the history of film lying a few feet away!

My freshmen classes are supposed to be working on brochures for their Utopias. It appears, though, that they've never been told much about the meaning of Utopia – or at least they don't remember much about it. I give them the whole shtick – the Greek root of the word, Thomas More, *Erewhon,* Edward Bellamy.

Sixth period is full of kids who remember me from Cucamonga. Muttering about referrals past fills the air and I attempt dialogue. One girl declares, "Middle school is evil" – an apparently full recovery. Their assignment was due today and they've got nothing else, so some start to get into yearbooks that are lying about. One girl finds her mother in the 1991. Mom sure wasted no time.

URBAN ED – *Math, Dolores High, December 1, 2005*

Thirty-five on the first period attendance list. Sixteen here when class starts, five trickle in later, including one who says, "Ms. M's not here? What the fuck did I come in for?" She actually turns out to be a reasonably polite student – just to give you a bit of the flavor of modern urban academia. The newspapers have recently been reporting the district's problem with losing funding due to non-attendance – they're only reimbursed for students actually showing up – so at least she's helping with that. I don't mention this, though. The class has a three-dimensional graphing assignment. The seven Chinese kids are doing it. As for the rest, three girls are playing with their cellphones, a couple are warming themselves at the radiators, and the others, other.

LUNCH – *School Age Mothers Program, Johnny Rotten High, December 6, 2005*

Described as "Health" on the machine. This place is so thinly staffed that when you enter the office you have to wait for someone to appear. I'm listening to a few guys lurking outside thinking this is not the big city so they're probably not going to be all that rough. But I soon learn there will be no guys at all in my class.

This is a class for pregnant students (six here; one absent) and the program is kind of all about food. My first task is calling in tomorrow's lunch and snack order. The instructions further explain that the girls are often hungry and snack throughout the day and that they frequently need to go to the bathroom. They are on individual work plans. One's reading *The First Year of Life;* another *Giving Birth*. And there's *School Age Parents: The Challenge of 3 Generation Living*.

I introduce myself, take roll, offer general help, and keep to the schedule:

9:05	Snack and lunch delivery. Put in fridge.
9:10	Infant Center calls; they want Maureen. Start checking on snack availability.
9:45	Heat up snack. (My educational moment arrives when a girl mentions Malcolm X and they hear more about him than they might have really wanted.)
10:15	Snack break.
11:15	Public health nurse (appropriately named Michelle Eatmon) gives them a Maternal/Child Health class for an hour.
11:45	Start heating lunch.
12:40	Lunch.
1:25	Lunch over.
1:30	Dismissal.

Long discussion on stretch marks in which I don't participate, nor in the one on how you put a condom on someone who is not circumcised:
"When you've seen one, you've pretty much seen them all."
"We're talking about this and the teacher's a male!"
"If the dick looks like an anteater, it's uncircumcised."

UNIFIED SCHOOL – *English, Sonny and Cher Bono High, December 7, 2005*

What made me come here again? The two and a half hours of fitful, interrupted sleep? The late call at 8:30? That it's supposed to be an ESL/Bilingual Spanish program? Office is disorganized as usual, although at least not unfriendly today. (There's a somewhat dottering sub ahead of me of the sort that make me marvel that they get though the day.) The secretary tells me this is English, not ESL, and gives me an inoperative bell schedule.

The teacher next door says that the one I'm replacing was hit in the head by a light that fell out of the ceiling yesterday, presumably sitting at the desk where I am. Indeed, the fixture above it is the only one without a covering. A poster seeks opinions as to whether the school needs a Union Building Committee. Disorganized faculty/disorganized administration/disorganized student body – a unified school. But a sign for the Condom Availability Program on my classroom wall indicates that at least some things function here.

THIRTEEN – *Math, Freeway Limits Middle, December 14, 2005*

When I arrive, the teacher, here enroute to jury duty, starts telling me first period is going to be tough. There's a kid I should throw out at the slightest provocation and maybe the seating chart needs a few changes and he doesn't actually have any referral forms for me. Not good signs.

The students don't make a liar out of him either. The seating chart is useless. The indicated boy acts up quick, yells "damn" loud, and gets a quick thumb. When he's slow to leave, I call the office to have him removed. By the time the security woman comes he's gone, but as soon as she leaves the room, another kid calls me a liar, so I call her back to take that guy with her. Later, someone throws a paper wad in my direction and two of them get the heave ho on that. It eventually becomes quieter and we even do a little math – factorization and prime numbers.

This all has the look of a teacher who can't manage a class. At the end of the period, Kim B, my past summer school principal who's now some kind of teacher coach/mentor, sticks her head in because she's working with this guy. I say, "We're trying to help here, right?" and give her the rundown. "He's young, right?" She responds with a "but some people get it right away." I agree. Some can do it immediately; some learn; and some go into other things.

His notes for third period say, "This is an eighth grade algebra class who are rough around the edges." Uh huh. He also teaches off of his own worksheets which are, to my mind, pretty confusing as well. By day's end, I've ejected thirteen students – most to the room across the way which was suggested to me for such purposes. That's my highest number in some time and it takes the regular teacher

somewhat aback upon his return. The machine calls later with another math job here in the new year. I let that go.
Student Names of the Day: Jamil JJ Khoury and Jamil NN Khoury – cousins

TWO LAWYERS – *English, Appian Way High, December 16, 2005*
Second day of a calendar year-ending assignment. Ends at 12:30 and the fight goes to the final bell: As the clock runs out the day and the year, I'm issuing a referral to a kid who declares that he's got two lawyers and he'll write the referral himself. I have to wrest the stack of them out of his hands and most of the class has disappeared before the bell. Happy Holidays.

NO PARTY – *English/Journalism, Citadel Middle, February 1, 2006*
The teacher warns on the tape that her one sixth grade class is rowdy. They are: They start out wanting to read their assigned class novel aloud, which seems a good sign in kids I've been warned to watch out for, but they interrupt whoever's reading and whenever one of them finishes reading, he's got to start asking for the bathroom, water, ice pack, etc. I'm supposed to tell them that if they get a bad report, there'll be no birthday party for Johnny on Friday. Well, lo and behold, whom do I throw out of class but birthday boy himself? Calls me a faggot on the way out, etc. I'm guessing – or at least hoping – that the party's off. Life in the big city, even in the best middle school.

I'm thinking about these guys after I get home and on into the next day. A *San Francisco Weekly* article discusses the over representation of black kids in Special Ed and the fact that being in Special Ed also entails getting a lesser education. All true, from my experience. The solution is less clear, however. What it is almost certainly not is pruning the Special Ed numbers so that they mirror the systemwide racial numbers. Every time I read a piece like this and am reminded that only ten percent of San Francisco public school students are black, I am amazed afresh, as they constitute about sixty percent of the problem students I encounter. And I'd say that's a fair measure of how much more difficult their average life situations are. In this sixth grade class it was primarily three black guys (out of the four in the class) who acted like they might as well be the only people there. It obviously wasn't that they *couldn't* learn, but that they require, well, special attention.

Boondocks had some great stuff on Sunday:
"Ugh ... This video is terrible. Turn it"
"You say everything is terrible. You're a hater."
"Y'know ... the brutally honest critiques that you call 'hating' are why black people have always been at the forefront of music and culture. Artists knew that if they didn't excel, black people would yell and boo and heckle them off the stage. Tough audiences have always made our artists better ..."
"Uh-huh ..."
"Now if we could only get black people to start booing each other in math class ..."
"Whatever, hater."

A lot better commentary on education than you'd likely find in *The Nation*, for instance.
Student Name of the Day: Ruby Tuesday Rosa

I MISS HER – *Sixth Grade Math/Science, Freeway Limits Middle, February 3, 2006*

On her way out to a two-day training, the regular teacher told me, "Be mean." And her written notes said, "Be strick." (sic) so I am strick and some of the guys doing virtually nothing the first day are doing something today and one says, "I never thought I'd say this, but I miss Ms. C." Ah, I've made my mark! These kids are supposed to be ESL, but they're quite high level so far as I can see – in talking, that is. Listening, not so good.

GREAT – *Computer Lab, Francisco Palou Elementary, February 6, 2006*

Francisco Palou is right across the street from the Holly Park Projects, so I expected wilder conditions than I encounter. Kindergartners and first graders, granted, but I've certainly had out of control kids of that age. On her way out, one girl says, "You're a great substitute." I mark her down for evaluation.

INVERSE LAW – *Math, Appian Way High, February 13, 2006*

Three easy classes, two hard. That is, three classes are covering difficult material and are easy to handle and two are covering easy material and are difficult to handle. First period has the Pythagorean Theorem and I am happy to go over the ins and outs of that with them. The next class has DeMoivre's Theorem applying powers of complex numbers to spirals. I only even remember what complex numbers are because I recently read Roger Penrose's *The Emperor's New Mind*. I tell them that to the best of my recollection, I have never heard of DeMoivre but offer to read this over as a class if they think that would be useful. Not surprisingly, they opt to go it on their own. But one thing you can be pretty sure of is that a class studying DeMoivre is not going to be terribly unruly.

Some second period kids are discussing an assignment from another class and I hear a couple of them trying to figure out the meaning of moderate, radical, and reactionary, words that were apparently not in the reading. They figure that radical means crazy, so I can't resist butting in and asking them: if you're inside Nazi Germany and you say that this is all wrong, are you a radical? They figure that probably you are. So, are you crazy?

A GOOD BRIDGE – *Therapeutic Day School, Johnny Rotten High, February 24, 2006*

The tape simply described this as "TDS" and I wondered if it might be the pregnant girls again, but no. The note left for me says "Some have been referred due to psychiatric disorders. Some have severe conduct disorders. Others suffer from depression. Be prepared for anything." There are twelve kids in the class, of whom eight are here. There are three other adults in addition to me, so I am quite obviously a warm body filling a legal requirement – the instructional aide tells me

I can read the paper. I am introduced to the class, one by one, as they come in, as they are all on individual programs and there is no central instruction. I notice that one kid's got a language tape set and dictionary on his desk for German, a subject not otherwise offered in this system. And I hear that one kid's taking Portuguese, so they're not necessarily losing anything educationally being in this class, which is nice to see.

With only one period to go, I am told that this is an exceptionally peaceful day. I guess I must be exerting a calming influence. Last period is free on a good day like this, so it's back to the gym for a second PE class. The two depressed kids who were shooting baskets by themselves previously now opt for pool, allowing me to do my first actual instruction of the day – properly racking for eight ball and how to form a good firm bridge. Thank God for that pool table in the Regis Senior Room.

ROLL UP THE WINDOW– *Johnny Rotten High, March 2, 2006*

I had an English assignment at Cappuccino until Ms. K called this morning and said she needed me at Rotten, mentioning the fact that you get out at 1 PM as a sweetener. 12:31, actually, but it's the longest four hours you're going to spend. This is not the therapeutic class or the pregnant girls, but the basic Rotten. Classrooms full of kids I've thrown out in other schools all staring back at me. The pits in life's bowl of cherries; the kids parents hope their kids won't turn out to be; middle school minds in high school bodies; wall-to-wall jerks. Perhaps you're getting the idea that I don't like these children.

The teacher left what the principal (I don't think they actually call him that – warden, maybe) later described as a skeleton plan. First and fifth periods they were free to do their own ongoing independent work. First period they're not too awake, so it's not bad. The other three classes get crossword puzzles that I am to do with the class and they're not bad. One is history and science, the next is vocabulary. And if I can keep this moving fast enough, there are some of them who get into it. Speed is essential here; if the class slows down they just resort to trying to be insulting. Their puzzles don't take long enough either, so each class deteriorates at the end and the final period class are just rude, crude and useless and I basically have to keep my eye on them to keep them from starting to throw stuff.

I throw a few out during the day, but with the small staff at this place, there's not a lot you're going to do with them. A few are quiet throughout; some sullen, some not. I remember this article on the LAPD in the *New Yorker* piece that reported LA cops generally referring to their arrestees as "knuckleheads" and "assholes." I do know how they got that way. Some of these kids are now working their way into the criminal justice system.

As I'm driving away, I see two of my recent charges walking ahead of me on the passenger side. As I pass by, when I hear my name called out as I anticipated, I hit the button and my window rolls up. My one moment of pleasure for the day. Ms. K won't be stealing me for this class again any time soon, although she does try to do just that a few days later. I leave a message replying to hers telling her that I respectfully decline her kind offer and will let someone else enjoy these children.

LADYBUG – *Second Grade, George Chinn Elementary, March 6, 2006*

Always like coming down here to Chinatown where it feels like real San Francisco: *I Remember Mama* San Francisco, Beatnik San Francisco. You can see Coit Tower and each day I think I should be basking in North Beach. This class is in the annex directly across the street from the main building, but to get from one to the other we have to walk up to the corner to use the crosswalk and then back down. We have to do this for recess, lunch, hearing test, and dismissal, so this place is good for keeping the kids physically fit. During one of our journeys, a pair of tourists starts taking pictures of my entirely Chinese class. I tell the kids to look, that they are going to be famous and ask where that will be. Norway, the tourists tell me.

The day's highlight will be rescuing a ladybug from the school yard – one of the schoolyards, that is. I think there are four of them. Between the two buildings and three levels, I'd be totally lost without the kids showing me where to go. The PE teacher tells them they're acting like they've lost their minds now that their teacher is out, but I don't know any better. Twice I'm asked what I'm doing there because, I guess, as the aide lining the kids up for the hearing test says, "you look like a middle school or high school substitute." And she's right on that. The kids can be a sensitive bunch here. Merely writing names on the board for offenses like dancing in the aisle instead of sitting down may drive them to tears.

HOW DO YOU SPELL IT? – *SED (Severely Emotionally Disturbed), Freeway Limits Middle, March 8, 2006*

Home room is replaced by an extended first period today so that eighth graders can meet with counselors from the high school they're going to next year. The counselor assigned to my room forgets what school he's supposed to be talking about. He's actually from Cappuccino and starts talking to the students about it until one girl asks what if you're going to Appian Way and he remembers that he's actually representing them because they're short-handed. So, if these kids weren't already confused... He tells them to write down their middle school accomplishments and high school goals. These kids literally don't know how to spell college; two of them ask. And if Jose, one of my summer school kids, is answering the questions candidly, I figure he's trying to spell "violence" and "Juvenile Hall."

Something you notice in a lot of these Special Ed classes is the lack of a sense of reciprocity appropriate to the kids' age. They want everyone to listen when they read and a minute later when someone else is reading, they're talking.

Back the next day for a class of primarily sixth graders. This teacher does it all. First period we read about vampire bats. Second period is math and I'm explaining the concept of prime and composite numbers. Then Michelangelo and the Renaissance, then the geology of carbon-14. Last period is math again – combining like terms. They simply cannot do the math problems the teacher left me, however. Had I known, I would have taught the concept from scratch. All in all, a productive day at school. Shocking, but they do happen from time to time. This teacher is definitely trying to do something with these guys.

SEX BY THE BEACH – *Science, Calvin Coolidge Middle, March 17, 2006*

Videos all day – *Asteroids: Cosmic Travelers* for eighth grade and *The Kingdom of the Seahorse* for seventh. They are to take at least fifteen notes and generally it's really not bad. (Typically depressing sixth period – four black kids; three of whom take not a single note.) The seahorse video has what purports to be the first-ever-filmed seahorse sex and some kids talk about how they're watching porn. They're also very interested in the part where the female cichlid takes sperm into its mouth.

STILL WRONG – *Math, Cappuccino High, March 20, 2006*

The day's highlight is a girl I recognize from Cucamonga coming in after lunch and saying, "I remember the conversation we had about the war in Iraq and I admit I was wrong." Unfortunately, this discussion would be timely all the way through her high school career.
Student Name of the Day: Darling Pineda
Teacher Name of the Day: Ms. Speller – English teacher
(Author's note: As you may have noticed by now, the name is appropriate to far more teachers than you'd think, and that's based upon just what they're confident enough to write on the board or in notes.)

WASN'T HE JEWISH? – *Bank & Credit/Career Education, Millard Fillmore High, March 21, 2006*

Machine called this Computer Lab but there are no computers. First two periods are Bank and Credit. A note says to give out worksheets on the desk, but there are numerous worksheets on the desk. No seating chart or scantrons for most classes – I'm supposed to use sign-in sheets. During second period, I notice I've got extra bodies and start trying to roust them and am thinking about locking the back door when I realize I can't find the key, which I apparently lost. I have to beg my way into a men's room during third period prep. It's that kind of day.

Two periods of Career Ed watch a video about difficult situations in the workplace. One day, these guys will *be* difficult situations in the workplace. A couple of kids in sixth period career class think Hitler was Jewish. Oy vey! And we've got a girl outside calling into the class to the TA to tell her that she's there, but not there. I tell her she needs to stop; she tells me to fuck myself. Kids start leaving ten minutes before the end of class. I take attendance a second time, leave the teacher the names of nine of them who cut out early, and say good bye to these nice boys and girls. Add this one to the Don't Return list.

The next day when I am back for a different job, the secretary says the principal wants to talk to me about the key. He informs me that I should have told them earlier, etc. He says thank you at the end of the conversation – and clearly doesn't mean it. I reply – you're welcome – and I don't mean it. Going back through the secretary's office I mutter "Pleasant fellow" loud enough for her to hear. I've previously noted a foreman-type tone in his printed communications and now I've had the pleasure.

Rich D's note says to keep on the iPods, etc. – the kids should be working quietly or napping. You just never know what goes in a particular class – so napping is okay here it seems. At one point during first, there's eight of them with their heads down.

There was a discussion this morning on the KFOG morning show about public and private schools. The private schools are better and you're doing what's right for your kid, etc. One woman says it's just racism that makes people take their kids out of public schools. A guy says that the public schools can't throw out the troublemakers. Another guy says that the testing measures nothing and, as long as the entrenched politicians are in, it won't get any better. There's the usual mention of good and bad school systems. Report comes in on improved public schools in the Bay Area. And what leads the pack? Why Marin, of course.

People seem able to deal with the understanding that education recapitulates economics, but the black/white divide and the extra grade point difference involving black kids remains a topic that few know how to publicly discuss in a useful way.

And then we have this news from the front:

40 mm shell paperweight severs teachers hand
VENTURA – A teacher who kept a 40mm shell on his desk as a paperweight blew off part of his hand when he apparently used the object to try to squash a bug, authorities say. The 5-inch long shell exploded Monday while Robert Cola was teaching 20 to 25 students at an adult education class. – AP

Must make note – touch nothing on teacher's desk.

WITNESS PROTECTION – *Assistant Principal, Excelsior Academy, May 9, 2006*

Late call, half-day job – the best way to try out a new school. From the name – which says trouble – I'd thought this would be a high school but it's actually a middle school. Assistant Principal today – office with private bathroom! Other than a little lunch time yard duty, my main assignment is calling kids' parents to see if they received the summer school letter and ask whether they want to send their kids. I get one – whom the secretary realizes she should have crossed off the list – who starts explaining that her brother was murdered and how she's taken the daughter to another school because they're in the witness protection program, etc.
Student Names of the Day: Princess Precious Pope; Lord Matthew Ramsey

ROLE WITH IT – *English, Millard Fillmore High, May 16, 2006*

The *English* teacher I'm replacing asks that I take attendance in his "role book." Hoping, I assume, that I will be a roll model.

TWO WITS – *Economics/English/History, Appian Way High, May 24, 2006*

In last period, two Arab kids explain the role of Arabs in world history to a couple of Chinese guys – from inventing our numerals and cultivating livestock, to taking down the World Trade Center, inventing airport security, and going to the head of the line at the airport.
Student Names of the Day : Lufthansa Castro, Stella Blue Kraft

TO THE BARRICADE – *Sixth Grade Language Arts/Social Studies, Freeway Limits Middle, June 2, 2006*

During the day a girl says, "I'm sitting with crazy people" and I'm pleased to explain to her that this is very common in middle school but that most of them will grow out of it.

I haven't received my San Francisco check yet. At the beginning of the year, the District announced that we would now have to get our demand sheets in on the 20th or wait a month to be paid. If you're subbing that day, fine, the school sends it in. If not, you now have to take a trip down to Van Ness. I mean, really, how could they be expected to process our checks in under ten days? I've been calling since yesterday afternoon and today someone tells me that my envelope is postmarked on the 19th and received in their office on the 31st. They pulled this on me two months ago and I let it ride, but I can't afford to this month. I leave numerous messages explaining that I expect to pick up a check this afternoon and that I don't want to make a scene, but that I will if I have to. Heading down there reminds me of what it felt like going to my draft physical. Knowing that I may not be able to achieve my goal of walking out with the check, I ask myself what I am willing to do. Get arrested? Self-defeating. Be escorted out by security? No problem. Curse someone up and down if they say the wrong thing? That could happen.

When I arrive, I tell the first person I encounter that I want a check. She says I can't get one and shows me the envelope that I've heard about on the phone. I ask to speak to Marlena, on whose machine I've left two messages and find out that I am already speaking to her. She hands me one of their instruction sheets that informs me that the problem is all mine, as it is my responsibility to see to it that the sheet is there on the 20th. Nine or ten days to move a piece of paper within their system and this is my fault! I inform her that I really don't care what this piece of paper says and that I want a check now. I am slamming down on the little attention getting bell that you find in offices like this. She pulls it off of the counter with a look of great alarm, so I just pound on the counter. After enough of this, I ask if there's anyone in charge and she tells me that the CFO is next door.

I head into his large office and find the secretary who tells me that he's at a meeting but she'll try to find him. I am calm, but skeptical. She fails on first try and I figure that's it, but she pursues it and says she's located him and he'll try to be up in a few minutes. Again I am skeptical, but indeed he shows up in a few minutes. I explain. He goes off to the sub office and returns saying that they can't get me one today, but could do so on Monday. I explain that I am leaving town tomorrow and my health insurance bill will be deducted from my bank account on

Tuesday. He asks could I get them a deposit slip. It's 4:00 PM on a Friday afternoon and getting back and forth from Bernal Heights is going to be a problem. I ask if there's a reliable way to leave one for them on Saturday. There is not. So he says he could stop by my house on his way home and he actually knows Bernal Heights. So that is what the CFO does. But while I am astounded by and grateful for this personal assistance, this is a systemic problem and I intend to force them to fix it. Otherwise I will be down there until it is. And I am otherwise a defender of public employees!

*****

FINGERPRINTS – *Art, Freeway Limits Middle, August 24, 2006*
    Yes, it's August and I'm in a classroom. I'll never get used to this before-Labor Day stuff. This is what happens when you take God out of the schools. I'm only here because my fingerprints are on record and those of the teacher hired for this class at 9 PM last Tuesday are not. My only real responsibility is to finish one class and start another while she goes off to Redwood City to get her fingers done – she got out of Ed school in the spring. There's a new principal here who thanks me for being there at the end of the day. *Thanks me?* I think they better run another check on *this* guy's fingerprints and references.

    And just to add the proper substitute teacher ambience, my 85 Buick having been given a not-worth-repairing diagnosis, I am now the proud owner of an 81 Volvo station wagon with 230,000 miles on it (before the odometer stopped working.) And today I learn that I don't know how to get it into reverse and have to push it out of my parking space at the end of the day. This will hopefully provide the students some warning of the dangers of not going to graduate school.

    A couple of weeks on, a teacher will tell me she thinks the school's better this year – the principal is more in evidence and male, which she thinks probably matters here. The kids can't hang around the office and watch TV anymore. I notice a master schedule on hand now which there never was before, so far as I can recall.
Student Name of the Day: Sancta Sophia Paran

LOOSE TEETH – *Second Grade, William Elementary, September 15, 2006*
    Democratic Club meeting ran until 10:30 last night, then there was ballot counting, so we didn't get to the Wild Side, the lesbian bar on Cortland Avenue until late and I didn't leave until 1:30, at which point I told Geoff I could get called in four hours, which I do. It's PE at Worcester and they're asking for a female, though, so I pass it up, along with another PE job, before taking an Art job at Appian Way at 7, when I am significantly readier for the day. The phone rings again immediately thereafter, however. It's Ms. K: The art teacher changed her mind and I wind up with this elementary job. And all of this has happened before many of you Americans have eaten breakfast!

    The classroom features a chart for keeping track of teeth that fall out – and one goes today! Lunch room discussion of an upcoming field trip – true suburbanites – they don't want to drive in the city.

    In the afternoon we make a collage about healthy food for which the kids cut things out from ads. The results include beer. Good kids.
Student Name of the Day: Love Lee

POORLY – *English, Appian Way High, September 28, 2006*
    Today I am in for Ms. Poore. I'd say it's because she's feeling poor, but she is an English teacher, so I must say it properly and use an adverb – she is feeling poorly. I find that most of her classes are poor, though.

Fly on the wall: Boy asks girl, "How much do you weigh?" "122 pounds; ten percent of that is my boobs."

ALWAYS HAVE TO DRIVE – Economics/Psychology, Cappuccino High, October 5, 2006

The teacher has an "I love farting" magnet on the board behind me. Perhaps a recent transfer from middle school.

Three periods of Psych, showing *Drugstore Cowboy*, during which the kids are to write three "critical thinking" questions. Now this film happen to have one of my all-time favorite lines in America cinema: It's the female lead complaining to her junkie male counterpart, "You never fuck me and I always have to drive." Of course, it might be deemed, uh, inappropriate to specify it, so I just tell them I think there's a great line in the movie but I can't tell them what it is. It comes right up as we watch, but in a low voice and goes right by them. I feel I have failed them on cinema appreciation.

Two periods of presentation from the California Culinary Academy. These for-profit schools sure have their people out hustling. The presenter's not actually talking about cooking, but job hunting. (I wonder if they actually teach cooking there.) At one point, she says, "Ladies, watch your cleavage," which predictably sets off a stir, the upshot of which is that the girl who's the target of this says, "I got my last two jobs that way. I'm in the men's clothing business." Apparently gentlemen watch her cleavage, even if she won't. The presenter does not raise the point during her second presentation.

Other recent experiences here include a Spanish class that could not understand me when I introduced myself to them *en Español* and an Economics class where a student accepted delivery of a package of raw chicken. Lots of deliveries come to class, but this was the first raw meat, so far as I can recall. Cooking class assignment, apparently.

Major educational policy advance here: No more bathroom passes. Students now just take an orange vest with the room number on it. Wonder if a consultant was behind this. Hope the education policy reviews are taking note.
Student Name of the Day: Lady Jane Pacaldo

TIP-OVER – Music, Appian Way High, October 10, 2006

To bed at 1:00 and woken at 5:30, so I sack out on the carpeted floor during my prep period. That was before the girl playing the bass clarinet tipped her instrument over and deposited a puddle of her spittle on the floor. Yum. Note to self: Do not nap on music room floors.
Student Names of the Day: Mark Anthony Bacho, Genesys Canizalez

HUMAN KINDNESS – Life Skills, Appian Way High, October 31, 2006

Called for English, switched me to this Special Day Class of eight mentally retarded students – 18 to 21 years old, but they look much younger. The day's big event is walking to Albertsons to pick up things for the afternoon Halloween Party. (There are two aides.) A woman working at the bakery gives them each a cookie. Coming back, we pass a little set-up with an inflated slide and a couple of bouncing rooms and the woman in charge of the slide lets the kids all take a ride for free. Then to See's Candy where the aide is buying everyone a chocolate for the holiday, and the counter girl also gives everyone one. Not health food, I know, but the nice thing about being around these kids is the way they bring out human kindness.

I ran into a sub I know around at a Halloween party Saturday night. When I raised my standard reflections on the plight of black America he compared a classroom of black students to walking into a room of people who had drunk a lot of alcohol. (He was drinking water at the time.) He said what kept him in the system was the polite Chinese kids and the free time within the job.

WAS IT CANADA? – *SED, Worcester Middle, November 14, 2006*

No one in class can tell me what country's rule it was that the American Revolution overthrew. Special ed – but still.

SHOT – *Language Arts/Social Studies, Citadel Middle, November 21, 2006*

I stop in on Mr. S's lunch group and one woman starts talking about the number of students she's had who've been shot – and this is Citadel! A black female teacher says black kids don't expect to grow up; her middle class nephews from 19th Ave. (out in the sedate Avenues) had friends shot, so they just assume it'll happen to them.

The *New York Times* reports: "Despite concerted efforts by educators, the test-score gaps are so large that, on average, African-American and Hispanic students in high school can read and do arithmetic at only the average level of whites in junior high school."
Student Name of the Day: Karl Jung

FROM THE BRONZE AGE – *Reading, Pamplona Elementary,*
November 29, 2006

I'm cleaned, dried, dressed, and sitting to breakfast in front of the computer about 7:10, when Ms. K calls to cancel a roving job at Appian Way Hi. Muttering about regretting picking up the phone, I eventually find this job on the San Francisco machine.

I'm replacing a reading teacher who usually works with students one-on-one, but today I help out in the students' various classes. One of them I've been in once before and been impressed with the teacher's performance. For one thing, she's got a Kinky Friedman quote on the wall: "It's a small world, but I wouldn't want to have to paint it." She's from Texas and we talked about when we'd seen Kinky. She has a TV monitor hooked up listing the class program for the day. Today she happens to write "planetes" on the board, Greek for wanderers, the origin of the word planet, so during a lull in the action, I tell her I could write it in Greek, if she'd like, which wows the boy who'd been trying to look up *antidisestablishmentarianismophobia* earlier. The teacher later tells me she thought I might be able to write that in Greek. *She thought I might be able to write that in Greek?* She said it was the professorial look. Seniority, I suppose. Perhaps she thinks I served under Xenophon.

In another classroom, I point out to one of the girls working on a writing project that she's left the second "a" out of pharaoh. She tells me her teacher (who has misspelled a word on the board) spelled it this way, but I tell her to trust me on this now and check it when she gets home, at which point her friend says she's seen it in the dictionary and my spelling is right. So it will be our little secret from teacher.

JUST FOLD – *Home Economics, Cappuccino High, December 1, 2006*

Yup, that's right – Home Economics – one period of Interior Design and four of Foods. And just to prove how inappropriate a placement it is, before I even start my first class, which is second period, I see that I've already blown my first assignment to take the pasta salad from the refrigerator – the refrigerator labeled "eggs" – to the teachers' lounge for the potluck. I'll have to hustle over with it during lunch time, I guess.

Interior Design is working on their "service and work areas" project. Sixteen girls and three boys, one of whom is absent. I have no role other than to take attendance. I suppose I could try to get some ideas, though.

A whole column in today's *Chronicle* on my tiff with Bank of America over its refusal to allow me to see the security tapes from the camera at its cash machine where the kid ripped the money out of my hand and ran away. It reports my response to the writer's inquiry about my eagerness to confront the kid who stole my money (I belatedly chased him and his little girlfriend for several blocks): "I'm a substitute teacher. I deal with these monsters every day." A friend thinks I may get trouble over this. Nah – no one reads the business page.

The sixth period TA wants to know if the teacher's coming back tomorrow because he's wondering about whether to put another load in the washing machine. I don't know, so he just folds.

SHE NEEDS A SUB – *Health/History, Appian Way High, December 5, 2006*

Not looking forward to this job when I find that part of the program is Health, figuring I've got the football team again (which I had in Ceramics yesterday), but my first class is actually really quiet watching *The Secret Life of Mary Margaret: The Story of a Bulemic.* Next one is an ESL History class watching the Pickett's charge section of *Gettysburg.* That is to say, the Chinese girl is watching – sometimes. Besides her we've got four with their heads down, two talking, one looking at her fingernails and occasionally watching, and one reading his drivers manual. I don't know that the message of American history is taking these days, at least out here. Gettysburg can seem a lot more remote here in California than it did back east anyhow.

In the teachers room for third period because there's another class in my room, I hear a teacher telling an aide that she had a student be so rude to her that it brought her to tears in front of the class. Wow! Sounds like she could use a sub.

Had a quite interesting phone conversation this weekend with a lawyer from Oakland who read the *Chronicle* story and called with advice on getting a case against Bank of America into small claims court. He's a Jewish guy from the Grand Concourse with a black girl friend who thinks blacks have to pull themselves up by their bootstraps, although he doesn't put it exactly that way. When I told him that I considered what I saw in schools and the situation of blacks in general to be a legacy of slavery, he had what I thought was a telling response – that it was too big a statement and that no one was going to deal with that. I tried to impress upon him the difference between what he'd just said and saying that it wasn't true. To my mind, this is the kernel of the problem – it's too big to discuss, so we'll just act as if it isn't true and seek all our solutions in smaller stuff.

CAN YOU HEAR ME OUT THERE? – Music, Worcester Middle, December 13, 2006

How big is Advanced Band class? 61. How big is that? The teacher has lately acquired an electric megaphone – for use in the classroom!

I read today that some thirty-five year veteran teacher in Bakersfield has been suspended for duct taping a student's mouth closed. As My Friend the Evil Substitute Teacher says, they tie the teachers' hands and they wonder why the education system is failing.

HONORS – PE, Appian Way High, January 17, 2007

I didn't like PE when I had it in high school and I still don't like it now. But you didn't ask me about that. Other than taking attendance and such, my main activity to keep my mind from idling all day is studying the records of past basketball and baseball players written high up on the gym wall. L. Lucca scored almost 30 a game one year in the 80's, but only appeared to play two years; in baseball he set the single season hit record and fielded 1.000 at shortstop. Wonder what he's doing today. Also notice four retired football jerseys above the office door; one was a High School All-American. No similar listings for top students or social activists anywhere around the school, that I've noticed.

Back here a couple of days later for Special Ed. After the kids in the first two periods do their drafts of an essay on the idea of credit cards for high school kids, they get to pick a movie. They choose *Scary Movie 3*. I have to tell a kid to turn back to the movie from the *Spongebob Squarepants* TV show he's turned on because the lesson plan calls for a movie, not TV. Why is watching *Scary Movie 3* more educational than *Spongebob Squarepants*? Well, I never got my education degree, so I don't know.

Most of them are on one or another of the computers anyhow and I sure can't see why I should roust them from there to watch *Scary Movie*. This kind of looks like another football class – linemen. But when a security guy comes by to give out Saturday school notices, three of the six of them get one, so they've got a pretty high class average on that, anyhow.

The other classes get to go right to the movie. Third period picks *Laura Croft, Tomb Raider*. Fifth/sixth goes for *V for Vendetta*. On days like this I rather enjoy writing the titles down on my report for the principal's perusal.

I do have an actual brush with education, though, filling in for a Senior English class, answering questions on a speech by Queen Elizabeth I to her troops.

In the lunchroom a teacher who's obviously been at it for decades recalls the course she took in classroom management from a guy who hadn't been in a classroom for decades. He told them that as teachers they must never raise their voices in a classroom, but instead go up to each and every misbehaving student and ask in a low voice why they're doing what they're doing. After attempting this in her first class of screaming children, she ended up screaming, "Shut up!" And it worked. Later she bought a whistle.

TUESDAY – MUST BE LOONEY TOONS – *Health/History/PE, Cappuccino High, January 24, 2007*

If this teacher's program sounds like a joke, well ... The PE comes as a surprise to me – only so many subjects'll fit on the tape. It's first period and there's some chatter among the students as to why he's absent so much, but it turns out he's got jury duty, a concept with which not every student appears to be familiar.

The assignment for the three health classes is watching *Remember the Titans* – it's about football, you know, and that's exercise, which is healthy. And it's Spirit Week. For some reason, this means that students – and teachers – are desired to dress up like cartoon characters. It's *Looney Toons* characters today; Monday was *Nickelodeon/Peanuts,* then the *Simpsons*; tomorrow, *Hanna Barbera* and then *Disney* characters. Hey, student government's got to do something. Just reporting it from the educational front lines, as I find it.

CIVIL DISOBEDIENCE – *English, Appian Way High, February 5, 2007*

The junior classes have to read *Civil Disobedience* and answer questions. A student comes up looking for help on the first one: "What kind of government commands your respect?" Do they want her personal opinion, she asks. Yes, I believe they do. Well, she doesn't care. How about if they didn't allow you to vote? That wouldn't bother her. How about a 10 PM curfew? That would bother her. I suggest she think on the matter. We seem in little current danger of building a populace that'll balk at things like going to war, any time soon.

SHE QUITS – *Math/Science, Freeway Limits Middle, February 12, 2007*

The teacher is not absent but has been taking personal time and they think she may leave. In fact, after I arrive, she decides she'll quit right now. The principal comes by and warns her that this might endanger her credential as she will be abandoning a position. She's a young Vietnamese woman who took over after a veteran teacher left it in November and the class had subs for a couple of weeks.

Before she actually decides to quit, she asks what I do to maintain order. She figures I may get more respect being older and male. People told her this would be hard, but you only know when you do it. Says all of her recent referral forms have been returned with no action taken (reason enough to walk, in my book) and she could be doing secretarial work for the same money, without the aggravation.

The first of her intervention classes immediately rises to the occasion and I throw one guy out in the first minute for shining a laser pointer at me and refusing to surrender it. Fifteen minutes later, security comes and pulls out the pointer's probable owner, who has been a continual nuisance. I eject another one who won't shut up. As you might imagine, I've seen worse, though. Another ejection in fifth and no bathroom passes issued all day. At the end of the day, I feel a certain appreciation for these guys – as worthy opponents, you understand.
Student Names of the Day: Kristina Aliana Goduco; Kristina Frances Goduco (twins)

ALL RELATIVE *– Language Arts/Social Studies, Citadel Middle, February 13, 2007*
Today's irony will be working on quieting the black kids who are talking while the class is supposed to be watching *Roots* and learning about the history of slavery. I throw one guy out in third period after he's thrown some object or other, stuck his head out the window, laid down on the floor, and told me he's not going to listen to an "evil-ass teacher." An aide tells me the police were here for him last week. Another kid gets a referral for a seized cell phone, throwing and breaking a mirror, and much thundering. At the end of the day, the secretary asks how my day was. When I give her a look, she asks whom I was in for. When I tell her, she withdraws her question. This is the best public middle school in SF and my day was about the same as yesterday, when I was in a class that has driven two teachers out of the worst middle school in South San Francisco.

FLAW IN THE PLAN *– French, Appian Way High, February 14, 2007*
Coming off of two days of middle school battling, I start the day with a hard ass substitute teacher move when an SUV tries to get in front of me in the parking lot and I make it back off. Probably would have let it go if it weren't an SUV. And then another car wants to block traffic to let the kid out, in a typical "there's no one else in the world who matters but us" move. I think I see a parent glaring at me. Let em glare, I've met worse – their children.

The French teacher's message says that she's emailed her lesson plans to the Italian teacher next door. But she's out too – a fatal flaw in the plan. (Mediterranean work habits, I guess.) So we wait. The day's highlight is ten girls arriving during third period and singing "My Guy" to some guy. It's Valentine's Day, you know. There are red rose deliveries in fourth and we have quite a lot of billing and cooing from one couple during first. Even necking. But with no lesson plan, there's no reason to stop it, I figure. And, hey, it's French class – this is the

room with the postcard of a woman's skirt being blown up – and it's a female teacher. They're card playing and iPod listening today – the teacher has failed to deliver.
Student Name of the Day: Kristle Leyson (say it fast, you Catholics of a certain age.)

SOME PRICK – *ESL Science, Appian Way High, February 15, 2007*
Comparing notes with the aide after one class, I start my standard rap about how nice these kids are because they're not Americanized and she says it's sad that in two or three years they'll be "normal." After school, there's a knot of boys, presumably from Cappuccino, talking at Trader Joe's. I'm waiting on line and one kid's mention of "penis" catches my ear so I tune in and that guy says, "I recognize him from somewhere," referring to me. I tell him it was probably in class. He then realizes he had me as a substitute and starts explaining that he was "a prick" (rather than a penis) last year and telling the other guys that some incident happened while I had his class. I say, "Well, you grew out of it then." He says mostly and I assure him the rest will come. A memorable moment of maturity and apology. I actually don't remember him at all – it can be hard to distinguish one specific prick from the crowd.

COUNT THE RASCALS – *Math/Science, Freeway Limits Middle, February 20, 2007*
The teacher sent the wrong lesson plan. The fallback is – guess what – movies. For Science, *Jurassic Park*. – that's some good science. As for the Math classes, which are notoriously difficult for film programming, it's going to be – and you're not going to guess this one – a *Little Rascals* movie. Maybe the idea is that you have to count to see how many Little Rascals actually appear in it. (You could probably use one for History too – they're in black and white.)

REDEMPTION – *Language Arts/Social Studies, William Howard Taft Middle, February 21, 2007*
The teacher having posted a list of proscribed items on the door, I seize a Gameboy early in first period and a cellphone later. Gameboy in the left pocket, phone in the right – to be delivered to counselor at lunch. And a girl who is up and loud continually is up again, doing a peer's hair. She should stop and sit. I should shut up. She should repair to the counselor's office. She ignores the directive. Phone is busy, so I send down a note to the office for Ms. M to send security.
Closing the windows at the end of a full day of middle school dreck, another girl – a nice one – hangs around to tell me that this isn't a very good class. I ask her if she thinks it's worse than the others around here, because I know that kids act like idiots when there's a sub, etc., although of course I don't mean everyone, like I don't mean her for instance. In the midst of this island moment of sanity, the girl whose cellphone I hold shows up to plead for its return. And whom

does she bring to help argue her case? The girl I had to call security on this morning.

Now, this is a poor choice of counsel and I am unmoved. We head down to the office where the two start pleading with Ms. M after I turn over the phone. So I leave on an up note, with a previously brassy girl sniveling in the front office. All's well that ends well!
Student Name of the Day: Lyric James (girl)

WATCHES – *Basic Math, Appian Way High, February 26, 2007*
After I go help a student with a problem, I find a note has been deposited on my desk: "Mr. Gallagher watchs gay porno on his computer." I go to the board and spell out "watches" and explain that even though this is math class, spelling counts. I would hate for some young man who obviously has so much to say to be taken for an idiot because he can't spell.

REMOVE THAT - *Science, Appian Way High, March 2, 2007*
The current openness about menstruation seems to be getting a bit out of hand. Today a boy deposits an apparently used menstrual pad on the teacher's desk. (I just report the facts here.) I make him remove his pad. Perhaps a misguided notion of what was appropriate to a science class.

TEACHER'S PET? – *Special Ed, Citadel Middle, March 12, 2007*
Instructions from the teacher: "Teacher's Manuel on table." But he wasn't.

CONNECTION – *Math/Science, Worcester Middle, March 21, 2007*
I make what may be my strongest connection ever with a middle school group. When spending last Christmas in Ireland with my friend Ray (whose last Christmas it would be, due to pancreatic cancer), his two young sons were all over us to watch their video of the *Family Guy Movie*. When they finally prevailed upon us we were roaring laughing and I've been a fan ever since. So today, as we're reading a section on condensation, I ask does anyone watch *Family Guy*? "Yes," shouts back what seems like two-thirds of the class. So I ask if they remember the one where Peter (the father, of whose name they have to remind me) plays football for the New England Patriots and goes off to England and watches BBC television, which is so boring that at one point he's watching a program about condensation. For a brief moment I felt like I had respect.

ALL? – *Roving, Worcester Middle, April 20, 2007*
Most noteworthy event was the seventh grader falling out of her blouse in the first row. The St. Athanasius uniforms did not allow for that problem. (Although, recalling that seventh grade pregnancy when I was in eighth, I realize some got out of the uniform somehow.) I tell a kid not to be a nuisance if he's going to want to go to the bathroom. "What's a nuisance?" "It's a pain in the ..." He understands. Perhaps we could get them all "street dictionaries."

No prep period today and in most schools the secretary would just routinely mark you down for an extra period, but it would be foolish to assume that here. Indeed, when I mention it to the long suffering secretary, she says, "Did you work every period?" When I reply that I did, she says, "Did you work all of every period?" For her to know that would have required her to actually read the schedule she gave me and that, after all, is my job, not hers, so I give her back the schedule so that she can check for herself.

TELÉFONO – *Economics/History, Appian Way High, April 23, 2007*

Fourth period is student government. They're discussing next week's planned events. Some will stuff their mouths with marshmallows and say "chubby bunny;" others will play telephone in Spanish, because it'll be Cinco de Mayo. And we wonder why the U.S. embarrasses itself at the U.N.?

Back in a few days for the English program that deteriorates badly as the day goes on – starting with AP Seniors and descending to the dregs. When the seniors are quietly settled in, I ask if the teacher ever tells them how much she appreciates this class. They say no, so I explain that, for instance, she has what are essentially fifth year middle schoolers in her fifth period class. At this point one says, "Oh, like the rest of the school."

And, indeed, fifth period is rock bottom today. I eject a guy for talking out after I've announced I will eject anyone who talks out. He is, of course, shocked. These classes hit you by surprise the first time around because they're "college prep," but about a third of these guys should not be planning on attending any currently accredited institution.

I greet sixth period with enthusiasm, simply for not being fifth period. And then my student "aide" arrives, late and noisy. I happily facilitate his desire to go the library, noting to the sophomores afterwards how hard it is to get good help these days.

DIDN'T WANT TO WATCH – *Russian, La Boheme High, May 4, 2007*

The issue in Russian 1 is to get students to stop playing their guitars. The Russian 3 kids drop in remarkably late; one says she just got off work; almost no concern is shown for the assignment. Students enter and leave class at will. Pretty much what I expected at an "arts" school. And how do they get away with this? Well today, obviously because I allow it. And how does that happen? Because they are pleasant and act like this is their regular routine.

After my last class (at 12:10), I'm informed that I'm expected to answer the phone in the office until 2, during which time an administrator comes by and says he needs to clear up an urban legend. Apparently a number of my students were found in Starbucks and claimed that I told them that if they didn't want to watch the movie they could leave. Of course, there was no movie for them even not to watch.

Student Name of the Day: George Washington

SENIOR CARTOONS – *English, Appian Way High, June 1, 2007*
    Third period senior class gets to see a movie – choice of *The Lion King* and *The Motorcycle Diaries*. I explain that *Motorcycle Diaries* is about Che Guevara. They overwhelmingly choose the cartoon.

EXILE ON MAIN STREET? – *Assistant Principal, Citadel Middle, June 5, 2007*
    Among other things, I am outfitted with a walkie talkie, just like in Bosnia, and told that I've got the front entrance for passing period, the breeze way for lunch, and California Street bus duty after school. While I'm in the hall, the Principal, Mr D, comes by and asks if I follow music. He then takes out the *Rolling Stone* all-time top ten album list to discuss. Five Beatle albums? I mean, really. And the one Rolling Stones is *Exile On Main Street*? He doesn't know the Clash and I tell him a little bit about them. This has got to be the only principal who'd stop to have that discussion.

*****

CUTLERY– *Home Economics, Appian Way High, August 24, 2007*
Same assignment on the board for all classes: Finish the utensils worksheets from yesterday, read the text (*Guide To Good Food*) section "Getting Started in the Kitchen" and do the worksheet. They are studying cutlery.

In the "And you thought you couldn't go lower" department, a note arrives from San Francisco saying that the District has agreed with the union that sub lists will be cleared of those subs who worked fewer than 36 days last year (once a week), so unless I want to explain why last year was an aberration, I'll be out. This turns out to be a blessing in disguise, though, as I check my records and discover that I actually did work exactly 36 days – counting the two days I discover on a green sheet I never submitted. Not turning in my worksheet – now, you don't get rich that way, now do you?

Continuing my South San Francisco turn for another year, this will be be the first of sixty-five days I will spend at Appian Way High In the course of this school year. In those sixty-five days I will preside over classes in Algebra, American History, Art, Biology, Broadcasting, Ceramics, Chemistry, Economics, English, English Language Development, Foods, French, Geometry, Health, Home Economics, Independent Living, Italian, Life Skills, Life Science, Psychology, Phys Ed, Spanish, all levels of Special Education, Physical Education, Typing and World History.

These classes will cover utensils worksheets, money logs, shopping and baking chocolate chip cookies, "Getting Started in the Kitchen" from *Guide To Good Food, The Autobiography of Frederick Douglass,* "A Raisin In the Sun," *The Giver, The Night, Catcher In the Rye,* "The Knight's Tale," the *Iliad, Huckleberry Finn, Beowulf, The Autobiography of Anne Frank and One Hundred Years of Solitude* (which one girl proclaims her favorite book ever and can't stop talking about how one of the characters has a "big dick") and various linguistic, mathematical and scientific topics.

I will show *Beetle Juice, Freedom Writers, Hotel Rwanda, In Search of Shakespeare, Jurassic Park, Kandahar, Pearl Harbor, Planet in Peril, Pocahantas, The Young Frankenstein* and videos on the American Revolution and Leonardo DaVinci.

I will attend the Folklorico dance spring assembly. I will enter a classroom head first through the window when I don't have a key. I will watch a student's mother yell, "You gotta move that shit; we've gotta get to work" as another clueless parent in a huge SUV backs up traffic at the school parking lot by trying to go in the out driveway.

I will eject three girls from one class for obsessive/compulsive grooming, thinking that my three cats are obsessive groomers too, but they're much nicer. I will finally learn the cause for students threatened with referrals also expressing a need to go to the bathroom at a much higher than average rate, when one of them explains that it's because they pee themselves with fear over the referral.

I will pose the question: Why do people do pottery, when most of it is just so heavy and shatters if you knock it over. (Give me – as Nanci Griffith used to say – unnecessary plastic objects from Woolworth's any time. But there aren't any

Woolworth's any more, are there? Hopefully my ceramicist friends are only skimming by this point.)
    I will encounter a student wearing a tie.
    But I will not be offered tenure.
Student Names of the Sixty-five Days: Jazztina Lopez, Judas Ochoa, King Tautoa, L'Amour Verdon (male.)

BLACKBALLED, AGAIN – *Special Education, Cappuccino High,*
    September 17, 2007
    I'm only here because there was a screw-up with the job I was supposed to have at Appian Way High and they're lacking a sub here, which makes me realize I must be blackballed here. I haven't been here since January and I have no inkling why.
    On the other hand, I've received notice from SFUSD that they will now accept demand sheets postmarked on the 20th, as opposed to insisting they be in their hands on the day the pay period ends. Given that the suggested solution of the union's new Substitute Division Vice President's was to mail them in on the 18th, I don't figure that she's behind the change. Did my vanguard action of pitching a fit at the sub payroll office have anything to do with this? One of life's small triumphs?
    Meanwhile, in the news, yesterday's *Chronicle* reported a study showing white and Chinese parents avoiding specifically black schools, as opposed to just poor schools.
    And, oh yeah, around here, it's pretty standard special ed fare; they do some homework – and they eat.

NICE! – *History, Novice High, November 27, 2007*
    A school I haven't been to before. This is a one-year, new immigrant program that's been in a few locations and now the Inner Sunset. There's a metered parking lot next to the building, so I take a spot and ask in the office. The secretary says why don't I park in the schoolyard like the other teachers, which I gladly do. As I'm getting out of my car, the person pulling in next to me asks am I there for the day because I'm taking someone's spot. I say the secretary didn't say any spot, but this person says subs have no spot. *God, they can be so welcoming!* But well, he considers further, maybe people can just move over. Ya think?
    Anyhow, five classes to take to computer lab to work on a major religion in Power Point which allows them to write simply, in few words. I go over their writing and they all thank me. A school where every student is nice! They should bring old teachers dying of cancer here, or something like that.
Student Name of the Day: Bail Nixon

NOW, THIS I KNOW – *Detention Room, Gilbert Middle, December 4, 2007*
    Very late call. I arrive at 10:40 and find the office manned by a child. When the secretary arrives, she has to call around to find out the status of the program. Eventually a student takes me to counseling where they call around

some more and send me downstairs to the detention room. Enroute, I notice students pushing and shoving each in the corridors during passing time, in full view of adults, so I still won't be taking a classroom job here. Anyhow, the room's locked, so it's back to the counselor's office and then back to the secretary for the key.

The program is that students are to sit here and copy from sheets explaining why they've been sent here. They can also do school work, but apparently these guys don't often bring that with, or admit to it anyway. Eventually a counselor calls and says she's sending a student, but he never arrives. I don't see my first until after noon. He's here for lunch detention which the regular teacher has noted he doesn't find very effective and would like to see eliminated. Another kid also arrives, but upon checking I learn that he just appears here regularly and is to be told to leave.

The guy who's actually supposed to be here says he can't remember his home room number – and the like – and eventually writes a little. Another guy is sent in and he quietly writes. A counselor brings another who won't write, but he is quiet. Another shows up with no paperwork, but he disappears. All in all, I am not very much disturbed during the day. I guess this is sort of the eye of the hurricane.

TOLERABLE– *Science, Pizarro High, December 6, 2007*

A guy in the Conspiracy of Beards (that's my acapella men's choir that sings only Leonard Cohen) works here this year and says Pizarro is okay now. It looked okay when I was at Gilbert across the street two days ago and I've been going back to Copernicus the last couple of years because it's changed for the better, so I figure I'll give it a shot. He's essentially right. The classes are long – hour and eleven minutes – and you wouldn't say the groups were ideal, but they are manageable. It's about on the level of Dolores High. A lot of security and no bathroom passes. If they really gotta go, you call security to escort them. Four ejections, but I call it not a bad day. Not a great place, but the atmosphere is not menacing. Of course, I've only had freshmen. Would I come back? Yeah, I guess.

TALKING SHOP – *Government/Psychology, Millard Fillmore High, December 12, 2007*

The student teacher in fourth period asks if I've ever been a teacher. My answer about not being interested in taking the requisite education courses gets him going. He says he has to take five three-hour courses and that maybe twenty minutes a week is useful and that might be a conversation with another student. Teachers run out of things to discuss; they'll show a classroom section of *Ferris Bueller's Day Off* and ask what the teacher's doing wrong. He thinks the training needs to be vocational – in the classroom, but you have all these ed schools full of professors who are no longer in the classrooms they teach about.
Student Name of the Day: Pandora Lau

PERCEPTIVE – *Math, Dolores High, January 2, 2008*
   The teacher has left an assignment on the machine, but no first period student makes the slightest move to do anything. Supposed to be Advanced Algebra; nothing looks too advanced. Generally unpleasant – and it's quite chilly in this room, to boot. An announcement follows that they've called downtown on that. It's early in the year and maybe some of the heating people extend their holidays as well.
   Second period's not as bad and one girl even goes so far as to ask where the books are. Well, no one asked that during first – I just assumed they had them, but then that was a moot point, anyhow. She also asks for a pass to another room because some assignment is due from over the break. You mean you actually want to do something? Well, I can think of no argument against that.
   I'm supposed to help in the library now, but the secretary says that some teacher has to leave suddenly and could I cover there. The teacher, who's still there, tells me they can be pretty rough and shows me the referrals. Some kids do math, but there's a few guys frequently out of their seats playing. When I indicate they need to stop doing that one of them says, "You look like you don't even want to be here." "Perceptive kid," I respond. Unfortunately, they don't appear to know what "perceptive" means. Not looking forward to coming back.
Student Name of the Day: Christ Baltazar

CANDY – *English/Social Studies, Johnny Rotten High, February 7, 2008*
   Mainly we're all in here today just to run out the clock, without illusions to the contrary. I think the smart money would market this place as some kind of existentialism magnet school.
   I run into George M who was my home teaching student (you do it in the library, actually) last semester after he got expelled. He was in no way a thuggish kid. I tell him the place is much as I remember it and my advice is that he should keep to himself.
   Various projects are up on posterboard on the wall; one is an autobiography in which a girl says her grandfather was a pimp. At the end of class, I erase my name from the board. I don't always think to do that, but in this case, I'd like to remove all evidence of having been here.
   (The markers were kept in the teacher's desk because you couldn't leave anything out here without the kids taking it. I stopped one kid from getting into a filing cabinet from which he intended to steal a bag of candy. That's what this place is like – high school kids trying to steal candy.)
   On my way out I see there's some kind of altercation on the street corner to which all available adults are racing. Me, I'm off the clock and I hope to be off the clock here for a long time.

RACE CARD – *Biology/Marine Science, Millard Fillmore High, March 3, 2008*
   I've got one little a-hole in third period who wants to push it: "What the hell are you talking about?" etc. Eventually he goes over the edge, but I've got no referrals and no seating chart. I call over to Rich D, who's on prep two doors down,

and he sends over a referral form. Now for the name. The student tells me "Don't worry about that," so I call for security. As this develops, I hear a kid tell him to "Play the race card" and he starts telling the security guard that I'm a racist. I actually don't know what "race" the kid is – Filipino, Latino?

At the end of class, I inform a kid that there's a piece of paper in his hair – there had been a certain amount of paper throwing earlier – and he starts into how he hates teenagers. He's pretty funny actually. Little kids are okay, he says, because they'll listen, but teenagers! He says he's amazed I haven't killed one in years of subbing. And tells me about some Japanese movie where kids are put on an island with weapons and hunt each other down. These moments of connection with students are all too rare in the educational system.

Student Name of the Day: Tranea Boyland

IN MY ESTIMATION – *Math/Science, Freeway Limits Middle, March 7, 2008*

One period we have what the aide calls "new math" – it's done out of a book with cards and it involves estimating – that is, teaching kids how to calculate the wrong answer. Seems to me that everything you teach off the main point is a potential blind alley for students to get lost in, and a method from which they will have to be weaned. Kind of like paper training your puppy, I think – not that I think teaching middle school is in any way like picking up dog doo, mind you.

ME AGAIN? – *Math, Worcester Middle, April 16, 2008*

The regular teacher is in the classroom with his maybe five year old daughter when I arrive. Thanks me profusely for coming. Says things have been getting difficult around here lately. They divide the math kids up between high and low achievers and this is his year for low. "And you've got the nice low-achievers and then you've got the - what's the politically correct way to say this?" he says. "Jerks," I offer. Worcester, he says, has been getting the kids expelled from Freeway and Cucamonga and now there's two or three in every class and the referrals have been moving at a great clip. His notes classify third period as "horrible."

On my way in I thought I'd noticed a kid I once threw out of a Freeway class twice in the same period. (Guys getting thrown out twice in a single period constitute quite an elite group, so they tend to leave an impression.) Sure enough, his name's on the first period problem list and the teacher can't believe I recognize the name. His next ejection takes only about fifteen minutes into class when he denies he has a cellphone in his hand when he quite obviously has a cellphone in his hand, one which I must assume he is using as a calculator, which is proscribed during the quiz. "Why do you always do this to me?" he wants to know. I notice a swastika on his binder, along with the words "swatstikon" and "Nazi perophalia." Bad breath, too.

This is the class with the great rock collection and all the California Stock Market Game Awards. Can't really say I approve of the values inculcated by the stock market game, but I've got to approve of the effort. And I love the rocks.

NOI – *Language Arts/Social Studies, Freeway Limits Middle, May 9, 2008*
Battling through my second day here. The teacher's left a long, somewhat involved packet project with three poems that's proving a pretty tough go with the first double period group. We've got nine tardies for first period and six for second – that's six of them late getting back to the room they were just in. I throw one out within five minutes of the start of first period and write another referral after the bell ending second period, so it's pretty much start-to-finish competition.

At lunch, a teacher asks if I'm working every day next week. She says some of the subs get run over by the classes here. She asked her class if they wanted me to sub for her and they said, "No," so she knew she wanted me to. They may run into problems in South City filling classrooms like these, of San Francisco-level difficulty, at the South San Francisco-wage rate.

Back in a week for an old fashioned morning of throwing kids out. My instructions say to send them to specific other rooms, but one teacher returns them and they are found in the bathroom. Four referrals one period – the edge of total revolt. The first period aide says subs are refusing to come back. She's quite surprised when I tell her that most of the middle schools in San Francisco are worse

REFUTATION – *English Language Development, Millard Fillmore High, May 13, 2008*
The newspaper tells us that a first grader showed up with a loaded gun at Cleveland Elementary School yesterday. My Friend the Evil Substitute Teacher calls to bemoan the fact that we're being outgunned by first graders now!

These are Rich D's classes and the afternoon guys continue to refute the proposition that all ESL classes are nice.
Name of the day: Wallyson Jian

NO RETURN – *Careers/History, Millard Fillmore High, May 20, 2008*
I generally wipe the "Don't return" class slate clean at the end of the year, but this should have been in my permanent record. Three periods of Career Education video on workplace problems that these guys probably think is a "How to" training film. Two of these classes are major pains but the teacher's left me no seating charts or referrals. I leave him a note that I wouldn't take this job again. I just hope I live up to my vow. There've been plenty of situations I've haven't planned on returning to, but I won't leave a note to that effect unless I feel that part of the problem is the teacher's laxness. You might get away with that in Cabot, or most of the classes here even, but not these.

HIGHER LEVEL – *Math/Science, Freeway Limits Middle, May 27, 2008*
Most of the kids are off to Discovery Kingdom today, so the three remaining in first period watch *Shrek II*. Not *Shrek I*, mind you – this must be the advanced group.

NEVER GETS THEM THIS QUIET – Book Stamping, Shady Grove Elementary, June 6, 2008

Listed as Computer Lab, this turns out to be a book stamping job, a qualification I carry on my resume. Plus some fill-in for a fourth/fifth grade class with a coloring assignment and a history project – and a retired government-worker-from-the-neighborhood classroom volunteer. The kids are allowed to talk, unless they get too loud, at which point my instructions say I am to forbid talking entirely – which I do. At one point, the volunteer tells me, "She never gets them this quiet for this long." That's what can happen when you bring middle/high school-level firepower to an elementary school.

JOY LUCK – Special Education Reading, Sonny and Cher Bono High, June 23, 2008

First day of summer school. The secretary and the principal don't know the place and can't even find me a key. The principal can't tell me if I have an aide. When someone finally shows up to open the door, the first thing I have to do is move the desks and chairs. No lesson plan, curriculum, class list, or even markers. I call the secretary to report this. Nothing happens. At the suggestion of the special ed math teacher next door, I call down and try to speak to the AP who's in charge of curriculum. He's not in his office and nothing happens. A student arrives and his assignment sheet says this is a Reading class, so that's how I learn what subject I'm subbing in. At the beginning of class we have two students; eventually this swells to five.

Nosing around the room, I check out the file cabinet and find a drawer full of worksheets. Of course, as the "reloj" label on the clock should have told me, this is normally a Spanish classroom and so the worksheets are in Spanish. The only thing I've got is a single copy of the novel *Joy Luck Club*. I ask the aide who has now shown up to photocopy me the first chapter for second period. I get one kid to read a little, but not unexpectedly – given the nature of the class – she doesn't do that very well, so I read virtually the entire chapter to them. This only takes about an hour and the class is two and a half hours. Tomorrow I'll try two chapters. This is appalling.

Second day, it's read, read, read. A bit of help from the students, but mostly me. In the second period, as I'm starting to read, a girl actually asks if she can and I am delighted. Of course, after she finishes she puts her head down and doesn't pay attention pretty much the rest of the way out. But the way I've got to look at it today, as long as they're quiet, I'll take it. (We're now up to 11 out of 31 students present in first period – I've gotten a class roster by now.)

In second period, I've got one sacked out on the floor in back, but I'm not even going to try to stop that. What would be the point, really? Everyone knows I'm filling time; I've made that quite clear to the kids. One girl pulls out a phone and continues to talk as I tell her to stop. I call the secretary to ask for security, but no one ever comes. The only time I see them was when I let a kid out to the bathroom and they came to tell me that the kids could only do so in their company. They take five boys to the bathroom and say they'll be back for the girls, but I never see them again.

When kids start to make noise, I walk over and read while standing right above them. I read right to the closing bell so as not to give the crowd any time to start up. Man, is this ridiculous!

The para in this class lives on the Peninsula and is thinking of seeing if she can work down there, as she is none too impressed by what goes on in the city.
Administrator Name of the Day – Assistant Principal Payne

*****

WHY A DUCK? – *Chinese, Millard Fillmore High, August 28, 2008*

A guy I met here a couple of days ago says he taught summer school at Bono for two days and a kid threatened to shoot him, so he left. Makes my two days look good, I guess. Anyhow, yes, I'm a Chinese teacher today. Fortunately all of the students are ethnically Chinese, (although a couple of gaijins will join us on day two), so someone knows what they're doing. They have an assignment to copy all words in hanzi, pinyin, (traditional and modern as I understand it) and English. I ask whether they actually already know Chinese but are in class to learn to read and write as you might find in Spanish classes. Someone explains that they know Cantonese and this is Mandarin. I've had this explained to me before and I don't claim to understand it, but apparently the written versions are quite similar while the spoken are not – "The chicken talking to the duck" according to a Hong Kong saying.

The only bad part of this job, really, is listening to the high school kids talking on the bus. (I sold the Volvo to the state as part of a program to get "gross polluters," as I believe they unkindly referred to my former vehicle, off the road. So I'm now a regular public transit rider.) They're not actually aggressive, but they do sound that way. As My Friend the Evil Substitute Teacher says, the surest way to maintain public support for public education is to keep the kids off of public transportation. Make sure the public can't see what it's supporting. Make the kids walk; put them in cabs if you have to.

Which somehow brings to mind the most important school story of recent days – the decision of the Harrold Independent School District in Texas to allow teachers to carry concealed weapons. According to Associated Press: "In order for teachers and staff to carry a pistol, they must have a Texas license to carry a concealed handgun; must be authorized to carry by the district; must receive training in crisis management and hostile situations and have to use ammunition that is designed to minimize the risk of ricochet in school halls."

Ammunition that is designed to minimize the risk of ricochet in school halls – now, doesn't that have a ring to it? It seems the school is a thirty minute drive from the Sheriff's and as the Superintendent sees it, "When the federal government started making schools gun-free zones, that's when all of these shootings started. Why would you put it out there that a group of people can't defend themselves?" (Or, as they used to say in Rome, "Cum catapultae proscriptae erunt tum soli proscripti catapultas habebunt.")

As you might imagine, My Friend the Evil Substitute Teacher called and said he's moving to Texas. I'm not sure if he's serious.

Student Names of the Day: Parris Bender, Yu Hu

SHE WORE WHAT? – *Business Education, Appian Way High, September 24, 2008*

Lunch room discussion on girls in scanty clothing prompted by a short shorts sighting this morning: the girl in the bra on Halloween and the one spread over the desk in short skirt and thong. So, yes girls, they do talk about it in the teacher's lunchroom.

Ms. S spots me and asks if I'm available for her English Language Development class next week and says. "Goody, they always do their work when you're there." Appreciate an evidence-based vote of confidence. I rather enjoy this one because I try to get to the fine points of grammar and pronunciation and empathize about the difficulties of English pronunciation. Having somewhat seriously studied Latin, Ancient Greek, German and Spanish and dabbled in Russian, Serbo-Croatian/Bosnian and Irish, I may be fluent in none, but I do at least know something about what's difficult in learning a language. When I've spent time on pronunciation in ESL classes, I've been told by aides that it doesn't happen normally and I actually cannot think of one set of instructions I've ever gotten in an ESL class that directed me to work on it. Odd – if you're learning a foreign language you generally want to learn precisely how it is properly pronounced and yet this doesn't seem to come up in public school. These days, I wouldn't be surprised if there's a school of thought that working on eliminating kids' accents was racist.

Experimenting with taking the Mission 14 bus for the last leg of the trip home. At this hour of the day it's sort of a rolling take of Chaucer's *Canterbury Tales* – there's just all sorts of stuff happening. A young woman explains God's will to a young man in front of me as others throw spare food in the stairwell and such. The guy behind me tells someone on his cellphone, "This is the ghettoist fucking bus I've ever seen." And these are just the pilgrims at the back of the bus.

BODILY FUNCTIONS– *Roving, Freeway Limits Middle, October 16, 2008*
Two sixth grade classes of I.B. Singer's *Zlateh the Goat,* two seventh grades of Mark Twain's *The Californian's Tale* and then a showing of *Osmosis Jones*, a mixed live-action/animated movie about the digestive system starring Bill Murray that is arguably the preeminent Hollywood release on bodily functions over the past several decades.

NEBRASKA'S NICE– *Electricity/Photo, Appian Way High, October 24, 2008*
On Tuesday, two separate Citadel teachers called me to sub but had given the job to someone else by the time I called them back. Now that was annoying. I'd resolve to quit, but what good would that do?

Lots of discussion in the press lately about that Nebraska law allowing parents to drop off their children if they think they can't handle them – to prevent child abuse, I believe the idea was. Someone has now dropped off a seventeen year old and another parent showed up with a kid from Georgia, I think. I'm wondering if maybe the parents of some of these guys here today would spring for one-way plane tickets.

Today's lunch room discussion includes a section on female students with stripper's poles at home – facts wafting out from MySpace or something.

The South San Francisco machine calls shortly after I get home, so I'm thinking maybe next week won't be so bad, since I already have jobs for Monday and Wednesday and this call will presumably make it three days. Wrong, Mooseface, it's a cancellation of the Monday job!

JUST FOOLING – *Math/Science, Freeway Limits Middle, October 27, 2008*
    Phone rings at eight thirty-something and it's Ms. K. Although they canceled my job, they still apparently thought I would show up at Freeway. Some kind of loyalty test, maybe. Off I go.
Student Name of the Day: Caribbean Cruz

RETURN? – *RSP, Appian Way High, November 26, 2008*
    Nine in first period; seven present; all male – boring and obnoxious. The aide, whom I've worked with before, seems to want me to write referrals. I write her a shelf referral for one guy who keeps saying "You want to get shot?" to no one in particular. The others seem to have similarly limited repertoires.
    The teacher returns from jury duty before the end of the day; asks if I'll ever be back again, due to the first period. Says most of them have been incarcerated and now it's become routine for them – they know they can do it. Had to move one kid out of the class because he just couldn't take the rest of them. Seen worse though.
    My Friend the Evil Substitute Teacher calls. Says he was hoping to get together a major scholarship fund together to deport some of his students to Nebraska and then the legislature went and amended the law so that they would only take infants from Nebraska – just like any other state. Nothing good ever lasts.

MELLOW YELLOW – *English, Appian Way High, December 1, 2008*
    First period Junior Honors reading *Legend of Sleepy Hollow* aloud. Don't know that I've actually ever read it before. Towards the end of class, a guy right in front of me doesn't want to read when he's called on by another student, popcorn style. Seems a bit unusual for a student to be reticent about reading in an Honors class, but all is clarified a moment later when he throws up on the floor. Another first for me, so far as I can recall. I guess it's new experiences like this that keep me subbing. The janitor is summoned and he arrives with what used to be the green stuff – but is now yellow – for the cover-and-sweep operation that takes me back to first grade and the heyday of throw-up.
Student Name of the Day: Lady Angelique Oliva

THE N WORD – *ESL, Millard Fillmore High, December 4, 2008*
    The bus is maximum crowded because there's only the one starting time at Fillmore on Thursdays, as opposed to the usual staggered start. Listening to kids going on about "Hey nigger, he dunk on you?" and that sort of stuff, I think of my friends who went on the road for Obama who seemed mildly shocked that people would tell them they were voting for "the nigger."

A COLD DAY – *Computer Lab/PE, Ocotlan Elementary, December 10, 2008*
    Apparently I'm here is because it's a *Day Without a Gay*, an event of which I was heretofore unaware – a takeoff on a *Day Without Immigrants*. But

these days, it sort of figures it'd have to be a day when you can't even find a gay in San Francisco before they'd call me.

I stuff Wednesday envelopes; conduct frisbee and dodge ball classes (which I dread, but from which the kids emerge seemingly injury-free), computer lab; and perform lunch duty. At which time, two cafeteria workers are appalled at the individually packed and wrapped food items thrown away at the end, even if unopened. Everyone comments on the irony of the schools hurting for money.

And, oh yes, someone has turned on the air conditioner on in the computer lab because it's in the sun – while there's heat on in the rest of the building. I'm sitting there with a sweater and hat on and thinking of putting my coat back on.

LETTERS – January 15, 2009

No work, but there is mail. Yesterday, Chris, the secretary at Freeway, asked if I had gotten an envelope and here it is – a classful of letters dated 11/21 from Ms. D's art class. They are apologizing for misbehaving. I believe Chris had walked in during class that day and apparently mentioned her observations to Ms. D. Me? I can barely remember it. It certainly didn't stand out in my mind as beyond the norms of substitute experience, particularly at Freeway. Hopefully the kids at least had an unpleasant time writing this.

COOL IT – PE, Worcester Middle, January 16, 2009

Assembly where a guy with long hair and a colorful outfit does an almost circus-like performance with dry ice, liquid nitrogen and such. When he pours the latter on the floor it turns to gas immediately. No kids were frozen during the performance or anything, but My Friend the Evil Substitute Teacher seemed very interested when I told him about it.

NOT ON MY WATCH – School Age Mothers Program, Johnny Rotten High, January 21, 2009

Back with the girls who flunked sex ed. "This class is like a supervised independent study," as the notes say. Eight girls present today; all Latina; all well behaved. I recognize one from fifth grade math summer school. The only real issue of the entire day was giving a few warnings to a girl who took her cellphone out. I feel obligated to keep them from going on any more dates, you know.

VERY TWENTY-FIRST CENTURY – First Grade, Bonanza Elementary, February 19, 2009

Having decided economic exigencies required it, I'm here for my first first grade in a long time. Hard to describe because so much goes on in the low grades that the teachers can't even write all their instructions down. Likewise, I have trouble even remembering what all happened if I try to write it down the next day. I am particularly struck by kids learning the greater ($>$) and less-than ($<$) signs that we didn't take up until high school. One kid is on a program where you draw a happy or sad face for each time block. He gets sad faces all day and I even send him to the office for a while, but there are really no serious problems. And, btw, I'm now getting jobs via cellphone! I've arrived in the twenty-first century – only nine years late.

JUVENILE DERIVATIVES – Math, Appian Way High, March 2, 2009

Third period, in walks a kid saying, "Mr Gallagher, I haven't seen your ass since Freeway." After informing the young man that he didn't see it then either, I realize that it's JP whom I kicked out of summer school two summers back. Other than that, good program here. First period is asleep; second period is ESL and tiny (5 out of 6 present), and this one is large and awake, but within tolerable bounds. The afternoon class will be doing derivatives and you just know there aren't going to be a lot of juvenile delinquents doing derivatives.

On my second day, the fifth period kids keep claiming that someone has something that's making a high pitched noise – but I can't hear it. Don't know if they're making it up or whether it's that kids hear higher pitched sounds, but it does make me think maybe I should invest in a really annoying dog whistle.

My next stint here, Ms. S's note asks me to make sure they don't cheat, and indeed I see one with the answers on his hand. When I send him to the bathroom to wash them off (Hey, kids! There's a tip – Want a bathroom pass? Write the test answers on your hand) he takes an awfully long time because, of course, he had to rewrite them on a piece of paper which he somehow doesn't think I'm going to notice him copying from. Of course, if they were geniuses, they probably wouldn't be copying in the first place, now would they?

And then we have the girl who comes in early for sixth and says she was supposed to read the regular teacher's tarot cards, so could she read mine instead. It's her senior project, she says. Very California.

Finally, My Friend the Evil Substitute Teacher calls very excited about this story; he thinks the idea has fundraising potential for hard-up schools:

Report Says Principal Put Students in Cage to Fight
By Gretel C. Kovach, March 20, 2009
DALLAS — A high school principal and his security staff shut feuding students in a steel cage to settle disputes with bare-knuckle fistfights, according to an internal report by the Dallas Independent School District.
The principal of South Oak Cliff High School, Donald Moten, was accused by several school employees of sanctioning the "cage fights" between students in a steel equipment enclosure in a boy's locker room, where "troubled" youth fought while a security guard watched, according to the confidential March 2008 report first obtained by The Dallas Morning News.
Mr. Moten, who resigned from the district in 2008 while under investigation in connection with a grade-changing scandal, denies the cage-fight accusations. "That's barbaric," he told The Dallas Morning News. "You can't do that at a high school. You can't do that anywhere. It never happened." But investigators with the district's Office of Professional Responsibility gathered testimony from two

employees at South Oak Cliff High who said they had witnessed students fighting in the cage from 2003 to 2005, among others who heard about the fights. One employee overheard Mr. Moten tell a security guard to take two students who had been at each other for days and "put 'em in the cage and let them duke it out," the report states, and the practice was so embedded in the school's culture that one student remarked to a teacher that he was "gonna be in the cage."
Mr. Moten, 56, is a former Dallas police officer who once lied about being kidnapped and robbed at gunpoint to get out of work, for which he was placed on administrative leave.

Do you know where your principal came from?

HOW'S THAT GO AGAIN? – PE, Ishi Middle, April 13, 2009

Replacing a teacher who apparently was a replacement player with the Giants during Spring training following the 1994 strike. He's left no instructions. A student teacher runs the first period and attempts capture the flag, but fails. Since I don't actually know how that game is played, the other teachers tell me to do kickball. By the end of the day they're telling me to let the kids do whatever.

At one point, when three or four girls just start to pile on one another (in friendly fashion), a boy announces, "If you're grabbing pussy, you're a lesbian, just like if I'm grabbing dick, I'm gay." So the sex ed stuff seems to be working here.

Fourth period I am alone in the gym, counting the minutes. I confiscate a yardstick being used as a sword; no bloodshed, though, which counts as a good day in PE at a city school. Three guys take off, which is all right with me. They return with an AP following. He asks if I've been given any passes. Negative. I've been left exactly nothing by this teacher. I tell him I'm utterly powerless over these guys. He says, "Most of us are." Wishes me good luck. There are seven blacks and one Sikh (all males) shooting hoops. No one else does anything. Last period I am watching over four kids on the tennis court. During the day, a black kid calls me "nigger," the first time that I've directly, unambiguously been called such by a black student, I believe. That does it! As they used to say, "No Vietnamese ever called me nigger."

NO PASSARON! – English, Appian Way High, April 17, 2009

A couple of classes are studying existentialism and I am to read them Sartre's *The Wall*, which I am glad to do – first time for me. Any day I get to talk about the Spanish Civil War and explain the International Brigades and the "falangists" is a good day by me.
Student Name of the Day: Courage Nwaopara

JUST WATCHING – TDS, Johnny Rotten High, April 24, 2009

Back with the severely emotionally disturbed program which has three other adults and ten or eleven kids. Most of them are getting to see movies all day because they've been good and three are doing schoolwork in outlying areas. I watch.

Late in the day, George M, my first home school student comes in. He's graduated now, doing some college work, and working on getting his record cleared. I more or less confirm from him that there were ethnic slurs involved in the incident that got him thrown out of school. (He's Lebanese.) The teachers here tell me he got placed in this class after the guys in the general population class picked on him. That seems like it was probably a good thing for him, although he says when one of these kids here goes off, wow!

THE U.N. – *Fourth Grade, Scarlatti Elementary, May 1, 2009*

I am advised upon entering that the kids will be tough and will push it with a sub and they do – within suburban bounds, that is. One of the day's first events is a tiny little girl handing me a small power pack and a microphone to put on my shirt because she says she can't hear me otherwise. (She's wired on her end, too.) I'm afraid I've given her an earful by the end of the day.

A class survey turns up eleven kids of Philippine origin, plus three halves; four Chinese and a half and a quarter; one and a half with origins in Nicaragua; one Japan; one Israel, one Tonga; three halves Mexico; two halves El Salvador; and halves for Spain, England, Peru, Pakistan, Fiji, and Ireland.

SOMETHING HAD TO GIVE – *Fourth Grade, Skyline Elementary, May 7, 2009*

For math we're doing perimeter and one of the review questions in the book was a simple algebra problem. This is fourth grade. What did we do in math for all those years when I was in grade school? Learned the times tables, I guess. On the other hand, I teach these guys the "i before e" rhyme which they've apparently never heard before. I guess they've given a lot of the old spelling time slot over to math.

REELITY – *Health/Modern World History, Appian Way High, May 11, 2009*

Health class is finishing a "What would I do" worksheet on sex and pregnancy, followed by one on "Reel sex versus real sex" and then a group activity on choosing the appropriate method of birth control. I wonder what the families of the two girls in head scarves in the ESL class make of all this. Ms. L comes in part way through class and I raise this matter of conjecture and she says there was one day when they were supposed to deal with male anatomy and the girls wouldn't even look at the paper and the teacher said to her, "I think I'll just excuse them."

The Modern World History classes are watching *Platoon*. Now that's some rough stuff. We're on the section where they massacre the village. I don't know if students make the connection between this "reel war" and the "real wars" the country's currently engaged in. It'd be a lot more controversial to raise that question than the sex question, me thinks.

One girl to another: "You look hella ghetto today."

FACTS OF LIFE– *First and Second Grades, Strawberry Fields Elementary, May 13, 2009*

Another first time school for me. Heading in for what is now becoming my daily dose of cuteness. Mixed class: eight first graders to my left, nine second graders to my right (and one absent.) You work with one group while the other works on its own. Apparently it's what you do when you have two and a half classfuls of students.

The second grade journal topic: What did you do this weekend? turns out to be left over from yesterday, so I replace it with What would you do if you went to the moon? They like that. Make em look forward to subs, you know.

Lots of "He said; she said" today, but no big tears. Did some shoe tying: Not too tight and double knot, please. Oh, and "She's telling secrets." I will admit that I am totally out of it as to having solutions to problems like that, but I pretty much nod through it and they seem to survive. If it's "She pushed me," etc., well then I'll ask her and usually she'll say that's not what she meant to do and it'll be all right.

I read to them from a picture book in the afternoon while they sit on the rug, which is a common enough routine, but this book turns out to be about a young student who has cancer and loses her hair in chemotherapy, so all of her classmates and her teacher shave their heads. But after a while the kids realize that the teacher's not growing her hair back and that she has cancer too. Turns out she has breast cancer and she tells them she's going to have surgery. The kids start saying that you'll be flat-chested like us and how super models are flat-chested and look how beautiful they are. Wow! And it turns out it's a true story and pictures of the teacher and two girls from the class are in the back of the book. Sister John didn't read us that one in St. Athanasius.

GOOD PERFROMANCE– *Math, Millard Fillmore High, May 15, 2009*
Sign outside the Brotherhood and Sisterhood rally: "Backstage Area: Perfromers Only."

This teacher's got a 286 page book entitled *Discipline in the Secondary Classroom: A Positive Approach to Behavior Management.* My Friend the Evil Substitute Teacher says he has one too. It's called "A Field Manual for Handguns." Task Three In Chapter Three in this book here is entitled "Decide on a Signal You Can Use to Immediately Quiet Your Students and Gain Their Full Attention." My Friend the Evil Substitute Teacher says that his is a warning shot.

San Francisco teachers union e-mail lists 25 schools classified as "hard-to-fill" where teachers will qualify for an extra $2,000 stipend next year. I can vouch for 23 of them; haven't been to the other two. Doesn't say anything about a bonus for subs.

*****

WHAT SHE HEARD – *First & Second Grade, Los Montecillos Elementary, September 18, 2009*

Tiny first grade girl calls me over to tell me, "He said motherfucker." When I tell the teacher upon her return, she thinks maybe I heard it wrong. Uh, no.

Student Name of the Day: Heaven Takapu

DOUBLE DOWN – *September 23, 2009*

Supposed to be a rover at Pine; they canceled the meeting. Morning call for half day at Appian Way; canceled. How low can you go in the job market?

OVER THERE – *Language Arts/PE/Social Studies, Worcester Middle, September 24, 2009*

Countries located by students on Middle East map quiz include: Tucky, Saudi Africae, Afiransce (apparently Afghanistan), Omen, Mesopatina, South Abariba, Sahira, Alfansestan, and Sandaria Arabia.

BONUS – *Fourth Grade, William Dawes College Preparatory School, October 15, 2009*

My first day back in San Francisco after being reinstated. For three years now the union has allowed the district to drop subs with less than thirty-six days worked and I because worked so much in South City, I wasn't close to that number up here last year, so with the assistance of the union rep, I am back at the district's sufferance – in a "bonus school" naturally.

A little taste of why it's hard to get teachers in the bonus schools: At the end of the day, as I'm trying to get the kids in a line to release them, I reach behind me for the doorknob and find it's wet. Two girls tell me that it's because Angel spit on it. Angel's this spaced out girl who has not done much of anything all day, has never been in her seat, but has not caused too much of a problem – up til now – so I've let her be.

There were, you see, others more demanding of my attention like the overly-large-for-his-age boy who's been filling out some form the entire day with the assistance of a girl at his table. Obviously he is on some behavior monitoring program – which has not been explained to me – but they appear to be on top of it, that is so far as filling out the form goes. Substantively, he engages in just about every type of annoying behavior going, throughout the day, culminating in crashing to the floor as his chair falls backward. At one particularly frustrating moment, he announces, "I want to hurt someone."

We also have a very large girl who alternately screams and cries. There's even a Chinese girl with a bad attitude – *and you never get that.* A number of other girls also obviously have fairly delicate psyches that I am far from able to deal with. You just try to make it to the bell on a day like this.

ALSO FAILING – *Roving, William Elementary, October 16, 2009*
Three different classes where even the kid whom I have to spend the most time quieting says that he likes having me in the classroom. We have group activities with genuine interaction of the entire group. Absolutely nothing like that occurred yesterday at William Dawes, where the kids who seemed like they were probably doing okay academically were just on their own and group activity was out of the question. And yet, later this school year, both places will appear on the same state list of failing schools. It can be hard to know even where to start talking about what's wrong with the school rating systems – not only is the whole "failing schools" thing a misleading concept, but these systems obviously don't even measure what they think they measure.

SHOCKED, I TELL YOU – *English/ESL, Appian Way High, October 23, 2009*
Ms. L, the para, says all the teachers I replace like me because I make the kids work. Pleased to hear and not entirely shocked because the ESL classes generally have more basic plans and more motivated students, so one usually *can* make them work. But a couple of weekends back, I ran into the teacher from across the hall in summer school at the Hardly Strictly Bluegrass Festival in Golden Gate Park (the city's absolutely superior bread and circus event, for those of you who don't know) and she introduced me to her husband as "a sub who gets students to do work." Wow.

PADRE PIO DAY – *Librarian (not really), Nathaniel Hawthorne Middle, November 2, 2009*
I know – I said I'd never come back here. But, hey – it's been ten years (Yikes!), long enough for every other sub in the city to have subbed here, so it's probably my turn. Officially, I'm replacing the librarian but the library is not open. First assignment is carrying a computer and boxes of books upstairs to store. You might think that this is simple, but it takes quite some time for it to transpire – getting the keys and such, you know. Anyhow, as any soldier'll tell you, providing logistical support beats actual combat. Then lunch periods in the yard, helping out in the boys locker room at the beginning of PE class, and a Padre Pio assignment where I'm supposed to be in the locker room at the end of the period while simultaneously watching the third floor hall. (For those of you without the benefit of a Catholic school education, at St. Athanasius we learned that Padre Pio, then alive, since promoted to Saint, was so busy that he occasionally had to bi-locate. There really was nothing like nuns' theology for the real skinny.)

Eventually I locate the teachers room to which I repair between bells. They're having to think up things for me to do, so I figure I'm less of an irritant being here.

NOTHING BETTER TO DO – *Economics/Video, Appian Way High, November 5, 2009*
A DeVry University advertising day today for all classes. The presenter gives away pens to students who answer questions on the PDAs she distributes.

They create their own "avatar." She informs us that there are four words in the English language that don't rhyme with anything – orange, purple, silver, and month. That's what we learned at school today.

THE WIRE – Science, Oskar Schindler Traditional High, November 13, 2009

Typical start-of-the-day signs of a difficult school – no key, no schedule, no attendance sheets. The guy who eventually shows up with a key looks familiar and, indeed, he was the counselor at Mateo during my miserable two weeks a few years back. I guess this is some kind of step up from that.

The teacher has left directions, at least. Four periods of Chemistry, which I assume will be fine, and one of Integrated Science, which I assume will not be. After letting a girl out to the bathroom (and even finding the teacher's pass!), I find an instruction sheet apparently given to yesterday's sub that says students are not to be allowed to the bathroom unless accompanied by security guard (not because the halls are so dangerous, I'm told, but because the kids are known to bolt). They send a sub as an escort, there apparently being a surfeit of them as some of the teachers they're replacing don't leave until later in the day. They later send a second sub to be in my classroom all day with me, minus the one period that she's actually been called in to work.

Home room is about what you'd expect – no one listens to announcements and a student comes with an empty jar seeking donations for something, maybe AIDS and leaves with no more than she started with. They can be hard in the big city.

Integrated Science could be worse, which is to say there's only 23 of them instead of, say, 35. Someone tells me that they've done the assignment yesterday. Just waiting out the clock on this one. There are some doing the assignment, but there's a clatch of four black kids pretty much right out of *The Wire* – "Barely housebroken," as one guy says in the show. At one point the boys are on a skateboard and I have to pick up the phone to get them to stop. I have to keep threatening one guy toward the end as he's grabbing other people's stuff to amuse himself. He calls some girl a "racist piece of shit," but then no one seems to take him seriously. Such are the gains of the civil rights movement.

(Speaking of *The Wire*, like many substitutes – I'm guessing – I don't even have basic cable, much less HBO, so *The Wire* had to make its way to the public library on video before I saw it. My immediate reaction was more "cops and robbers," but once I got beyond that I was amazed to find it consistent with what I imagined the home scene was like for some of the kids I saw in San Francisco. Not that I really know much about what's on TV, mind you, but I sure didn't expect to see this, if only because it painted such an unflattering picture. For the first time I feel like I have some public point of reference to describe my experiences to people who often clearly have little idea of what it's like out there.)

Anyhow, I tend to forget that first periods are generally better than what follows because the kids' are still sluggish because the sun has still not warmed up anything past their lizard brains at this hour – my forgetfulness no doubt also due to much the same phenomenon. I actually enforce the no electronics rule in first period when the other sub figures it's not worth it. By third, I'm not going to try – or try to stop the card games either. But on the accomplishment side, there's no one on a skateboard and there are no objects flying through the air. A kid rapping along with his iPod reminds me of hearing the landlord's son working on his rap in the basement studio the other day – his refrain was "All my niggers and all these hos."

The other sub is Russian. The fact that I know more of the history of the Russian Revolution than she is not so surprising, but what does surprise me is that she appears to think there may be some real science behind *2012*, the current the end-of-the-world sci-fi movie, even though she obviously has a science background – she's working on some math in her spare time. Most interesting, though, is that she thinks socialism would be a good idea, just not the way they did it in Russia.

MUY BIEN – *Third Grade, Hully Gully Elementary, November 16, 2009*
Nice class and maybe it's a nice age. We talk about Ireland – the origin of my name, my old favorite *triskaidecaphobia* (we're in room 13), King Tut, living museums and lots of other stuff. As is often the case, I found the math lame – grouping by fours and stuff like that – the four times table works just as well or better, thank you very much. I have a girl pronounce some Spanish words and when I give her a *muy bien*, she's thrilled. And the more I think about the class, the more impressed I am – no table points, no quieting device, nothing.

SIMON WON'T SAY MUCH FOR ME – *PE, Benjamin Banneker Elementary, November 17, 2009*
There've been some changes here. The school day now goes to four and there's only K-3 kids at this location, for openers. It's nearly ten by the time I arrive and it turns out to be mostly one of those *What can we do with this guy?* kind of days – a couple of recesses, then a couple of lunches. First I'm minding a table and opening stuff for kids and then they just put me out on the yard. Then help out with a class where the kids are just a continual problem and the teacher is really frustrated. I try to work with a couple of girls on money counting, but can't get anywhere.

The last hour of the day, they give me a PE class. I take over from this aide of some sort who's very good with the kids. I watched him at lunchtime – he kicks a ball really, really high in the air which thrills the kids. He's playing Simon Says with them when I come and I ask him what to do and he says "Whatever you got." So I try more of that but it doesn't work. I've got no lesson plan, no equipment, and not even a class list – I don't even know if I've got all the kids. So they spend the time on the play structure as I count the minutes down. Not going to make a fuss, as they have hardly driven me hard, but this ain't the way it's supposed to be – but then nothing new there. And then they give me the forms to get my extra hour's pay because of the longer school day, which I would not even have bothered them about, given my arrival time.

The bus going home leaves from a different spot than the one coming there, so I have to do a little perambulating around – long enough to decide that I really don't want to be spending too much extra time around there. Darkness falls early now and it's after four.

MY GODDAMNED HEAD – PE, Shady Grove Elementary, November 24, 2009

The place seems not to be filled with pretty young teachers which is a good sign, in that it means teachers don't transfer out of here. Benjamin Banneker is, because they haven't been around long enough to transfer out. Was not really looking for PE, but it is a gorgeous day to work outside. Wind up with three periods. The guy's left a plan that I cannot fully interpret, even in concert with the kids, but good enough. The first graders can't replicate the drill – warmups, etc., at all, but they just run themselves silly on races and it takes care of itself. At lunch yard duty I observe a boy on the ground crying. Am told he hit the back of his head. Another guy says he'll go for an icepack – something they generally love to do, but he's never heard from again. Maybe he used it himself. Another kid comes by and asks the kid on the ground what happened and he says, "I hit my goddamned head on the ground; that's what I happened." I decide to leave his goddamned head to heal on its own.

Okay, so there was this amazing young female teacher I saw on my way out as she led her charges into the classroom. Basically my point holds, though, I think.

DAY AT THE SYMPHONY – Second Grade, Stokeley Elementary, December 2, 2009

First things I see here are a picture of President Obama with a "We did it" note on it and a recognition of his Nobel Peace Prize. I understand the interest, of course, but he just gave his second Afghanistan escalation address last night and I'm not exactly feeling warm and fuzzy in his direction.

They start the day here with the outdoor pep rally type of thing that you sometimes find in difficult schools – we have to try harder – that sort of idea. Appears to be only grades one to three here now, like at Banneker, so it's small and I am even introduced by the principal at the get together. I'm pleased to learn that mine is one of three classes on a field trip to the Symphony – pleased because I'm accompanying a Resource Room teacher who'll actually be in charge of the class. They wouldn't have sent them with a sub and she volunteered to go so the class wouldn't miss out on account of the teacher's absence.

After a long bus ride across town, we arrive after the half way point in a half hour program. The kids are crawling up the carpeted stairs and all sorts of stuff – "totally out of control," as an usher observes. The show does interest most of them, but it's pretty tough to keep them in their seats and we're in a small balcony with rounded edges that looks like very precarious placement for these guys. They all manage to stay within it, though, and it's decided that we'll stay for the next presentation since we were so late for the first.

In the interim, kids eat what they've brought along on the steps of the Opera – almost the only times that they're good during the day are when they're eating. Staying for the entire second session not surprisingly proves too much. These are supposed to be small doses for little kids and they've now had a dose and a half and very few are into it by the end, particularly since, now that they've eaten, everyone's got to go to the bathroom.

Back at school at maybe 12:30. It's now recess and then to the cafeteria to eat the uneaten school lunches. When we return to the classroom, the other teacher stays, for which I am most grateful. She has the pace down for getting a little bit out of them and has them write a couple of things about what they learned – which I'm sure I couldn't have done. She lets them play the math games to end the day, which means dominoes, and a couple of boys start fighting, and she declares that a mistake. The kids are not supposed to write on the board. (They started the day by erasing the bonus points of selected kids and by the end of the day they're all gone.) When I actually try to enforce the ban, a couple of girls write "stupid sub" on the board – at least they spell it right.

At the end of the day, I tell the resource room teacher how grateful I am that she was there and mention how rare and useful it is to get of glimpse of the behavior norm for a class under something closer to its everyday circumstances and how I might have otherwise assumed they were only being that bad because I was there and not their teacher. She seems a bit taken aback when I put it that way, probably herself wondering if maybe she couldn't have gotten them to be better, although I wasn't meaning to suggest that. But I'd say that, like Dawes, this place has passed a tipping point – bad behavior is the norm.

I'm not breaking any new ground here, or anything. A big part of the argument for busing is to try to break up or at least dilute places like this. It's hard to imagine an informed parent with options wanting to send a kid here. A Muslim woman wearing a head scarf has come on the field trip with her first grade daughter and stays with her at recess. I wonder what she makes of all this.

COMPARISONS – *Fourth Grade, Buenos Dias Elementary, December 3, 2009*

I'm replacing the afternoon English teacher in a team teaching pair. In the morning, I reconstruct decks of math cards while observing the Spanish teacher. For her, the class is very well behaved and she quiets them very easily. During recess, I mention where I was yesterday and she says she was very lucky in getting assigned here in her first year and told herself that eventually she'd switch to a more difficult school, but after eight years she finds herself still there. This, of course, is why they've started paying stipends to teach at Stokeley.

At day's end, I leave the English teacher a note explaining that I would have said the kids were pretty good for me – had I not observed how much better they were for the morning teacher. I spot a note from yesterday's sub saying how good they were for her and how she'd love to come back. So I think: Did she not see how they were for the morning teacher, as I did? Or is she just really good? Or is she a sap? Personally, I never claimed I was cut out for elementary school.

BACK TO REAGAN – *Math, Worcester Middle, December 4, 2009*

Back to the classroom with the stock market stuff and the picture of Ronald Reagan. Weren't no pictures of Ronald Reagan at Stokeley. This guy has drawn the difficult math classes here this year, though. I'll be back here another day and eject three, call in an assistant principal and issue a very satisfying referral at 3:01 on a 3:00 day. Oh yeah, I'm known as the sub with the skinny jeans here, even if I'm not wearing them. Any little statement I can make against baggy, falling-down pants, I'm happy to help.

"FAILING SCHOOL" IN ACTION – *Reading, William Dawes Elementary, December 10, 2009*

Sit in for a while on the class I recently subbed in. The teacher calls two parents on her cellphone while she is teaching. Really doesn't break stride – keeps moving around the classroom. One time she puts the kid on, the other she leaves a message. Her overall m.o. is to quiet the most far-removed from the pace, although she can't really do much more with them. If she took the time it would require to get to their level, she'd lose the rest of the class – so a couple do nothing. The standard order, really, but it's always good to be reminded that it's not just you. And a good reminder of the general uselessness of most of the public discussion about rating teachers. This woman is doing some of the hardest work around and it's hard to imagine someone doing a better job of it and yet I suspect very much that the "output" of the class will show up as "failing."

90 MINUTES! – *Art, Henry Clay Elementary, December 11, 2009*

The teacher is here when I arrive and comes to my first class with me. She tells the kids she feels better than yesterday but still feels sick, so she's going home so she won't be sick for the holidays. (She'll be sick for the taxpayer, instead.) Now I don't know the current status of the ethical debate about coming to school if you have even a bit of a cold, but she wasn't very sick, seemed to me. Anyhow, the big news is they have ninety minute periods in elementary school!

The third and fourth grade group is not half bad – they pick from a sheet of African symbols, draw and color. The first grade was described in the teacher's notes as "squirelly" and the plan is pretty much a wipe-out by half an hour in and I'm just keeping the lid on. There's a boy in first row who goes off real quick – "I can't do this," etc., and soon he's on the floor. There's an aide here and I'm quickly asking whether we've got an option of sending him somewhere, but instead she takes him to the back of the room and he produces one of the best works in the class. So not only doesn't he disrupt, but he produces – what an aide can do!

I am talking real loud and stern to the third/fourth group just before a tour of about ten parent-looking people comes walking through unannounced. One says "You subbing here? Come here often? Would you ever come back?" I tell her it hasn't been bad, but I would have thought they might have wanted to tip me off about the tour. That, however, would have required treating me as something more than a piece of furniture and the assistant principal or whoever it was that was around did not interact with me at all in this process.

MEMORIES OF MARIA – *Kindergarten, Hully Gully Elementary, December 14, 2009*

I'm sprinkling glitter on names written in paste and doing other things I haven't done for a while. And we read *Get Well Santa* and *Amy Loves the Snow* (a dud), do some math, some language, and some Scooby Doo video. At the end of the day the secretary has noticed my time sheet has three days at Appian Way High replacing a teacher she says is her son's best friend. "That's special ed, right? You cover high school special ed and kindergarten?"

This brings to mind Terence, of course, but also an old interview with the opera star Maria Callas I once heard rebroadcast on the radio. The interviewer made some mention of Callas's "rivals." Callas, known for her broad range of roles, from Italian bel canto to Wagner, took umbrage at this. As I recall it, she said something like: "Excuse me, but I have no rivals. If one plays the violin, one does not say 'I only play Beethoven,' or 'I only play Brahms.' One plays what is written for the instrument. Likewise with the voice – one does not say 'I only sing Verdi,' or 'I only sing Puccini.' One sings what is written for the voice. When my so-called 'rivals' are willing to do that, then perhaps we can speak of my actually having rivals."

I think Maria spoke for all of us "real" substitute teachers that day. The true substitute does not say "I sub for math," or "I sub for elementary school." The true sub subs for what is taught.

CONGRATULATIONS – *Fifth Grade, Gavin Newsom College Preparatory Academy – Dream School (When they have to use a name this long, you know it ain't gonna be easy), January 4, 2010*

Gavin Newsom Middle School finally caught up with me. Steeling myself, I recall that thus far none of the other presumed difficult assignments I've recently taken have turned out to be that horrible. Plus I am just back from the east coast where I believe we had a temperature of nine one night and it's supposed to be 63 degrees here today, so whining – even silently – would be unbecoming.

Upon arrival, I am asked how I would feel about taking PE instead of the English Language Development job on the tape. Well, this cancels my no whining resolution and I groan. Apparently a pregnant woman took that job and the male administrator just figured it'd better to have a man. I wind up saying that I'll do it, but he says nah, that's okay. Guess I groaned effectively.

This is the old Third Millennium Academy, turned into one of the Dream/Nightmare Schools. Watching the principal struggle (largely unsuccessfully) to get the kids to line up after lunch gives you a pretty good sense of what they're up against here.

The class is already in the room by the time I arrive – actually only three at the moment, plus an aide for the morning. Journal writing assignment on the board and the aide starts them on it – "Dreams, hopes and expectations for 2010," that sort of thing. One kid volunteers his holiday experience: "I went to a party and the people drank a lot of wine and they got sick and they had hangovers." She tells him to come up with something else. Someone says "I hope no one gets killed."

We read a story and do vocabulary and comprehension. After two disruptive girls are removed and one of the boys falls asleep with his foot on his chair and his head on the desk, I'm able to proceed pretty well with the remaining four students. Did I mention that the classes are very small here? The whole place might be special ed or something, but it is the school's saving grace, although that's probably putting it too strongly, as it's a stretch to say anything's exactly being "saved" here.

When I bring them to lunch from computer lab, a black woman who was briefly in the room in the morning comes over and says, "Are they kicking your butt in there?" Says she's from the 50s; that's when she went to school – in San Francisco – and these kids are very different. "My mother'd just have to look at you ..." I mention seeing one of my students talk quite disrespectfully to an administrator this morning and she says, "He can't handle em himself. They're lucky to even get subs here. I congratulate you for getting your butt in here" and gives me a fist bump.

After lunch, it's more than three straight hours of class, this being a 4 pm school. The aide has given me the list of home phone numbers and I'm making big use of them by the end of the day. I talk to one guy's grandfather twice and the grandfather has the mother call, but it doesn't do much. Another kid goes after the above kid in the middle of class. This second kid's father actually comes into the classroom during the day. I don't realize whose father he is until after he leaves, but when I do, I call him back to tell him his son has started fighting in the middle of class. He talks with him, of course, and after he leaves the kid does it again. One girl I bounce thrice during the day. The other trouble girl apologizes later in the day. There's too much time, the sub plans are half-assed, and I don't have a bag of tricks.

Meanwhile, a *New York Times* article on college courses studying *The Wire* quotes William Julius Wilson saying it's the best thing to come along to show the nation the nature of the educational problems the black community faces. Glad someone's talking straight. (They also ran an op-ed by a sub whose byline says she's working on a memoir about subbing. Apparently she's only done it once a week for two years, if she's already getting published in the *Times*, she's obviously got a major leg up. Better get cracking on this book.)

When I return home, there's a message from the San Francisco machine and a look online confirms that they're asking me to come back to the class I just survived. I duck em.

CLEAR PLANS– *English, Cappuccino High, January 11, 2010*
Today, first day back here after ascertaining that I was on this school's black list and getting myself removed, I learn that there are kids here from Colma because the living population of the town is too small to support a school system of its own and it is across the street. The City of the Dead has been on my mind recently since watching a dvd of *Colma, the Musical*. This being one of the most

improbable films I've ever seen, I'm not terribly surprised when no one has heard of it in my first couple of classes. But third period Juniors Honors not only has a kid from Colma, but several students also know about the movie – that's why they're in honors. Who knows, this could be the only academic discussion of that work of musical theater ever held. Plus one of them also knows the heating system which I have not previously gotten to work properly and now we're warm. I love this class.

JE NO PARLE PAS FRANCAIS – UNFORTUNATELY – French, Cabot High, January 21, 2010

The phone rings at 5:15 AM – it's San Francisco calling live because I've apparently slept through a call from the machine and I've been requested directly. Figure this means I'm going right back into *The Wire* – which I was watching until 1 – without passing through REM sleep, maybe to Gavin Newsom Academy – from the world of my dreams into a Dream School. But, no – I've been requested at Cabot.

I'm replacing the wife of a Citadel teacher who has sometimes requested me. A note on the board explains that his father died last night. When I arrive in the room, I learn that I am a French teacher today. I use one of the few phrases I've picked up for trips to France and Canada: *Je no parle pas francais.* A couple of kids whisper to each other so low that I cannot hear them ten feet away. Later kids seem more normal, i.e., they make audible sounds and move. Only one kid absent the entire day. Kids thank me on their way out of class! Once, when I'm having trouble getting their attention, I warn I'm about to use my middle school voice and they don't want to hear that because they've spent their time succeeding at school so they wouldn't have to listen to teachers talking like that. Unfortunately, the school apparently plans to secure the services of a teacher who does *parle francais* for the rest of the teacher's absence.

CHRIS – Spanish, Appian Way High, February 1, 2010

On my way back into this virtually windowless (there are actually three, but they have metal shutters on them) and ill-lit "portable" after lunch, a guy stops me and asks could I call him Chris when I call roll. I ask what his name is listed as and he says Christine. I see the issue.

FRIES WITH THAT? – Drama, Gavin Newsom Academy, February 9, 2010

Three out of four classes are tiny – seven or nine kids (I assume this means they're Special Ed) and they go all right. We start with a chant, *Voice of the People* – Martin Luther King was a Voice of the People, etc. The kids know it and do it. Then we do readings of a little play the teacher has written about an interview with Franklin Roosevelt and then some biographical info on Harriet Tubman, Ida B. Wells, and W.E.B. Dubois for them to do pretend interviews with. (This is Black History Month.)

When I show up an hour early for the fourth one (because my schedule has the wrong time), the aide says, "I'll pray for you." It's got about 14 kids and when the teacher and aide leave, it immediately devolves into the scene from

Pryzbylewski's first class on *The Wire*, which I was up late watching. Just chaos – utterly unmanageable bickering and screaming. They're younger than the TV class and no razor is pulled, but they could definitely hurt each other. I call the office to tell the secretary that this class is totally unmanageable and they need to send someone in. A student depresses the hook on the wall phone and disconnects me the first time I call, so I need to hold her off to complete the call. We're talking brass here.

When no one comes quick enough for me, I just step out into the hall and start shouting, "Where is security?" Quite a scene. Eventually someone arrives. He can't do much with them either, but at least there's someone there. 14 is too large a class at this school! Kids claim it's time to go to some other program, which they may genuinely think, since they can't tell time. During lunch, I leave my newspapers on the table while I go to the bathroom, since no one else is in the room. When I return, someone has spread his lunch out on them. I toss a french fry and a straw wrapper into his McDonald's bag. Staff manners match the students'.

But My Friend the Evil Substitute Teacher does call and cheer me up, quite excited about a couple of items in the news. First there was the one about the girl in Junior High School 190 in Forest Hills, Queens who was handcuffed and detained at a police precinct for doodling on her desk with an erasable marker. The story also mentioned a 5-year-old handcuffed and sent to a psych ward after throwing a fit in his kindergarten in New York City in 2008. And I see that there was one in my old neighborhood – a 12-year-old sixth-grader arrested in March 2009 for doodling on her desk at the Hunts Point School. Now that's discipline.

THEY DON'T KNOW– Kindergarten, Ernest Everett Just , February 17, 2010

Long ago, I vowed I would never come back here – but that was long ago and work is scarce. Early morning call and I just grit my teeth and go. By the time I arrive the kids are getting their hearing checked in a van in the schoolyard with a young, very pregnant woman tending them. I immediately hear one calling another "bitch" – this is kindergarten, remember. Apparently there's a para attached to the class, but she has just gotten injured and this woman stays here the whole time before lunch. As soon as we get back to the classroom, she addresses them as "achievers," so you know that's going to be trouble. She sure has the little child noises down though. She says, "Bum badda bum bum," and they say, "bum bum," and that works. I use it a lot in the afternoon when she's gone.

The lesson plan is much harder to carry out than yesterday, when I had a kindergarten at Bruce in South San Francisco, because it involves deciphering the teacher's manual and locating the related material, where yesterday, I had specific instructions and handouts next to them. But then, one way or another, just about everything works out to be harder in a place like this.

In the afternoon, with no assistant, I wind up having to do some serious yelling. I'm embarrassed to be doing it – these are really little kids and these are open classrooms. It seems inappropriate, but it's what works. I send one kid to the office, but in the afternoon, the kids sabotage the discipline system – the usual clothes pins on sheets of paper color coded to behavior – by moving kids down to the bottom who shouldn't be there.

We do surveys and charts after lunch which ain't bad, really – I ask if they have a sister and plot the answers on a bar graph and then they do their own surveys. But it will not fill the amount of time it's allotted so I start "centers" early but these are kids who can't handle playtime because they bicker and fight and I have to send them back to their chairs. I try reading out loud. A poem is useless, but I find *Green Eggs and Ham* and do a very animated reading which does grab them. Eventually I let them back to centers and it works much better. There's points where I'm ready to tell the school – at the slightest provocation – that they could just put me on their no-call list – it's that hard to remember that it's just kindergarten kids and in five minutes everything's forgotten.

I tell the bitch story to some friends and one says, "Five years old! I thought it didn't start until the third grade when they realized they were behind." This is why I tell people these stories. They think they know – and, generally, they don't know.

And I also think back on a day long ago, not even sure what the school was, watching kids – first graders I think – on a play structure and seeing this tiny boy try to stick his hand up the girls' dresses, with them not having any idea of what he was doing – not that he had much idea of what he was doing either. I'm not sure if I've ever mentioned that one to anyone at all.

GOOD EATING – *Art/Math, Ghiradelli Middle, February 18, 2010*

Back to one of my normal weight classes. Have to copy an emergency lesson plan for math – a worksheet of graph plotting to be followed by a video – if I can come up with the equipment. One girl starts the day making a lot of noise and whacking someone else in the head, so I call the assistant principal on her, at which point the girl asks me "What the fuck" I want, so I put her on the phone so she can ask him. In fourth period, a boy makes the mistake of addressing me as "fool." Takes me about five phone calls before a large surly guy comes and takes him away.

Eventually I secure the video equipment, but the video is the *Simpsons*. I ask the opinion of an aide of some sort as to whether that's what I should be showing and she says probably not and gets one on volcanoes. There are no instructions for Unified Arts class after lunch, though, so I let them choose between the volcanoes and the *Simpsons* – the *Simpsons* might be acceptable in an "arts" class, I figure. And when we watch the episode, it turns out to involve the cooking and eating of children in the school cafeteria. Had I known that earlier, I would have shown it all day. This evening I will call My Friend the Evil Substitute Teacher to make sure he knows about this episode.

The teacher has a fifth period prep and a sixth of common planning time. By now I have the sense not to ask questions here that would more than likely get me a stint answering phones, so I sit tight in the room.

FUN? – *Kindergarten, William Elementary School, February 23, 2010*
    Down in LA this weekend, I mentioned having done kindergarten recently, to which my friend Mary said, "Fun?" and I told her that in a place like here it was, but in a place like Just, kindergarten isn't even fun. Today I repeat that conversation chatting with the other kindergarten teacher as we pick up our kids and *she* is surprised. I tell her I talk about it because even teachers in the next town have no idea. But here we have fun.

GOOD FOR THE FISH – *Special Ed, Bonanza Elementary, February 24, 2010*
    Nice kids, but difficult job. Couple of different grades and divided into six groups that continually shift. My instructions say to meet them at the buses in front, but I can't find a one. There is, however, an aide, which, as usual, makes all the difference. In elementary school you do it all – in the afternoon we're teaching basketball.
    My main contribution, or at least attempt, is to leave the teacher a note about the betas (a.k.a. Siamese fighting fish) in small bowls near the door. I am closing the door all day to protect them from drafts and the aide tells me they're new acquisitions, so I leave a note detailing what I assume their temperature needs will be, as they are tropical fish. (I am fresh from telling my LA friends that their goldfish needed a larger bowl.) I try to be a good sub for the animals, anyhow.

AM I BLUE? – *ESL, Appian Way High, February 25, 2010*
    One girl likes my blue eyes, something I get from time to time, particularly in ESL, where the kids are usually Latino or Chinese. Another asks why some people have them. I do my best to explain how they come from northern Europe, but as I'm talking I realize that I don't know actually why they emerged; the last time I'd really considered the question having come before the consensus that all humans emerged from Africa. (And looking into it later, I realize that "Science" doesn't know much about it either.)

REALLY BORING LIVES OF THE SCULPTORS – *Art/Computer Lab, Cappuccino High, March 1, 2010*
    I'm supposed to borrow a movie from next door for my two art classes. The teacher there says she's already sent a couple last week. *The Lion King* and *Toy Story II* were on my teacher's desk, but I ask if there might be something more grown up for high school. She explains that they look upon it as animation, but scares up some lives-of-the-sculptors videos (she does ceramics) and I show them Louise Nevelson and Henry Moore. These films elicit not the slightest interest among the students – and some people do make a good living in cartoons in these parts, but I'm sticking with showing em the sculptors. Too much *Shrek* over the years, I suppose.

NO STUDENTS HARMED – *Sixth Grade, Gavin Newsom Academy, March 8, 2010*

Phone rings at 7:15 AM – I know it's going to be bad. Fourth grade at Gavin Newsom. I catch the 67 bus in a sun shower but it's all gray when I reach the other side of the hill, nature foreshadowing the day of unrelenting unpleasantness that follows.

As I arrive in the classroom, another teacher is finishing up first period in what I take to be a sixth grade class. Right away we have a kid throwing a bottle of water. This I note and say I'm not going to allow. The teacher says that's right – Level two referral – shows me the forms. She also asks do I want her to take anything valuable to the office for safekeeping as things tend to disappear here.

An aide arrives for second period Language Arts. We have a packet that starts with a warm-up. I ask should we all go over it together. He says yes, but no one listens when I try. I scrub that plan. One guy is already lying on a table. The aide takes a couple of guys at one table, there's a also a one-on-one aide who works with another student, and I'm able to get one other to work with me. There's a table of four girls that is just *unpleasant;* I have to tell two of them to get off the classroom phone that they pick up as they please.

The aide asks me to give a referral to one guy who's been throwing things. I do and call the office to have him removed. The kid says to him, "Why you siding with him? I'm just trying to do to white people what they been doing to us for the last 50 years." He and another guy with a later referral are both sent back to the room. The aide tells me not to feel bad because a lot of these kids don't want to work.

We have a long talk after class. He asks if I've also been to "good schools" and what I think the cause of the difference is. I tell him I think it's mostly the circumstances of the kids' lives. He's in his second year, pretty young. Says the principal parks his BMW out front one day and his Escalade the next and figures there's some money misspent there. Says they don't suspend kids here because if they do, they'll go home and play video games. Says some kids are like a cancer; some days you'll notice things are going okay and you wonder why and then you see so-and-so is absent.

Social Studies starts the afternoon. The assignment is too easy. All multiple choice – they just have to fill in a few bubbles and they can say they're done. Six of them are at the computer after they "finish" and I don't even want to know what they're doing. Another six are on a couch. My main goal there is to periodically break up any wrestling. This is completely a "no blood, no foul" class.

No classroom aide in the afternoon. The woman I talked with in the cafeteria in the past comes in after lunch to pick up a girl to work with; says her usual, "They haven't chewed you up yet?" A girl arrives from somewhere and asks, "They been rude to you?" And says, "Never teach at this school." This is before she herself joins the rude parade.

I have a couple of walkouts by kids I won't give passes. I call the office on them and the counselor comes down, but in the course of the day I give four referrals and all of the students are allowed to return to class. But then, as the aide said, what are you going to do with these kids? On the other hand, I wonder what does it say that neither the school nor the teacher has left any directions as to pass policy, expectations, etc. But maybe this would just be a waste of paper. This place is off the cliff. But saying that, of course, doesn't negate the fact that someone's got to try to do something with them. About the best I can say is akin to what film makers can claim as an accomplishment at the end of even the worst movie: No students were harmed in the making of this school day.

Gavin Newsom College Preparatory closed at the end of the 2010-2011 academic year. Down the road I will observe a teacher become the object of some awe in the Moonlight Elementary School lunchroom when she mentions she worked at Gavin Newsom for seven years.

JUST LIKE YOUR MOTHER – Kindergarten, Pine Elementary,
March 10, 2010

The first of several days here this spring. A teacher will leave me a note about how rowdy her class is and how I shouldn't hesitate to be strict, but really about the worst I hear is that "She stuck her tongue out at me." And a mother in to help for the day says my name sounds familiar and did I ever sub at Nations of the World Institute? Only once. Middle school? Nathaniel Hawthorne. That's it. *Kid, I threw your mother out of class.*

A Walmart employee will come to my room for Junior Achievement Day. This is the store that tries to make its prices low enough so that even its own employees can afford to shop there. I guess this is their corporate contribution to education. Nice break for the teachers and all, but no value added. Better they should pay taxes. Never been in a Walmart myself, so this is my closest brush with the famous company.

Fifth graders come in to read to one class, with their teacher who left the stock broker world fifteen years ago; says he's never regretted it, even if he makes half the salary, maybe a third, if you consider inflation. (When I experience the common – for me – kindergarten problem of not understanding what some kid is trying to say to me, he says he doesn't understand them either, if that's any consolation. It is.)

On Friday we have Free Choice – blocks, sand table, rug, and playhouse (which includes costumes). All in all, it's a lot of "He's not being a good friend," etc. in a room full of witches, power rangers, girls who have found roly polies (they're bugs) and intend to bring them home, and others who are "not sharing." But I continually shake my head at how much more gentle it is than, say, the Bayview District in San Francisco, although this is certainly not what you'd ever think of as one of San Francisco's wealthy suburbs. It's that level of amazement that I keep trying to figure out how to convey.
Student Name of the Day: Love Bhusal (boy)

WEST COAST ANGLES? – *Math, Oskar Schindler High, March 19, 2010*
    Thinking about the sainted Sandra Fewer on my way in, having gotten up at 5:45. She's the San Francisco School Board member who has proposed not starting high school until nine. Must do something to help her re-election.
    Upon arrival, I find that I am only a back-up and there's another teacher there who clearly does not want to say a lot about the status of the teacher I'm replacing. Eleven students when I arrive; double that by the end of this double period class. My only useful function will be to collect tardy slips at the door and send the students who don't have them to the office to get one. The other teacher asks if I know math and says I could go around helping students, but does not so much as introduce me to the class – or even ask my name. Some sort of preliminary grades are distributed and apparently only three are passing. Not terribly surprising on the basis of what I see.
    Second period has only 11 and is much better, but I am delivered from there when another teacher arrives to tell me I'm to take his afternoon classes when he will be in San Jose. First one is Honors Algebra which he's not particularly concerned about, but turns out to be the worst class of the day. The sixth period text book is *California Geometry*. California Geography I knew about, but California Geometry?
    I draw the same assignment in a couple of days when it turns out to mean replacing the art teacher – five periods supervising kids painting, with specific instructions against iPod's, etc. I try to enforce, but simply cannot and have to call in security. Mainly, they're just loud – and let's raise that to obnoxious. Last period, a district employee comes by with a work order that says there's a filing cabinet in the room that needs keys. It's dated August, though, so he allows as how it may already have been taken care of.
Student Name of the Day: Pansy Au

YOU MEAN THERE'S A BOOK? – *English, Appian Way High, March 25, 2010*
    My first (of three) sophomore classes is finishing up watching *To Kill a Mockingbird*. But no, they haven't finished reading the book. And they're not going to. They're only watching the movie!
    Next day is the pleasant little Special Ed class. Ms. W, the aide who's really in charge here, tells me Mr. R is getting 86'd as principal at Freeway because of test scores. I saw Freeway on the list of "failing" schools slated for dismantling in one way or another, so this is not a complete surprise to me, but I count it as a mark against the current misguided fix-the-schools-and-ignore-larger-reality movement. So far as I could see Mr R. was an involved principal. I barely saw his predecessors, but I always saw him and I knew him. I figure when they're interacting with *substitutes* on a regular basis, they're *there*. The school is still tough, to be sure, but so far as I'm concerned, it's notably better. How much of that is due to him, I can't entirely say – one aide attributed the change to the hiring of a second assistant principal. But whatever the cause(s), the place is better. Apparently the test scores deny that, though. Ms. W tells me there is some glee at his demise, stemming from the perception of a certain ruthlessness to his

now officially failed efforts to turn the school around – supposedly once walking past the various classrooms noting aloud which teachers would go.

South San Francisco's officially "failing schools" include Los Montecillos, Bruce, Freeway, and Pine. The only one that ever struck me as a "problem school" was Freeway.
Student Names of the Day: O'Shea Calacal, Romeo Noniscan

THEY DIDN'T KILL EACH OTHER – *Severely Handicapped,*
Annunciation Gulch Middle, April 6, 2010

Another place I haven't been for a while. Y told me some time ago that Annunciation Gulch wasn't that bad these days, if only because it was small. It's a gorgeous day and I'd forgotten just how beautiful the setting is here in the unknown San Francisco abutting McLaren Park, the city's second largest park.

The maximum number of students we'll have here today is five and there's three periods of four. My instructions indicate that second period deals with tooth brushing and deodorant use – another thing those "failing" public schools have to handle these days. I've got home room and first period free and my first sight of kids comes as they start popping into the room looking to hide, with an adult in pursuit.

As one of the second period aides (four students; three adults) says, it's a struggle every day. The severe handicaps, btw, are clearly psychological. The kids say that they've already brushed their teeth and put on their deodorant, so we're ahead of the game here. Then they do an NFL word search (it's all boys) and we do have some discussion and it's okay. Of course, the class started with the aide dragging one boy out for continually cursing. Third period, shift of aides, and they watch *Ice Age*. The kid who was dragged out flees the room following his next outburst.

Sixth period there's no aide and five of them and I. I call the office when two flee and get the security guard to take away the two skateboards they continually ride around on. Then they start hide and seek, sitting on the floor, etc. They stop when I call the office – at least for a while. They all have to fill out a form assessing their day and I fill out a parallel column. They seem to think they were great, but I didn't see it that way. But, as the last period aide says, "They didn't kill each other." And that, as always, is the bottom line. And in that regard, I still have a perfect record after all these years.

KICKING AND SCREAMING – *First Grade, Ernest Everett Just Elementary,*
April 9, 2010

The South San Francisco website now carries a notice that "Substitutes should check their assignments daily online to make sure job has not been CANCELLED." So I did that last night and today's assignment at the Bruce School wasn't there. Here at Just, I have to physically separate two boys fighting and end the day with bus duty which involves carrying a screaming, kicking girl down the block to put her on the bus. In between, they are almost never good, except when a school regular sticks a head in the room and instills fear in them. They are bad enough that the principal makes them all stand in her office for ten minutes after computer lab and before the musical presentation – both of which periods I am extremely grateful to have. In the teacher's notes the students are universally referred to as "achievers," as in "walk the achievers back from lunch."

THE BACKGROUND – *April 13, 2010*
Bay City News reports:
A 19-year-old San Francisco man was arrested tonight on suspicion of shooting at two private security guards, triggering an exchange of gunfire in the city's Bayview neighborhood this morning ... police spokesman Officer Samson Chan said ... The suspect shot out the windows of a white Dodge Charger carrying two security guards at about 10:20 a.m. near the intersection of Keith Street and Newcomb Avenue ... security guards returned gunfire, but no one was injured in the shooting ... about 10 shots were fired.

The shooting occurred about a block from Ernest Everett Just Elementary School, which was locked down until about 12:40 p.m. According to Chan, some of the public housing communities in the Bayview District hire private uniformed security guards to protect the area. The guards are armed, he said. During the Ernest Everett Just school lockdown, classes continued inside, but no one was allowed to enter or exit the building, San Francisco Unified School District spokeswoman Gentle Blythe said. Blythe said the lockdown was just a precaution and that school staff members are familiar with the procedure because police activity in the area is fairly common. "The school is really a safe haven in that neighborhood for those children," she said. Violence around the school has never entered the school, that I know of."

When I mention this to my friend Bob and tell him I had just subbed there and the kids' behavior was consistent with this sort of experience, he says they probably have Post Traumatic Stress Disorder. And I'm thinking that sounds about right, except it's not "post;" it's ongoing.

ON THE ROAD – *Pamplona Elementary/Sojourner Truth High –*
but not really, April 14, 2010

A call comes through for Gavin Newsom in a program described as "Aphasia," but I figure that'll describe me if I take it, so I let it go. Instead, a rare trip to Mt. Davidson, another San Francisco the tourists don't see, one where you can find Meg Whitman for Governor signs. This is a "location, location, location" neighborhood – there's nothing special about the houses I'm passing – they're the general San Francisco one-floor-over-a-garage's. So I'm sure a lot of these people up here don't feel that they really have a lot because they don't live in fancy houses, although their property values might suggest they do.

Arrive maybe forty-five minutes into the day to learn that they already have the sub they requested. Call into the sub office where they say it was their mistake and would I go to Morgan and pick up a para position for sub pay. While I'm waiting for the bus outside, someone comes out and says they called back. I get on the phone and they want me to replace the IRF (Instructional Reform

Facilitator, in case you've forgotten) at Sojourner Truth – a four bus trip. I am off to Forest Hills Station, then through Golden Gate Park, then I outwalk the Fulton bus and am over to Alamo Square.

Today is the day the *San Francisco Bay Guardian* and the *San Francisco Weekly* come out, so for me it is a five newspaper day and I've finished three by the time I arrive at Sojourner Truth to find that they too already have the sub they really wanted. The sub office first says why don't I drop by and get my form filled, but decides the secretary can do it herself and that's it for the day. Beats Aphasia at Gavin Newsom, I'd say.

FEELS LIKE FLYING – Language Arts/Social Science (sort of),
   Wolfpack Middle/High, April 28, 2010

The kids here are all on suspension. The plan calls for writing fifteen vocabulary words on the board, having them look up definitions and write sentences, going over that with them, reading a story from *Multicultural Voices,* and then switching classes with the Math/Science teacher in the next room. But he comes in and says that on sub days they usually combine classes, so they all come in.

He seems quite hesitant about the vocabulary assignment and eventually I ask if he'd like me to go with the vocabulary and I do. Bravura performance, if I do say so myself, running through "resilient" and "sagacity" over (in the sense of having to talk *over* the din) a class of 28 (25 boys). It's the only focus a human will bring them to for the entire day.

When it comes time to read, the other teacher says we won't have enough books as the classes have grown large (a semester starts with a small number and accretes suspendees – and we've combined classes), so he suggests they just watch a movie instead. Today's feature is *Blindside,* a recent Sandra Bullock film about a rich white family in Tennessee that takes in a homeless black kid who becomes a football star. Subbing's kind of like flying in that you see all sorts of movies you'd never go to on your own – that is, flying before they charged for movies.

The other teacher describes things as more "relaxed" around here; says many of the kids are here for things like smoking or selling pot in school. So we have the potheads here. That's cool.

"WHAT THE FUCK?" – Seventh Grade Math, Worcester Middle, May 11, 2010

The difficult math classes again. By fourth period, I have ejected three and called an assistant principal in. And today the fight goes past the bell ending the final round. I've told the last period class they'd have to stay after for being so loud and one of them (the little darling who has spilled a cake all over the floor) then yells "What the fuck?" which gets him a rare 3:01, after-the-final-bell referral that I deliver with pleasure to the assistant principal on my way out. And, oh, yes, we combined like terms in the addition of polynomials all day.

I SEE THAT – *Fifth Grade, Juan Crespi Elementary, May 13, 2010*

Today's student teacher had me as a sub; she's not sure whether at Cappuccino or Worcester. And it turns out that I had her brother in math yesterday so she tells the students I'm a good guy. Otherwise, it's a typical elementary school whirlwind: Announcements come over the PA and students leave on some cue and I don't know where they're going, but everyone else seems to.

And we plow through the spelling, grammar, punctuation, multiplication by two digit numbers, similes, metaphors, novels about plane crash survivors, PE and all the rest that makes us the nation we are today. My best trick is walking around reading the novel to them while picking off toys and other items spotted via peripheral vision.

WHILE THE IRON IS HOT – *Clothing/English/Health, Cappuccino High, May 17, 2010*

Fourth period Clothing class – another career first. Instructions say: "Self-paced class. The students will each work on their own project. Make sure the iron is unplugged at the end of class." Sewing machines and fabric strewn about the room. A kid says, "No one will do anything, but that's okay with Mr. C." But three of them actually do! Apparently no one plans to use the iron today, though, so I get it unplugged right away, completing the most important part of the assignment – from a public safety point of view anyhow.

YOU, TOO? – *First Grade, Los Montecillos Elementary, May 20, 2010*

A high school student shows up in the afternoon to work with the kids. I ask if I've subbed in her classes. Many times, she says. By now I'm starting to wonder if I had any of the principals in these schools in class. She also says that the kids in this class are always the way they are today with subs – out of their seats and talking. And all subs have trouble with the teacher's lesson plans, as I'm having.

YOU SAY THAT, HOW? – *Sixth Grade Language Arts/Reading/Social Studies, Citadel Middle, May 21, 2010*

Rough start to this six-day assignment (for which I have passed up working an election in Georgia – that's the one that used to be in the U.S.S.R.) She's left me inaccurate seating charts and when I tell a kid to take his assigned seat, I get a "Fuck off!" Special ed kid, ya know – very special, but I had no warning.

I am corrected on my Greek pronunciation both morning and afternoon. Well, no stinkin little sixth graders are going to correct an alumnus of the Regis High School Homeric Academy, so I write the word αγορα (agora – market) on the board by way of illustrating that there is no "right" pronunciation and explain that they may inform me of the pronunciation in use in their class, but they are not to think to correct mine. When I am asked did I learn to speak it, I recite the first two lines of "The Odyssey":

ἄνδρα μοι ἔννεπε, μουσα πολτροπον, ὃς μαλα πολλα
πλάγχθη, ἐπεὶ Τροίης ἱερὸν πτολίεθρον ἔπερσεν

although I do also explain that we never really spoke it.

In the course of discussing Athenian theater with them over the week, I've asked if they know other examples of theater where there were no women and they know about Shakespeare. So I tell them that my high school used to be that way, with boys playing all the roles in the plays but they started importing girls back when I was there and that I've recently learned that Lady Gaga sang in the school play a few years ago (this, the biggest Regis news in some time). Now that gets their attention, although not everyone seems to be exactly understanding: A girl asks did I know Lady Gaga. But another girl says, "He's like fifty and she's like twenty," and then puts her hand over her mouth looking like she thinks she shouldn't have said that. And I'm thinking, "Fifty, huh? An A for you."

WHAT I REALLY WANT TO KNOW– August 9, 2010

A mid-summer subbing story, of all things! Saturday night, waiting for a bus home from the Sea Chantey Sing at the Hyde Street Pier, someone says, "Mr. Gallagher!" A past student, who tells the guy he's with, "This is the best substitute ever" – so obviously he's been drinking heavily. Says he had me in Cucamonga, Worcester, and Appian Way High. He and his friends get on the 47; I wait for the 49. And then they appear on the 49. He explains they got off the 47 when their alcohol container broke. Says he'll sit with me. I am not enthusiastic about this, but ...

Tells me I threw him out of class a number of times, but I as a sub I was just right – the other subs, they were too strict or too lenient, "but with you it was 'If you're not going to learn, you're out of here.'" Remembers telling me his name was George or something in Music class at Worcester once and I told him there was no George on the class list and threw him out. I am genuinely shocked by this testimonial. But he says he does have to ask one thing: "So, were you really watching porno (on my computer), like they always said?" Now this is more what I expect. So I explain how I use it to read and write and he allows that anyhow, so far as he knows, "there's no rule in a book that says you can't watch porno if you're substitute teaching." Quite open minded of him, I'd say, but then he's a graduate now, you know.

Apparently he lives in the projects in Hunters Point in San Francisco but used his grandmother's address to go to school in South City. Eventually he rejoins his confreres who are generally behaving badly at the back of the bus, asking other passengers to give them a beer, etc. He's still on the bus but I do not opt for further communication with the group upon my departure.

I tell the porno story to my friend Ian who subs in New York. He says that he frequently brings water bottles with him, so the story that goes round about him is that he's drinking gin or vodka in class.

*****

KEEP YOUR SHOES ON – *Southern Futures, August 23, 2010*

New year; new frontier: my first full-day pre-school job – did an hour or two once. As I assumed, there's someone else here actually in charge – I didn't imagine they'd really bring you in off the street and put you in charge of a day care center.

Turns out pretty boring, actually – as bad as PE. What's nice? The big tricycles they ride around the yard; the two-hour afternoon nap – one til three, when it's "wakey time." I have lunch for 45 minutes of it and sort two colors of little blue crepe streamers during the rest. The kids nap with their shoes on – in case of fire.

Opened lots of ketchup packets at lunch, which was a particularly horrifying meal: potato puffs and orange slices. For a snack they get a brownie. Weight reduction programs don't start for another couple of years, I think.

WET – *Kindergarten, William Elementary, August 30, 2010*

Angel starts the day crying because Ms. K isn't here. Immense bathroom activity, but one's too slow on the draw and we've got a puddle on the rug. It's only the third week of school in their lives and already the kids are programmed: At 1:10 I play their clean-up song, "The World is a Rainbow," and they start cleaning up.

The second day Angel stands in front of my desk before school starts. He doesn't say anything and finally I ask if he wants something. He says, yes, he wants his teacher. But he doesn't cry today

Within a month, I will have been in this class five times and I don't think the teacher's actually been absent once. Everyone notes that the district seems to be doing an unusual amount of training and testing this year – the preferred national solution to the "education crisis." By now, Angel doesn't cry anymore, but Vincent does – and runs at the sight of me because he figures he's going to be in trouble. The aide finds him on the lam outside one day.

On one of my trips here, I'm about two blocks from home when I look down and notice the brown shoe on my left foot and the blue on my right. I think about just going on, but figure two different color shoes would drive the kindergartners wild. (I understand that people get married to avoid situations like this.) On another, a mother ushers in her boy with pinkeye. I suggest she go to the office, where they apparently send him home. If I don't die from one of these kindergarten classes, I figure I should build up enough immunity to be immortal.

ICE – *Librarian (but not really), Nathaniel Hawthorne Middle, September 17, 2010*

The machine said that this was a librarian job but that I'd really be doing something in the office. After a bit of a shuffle I am in the counseling office issuing tardy passes, permits to leave school and band-aids. And ice packs! They all want ice packs. We got along just fine without them back in St. Athanasius, before there was refrigeration.

I've also got a couple of study skills classes in the afternoon. The first is pretty bad: eight kids, insulting each other, cursing etc. They have three worksheets, one of which is on cursive writing – and these guys are in eighth grade. But then, writing does not necessarily mean cursive any more, even for grown-ups.

NO ESTIMATES – *Fifth Grade, Juan Crespi Elementary, September 23, 2010*
I tell myself I've been remiss lately in checking out the teachers lunchrooms, so I go and – I'm the only one there. So much for resolutions.
We're supposed to do estimating problems, but the kids say the teacher tells them not to estimate, just to do the problem. A teacher after my own heart, aiming at correct answers not "useful" wrong answers. You know, as Tom Lehrer once put it, "The important thing is to understand what you're doing, rather than to get the right answer." As I'm leaving, the secretary tells me the regular teacher said, "I love my sub," after seeing me in the classroom. Perhaps she's gotten wind of my firm support for her mathematical principles.

MARINES? – *Fifth Grade, Strawberry Fields Elementary, September 24, 2010*
Apparently these guys had a sub yesterday who reported a rough day. So I open up fierce, to the point where one of the indicated problem students asks, "Were you in the military?" Music to a substitute teacher's ears. I tell him no, I chose this path instead. Teachers here are amazed that I sub in San Francisco. One tells me about Tony Danza's reality show on teaching in inner city Philadelphia, apparently the closest she comes to such places.
Student Name of the Day: Knowledge Kendrix (says he has a younger brother called Wisdom)

JUST SLEEPING – *Second Grade, Scarlatti Elementary, September 30, 2010*
Immediate fire drill whereupon I meet the sub next door who's confronting a problem I'm happy to say I never have – the death of a mammal. The class hamster appears to have expired overnight. Apparently it looks enough like it may still be sleeping that the kids don't know. He's going to the office to confer.
What do I do in elementary school classes? Talk about my cats a lot, and ask who's sillier – the cats or the kids. Say that students who talk should be stuffed in the closet until the regular teacher lets them out tomorrow. Tell them they sound like chickens when they all talk at once.

FILL IN THE BUBBLE – *First Grade, Los Montecillos Elementary, October 19, 2010*
This is a big day in these first graders lives as I administer what appears to be their first standardized test, initiating them into an activity that will dominate the next twelve years of their education. Otherwise, it's Duck, Duck, Goose at PE, etc.

THAT'S SPELLED N-O *— Second Grade, Benjamin Cardozo Elementary, October 27, 2010*

The teacher is here but has to do some kind of other yadda yadda, as is so frequently the case these days. Says her sub plan's not quite finished and asks if I speak Spanish. I don't know if it's any kind of official bilingual class, but obviously a lot goes on in Spanish.

It is a battling day. The only really good part is when I read an Amelia Bedelia story to them. I can command their attention with dramatic reading and little else. The teacher tells me to send problem kids to the adjacent rooms to write of their misdeeds. I utilize this to a degree I would not have imagined. I send one guy there three times plus once more to the office; a few others take trips as well. If I coulda dumped two or three boys and one girl, it could have been an okay class though.

English Language Development class after lunch is a mix of all the second graders with the least English from two classes. Includes a kid from China whose English is sufficiently minimal that he can't tell me where he's from. He is, however, able to go into a tantrum in order to demand a red marker when we get to the writing part of the class and I'm scavenging markers from all about the room. Well, I am all over him. I even have another girl telling me that he doesn't understand and I am quite aware of the absurdity of the situation, but where I am struggling to assert control no kid is going to get away with a snit, I figure. I am fairly certain that by this point he at least understands the meaning of "No" and if he doesn't, he's going to learn it today. Oh Lord, deliver me from these elementary schools.

I bring one boy to tears after he has caused the entire class to be brought back up stairs from going to lunch because he bolted into the yard before being told to. I did say I fought just about every minute, didn't I? The school security staff is very helpful, though. When they see the kids pulling shit in the halls, they're on them. Hopefully I make my gratitude understood.

A few nights later I will use this class as an example of my "it ain't rocket science" educational theories. I imagine the regular teacher doesn't have this much difficulty with them (although when I chide one of the boys about what his regular teacher would think, a girl says "He doesn't listen to her either"), but if she did, an aide to help with the three or four problem kids might go a long way. A single aide to try to get the distracted and distracting kids to follow the teacher's directions while the teacher dealt primarily with the non-problem students could dispense with the need for a lot of higher-priced training and consultants, me thinks.

WELL PUTTED *— Seventh Grade Math/Science, Calvin Coolidge Middle, October 28, 2010*

The *Hawkeye News*, the school newsletter (produced by the administration, not the students), says, "Winners [in the Yearbook Art Competition] will have their artwork putted in the Hoover Year Yearbook 2010-2011 edition. Good luck to you all!"

And good luck to you in the next staff grammar bee!
Student Names of the Day: Tiernaee Cato (that's pronounced "tyranny"), Cien Du (pronounced "see and do")

DON'T SCRATCH – *Math, Cappuccino High, November 1, 2010*
Midway through third period a delivery comes for me to distribute to students – samples of an acne drug. Is there anything the modern school is not expected to cover?
Student Names of the Day: Bismark Gonzalez, Oarange Richardson (pronounced as the fruit), Jazzelie Varize

THE FUTURE – *November 3, 2010*
Coming home on a day when the Giants World Series victory rally has filled the public transit system to overflowing, I encounter a group of four girls getting on the bus accompanied by much noise, most prominently from one continually saying things like "Push over motherfucker, I've got a baby." And she does. She's maybe seventeen years old. I kind of think she won't be doing a lot of reading to that kid. And I could still be subbing when it enters the system!

A BIG SMILE – *Language Arts/Social Studies, Worcester Middle, November 8, 2010*
The day's highlight comes at the front desk where, in place of the most unhelpful secretary around who's been here for years, I find the one I know from summer school at Pine. After school I ascertain that the change is real and permanent. The other one apparently retired. And just when I was thinking there were no positive trends in education.

REALITY DOSE – *English/English Language Development, Appian Way High, November 10, 2010*
Yesterday's *New York Times* had a story entitled "Proficiency of Black Students Is Found to Be Far Lower Than Expected." If more of the education experts would enter a classroom from time to time they might not be so surprised.
Student Name of the Day: Hollywood Banayad

JUST TWO – *Emotionally Handicapped, Waterfront Middle, December 1, 2010*
This is why we soldier on down this broken career path – things we've never seen before. Today it's a class with only two students. And it comes with a para! Apparently this class started with five kids; one expelled; one now in some psychiatric situation; I forget what happened with the other. The para and I will fill the intervals when the students do not have to be pressed on their educational paths with long knowing conversations about the state of education. He thinks the kids ought to be mainstreamed; says if you want to be considered seriously weird by everyone else in your school, just be in a class with two students. Pointing to the college shirts displayed on the classroom wall, he says he thinks it's just totally unrealistic for these kids (who, as you might imagine, are genuinely

serious behavioral problems) and they ought to be given a program that isn't. I notice one of the kids writes about wanting to go to Stanford, have a big house and get a Porsche.

FRENCH DISEASES – Librarian/English/Math, Ralph Bunche High, December 2, 2010

I figure a library job is a good opportunity to take a flyer and see if Bunche is bearable these days. Sounds like I've never done this job before, right? It is a library job – for a while. Then I've got one English class, another period to supervise two TAs, and otherwise I'll help downstairs. The security guy who escorts me to the library says my second period class is "interesting." I tell him that doesn't sound good. He says he'll stop by.

Second period is not actually too bad. It does start with the common depressing pattern I'll see for the next two days. The black kids all immediately go to computers – we're in the library – rather than take the assigned seats. By the time they do take seats, I've already handed back the worksheets that carry over from yesterday and begun today's poem with the mostly Chinese kids who mostly work. So now we've got kids talking out about how they don't know what we're doing. I come down pretty hard on them, have the aide call security, and the class works out okay. Part of the m.o. here is that disrespectful kids claim you're not respecting them.

The downfall comes third period when I'm asked to take over a math class because the sub originally assigned to the class has disappeared. This is also not a good sign, but I do it anyhow. I take away playing cards and make them put the electronics away. The girl in front of me finds this "hella irritating." The kids from whom I take cards seem to expect me to hasten to return them after class. In their book they shouldn't even have to ask for them and they think it's bad form on my part to tell them that if that's their attitude they can ask their regular teacher for them tomorrow. Manners are not big here. Seven kids walk out during the class, so I do a second roll call. Another one walks out in my face. I call security, they take names and most eventually return – for better or worse.

During fourth, the office calls and says that the first sub has reported that he injured himself and left – without telling anyone – and could I finish the day in the math class. Well, I guess I can, but I see that the afternoon is two regular freshman classes – and the two advanced classes I had this morning were none too advanced.

A girl asks if I'm going to stay in the classroom during lunch as the regular teacher apparently does. I tell her I'll do so if it doesn't involve aggravation. A minute later, the door opens to a loud "Fuck" emanating from a student's throat at his discovery that the teacher he wanted to sign something is not there. I tell the girl I'm out of here and she'll have to go.

After lunch I have the reverse problem from the morning – a kid who's not in the class deciding to sit in because I won't know him. He leaves when I announce I'm calling the office because I have more kids than the scantron says I should have. Then we have an ejection for defiant phone use; then another walkout. I am burning up the wires to the office. This'll teach me to go for an "easy" job at this place. (In fairness, I should note that I am actually able to help a couple of kids with their math over the course of the day.)

During seventh (and last, hooray!) period the "extra" student from sixth shows up. I promptly throw him out for phone use and he is returned to me. This then sets me on a course of numerous calls to the office to have him removed again, as the students who answer the phone disconnect me on several occasions (which I attribute to incompetence rather than defiance). But persistence wins out in the end when he is removed again. Wrong! They send him back again. They will get a speech from me at the end of the day and I will never be back here again.

Pique, umbrage, and *ennui* – Ursula LeGuin once called them as "the French diseases of the soul." By the time I was out of my twenties I had pretty much decided I had no more time for ennui, but I still do enjoy the others. And I just love the taste of pique, really. So the principal gets a note from me about how this student learned that he could defy me with impunity because I was just a substitute and if they don't want us to bother trying to enforce their rules, they should just say so and I'll be happy to let them text away. It'd certainly make me much more popular – I wouldn't be "hella annoying" to the students or anything.

Since I called down to the office numerous times during the day, I can allow as how they may think that they gave me a lot of back-up. And perhaps I needn't have made my statement so drastic, but I do hold out some slight hope that it might have an effect. This school seems to me to be maybe within striking distance of order and the message that they need to back up someone trying to maintain it is something they should hear. And then there's the fact that swearing off this place is not all that great a sacrifice.

TAKE TEN– *Social Studies/Spanish, Calvin Coolidge Middle, December 3, 2010*
This job is listed as Spanish and continuing for the rest of the year, so I'm asking myself if I can pull it off. Do I speak Spanish? Well, no. But I've been in high school Spanish classes where I was definitely on top of the material and this is just middle school. Yes, I decide, I could probably do it.

Of course, none of this matters; the teacher's actually got 4 periods of Social Studies and only one of Spanish, and the first thing they deliver to me – even before any material to work on for the day – is a letter for each student telling them that the teacher is gone for the rest of the year and that another teacher will be taking over on Monday. And I even thought to bring my electronic dictionary!

Just as well, I suppose, since when a student refuses to take her assigned seat and refuses to go down to the counselor and I have her removed, the security guy brings her back because the counseling office says they're "not a holding tank." I wonder what it is that they actually do there. He's apologetic about this and I tell him that I guess I've got to at least give the counseling office credit for answering the phone, something they didn't used to do. Discipline and order shall

.not be my priorities today, then, at least not on the school's account, as it has again shown that it's not a high priority here.

Later in the day the teacher next door looks in, as she says she frequently does because this class is in danger of going feral, being without a teacher. When a kid won't take her assigned seat, this teacher says she'll write her a referral. Guess she doesn't know. When I give a kid a loud harsh monotone to the effect that I think he understands perfectly what I'm talking about and he should just sit down, the teacher says, "Ooh, that was good." I tell her it's not my first cruise, (preening inwardly)

At the beginning of the last period, yet another teacher comes in to asks if she can take one girl to help her clean up her room. I tell her not only can she take her but she can take ten of that girl's friends too, if she wants. She actually takes eight kids. I am amazed – and thrilled!

I've previously seized a phone from a kid in the Spanish class who was giving me a general wall of defiance. After school, he's back to beg for it. He's a real whiner and I will admit that I take more than a bit of satisfaction in listening to him go on about how he's going to miss his bus as I make him accompany me to the counseling office where I run into a sub I've seen around for more than a decade who's apparently a counselor for the day and to whom I deliver the phone. He says there's no real counselors there and just asks the kid, "You're not going to have it out it in class any more, are you?" and gives it back. I mutter "Not very impressive" and head out into the Sunset gloaming – not before getting a final bit of abuse from the (adult) crossing guard who takes umbrage at my stepping into the crosswalk without his say-so.

Student Name of the Day: Thunder Zachary

CHEERS – *Sixth Grade English, Annunciation Gulch Middle, December 9, 2010*

Generally, a phone call that opens with a pre-recorded chirpy "Congratulations!" signals the end of the morning's sub calls and the beginning of the telemarketing day. Not today, though. The school call comes in after the first sales call. So this'll be a very short day. It will, however, bring to mind the lyric from Paul Hardcastle's 1985 song, *Nineteen*: "In Vietnam the combat soldier typically served a twelve month tour of duty but was exposed to hostile fire almost everyday." This will be a *Nineteen* kind of day.

I will give this place high grades for back-up. When I hand in a cellphone at the end of the day, I am cheered by the counselor and two security aides who are in the hall. Cheered! One of them had been in my classroom attempting to restore order when I first arrived to replace the stand-in sub and I had her back a couple of more times, once to remove one of the little fellers. (Telling one of his peers, "I got it out of your mother's pussy" was the phrase that got him removed – in case you were wondering). And, by the way, the assholery gender gap has rarely been more profound than what I encounter today. Most of the boys should be frozen for a couple of years.

CONTRAST – *Biology, Appian Way High, January 14, 2011*
   In the lunchroom, the topic of Cabot High comes up. One teacher says she was offered a job there before she started here, but somehow did not take it. Another speaks with wonder of having sat in classes there and being just amazed that the kids were interested – and then coming back here.
   As I'm trading in my key at the end of the day, I recognize a female sub somewhere up around my age whom I've seen before at an elementary school who catches up to me after I leave the office and asks if she can talk to me. Says it was the worst subbing day of her life there. Math classes where no one would listen to her; they called her a bitch, etc. Apparently she'd been here just once before, maybe partial day for a not-great SDC, but this took the cake. She's never coming back. Not much like Cabot, ya know.
   I tell her that I assume it's not as hard if you're male and that if she ever decided to come back (and I'm not saying she should) she should just get on the phone and call security. Tell her that the principal himself has come to remove a kid from my class. At the end of the year, I will run into her again at a party where she tells me she is no longer subbing and is pretty happy about that.

THEY WALKED HERE – *Spanish Immersion, Gettysburg Middle,*
   February 17, 2011
   This is another school I'd stopped going to, but I'll give it at least one shot now. The morning is pretty uneventful, followed by a desultory scene in lunch room – three aides and a sign in blue wooden letters attached to wall:
   ETTYSBURG OWLS – PR DE AND TRADITION
   I spend the afternoon with another teacher, though, and this is quite interesting. I assume she's pretty new. (Her mother teaches Special Ed.) She tells me she walked in on the afternoon class with a sub once and couldn't believe how bad they were and the language they were using and what they were saying about each other's mothers because they knew the sub couldn't understand. (She runs her class entirely in Spanish.) I tell her we see that every day. Says she could never be a sub.
   She asks the kids who hasn't eaten anything today and I'd say nearly half raise their hands. About 20 in the class and she says it's growing. Says some of these kids have walked here from Central America. They've seen people killed in some cases. She mentions post traumatic stress disorder several times. The school's got two therapists and there's too much work for them. There's one kid who sits next to me who does absolutely no class work. The teacher says he's never been to school before. With just a sub, he probably would have just shoved all the papers on the desks to the floor, or something like that.

NO ME GUSTO' – *Spanish, Dolores High, February 18, 2011*
   Spanish classes like these must be about like the French classes of my day when it was the most commonly taught foreign language and kids came out of them knowing about nothing. I've got to show a transparency with a word of the day and a phrase of the day. I think a word a day may be the pace at which some

of these classes progress. A couple of kids in the last class tell me this is really easy, so they're not going to even bother writing it as per assignment. One says he's a Spanish speaker, but he can't properly translate both verbs as past tense.

No specific instructions left today on cellphones and iPods, so I'm not even going to try. I also have to take them to the computer lab to do Power Point presentations on various countries. I leave the guy a note about the inadvisability of sending a sub to the computer lab, but generally try to prod. There's a kid from another class there watching music videos and sharing, so I have him removed. Some actually work, but these are hour-and-a-half classes ... An administrator comes in during the second period and asks if the teacher told me to come here or whether I just decided to come here on my own. Like I'd want to be with these guys in the computer lab! Honestly, the things some people think. I assure her that I was directed to come here. She says she'll talk to the teacher.

FISH OUT OF WATER – *Second Grade, Ralph Bunche Elementary, February 22, 2011*

Last period, we go to the library for a nature session where they've got some poor flounder they take from school to school and move from tub to tub to show how it changes its colors – and the kids get to pet it. Some poor crab, as well. What did these creatures do in their past lives to deserve this, I wonder.

DOWN AND OUT – *Language Arts/Social Science, Waterfront Middle, February 24, 2011*

Fourth period is Leadership (and let us hope that the nation's future does not depend on it.) They are watching a video on Obama (while I am writing an article about how he should be challenged in next year's primary). One kid immediately starts laying out his Magic cards on his desk. I immediately take them and put them in the teacher's desk. He proceeds to quickly write his required ten facts on the film and then generally screw around. At the end of class he asks for his cards back and I tell him he can get them from the teacher tomorrow. He tells me that I have to give him $40, in the usual respectful manner to which I have grown accustomed. After the class has left, I look toward the door and see him on the floor, crying about not getting the cards. I think I can honestly say I've never seen the like of this past about second grade. Eventually, he crawls out the door – yes, crawls.

Ms. F, who used to be the assistant principal at Taft, seems to have created a pretty chilly atmosphere for subs. You're now supposed to notify the office if you leave the premises during lunch or prep and on your way out the secretary asks if your classroom is clean. I mean, one tries to do what one can, but I'm afraid that order comes before cleanliness in subbing and when you're spending all your time trying to keep them quiet, you don't always notice the floors. And I don't really recall ever being asked that on my way out before.

CONTRAST – *Math, Ishi Middle, March 3, 2011*

One of the home room hotties expresses admiration for my bright blue super slim jeans. I am delighted. I figure if the 13 year old girls like em, their grandmothers will surely follow.

So I told My Friend the Evil Substitute Teacher about the kid crying on the floor at Waterfront and he said, "You got a picture of that, right?" I reminded him that, in the first place, I have an old-fashioned cellphone that only makes phone calls. And besides, how could he think of such a thing – photographing a student in a debased situation like that? Well, in addition to the expected lecture about how this was another example of why I needed to upgrade from my current phone, which is only of average intelligence, he told me that I owed it to the sub brotherhood and sisterhood to record such a moment of triumph. "Remember that woman you told me about that they drove out of Appian Way High? Don't you think she should be able to see that? You'd give her hope, something to aspire to." I got off the phone as soon as I could. The dark side was too near.

Anyhow, here it's administering five periods of math assessment tests. Remarkable contrast, really. First three classes are like perfect, but the next one brings out the grrr in Gallagher – I'm raging at this one to get quiet for the test. The last class is really fine and pretty small, but a couple of boys start a bit of trash talk across the room at the start and they get full decibel treatment from me. During all this, the teacher across the hall sends me a kid because she's been disrupting his class. I'm guessing he didn't realize there was a sub here, but in any case I've got her. Not surprisingly, in about two minutes, she's calling out asking if she can go to the bathroom. Well, I'm quite worked up dealing with these guys and the NO she gets from me is sufficiently ferocious that she is visibly taken aback and asks if she can go back to her class shortly thereafter.

This comes to mind a couple of nights later when my cats and I are on one of our occasional walks up the hill at the end of the street. We only do this at an hour when we hope all of the dogs in the neighborhood will have gone to bed, but on this night a couple shows up with two dogs while Gracie is still straggling on our way home. She, of course, immediately goes into battle form, but when the dogs seem reasonably out of the way, I decide to pick her up so we can get going, only to her have slash my hand. The moral here is never go near cats or substitute teachers before they've had time to calm down.

My cats, by the way, have become famous, the story of our midnight walks having appeared in the *Chronicle's* weekly pet column, a laminated copy of which becomes one of my lower-grade staples. Once when I told a Los Montecillos first grade class that I'd forgotten to bring it to show them they told me they remembered it from kindergarten.

ON THE NOSE – *Learning Handicapped, Francisco Palou Elementary, March 8, 2011*

This teacher's been out three or four weeks since one of the kids was swinging a milk crate, hit her in the face and broke her nose. But the aides assure me the class "isn't scary." Only two students here when I arrive, actually. One spends as much time in the corner lying on beanbags as he can. The other says, "Get the fuck away from me fat ass bitch – stupid Chinese lady" – that's to the principal. She will overturn a desk at one point.

On my second and last day of what could have been a seven-day job, we've got three kids, including the beanbag guy who's a third grader, a fifth grader who I think may have been the one who broke the teacher's nose and another fifth grader, who announces she doesn't want to be here with me. Professional responsibility prohibits me from telling her the feeling is mutual. But after watching her be coddled all day – and I don't mean to say that I think the aides' approach is necessarily wrong; I don't claim expertise here – I do finally inform her at one point when she's yelling in my direction, that "These people have great patience for you; I do not." Her response? "He don't like black people."

Tine, the aide who can get the beanbag guy to do a little work, says I'm the only sub who's showed up "who had all the lights on," but while I help as much as I can, I tell her I think a fencepost could do what I'm doing. Janet E, an aide I've known from past union work, says these five kids (the total population of the class) have the school in knots. She says they – the principal, etc. – make you feel like it's your fault, but dealing with these kids is a hard job. I continually say to the aides that the general public just has no idea. You know that charter schools are not going to be jumping at the chance to get these guys. And they'd be thrown out of Catholic schools.

Society's responsibility to rude children – what is it? You just wonder if any of these kids have any sense of the consequences of their actions. And what do their parents make of the situation? At one point we have the kids outnumbered, four to three.

THEY NEVER CHANGE THE HOURS – *March 16, 2011*
My Friend the Evil Substitute Teacher calls about a story in the newspaper:

A man posing as a government official took over a rural high school, where he beat students with a cane and leather belts and arbitrarily changed school hours, the police said Friday. The head teacher and others at Golden Grove High School in eastern Guyana initially accepted the man's claim that he had been sent by the Ministry of Education to run the school. But they became suspicious when he began using different names and they noticed his poor grammar and spelling, police Commander Gavin Primo said. After two weeks, they called the ministry, and the man, who was not identified, was arrested.

To the extent that my American experience is a guide, his spelling or grammar wouldn't have given him away. Must have been changing the hours.

NAKED? – *English/English Language Development, Millard Fillmore High, March 18, 2011*
Ah, the duties of the job! I've got to continually shush the class, even when one girl is telling the class that she went through In and Out Burger naked.

"Well, no," she allows, when challenged, "I had my bra and panties on." I assure them that I'm as interested in the conversation as anyone, but we do have to have it quiet enough to do the assignment.
Student Names of the Day: Shang Shang and Yang Yang

A PORCUPINE! – *Special Education, Bonanza Elementary, March 21, 2011*
      Best assembly ever – wild animals. We get a fox, opossum, porcupine, red tailed hawk and great horned owl. A porcupine! How ya gonna beat that? At the end of the day, the school secretary says that there was a baby opossum outside her house once and her husband called the SPCA and they came and picked it up. I figure it might have been the one we saw today and probably grown-up opossums warn their offspring that "If you're bad and you don't listen to us you'll wind up spending your whole life going to assemblies of school children."

NO BOO, THOUGH – *Librarian, Vallejo Elementary, March 22, 2011*
      A Twin Peaks/Noe Valley school with lots of kids with hyphenated last names and two named for "To Kill a Mockingbird" characters – an Atticus and a Scout.

ABOUT THE SAME – *Counselor, Mateo Middle, March 24, 2011*
      With the greatest trepidation, I decide a one-day stint here will be a reasonable gamble. And when I arrive, the secretary is speaking Chinese – always a good sign – but this will be the highlight of the day. My main duties will be covering the second floor during passing periods and the cafeteria and gym (it's a rainy day) for two lunches. I pretty much just stand around and observe halls full of kids wearing hats and talking on phones (proscribed activities) who don't listen to the security guard – so they're sure not going to listen to me.
      During last period, the principal (different one than when I was here last) comes in to the counseling office where I am holed up and tells me to process a bunch of kids who are waiting outside. Apparently I'm the only "counselor" in the office at the moment. It's my job, she says. Well, I have been left no directions about how kids are to be "processed" at this school, so I follow her back to her office and ask what she means. Bring them in; find out why they're there; call their classroom, she says. Of course, none of them will listen to me and I am headed back to the principal when a regular counselor comes in and she clears the kids out.
      During the last few minutes of the day, a couple of kids wait for their counselor in my office. One asks how I like the school. I just smile. The other says, "No subs like this school." So, nothing's changed in seven years except the identity of the principal. And, by the way, I don't think unpleasant principals make unpleasant schools. I think unpleasant schools make unpleasant principals – mostly. I don't want to come back, but this was a good way to find that out.

LIKE KOTTER – *English Language Development, Dolores High,*
April 8, 2011

Difficult, but somewhat rewarding two-day assignment. Another sub before me got sick and I don't have lots of things I'm supposed to do, whether because the teacher didn't provide them or they were lost in the shuffle, I don't know. The guy I threw out for general childish behavior was emblematic of the experience. After his return, he was my pal and asked me lots of questions and told me I corrected them in ways that their teacher didn't. (I try to explain that their teacher may emphasize fluency over correctness.) The class was kind of like what you see in those heartwarming movies about "urban education" where the teacher ultimately wins the students' respect and can get them going. It wouldn't have happened if they had been native-born, though.

And today I noticed a girl using her iPhone as a mirror for the first time. I imagine it won't be long before they'll be asking what those things on the bathroom walls are for.

MY KIND OF PLEDGE – *Kindergarten, Bonanza Elementary,*
April 15, 2011

Pledge of allegiance on the wall in this classroom: "I pledge allegiance to the earth. To cherish every living thing. To care for earth, sea and air; with peace and freedom everywhere."

AVID TIC-TAC-TOE – *7th Grade Math/Science, Nathaniel Hawthorne Middle,*
May 3, 2011

Eighth period is an AVID class – Advancement Via Individual Determination – an extra tutorial for kids who might not otherwise get to college – their parents have never been, etc. I don't know that I've ever seen an AVID class in middle school before, though and this class demonstrates why it may not be such a good idea. After I've told a girl to stop playing tic tac toe and do something else, she's playing again, so I take the notebook she's playing in and put it in the teacher's desk. And now I realize that the kid's she's playing with is the tutor for this class who proceeds to get snippy with me and starts talking about how she'll help other kids with tic tac toe. So I throw her out. A kid says I can't do that, so I call the office on him. A security guard comes up and tells a couple of girls to stop eating lollipops and they start giving him lip, so he takes them too. So we've have had four ejections, which is certainly not what I expected to see in an AVID class, based upon my experience in South San Francisco, where they actually did seem to be the good kids!
Student Name of the Day: Francesca Kocks (I just called Francesca for roll.)

BIG BROTHER – *English, Appian Way High, May 4, 2011*

Today includes two showings of the film *1984*, 35 minutes into which I have to stand up and interpose a sign on a stick that says, " CENSORED! Big Brother doesn't approve of you watching this!" between the class and the sex scene on the screen. Of course, the kids are all over the fact that I'm watching behind the sign to see when I can take the sign down. A fifth period girl who's seen it before, previews the plot for the class: "He's gonna get in."

SOCIALIZATION – *Kindergarten, Anza Elementary, May 5, 2011*

Discipline's not great and I don't know the kids' names which doesn't make things easier. (In South San Francisco, Kindergartners often get name tags on sub days.) But after lunch, four boys go off to some kind of socialization program. And guess what? The class is a whole lot smoother when they're gone! They gotta teach em socialization skills in Kindergarten! Again, the general public has no idea. Failing schools, indeed!

NO BLOOD – *Fourth Grade, Pondside Elementary, May 6, 2011*

Switched to this from a fourth grade assignment I had set up in South San Francisco, but you generally don't switch up the pay scale to the big city without paying a corresponding aggravation price. The teacher has identified the likely problems, though, and suggested clever methods for dealing with them, e.g., ask so-and-so to bring a pencil to Mr. X. (Unfortunately, so-and-so says he doesn't know where Mr. X's room is.) And he's left me a great note saying to write him an explanation of anything he needs to know, such as "Why there is blood on the floor."

The highlight of the day (he said sarcastically) is the 46 minutes during which the whole school gets to go outside to watch the championship kickball game. I'm standing with the class, none of whom appear to have any interest in the game, in the spot they said they generally go to – as usual hoping that they don't just decide to all run away, since there's no way I could identify them – when a woman in a principal tee shirt comes by and says that fourth graders need to move to some other place. I tell her it's the first I've heard of it. She says, "Well do it now" and, as an afterthought, "please." The big city – rude children, rude principals.

YOU'RE WEARING THAT? – *Math, Nathaniel Hawthorne Middle, May 9, 2011*

Notice major cleavage across the hall between classes – I'm talking the teacher this time. Mrs. McCartney sure never dressed that way, so the style changeover appears to be complete. Three showings of *Jumanji* today, a movie with the redeeming feature of a plant that eats middle school-aged children.

THE WURST SPELER – *Third Grade, Benjamin Cardozo Elementary, May 11, 2011*

As you know by now, I've run across a lot of spelling challenged teachers and it's very hard for them to hide it in elementary school. A lot of teachers post a lot of stuff around the room – including their spelling problem. A teacher at Los Montecillos posted her "Pet pieves" and a sign asking, "What do Good Writers do?" and answering, "Generate thier own topics." They could study "homophons" and "synomyms,"or use words like "vacummed."

The teacher here has an envelope full of vocabulary words with pictures that the kids dump out on the rug to use during the day and she's got misspelled words among them. I confiscate "exhuasted." She's also pasted corrections over several "peices" on a math poster, but has missed a couple. And there's a "librian" on the jobs chart and a "but their too short" on a poster analyzing a story. When I wind up back here for a different class the next day, I introduce myself at the morning line-up. She thanks me for my spelling corrections – and appears sincere. Knowing you've got a problem is half the battle.

My class basically gets thrown out of PE (along with another class) for bickering and not paying attention on the second day of this job, probably a good measure of what they were like compared to normal. As for me, I'm not used to normal, so I enjoy this class (all Latino, I think, with one Egyptian) more than any in recent memory. I got a lot of hugs upon my departure.

THE UP SIDE – *Math, Cappuccino High, May 23, 2011*

They've divided boys and girls who failed math into separate two-period remedial math classes. I had the boys five days ago – 28 of them, playing with those toy skateboards that middle school kids favor, surreptitiously blurting out words such as "clitoris" and "uterus" for thrill value, and so forth. Today the girls and wow, is this better! I'm not sure what this all does for the boys, but it can't not help the girls to have them gone. I wonder if this is being written up somewhere.

WHATEVER I WANT TO? – *Fourth Grade, Strawberry Fields Elementary, May 26, 2011*

In a few year-end days, I have a fifth grade that comes with a "problem" list of kids who were so bad – according to some of their peers – that they made the long-term sub sick yesterday. We're talking making her throw up. Now, there've certainly been a few classes that I might have wanted to say *You make me puke!* to, but it was, you know, a metaphor. Anyhow, the school's kind of all over them this day – principal and other teacher in – and there's no throw-up today.

And a "heart assembly" (how to treat yours right, etc.) that is so boring as to be simply beyond the reach of the fourth graders I have that day, whom I nevertheless subsequently lecture on the rudeness they displayed there. Afterwards a discussion of a reading on the first guy to photograph snowflakes that leads to my discovering that they didn't know what century it is that we are currently in. At this point I accuse them of originating on another planet.

The last day of year ends with PE, for which the teacher's note says, "Take them out and do whatever you want to." Dangerous words so late in the day, so late in the year. I advise her accordingly in my note.

*****

PRACTICAL SKILLS – *Severely Emotionally Disturbed, Appian Way High, September 1, 2011*
A kid from another class comes in during lunch, says he's selling candy for $.75 to support sports programs. Turns out none of it's actually candy, so I get a tiny bag of Cheezits. And do I want any change? Apparently they're learning pan-handling skills, anyhow, and that's at least practical, right?

NO THANK YOU – *Equity Release Teacher, William Dawes College Preparatory School, September 2, 2011*
Yet another job title in the ever evolving education world. This one involves accompanying a cart full of laptops to a couple of classes so they can work on math and language arts programs. The second has a teacher who must be just out of ed school. When a kid does something "inappropriate," she identifies the behavior, tells the kid how to correct it, and the kid is then supposed to respond, "Thank you, Ms. K for helping me go to college." This entire protocol is written on the wall. This *is* William Dawes *College Preparatory* School, after all. Two black kids balk and say they don't want to go to college. I wonder how long she'll continue to try to make them say "uncle." I work with one of them who's clearly not making any sense of the computer's explanation for why her math answers are wrong. We resort to old fashioned pen and paper, with better success.

EXTINCTION – *Literacy Specialist, Grant Elementary, September 6, 2011*
Today I encounter the theory called "extinction" in an inclusion kindergarten classroom that has two kids "on the autism" spectrum, one of whom is in the process of tearing the place apart. He comes with an aide and does pretty well for quite a while until he starts ripping down everything he can. "Extinction" means you simply ignore everything he does; you don't even let him put things back; he's only doing it to get attention. A specialist's doctoral dissertation, I'm sure. The class ignore the outburst remarkably well as they go about the basic reading, writing and math manipulatives that constitute their lives' work.

COINCIDENCE – *Kindergarten, City Commonwealth School, September 16, 2011*
Anything that went according to plan here would pretty much have to be counted as a coincidence. After returning from the library, I consult the lesson plan and explain to the kids that I'm looking to see what we would be doing *if* we had a well behaved class. Irony presumably not in the kindergarten range, I guess I was talking directly to the camera.
Student Name of the Day: Miracle Hall

VERSATILITY – *Roving, Pine Elementary, October 4, 2011*
Today's work includes hanging posters off of dropped ceilings with paper clips, filling "hip pockets" (information envelopes that go home), feeding a black bunny, stapling first grade "books," reading a Davy Crockett story out loud – and

asking rigorous follow-up questions, having a class write on the topic of what happened "when I forgot my birthday" and overseeing production of pumpkin pictures.

DARK THOUGHTS – *Italian, Appian Way High, October 14, 2011*
    The teacher has left a form with space to list absences, below which it says, "Anything else I should know?" I leave a note that dark energy is now thought to comprise most of the universe.

MENU? – *Kindergarten, Los Montecillos Elementary, October 20, 2011*
    One of my students apparently bit another at lunch. They all know they're supposed to eat then, but apparently not everyone is clear about what's actually on the menu. Another nice thing about high school is that you don't have this problem so much.

LIKE LABOR PAINS – *Third Grade, Benjamin Cardozo Elementary, December 2, 2011*
    At least this one's close to home, I figure. They say that after a woman gives birth she forgets the pain; otherwise she couldn't go through another pregnancy. Subbing's kind of like that – classes here are not actually a picnic, but here I am. Some schools are like breach deliveries, though, I think, and you don't forget those.
    In today's paper: ***Officer handcuffs teen for burping in class, suit says.*** "*A 13-year-old was handcuffed and hauled off to a juvenile detention for burping in class, according to a lawsuit filed against an Albuquerque school principal, a teacher and school police officer."*
    Well, you certainly couldn't fault that principal for not backing his teachers up, anyhow.

NO TRAUMA – *Fifth Grade, Grant Elementary December 7, 2011*
    After agitated start – late, missed bus, unhelpful secretary, can't locate students – I walk into a class having an educational experience largely unhampered by public trauma. A kid asks if they're the most talkative class I've had. If they only knew! You can actually talk to these guys. I explain to them what RSVP means! Why that's French! One girl with whom I do individual reading tells me her father is a lawyer – it's that kind of school.

TEACHING OUTBREAK – *Fourth Grade, Strawberry Fields Elementary, January 17, 2012*
    We read "City Mouse Church Mouse" and one of the vocabulary words is eavesdrop. I decide I'll tell the origin of the word and what the eaves of a house are. Looking for a dictionary in the classroom, I find a big one which starts me rhapsodizing on the joys of owning a large dictionary which leads to how English has more words than any other language and where they came from. And the French influence and the Battle of Hastings and the Romance and the Germanic

Languages and the Celtic Fringe, on to the domestication of cats in Egypt and hunter gatherer societies. The teacher has other options lined up for me, like making *City Mouse Church Mouse* bookmarks, but I figure I'll go with world history for this hour. Mind you, I get through this – with much student Q&A participation – pretty much undisrupted. And I think of the latest wave of articles about how teacher "quality" is the defining factor in students' education, when I know there sure are a lot of other places where I couldn't be doing this and I'm not any better here today or Grant last week but I'm sure getting better results than at Cardozo or City Commonwealth, for example.

The next day's *Examiner*, of all things, has a piece about a trip to Yosemite for teenage black boys that's more to the point than most of the schools articles. An 11th-grader who went last year said, "If you're black, you have to scowl, you have to have your pants low. If you don't conform to the stereotype, you're ridiculed. But that doesn't happen at Yosemite."

ARTS EDUCATION – *Kindergarten, Los Montecillos Elementary, January 19, 2012*

I'm reading the kids the story of Olivia, the pig, who goes to the art museum where she likes the Degas, but can't make heads or tails of the Jackson Pollock. Johnny Otis died today, so I think back on that History of Black Music class at the Berkeley nightclub Ashkenaz with the speaker who attributed the rise of rap to widespread public school discontinuation of musical instrument instruction. And I wonder whether maybe they were laying off the drawing teachers when Pollock went to school.

SPECIALIZE? – *Whatever, Barlett Elementary, January 24, 2012*

Some kind of special ed job, I think. They tell me I'm replacing a coach and that I obviously won't be doing that. Does this mean a sports coach? Dunno, but they clearly regard my presence as pretty much of a loss for themselves. Would I go out to the yard before class? Stay for assembly; learn that tomorrow is pajama day. (Today looks like silly hat day.) Then, would I go up to the Computer Lab where there's a paper cutter and cut these two foot square pieces of manila cardboard into 3 by 5 cards? Not sure if they've heard that such things are carried in office supply stores these days – and at a much higher quality than I am about to produce. It brings to mind the Bob and Ray skit about the company that straightened out paper clips. Their employees made seven cents an hour and foraged for food on the outskirts of town. I do this for more than three hours! Did some cutting yesterday afternoon at Pine too, so I'm starting to wonder if there might be any district cutting-specialist contracts out there.

OLD, BUT – *Roving, Grant Elementary, January 27, 2012*

Additional body in a special ed class for the morning. They've got one of those kids who ties the school in knots here. He's maybe fourth grade. Says "motherfucker" a lot to try to get a reaction. Earns points for *not* spitting on the floor, that sort of thing. Predictably feels sick and has to be taken to the office to call home, but his mother's not buying it. In the afternoon a kid tells me, "You're old, but you're pretty smart." About the best I'm going to do these days, I think.

THERE'S A PLACE FOR YOU IN THE BUREAUCRACY – Science,
William Howard Taft Middle, January 30, 2012

Guy who's brought in late by security during seventh period doesn't want to do anything and why am I picking on him for talking when everyone else is talking, etc. When I decide I've finally had it with him, the guy next to him actually provides a referral form – from his own supply! The first kid then bolts, so I call in a missing person report. Soon I've had about enough of the neighboring group as well and tell the guy who provided the referral form to move. He refuses and offers me a referral to use on him and I have him removed. Very efficient kid.

Back here the next day when it's Health Benefit Supplement Enrollment Day and there's a guy selling insurance in the teachers room, which is common enough. After a consultation, a woman asks him about a certain disease and whether there's a cure and he says he thinks with a proper attitude and prayer, anything can be cured. I guess with the policy he's selling you should plan on praying some.

My counseling work today involves three periods standing in the halls and two in the yard. The security guy introduces himself since we will be co-workers all day. It's his second year here and, boy, is he happy to be here. "Quiet, huh?" he says. He was at Schindler before this, where there was drugs, alcohol, weapons and fights. Later in the year, the Skyline security guy tells me he's just spoken with his girlfriend who told him they found a loaded gun at Bunche that day. So, yeah, I imagine some of these guys are pretty happy about the places they're not.

The pigeons and sea gulls swoop in as soon as the bell ends lunch. Good eating at middle schools where much is lost between hand and mouth. I notice one sea gull with a foil packet of some type that it seems unable to open. When it gives up I go over to check and it's a couple of graham crackers. I think of saving it for my own species, but open it for the birds instead.

"Queer people of color" posters in the hall. Weren't allowed to call somebody "queer" when I was in school; "colored people" was still in, though.

ADMINISTRATIVE CREDENTIAL – *Science, J.P. Morgan Middle,*
February 3, 2012

In the afternoon, a woman just appears in my classroom and starts asking students if they contributed to some mess in the hall, without so much as acknowledging that I'm in the room. I figure that no one could feel that entitled to be rude unless she was the principal. A glance into her office on the way out confirms my intuition.

NICE WHEN THEY'RE DUMB – *Seventh/Eighth Grade English, Skyline Middle, February 8, 2012*

Up at 5:35. Bus up to Twin Peaks. Get off at Iron Aly, one of those staircase streets you run into San Francisco, and climb 143 wooden stairs. Then up three flights of stairs to a locked classroom. Back down and up again. I've just walked up 13 to 20 flights – depending on how many steps you consider a "flight" when there are no landings – and down three, before facing a student. I suppose if you had to do that every day before facing middle schoolers, it'd toughen you up.

A teacher in the lunch room says sixth period will be the worst. I tell her fourth was no picnic. She finds the ejections I name totally predictable. "I don't know how people do it. I could never sub," she says. Two more ejected, including one who threw something during the first minute and I warned would be thrown out if he did it again, which he did. Not sure he ever actually went to the office, but after the bell rings to end class, I happen to turn toward the door to see a wad of paper coming my way and its thrower already in flight. He is, however, conveniently wearing a hoodie which I grab – by the hood. He proves to be the earlier thrower and we march downstairs with him proclaiming that I can't do that and the usual. Close to the bottom, he says he needs to get his backpack, so we go back up for it. I switch my guiding hand to the backpack for the trip back down and he starts wriggling out of it when as we get to the ground floor – which I just let him do and then deliver the backpack to the principal. Gawd, I love it when they're dumb.

Man, this job's not for everyone, now is it? I'd say Skyline isn't what it used to be, but so far as my experience goes, I'm not sure Skyline ever was what it used to be, at least the middle school part.

OVER-RATED? – *Language Arts/Social Science, Ishi Middle, February 9, 2012*

Another teacher is in the room by the time I arrive and I'm struck by the difficulty she has keeping this 6th grade *Honors* class quiet. When I take over, first thing we do is answer questions on a reading on Jackie Robinson. Having written his entry in the "Encyclopedia of Baseball Biography," I qualify as something of an expert on the topic, which I proceed to demonstrate. This will be the high point of our relationship. In passing period, half the class leaves for water or the bathroom, which I imagine they're normally not allowed to do. The remaining half is quiet – like an honors class – but as for the entire class, nah. But they continually tell me wait until I see the other guys.

Third period is Honors Assembly, at the end of which teachers are asked to collect the Honors certificates to hold until after lunch, presumably so they don't accrete condiments. From the large number of certificates handed out in the assembly, I assume the award determination heavily weights attendance.

In the midst of my one period of "regular" sixth grade, I ask a girl who's reading out loud to repeat a couple of names louder. They're difficult, old fashioned names and I want to know exactly how's she's actually saying them before giving her the right pronunciation and I can't hear her because she's reading low and the class is talking loud. I still can't hear them the second time so I pronounce them, at which point she rolls her eyes in a way sixth grade girls are wont to do. I say something to her about giving me attitude, she starts crying and we just move on to the next reader. Well, toward the end of the period, the assistant principal arrives and after the bell says something about there being an incident and what is my side of the story. "My side of the story?" I ask. She says kids were going to the principal's office (after getting a bathroom pass from me, apparently) and reporting that a substitute "made a student cry." She starts telling me that some kids have limited English – like I've never dealt with that before. I am not amused. A room full of kids making it hard for me to conduct the class, then running the bathroom pass routine and telling tales on me. I suppose maybe this AP had to check it out, but it burns me. Ooh, I'm just waiting for them to say something to me in the office on my way out, but fortunately it doesn't happen. Hey, I've got an idea. Every administrator has to spend one day a year subbing at a school where they're not known. Might give em a clue.

I then watch a student teacher struggle though his uncooperative eighth grade class. The one advantage he's got is that he can hand out detentions – which he does. We talk during the prep period and I mention my skepticism about the value of ed courses. He seems to think they're valuable though, although he does allow that they were not *actually* useful for the class he's *actually* teaching. Ishi has lately been considered a good and rising school and I suppose it is in comparison to many, but it wouldn't bring a smile to your face or anything.
Student Names of the Day: Czarina Ayran, Jesse James

WAR WITHOUT END – February 12, 2012

The *San Francisco Chronicle* carries a note about "former first lady Laura Bush who was in the neighborhood the other day to gauge support for the George W. Bush Presidential Center's latest educational initiative, pushing the importance of middle school." First the Iraq War and now he's promoting middle school? The man is incorrigible.

MET AN ED PROFESSOR LATELY? – English, Appian Way High,
February 22, 2012

Today I'm in for a Ms. Marder. So I'm a substitute Marder. I've got a student teacher for one class. She's at SF State and says their professors tell them to do various things with the kids and the student teachers have to tell them that the kids are not ready to do that. Says she doesn't know if the professors have even been to the schools where their students are student teaching. And, you know, I don't recall ever running into an Ed professor in my travels and now that she mentions it, it does seem pretty downright amazing.

SHAKE ON THAT? – *Roving, Benjamin Cardozo Elementary, February 27, 2012*
   Overheard a teacher asking a kindergarten student a question that might dissuade some from working that grade level: "Did you wash your hands after you put them in the toilet?"

A LITTLE AFRAID – *Math, Ishi Middle, March 23, 2012*
   A fair amount of yelling to quiet these guys. A woman appears in the back of the room, says she's a special ed sub from next door and she's supposed to be in here for the first periods. Tells me I'm controlling them better than the regular teacher. Says this one girl "isn't afraid of anybody – I think she's a little afraid of you." We subs take our compliments where we may.

WELLNESS – *Counselor, Ruth Harrison Middle, April 2, 2012*
   The counselor I'm replacing apparently runs the Wellness Center, something I am not equipped to take over, as wellness had not yet been invented when I was in school. We knew only sickness then.

I WATCHED TV – *English/Travel & Tourism, John Adams High, April 3, 2012*
   Just when I might think I'd done it all, there comes a Travel & Tourism class. The assignment is to write two paragraphs about their spring break and then share that with three other students.
Student Names of the Day: Theodora Pasion, Queen Lee, Cinderella Situ

WHATEVER – *Vocal Music, Dolores High, April 9, 2012*
   A guy could get the idea that some electives are not taken all that seriously. Three periods are supposed to watch an Alicia Keys video, but before another teacher comes in and locates the video for me, I cannot get a single student to volunteer to walk down to the library to see if they have it. There's a list of questions for them to answer – ha! I notice a sign-in sheet from March 12 lying around – this does not seem encouraging. Dolores is fairly quintessential *Urban High:* Not horrible scary, maybe not exactly what "Harlem's Queen Mother Moore once described as 'idiot factories,'" as William C. Rhoden wrote of in today's *New York Times*, but little resembling an intellectual atmosphere.
   And by way of reality check, my friend Sarah, who has two kids in San Francisco public schools, has read what I've written about necessary teacher (or adult) to student ratios maybe running as low as one-to-five or six in some classrooms – regular classes, not special ed, that is. She actually thinks it's as low as one-to-three in some cases.

HIGH QUALITY? – *Counselor, Gettysburg Middle, April 19, 2012*
   This is a school where I'll risk a counselor job, but probably not a classroom job – although I realize the one could easily turn into the other. But no, I am escorted to a room where I am to issue tardy passes and proctor tests for any late seventh and eighth graders. (And make sure the eleven skateboards in storage don't disappear.) A fleet of adults, all non-classroom personnel, I think,

stick their heads in to inquire or introduce. I'm supposedly proctoring four kids taking the STAR test – a girl who's arrived late and more or less does it and three boys who've been thrown out of class. Of course, I have no impact on them and another counselor is actually proctoring.

Then lunch time door-guarding. The assistant principal advises me that there were three physical altercations yesterday. None today, though. Then back to the room where a couple of kids have to write out a "Think Sheet" about some incident. Not a lot of thinking seems to go into this, though. I'm supposed to call their teacher and ask if he wants to send down work for them. He says it's group work and they can come back if they're not going to start hitting each other. Says he sent some kids down yesterday and they came back eating chips like everything was fun and what goes on down there anyhow? I tell him that, of course, I am in little position to do much of anything but that my take on what I've seen is much like his. At the end of the day, the assistant principal thanks me and I demur saying I really haven't done much of anything. She says, no, my guarding the hall was important and that I'm the type of high quality sub who'd be welcome back at Gettysburg. Um, probably not.

BUBBLEHEADS – *History/Social Science, Appian Way High, April 20, 2012*

Last day of STAR testing. In my briefing, I'm told that the teacher had trouble with a couple of guys yesterday. Trouble in STAR testing? When the kids arrive, I recognize a few of these bozos and get the idea. These fellows won't be worrying about college placement or anything like that. A couple just bubble in anything and finish in five minutes and want to play. Actually eject two. No wait, a third – three trips from security – for testing! Man, have I gotten tired of this place.

SO THAT'S WHY THEY CAN'T SPELL IT – *Fifth Grade,*
Buenos Dias/Nathaniel Hawthorne, April 24, 2012

Overseeing a lot of class reading time today and lack an actual book (as opposed to a newspaper). I decide to look among the student books and find a whole box of Judy Blume. I pick out *Are you there God? It's me, Margaret* and there I find the part where it's written that the teacher "called the role." Well, since I figure that just about every female teacher minted in the past thirty years has probably read this book, how would we ever expect them to realize that a teacher's actual role is to call the *roll?* And as for the guys, well spelling is supposed to be the sort of stuff that the girls are good at, anyhow.

The para here says it's amazing how different they are with a sub. About a quarter of them try to help, as she sees it, and the rest are testing what they can get away with.

Buenos Dias, by the way, generally considered a very desirable school, has now been combined with Nathaniel Hawthorne, generally considered not so great, to form a K-8 school. We'll see how that goes.

WE JUST WORK HERE – *Dance/Reading, Citadel Middle, April 30, 2012*
      We start with proctoring some kind of standardized test in the library for the first two hours. As if sixth graders weren't confused enough, there are two different sets of numbers on the pages to confuse them when you give directions. But then, they didn't provide me with directions. And someone decided to do the test out of order and start it with the untimed portion that was supposed to go last. Two different teachers that I ask what's up give me the same answer – "I just work here." Even when the principal and the assistant principal are in the room, they act like they don't know who thought this thing up either.
Student Name of the Day: Zeus Cruz

BULLYING AS A CAREER? – *Counselor, Ishi Middle, May 7, 2012*
      I notice an announcement for a Bullying Academy. I wouldn't have thought they'd be teaching that, you know. But I suppose the CIA is hiring.

YOU? – *Learning Disabled, Aldo Leopold Elementary, May 8, 2012*
      I pressed the button to listen to this job again and accepted it by mistake and when I tried to cancel I was not given that option, so off I went – in case you were wondering about the science underlying substitute teacher placement. This turns out to be a Pre-K for autistic kids. Nine of them, all boys. I tell the aide I feel like I should know this, but was autism overwhelmingly male? She said she understood it to be about 75 percent but actually she'd been there 2 1/3 years and they'd only had one girl – for a month. One biter today, but really not a difficult bunch. A look of alarm comes over the face of a friend a few days later when I mention that I'd done a couple of Pre-K classes recently. I had to reassure her that they don't actually put me in charge of such things.

BUCKLE UP, KIDS – *Math/Science, Calvin Coolidge Middle, May 10, 2012*
      First period is pretty loud. The aide says it's always like this and thanks me for bringing some order. Same old same old here – I call counseling to have a student removed and someone comes and changes the kid's seat. I'm in a computer lab without a phone and have to rely on the people next door to call for me. The second time around, they are no better for the guy who comes in than they are for me. I'm just not even going to try to keep them on task next period in the lab. I do call security on one kid for cursing; he runs away. Thank you lord! I seize a couple of phones and deliver them to counseling. The kids hate that – so I like it.
      Apparently some of them are going on a class outing to Great America tomorrow and a bunch of them are looking at that website. Noticing the pictures of the roller coaster where your feet hang free and it looks like everyone's going to be thrown into space, something comes back to me: Did My Friend the Evil Substitute Teacher say something about getting a summer job as a mechanic in an amusement park? I don't want to think about it.

ANTHROPOLOGY – *Whatever, Buenos Dias/Nathaniel Hawthorne, May 16, 2012*

First job canceled This one doesn't come in until 10. It's a first grade job, but when I arrive, they say that class is actually on a field trip with another teacher. Pretty much spend the day doing yard duty through a never-ending succession of lunches, followed by a last period PE class that I'm added on to. There are these small yellow cones in the yard that are used for setting foul lines and such. A group of girls around the play structure have a couple of them and start jamming them between each other's legs so as to simulate penetration. I feel like I'm witnessing an initiation ritual that has been going on since well before the invention of plastic.

IS THERE A SPRAY FOR THIS? – *Math, Ishi Middle, May 17, 2012*

On the bus ride home surrounded by the inmates, I try to think what else I have ever experienced that was as annoying as middle school kids in large numbers. Some tiny flies that bit us all night once in Nova Scotia come to mind.

ONE NATION UNDER GOD – *Special Ed K-3, Los Montecillos Elementary, July 24/5, 2012*

Surprise summer call. The other Special Ed teacher (and with budget cuts, Special Ed's all that's left of summer school) offers me a ride home the first day, picks me up the next morning, and apologizes for *only* dropping me at BART that afternoon because she has a meeting after school. Absolutely unprecedented! On the second day, a kid is talking about platypuses and I ask if he knows where they're from. He doesn't, so I look for a map to show him, but there isn't one on the wall and over the course of the rest of the day I search all over with no success. There is a flag, though, of course.

*****

I CAN'T WHAT? – *Life Skills, Appian Way High, September 6, 2012*

My first day in Appian Way starts with a packet I have to sign off on that appears to say that subs can no longer issue referrals. This, along with a couple of days of arguing with the secretary over the quality of my note-taking (an aspect of the job newly elevated in importance), prompts me to effectively drop subbing in South San Francisco without further deliberation. This was Life Skills class, so this referral stuff was only theoretical, anyhow. But I'll wind up only working four days in this district the entire school year.

SPEECHLESS – *English, Annunciation Gulch Middle, September 14, 2012*

Lost my voice at Bayard Rustin yesterday, so I jump at this because it says a student teacher will conduct tests so maybe I can pull this off *sotto voce.* There is no lesson plan – something I will run into more often this year than in the past – but the student teacher lives up to billing. Although I lack a classroom voice, which the student teacher (who looks like a high school student) provides, we talk continually during the day. As she tells it, she's mostly just supposed to be observing this semester, but this teacher is retiring after first semester and the kids know it, so she comes all the time. Figures if you can cut it here, you can make it anywhere. She hears fellow ed students who were placed at Cabot and Morgan, etc., talking about kids coming in, sitting down and learning; discipline all the time here, however. But they remain tremendously supportive – a couple of security-type people appear at the end of the day and thank us for our work. I tell em it was all her. Later in the year Y tells me how the principal here once decided they'd have a school spelling bee and gathered the entire student body in the auditorium only to have chaos ensue – no one could hear. That is, until one of the security guards took over and ran it.

OH SHIT! – *Fourth Grade, Hanna Elementary, September 20, 2012*

First thing I hear upon entering the classroom is that the turtle has pooped in its food dish. I hate when that happens. And then a yoga teacher appears. The kids even do some "ohm"-ing.

NOT A "FAILING SCHOOL" – *First Grade, Rockefeller Elementary, September 21, 2012*

I used to come here as a union Area Rep, but I'm not sure that I've ever subbed here before. The teacher has left a morning message on the board, presumably for me to read to the class, except that they can already read the entire thing and it's September of first grade. The school website describes it as "a small, safe, and successful elementary school located in San Francisco's Inner Richmond neighborhood." No argument here.

TEXT ME – *Finance/Marketing, Millard Fillmore High, September 24, 2012*

     Some kids hang out here at lunch and watch a movie and ask if they can turn the lights off. Which I agree to – provided they're really watching, as I'd prefer to read. Some watch intermittently, in between looking at their phones. They probably consider this watching, I suppose. Watching doesn't mean not texting – life doesn't stop because of a movie, does it? I suppose it's sort of like old people checking their e-mail.

     Over the course of the year I will preside over Math, Spanish, Chinese, ESL, Special Ed, History and Economics classes here, in addition to today's specialties. I will commute here for an entire week and try to think afterwards if I ever saw a student reading a book, newspaper or magazine on the bus the whole time. (Although I suppose some of them could have been reading Chaucer on their phones.) But I will encounter a chorus of girls singing a "suck my dick" song on the bus one morning. Man they just don't write em like that any more, do they?

     And for the first time I encounter a student with whom I've played volleyball. Happily, our common past in no way affects the traditional sub-student relationship – I have to tell her to stop texting – twice.

Student Names of the Day: Pinky Lee, Master Lo, Maverick Pumaras

ON THE EDGE – *Journalism, Ishi Middle, September 26, 2012*

     Ishi will be my on-the-edge school this year – as annoying as I'm willing to go; a couple of others will go over the edge. Half of this place is Honors. That's supposed to be the manageable half – maybe. At about 10:10 one day, a girl in an Honors class asks when the period ends. I tell her 10:15. She says, "20 minutes?" I point to the clock on the wall. She says, "I can't read time." When I pursue the question, she says, "I'm really bad at math." I assure her that even people who are really bad at math can tell time, thinking maybe I should give her an attainable goal to aspire to.

     I'll be here on days when there are 22 and 23 subs in the school, so you know you're not going to get a lot of back-up on those days. There are reasons to return here though. For instance, the view's good – on some days, from some classrooms you can see the Farallones, 30 miles out into the Pacific. On the right day it's beautiful and usually there's not that much beauty in middle school.

     Gandhi's name is misspelled on the door of the Journalism class (Ghandi).

Student Names of the Day: Thomas Angst ("Angst in Middle School" sounds like something Goethe might have written), Syncere Austin

REFUGEE SCHOOL – *Art, Dolores Education Center, October 10, 2012*

     The secretary says she's been here since this school started in the 70s, but it was a new one to me. Pretty much a one-year-and-out introductory program for Spanish-speaking elementary kids – like the Sun Yat Sen Educational Center. One of the most overcrowded schools in the city in the 80s, at the height of the

Salvadoran civil war, they tell me. Small classes today, though, although the size apparently varies with parents' employment prospects. Five periods of coloring in pictures of Central/South American pottery with complementary and then analogous colors.

CHARTERED – *Resource Program, Threshold Middle, October 11, 2012*
    Second day in a row at a school I haven't been to before. Also only my second day ever in a charter school. The teacher I'm replacing is special ed and they're apparently the only San Francisco Unified School District employees here; they pay their own subs considerably less, I learn. Being in and out of classes here for three days allows me to observe just what a tightly scripted program they run – the two social studies classes seem to cover identical material daily.

RAPE TAG – *Second Grade, Pondside Elementary, October 18, 2012*
    Note says "You will be blessed to have taken this position," but unfortunately I am not blessed with a lesson plan. Class is small and not difficult and they have both Motion and PE classes during the day (How is motion class different than PE? Well, I don't have my elementary teaching certificate, so I can't answer that question properly – one was indoors and one out), but I'm winging it the whole way and leave a note expressing my displeasure. And while I'm at it, I am not that impressed with the office either. No lesson plan? Not our problem. Key? Well, I suppose we could give you one of those now that you're locked out of your classroom cause we didn't give you one in the first place. Of course, I'm late and don't know the name of the teacher I'm replacing, so I suppose they're probably not all that impressed with me, either.
    On a trip here later in the school year, I see a note the office has circulated reporting that some of the third grade boys "had been playing a very inappropriate game called "Rape Tag." Parents had been contacted and it seems to have ended and there didn't appear to have been any inappropriate contact, just language, it says. This would in no way be considered a scary school, by the way. Just keeping you apprised on modern urban education.

GENERAL DUTIES – *Third Grade (maybe), Yi He Elementary, October 23, 2012*
    I walk over Nob Hill, in the heart of the San Francisco that the world comes to see, brushing by deutsche tourists on the curvy block of Lombard, to get to yet another first-time-for-me school where I find a student teacher who's got the whole thing in hand. I never actually ascertain what grade this is, but it's a typical day maintaining order, helping out with math, reading aloud from a Roald Dahl novel and watching a Humphrey the Whale video.

CARCASS – *Spanish, John Adams High, November 2, 2012*
    Student poster on Venezuela says that Margarita Island is located "towards the northeastern part of the capital city of Carcass."
Student Name of the Day: Sparkle Wilson

JUST THE WAY IT IS – *History/PE, Skyline Middle, November 5, 2012*

I think part of what I don't like about this place is that it seems too small and ingrown. If so and so acts like a jerk, that's just the way it is – we've known him since first grade and that's the way it's always been. Every black boy I encounter here is a problem and I've experienced some of the worst behavior from white boys anywhere. Don't think I'll be coming to either campus again this year. This sure seems to be the year of my discontent on the middle school front.

LINCOLN, MAYBE? – *Third Grade, Annunciation Gulch Elementary, December 6, 2012*

I have to read them a story about Barack Obama. I ask does anyone know who the last president was. No one does. Somebody says George Washington.

OUCH, A PEST! – *Second Grade, P.H. McCarthy Elementary, December 11, 2012*

Upon arrival in the office, I encounter numerous binders – *Subs Sign-in, Key Binder, Visitors, Volunteers*, etc. And one called *Pest Log*. Why had no one thought of this before? An official log to record pests? So since you can see Nelson Mandela Middle School out the window here, I figured I was probably in for a difficult time and might be recording some names in the book. Wrong on two counts, though: The school wasn't like Mandela at all. And the log turned out to be about termites and the like. Nothing to stop someone from adapting the idea, though.
Student Name of the Day: Carol Ouch

A LOVE SUPREME – *First Grade, Vallejo Elementary, December 12, 2012*

Two student teachers. And they vacuum and wash desk tops at the end of the day. (I ask if they do windows, but they say no.) One of them is being graded by his supervisor, so I'll see an ed school person for the first time – or I suppose it's possible I just wasn't looking in the past. The kids have a Hanukkah word sheet so we talk a little about Yiddish and German. The other student teacher plays them John Coltrane. I am continually remarking to the student teachers on how much more the kids are exposed to when you're not continually dealing with behavior problems; how far from the Bayview this day feels.

STUPID STUDENTS? – *Astronomy/Physics, Pizarro High, December 14, 2012*

Physics for freshmen – what a stupid fucking idea. These guys should be playing with blocks. All review sheets – another sub yesterday – no discernible work goes on. My standard today simply becomes what it would look like if an administrator came in: Down off the tables and up off the floor and no cards; I don't even try to stop the phones. I hear one guy describing a friend who wanted to be a teacher and he asked him, "You want to teach stupid students?" Self awareness is to be admired in any circumstances.

PUFF DADDY, REVOLUTIONARY WAR AUTHORITY – *Nathaniel Hawthorne Middle – English/Social Studies, December 20, 2012*
    Chaos upon arrival; simply taking attendance is contested ground today. They watch a video on the American Revolution in which Colin Powell talks about how the Americans didn't play by the rules. *Ya mean they were terrorists, General?* Michael Bloomberg, Sheryl Crow, Sean Coombs (the former Puff Daddy), Newt Gingrich and Rudy Giuliani will also comment on the Revolution over the two days I'll show the film.

CHILD-PHOBIC TEACHER SUES SCHOOL DISTRICT – January 15, 2013
    You first read in the newspaper that "A former teacher is suing the Cincinnati school district, saying she was discriminated against because of her rare phobia: a fear of young children," and the story sounds preposterous. But then you learn that "Maria Waltherr-Willard, 61, who had been teaching high school Spanish and French since 1976, said that when she was transferred to the district's middle school in 2009, the children set off her phobia, causing her blood pressure to soar and forcing her to retire." And you realize that Ms. Waltherr-Willard is simply claiming that middle school children make her crazy. Now, you're not going to find anyone who's ever spent serious time around large numbers of middle school children telling you that they doubt their ability to bring on mental breakdown. Hopefully Waltherr-Willard Syndrome is recognized in the next *Diagnostic and Statistical Manual of Mental Disorders* and we can put this behind us.

PEOPLE COLORS – *Second/Third Grade, Harriet Tubman Elementary, January 17, 2013*
    Student teacher doing class and lucky for me, cause this ain't an easy bunch. She tells me that the regular teacher doesn't like to be absent because when she's gone there'll be fist fights in this class. Kids in foster homes, raised by grandparents, etc. A kid maybe ten feet from the board says he can't read it – some of them are waiting for glasses to arrive.
    Lunch time today will be the first meeting of the Math Club which means that they can come in and play math games and – the best part – chew gum in school. But first a boy and a few girls wearing head scarfs arrive, mistakenly thinking that the Prayer Club met in that room.
    I remind the teacher that there's a "c" in Barack so she can correct it on the board, figuring that teaching them how to spell the President's name wrong is sufficiently egregious as to require intervention. The kids have some kind of civil rights assignment, so they're doing bios of MLK, Rosa Parks, etc. I also enjoy informing the two kids doing Jackie Robinson that he was a Dodger. Of course it turns out that one of them doesn't actually know what baseball is, not coming from a part of the world where it's played. And today I discover people-color crayons, which is to say, a set of crayons of maybe twenty different flesh tone hues. One flesh tone in my Crayola box – and we were glad to get it.

RESTFUL – *Language Arts, J.P. Morgan Middle, January 28, 2013*
Four days in a row here that are so uneventful, I'm forgetting to write notes. The principal of Mountain Top Elementary is an AP here now. Says he wanted a rest.
But the Student Names of the Day are good – Tweety Doe, Tiger Kotsching, Philander Xieu

EUREKA! – *Second/Third Grade, Skyline Elementary, February 11, 2013*
We read a lot about saving whales in a largely trauma-free day when my main function seems to be distributing hand sanitizer – every time they walk in the classroom – start, recess, lunch. You'd think these kids were going to the International Space Station or something – only now do I realize the filth in which we grew up. But a far deeper epiphany comes when I'm explaining the idea of twiddling one's thumbs when one has nothing else to do and a kid replies that "I text when I'm bored." For the first time I recognize that in hindsight thumb-twiddling could be seen as a sign of humans awaiting the invention of texting – for centuries, if not millennia. Like waiting for the messiah.

CIGARETTE TREES – *Music, Bayard Rustin Academy, February 26, 2013*
A quite kinetic day. First and second graders singing "Big Rock Candy Mountain" and dancing around as the substitute music teacher introduces them to the concept of the hobo life.
Misspelling of the Day (on the wall – teacher did it) soilder

MORE SONG AND DANCE – *Conceptual Physics, La Boheme High, March 1, 2013*
Honest, at La Boheme High they call it Conceptual Physics – it's an *aaarts school,* ya know. One of their assignments is to write and illustrate a haiku about sound. The classes are quite advanced, though, in the sense that they themselves exhibit quantum mechanical characteristics – it can be impossible to definitively state whether a particular student is actually in the classroom at any given point. Some disappear; some appear, as if out of nowhere. You wouldn't confuse these with serious classes or anything, but when they start singing or dancing in class here, whaddya gonna say? This is La Boheme High – the kids have a TV script internalized. In third period a couple of girls have to leave to catch the Dance Bus.
Student Name of the Day: Madeline Tuning (at a music school)

UNAUTHORIZED READING – *Fifth Grade, Grant Elementary, March 6, 2013*
Some of the biggest problems today are kids reading stuff other than what they're supposed to. When your worst problem is willful readers, well ...

GRIM – *Spanish, Sojourner Truth High, March 7, 2013*
Alternative school for students trying to finish their degrees. I've got 18 on my list – on four different levels of Spanish; six show up. The teacher, who is herself apparently a long-term sub, has been out for several days with a different

sub each one. The kids claim they've already done the assignment – and that they don't use textbooks in any ordered fashion. One thinks the teacher just thinks up something when she comes in.

I suggest they do homework from other classes; they say they don't get homework here. I pass out novels (in English) from a pile on the front table, but naturally there's no interest in that. We do have an okay current events discussion for a while – North Korea, Iraq, drones, crack, etc. A girl talks about a hostage-taking incident in a marijuana grow-house in the Bayview yesterday and I take out my *Chronicle* and show her the story. The girl next to her even turns the page! Now that's education.

Here I will draw the line on the phone usage only at not using speakers. My perusal of the other classrooms while roaming the halls in search of the men's room suggested that this policy fit within school norms. The kids were mostly pleasant enough – there is absolute stillness at times, even, but this program I'm in would certainly appear to be a waste.

All third period classes are invited to watch one class's set of short dramatic monologue presentations. One kid acts out being in front of a judge; another talking to a cop; a girl who doesn't get a job and thinks racial discrimination was in play; kids who don't get financial aid or bank funding; one who circulates the spat-upon vet story, in this case about an Iraq War vet. Not sure if the overall assignment was to convey disappointment, but it certainly was pretty grim. I think the kids might call this a ghetto school.

THE BESTESTESTED SUB – *Third Grade, Juan Crespi Elementary, March 27, 2013*

Down here in South San Francisco because it's school vacation week up north. When they've gone for lunch, I notice a paper has appeared on my desk:
Dear Mr. Gallagher,
I think you're the bestestested sub in the history in the world. I would love if can be our every day and there'll be a pattern Ms. Ball and then you. I think that's a splendid plan. But to bad it's impossible. Sincerely, Katelyn.

Wow – I'm sure not in the big city, am I?

NOUN? VERB? – *Language Arts/Social Science, Citadel Middle, April 2, 2013*

I have such high expectations for my day here that I plan out what I'm going to work on during each period after giving them their assignment. And I am actually able to do that – the classes are that well behaved. But not everything is perfect: It looks like they may have assigned the production of today's Daily Bulletin to a non-English major. The Word of the Day reads, "Rank (noun): a position. Toy Story ranks as my favorite movie." (I also notice they're still using hall passes from the 20th century – environmentally sound, I suppose.)
Student Name of the Day: Miracle Marshall

NO FALSE PROMISES – *Peer Resource, Copernicus High, April 5, 2013*

One period of College/Career; three of Peer Helping, during which they go off to the cafeteria to work on some presentation; one period of Health, during

303

which they watch *28 Days Later*, a sort of zombie movie, on the Smart Board – because it's Friday or something. Student government candidate assembly – one girl says people should vote for her because she has a cheerful personality.

HANDS-ON – *Health, Pizarro High, April 9, 2013*
    Highlight of the day had to be the girl flashing a menstrual pad, colored – I believe – to make it look used. It made the rounds at her table and eventually to the floor outside. As I was returning from lunch, I saw the principal carrying it in. Compliments on his hands-on approach, I suppose.
Student Name of the Day: Zi Li

PEAK EXPERIENCE – *Language Arts/Social Science, Waterfront Middle, April 11, 2013*
    This place seems a bit more welcoming this year. One teacher left me a note with the name of the "assistance principle" – you know, the person who helps the principal. The faculty displays a lot of room for growth, I think is how you put it. One day I got to show the movie *Matilda*. Double period, so we pretty much see the whole thing, I've seen it before, but seeing it in a theater simply can't compare with watching the scene of a middle school-aged child being thrown out a school window by a wicked administrator while in the company of actual middle schoolers. And when the ogre headmistress says the best schools are the ones without students, well, it makes a lot more sense if you're actually sitting in a middle school classroom. A lot of subs will go their whole careers without experiencing a peak moment like this. On the way home the MUNI driver stops the bus and shuts the kids at the back of the bus up, says he can't concentrate. I consider going back there to help shut them up, but I'm off the clock.
Student Names of the Day: Limber Olan, Christ Martinez

TORTURE – *Fifth Grade, Shady Grove Elementary, April 15, 2013*
    A kid's tee shirt catches my eye: "Torture makes diamonds" and I'm frankly surprised to find a kid in this school whose parents have turned him on to the hazards of the African diamond trade at such a young age. Then he turns around and I see that it's a San Francisco Giants 2010 championship shirt. The fans went through "torture" that year, you see.

THE SAME TO YOU – *Chemistry/Math, Pizarro High, April 19, 2013*
    In case I've given you the impression that it's only middle school kids who can be mean, there's a note on the board that says, "Whichever students wished I had more family emergencies, how would you feel if your family gets sick?" It's signed by the teacher who was absent yesterday and I'm guessing this is somehow directed at his first period jerk algebra class. One girl does write, "We hope your family gets well soon."
Student Name of the Day: Bi Yu (I wonder if he could get a scholarship in Boston based on that.)

BOYS LIE – *Literature, Pizarro High, April 25, 2013*
      Two-day job taken with some trepidation, but they're seniors and juniors – perhaps it speaks well of the school that it has freshmen classes such that I wouldn't come back here if they were characteristic of the place as a whole. Another teacher comes in to cover *Hamlet* in third period – woman in her twenties, discusses the patriarchy, i.e., men controlling younger men and women. Detailed critique of Hamlet's uncle's speech: Shakespearean *bon mots* that are mostly cliches – "neither a borrower nor a lender be," etc., followed by a lecture to Ophelia that comes down to "Boys lie." Which portion said teacher endorses from the bottom of her heart – "When they're horny, boys lie. The first thing my father told me when I got to high school was K, boys lie." In case you were wondering where Shakespeare studies were at these days.
Student Name of the Day: Chairman Lin

INDIVIDUALIZED STUDY – *Music, Dolores High, April 29, 2013*
      Choral singing. No lesson plan. Not unpleasant, but the teacher sends nothing, so far as I know. Total waste. In one class, three kids play piano – the only music-related activity that occurs all day here, except for listening to iPods, of course.
Student Name of the Day: Fantasy Decuir

ADIEU – *Language Arts/Social Science, Calvin Coolidge Middle, May 2, 2013*
      Earlier this year, I asked S if the Counseling Office here was as useless as ever. He said it was – scandalous, actually, he thought. Nonetheless, he said there was one girl in fifth I should give the heave-ho if she started up – even if no one answered the phone in counseling. She lived up to billing and I did successfully divest the class of her. Today I will not be so fortunate, however.
      They've already worn through my patience here by previously deploying me as a security guard for an entire day. Today my second period class is supposed to go to a concert but my instructions say to wait for an announcement. When none comes I call the office and they say just go. But when we arrive we're told there's not enough room. Not enough room for all of the classes invited? What is it that makes me feel less than certain that this place is well run? On our way back, a kid says there's a monster in the hall. I reply that this is a middle school, so there's always monsters in the halls. That makes its way around – they like that. Glimmers of recognition.
      But eventually I've got me a little feller who wants to throw stuff in class and won't give me his name, so I call the office to have him removed. After four calls, by which time I've got a second kid set to go, security arrives but all he does is get their names. When I tell him I want them out, he says there's no place to put them. That'll be it for me for at this place. The room is such a mess that the last period kids note it – bad even by middle school standards – water on the floor, etc. I explain that given the maturity level of the last group, I can not be sure that some of them didn't wet themselves.

I say goodbye to S on my way out cause I won't be coming back here. The secretary asks if I want the job she mentioned this morning and I tell her the same. She asks if I want to talk with the principal, but I just shrug and walk out. Later I will tell Y about this and he says he had a kid acting up here once and locked him out of the classroom. The kid returns with the assistant principal and Y tells her the kid was doing this, that and the other thing. The AP says he's allowed to go to the bathroom any time he wants and she understands that Y was yelling at a child. Don't you think that's sometimes in order, he asks. No, she says she's been there four years and never has. Y says he still goes there now and lets them do what ever they want; only makes sure no one gets hurt. Not me, though. I did at least salvage a couple of
Student Names of the Day: Winky Fong, Valiant Nguyen

HIPSTER MIDDLE SCHOOL? – *Art, Nathaniel Hawthorne Middle, May 3, 2013*
Two day gig showing the movie *Frankenweenie* (pretty good, actually). They have an assignment and the classes are really not bad. Perhaps this is a foreshadowing of the change in Dolores High (due to hipster parents presumed to be sending their kids there) that is not actually yet as great as some might think or wish it to be.

IT'S CROWDED AT THE TOP – *Cabot High, Psychology, May 8, 2013*
For three days I'm showing psychology-themed movies for a teacher who's on jury duty to a class that's basically finished their semester's work – *Rainman, Donnie Darko, Memento*. When I run into predictable problems with the video equipment, I am struck by the absence of students stepping forward to get it to work, which you'll usually get. Is this because kids don't get to Cabot by watching TV?

This school is jammed. Being pretty much urban public school heaven, everyone's dying to get in. Another teacher and I hot-bed it back and forth between the classroom we share and the Social Studies office, which is a pretty hopping, crowded, collegial place with lots of students dropping in.

On the way in there's a group of black female Cabot students engaged in very un-Cabot sounding discussion at the back of the bus about fights and such. A couple of girls near me on the ride home are more like it: One asks the other if she's going anywhere this summer. She lists four countries as possibilities, including Switzerland and maybe the Bahamas.

GETTING IT RITE – *Special Ed and So Forth, Dolores High, May 13, 2013*
I'm immediately sent to a different class where no sub has arrived and there is a sign on the wall:
> The Principals of Right Speech
> Speak Truthfully
> Speak Kindly
> Avoid Idle Chatter
> – the Buddha

So far as I know, while the Buddha's exact language is uncertain, it seems pretty clear that it wasn't English, so I don't think we can expect him to know the Principles of Right Spelling, can we?

My real assignment is for one of those loosey-goosey special ed classes that actually seems to work, at least for one of the two periods I'm there as the kids manage to focus for long stretches on the Sherman Alexie novel they're reading. Gavin Newsom Academy comes up during a wide-ranging discussion with one of the paras who says he had a friend who taught there – fifth grade I think – and had a boy beat up a girl in class and tried to get the principal to do something to the boy, but his response was just – that's how these kids are. We talk about how difficult it is to be at a "bad school," where everyone is mad at everyone else, etc.

IN MY DREAMS – *Spanish, Copernicus High, May 15, 2013*
There are still a few more things I'd like to accomplish in my sub career and I almost got one of them today. At the end of last period we have a student who sleeps right through the bell and all of the other students leaving. I gather my effects and almost manage to clear out and leave him there, but he wakes at the last moment. I always imagine them waking up when it's dark out and the school is locked up. Guess I'll have to re-up for another year. Winter's the best shot at this, anyhow.

ADOLESENT SPELLING – *June 18, 2013*
I spot a job notice for a private middle school social studies teacher today that specifies candidates must exhibit a list of qualities that includes "joy and familiarity with pre-adolesence." I immediately forward this to My Friend the Evil Substitute Teacher who responds that this call for exultation in the debasement of the middle school experience surely must be a code notice for the opening of some sort of Nazi juvenile war crime academy. But to whom would we report this?

(Some might take the misspelling as evidence of adolescent forgery, but with our vast school experience we recognize that it falls well within the current spelling competency standards for school teachers and administrators. Come to think of it, maybe they've started teaching estimating in spelling now, just like in math – although I haven't seen it yet.)

EPILOGUE

As the publication of this book can only hasten the end of my "career" as a substitute, it seems increasingly likely that my earlier vision of how I would spend my final days will come to pass: Sitting on a park bench wearing an overcoat on a hot summer day (okay, so they don't have hot summer days so much in San Francisco – but it could be New York City), with a shopping bag full of my writings, asking passers-by if they'd like to see them. But at least now some of it may be bound. And if that career is indeed over, I'll leave it with two lingering questions: When are they going to decide what to do to that kid in Oakland for throwing the wastepaper basket at me? And when will *Dissent* decide if they're publishing my article?

The last word must go to My Friend the Evil Substitute Teacher who called recently to chat about the topic of middle schools and Catholic theology (at least Catholic theology as interpreted by the Sisters of Charity.) The distinction between Purgatory and Hell, we are told, is not one of degree, as the fire burns equally hot in both places, but one of time – and of the hope of redemption. The difference is simply that Purgatory will end one day, but Hell will not. He saw in this a parallel with middle school where the experience is equally excruciating for students and teachers (and especially subs), with one crucial distinction – the students know it will end in three years.

APPENDIX - THE ANTI-SUSPENSION MOVEMENT

I'd wish I could be enthusiastic about the current efforts to reduce racial disparities in public school suspension rates. The intent of the activists is obviously honorable and the increased attention to the plight of black kids within our schools is laudable. And if the net result is to steer more resources in the direction of the kids now getting suspended, I'm all for that. At the same time I can't help feeling that some of those involved would feel they'd accomplished something significant if suspension rates were simply equalized across races – although this would have as little real impact on any underlying problems as mandating racially equal grade ratios would on alleviating an educational achievement gap. And actually, it's often not even clear that everyone involved understands what's at issue here – the basic fact that removing a disruptive student from a classroom is not done primarily for that student's benefit, but to allow the rest of the class to carry on without disruption.

The Department of Education's Office for Civil Rights has found black students three times more likely to be suspended than white students. The immediate question is "Why?" An influential 2010 Southern Poverty Law Center (SPLC) publication, *Suspended Education: Urban Middle Schools in Crisis* suggested "the possibility of conscious or unconscious racial and gender biases at the school level." In a *San Francisco Examiner* article reporting that blacks constituted but 12.5 percent of students in San Francisco's public schools, but "half the students who face disciplinary action belong to this ethnic group," some School Board members attributed the disparity to "cultural incompetence" and "racial discrimination" on the part of school staff. Given this country's history, these reactions are hardly surprising. But is it racial prejudice or insensitivity that's the root of the problem – or maybe something bigger?

In San Francisco, for instance, an African-American, Barack Obama, has received 84 and 83 percent of the vote in the last two presidential elections. Comparable statistics are not available for the city's teachers, but everything we know about who goes into teaching makes it seem likely they're at least as liberal as the electorate as a whole. This, and years of experience as a substitute teacher at more than eighty schools throughout the city, tells me it's not teachers' racial prejudice that's the issue here. When the question came up a few years ago, the president of the city's teachers union went so far as to suggest that some teachers might actually be avoiding disciplining black or Hispanic students for fear that they would be accused of prejudice. About that, I couldn't say, but I can tell you that there have been occasions when I felt relieved at finally sending a white student to the office because the last several had been black. At any rate, I feel certain that not only are most teachers quite aware of the racial discipline disparity but that the vast majority of them are also uncomfortable and unhappy with the situation but generally lack the resources to handle both the needs of their classes as a whole and the needs of kids who are disruptive in class.

Taking the example of San Francisco, again, the December 29, 2012 *San Francisco Chronicle* reported the city's black infant mortality rate was six times that of whites. (It also reported that the city's black population had shrunken to a number too small to even constitute a statistically reliable sample – a trend widely attributed to the city's relentlessly increasing cost of housing.) Other markers of community well being show similar numbers. In short, the black community in San Francisco – and the nation – lives under considerable stress and, as anyone familiar with schools knows, kids don't leave their problems at home. So it's not at all that I fault the anti-suspension campaigners for overstating the difficulties facing black students. If anything, I fear that by focusing only on what actually transpires in school itself, this campaign may underestimate them.

Robert Moses, who gained fame as a Student Nonviolent Coordinating Committee organizer of Mississippi voting rights struggles in the 1960's, later turned to teaching math to black middle schoolers and co-authored a book called "Radical Equations: Math Literacy and Civil Rights" with another civil rights veteran, Charles E. Cobb. Moses came to understand from his classroom contact that "what young people are up against today is less clear than the raw racism of segregation laws and the Ku Klux Klan." Cobb, on the other hand, confessed that when first approached about the book, "I had not been involved with public schools for years and while visiting them ... it seemed as if I had traveled to another world," as he watched a mother attack a Chicago teacher in a hallway, and talked to one kid as "another kid walked up behind him and hit him in the head with a brick or something." I'm happy to say I've never witnessed anything that dramatic, but I recount the story as a reminder that wanting to do the right thing about education doesn't necessarily mean that you actually know much about school (although I do think the TV series, *The Wire* – particularly the season on public schools – has been helpful in delivering a picture of how rocky life can get for some urban black kids.)

This discussion has never been an easy one and in some ways it may be more difficult than ever. At one point in the past the conversation had a more historical dimension. In addition to questions of individual attitudes, people might speak of "structural" or "institutional racism" and of the residual impact of slavery. They proposed remedies like affirmative action or even some form of reparations for slavery. The reparations idea never made it too far out of academia (although in 2000, California Governor Gray Davis did actually sign the University of California Slavery Colloquium Bill, promoting research and publicity on UC campuses on the topic of reparations for slavery.) And much of the affirmative action thrust was blunted in the courts. So where we once might have talked about big issues like creating full employment or guaranteeing adequate housing or even substantially smaller classes in difficult schools, there is a much deeper pessimism about effecting such changes today. Instead we tend to talk more about things like suspension rates, about which we feel we can do something.

So far as suspensions go, Secretary of Education Arne Duncan states the obvious: "Students who are suspended or expelled from school may be unsupervised during daytime hours and cannot benefit from great teaching, positive peer interactions and adult mentorship offered in class and in school." And certainly, although there is an "out of sight, out of mind" aspect to suspending kids from school – you'd be hard pressed to find anyone who actually thinks that sending kids home to possibly watch videos all day – or worse – will make them better students. Why are they sent home, then? Generally because few schools have the resources to do anything with them within the walls of the school, but outside of their classroom. An "in-school suspension" would likely be a far better alternative in most cases, but it requires having people and space available to deal with the suspended students. Perhaps the anti-suspension efforts will ultimately lead to increased resources for alternatives – and, if so, we should all be grateful – but if they do, it will be in spite of the obviously quite limited understanding of actual classroom situations that some anti-suspension campaigners display.

The above cited SPLC report, for instance, suggested that "the high and disproportionate suspension rates being experienced by youth of color," and especially "the pronounced differences for Black males" were for reasons that were insufficiently specific: "disrespect, excessive noise, threat, and loitering - behaviors that would seem to require more subjective judgment on the part of the referring agent." This critique does raise a good question: Are the rules leading to school suspensions somehow structured in a way that will produce harsher results for one group than another? Certainly there are precedents for this in the criminal justice system. An example that readily comes to mind is the greater penalties attached to the use of crack cocaine than to other forms of the drug, resulting in black crack smokers drawing harsher sentences than white coke snorters. Are kids, for instance, being suspended for things like wearing hats in class? If so, are black kids more frequently affected? If an overall reconsideration of school behavior standards were to conclude that some of what schools were getting all worked up about wasn't ultimately all that important, well, again, that would be a positive outcome of the anti-suspension campaign.

At the same time, while the study's authors may be accurate in characterizing charges such as "excessive noise" or "threat" as matters of "subjective judgment," the fact is that these are anything but trivial matters when it comes to maintaining a classroom situation conducive to learning. The authors also appear unaware of or unmoved by the fact that the kids most negatively impacted by classroom disruption tend to be of similar background to those causing the disruption – something we know from recent studies showing how race-separated America's schools remain, even after decades of desegregation efforts. So if the fact that "certain racial/gender groups are at far greater risk" of suspension from school means that "harsh discipline policies becomes a civil rights issue," as the report argues, then the fact that the same groups will be at far greater risk of experiencing significant disruption to their educational process must be a civil rights issue as well. Could the writers really be oblivious to the fact that all parents want disruptive students out of their children's class rooms – with the possible exception of the parents of the disrupters themselves? In fact, a formidable part of the basis of the highly promoted charter school movement is the claim and/or hope that a charter school can deliver a better educational product if it doesn't have to deal with the "trouble-makers."

And as for the discussion of the presumed "gender bias" in middle school suspension rates, this only seems further evidence of lack of real world contact. I don't think we're even dealing with a particularly sensitive or controversial issue here, as it's hard to imagine anyone familiar with middle school-age children not being aware of the fact that there are far more behavioral problems with boys than girls among the age group.

But then, the two university professors who authored the SPLC study don't seem much less knowledgeable about classroom dynamics than some people far closer to public education. For instance, San Francisco School Board President Sandra Lee Fewer recently amended a proposal to ban "willful defiance" suspensions by adding a mandate to reduce the use of referrals – removing a student from class, but not sending them home – calling them "invisible suspensions." In other words – "Just keep the kid who's giving you a problem in the classroom and deal with it." Look we've made the problem go away! (Oh, and by the way, make sure to get those test scores up.)

If anything, San Francisco Unified School District Superintendent Richard Carranza went further. "We're talking about culture change," he said, "A culture where it's not okay for an adult to say 'get out.'" Now, I don't claim that my classroom experience is any more "normal" than a superintendent's – it's just at the other end of the behavior spectrum. I see kids trying out stuff they wouldn't pull with their regular teacher because they know they won't have to live with me tomorrow – hey, I might not even know their names. As for the superintendent, I'm guessing there might be a certain "Potemkin Village" aspect to what he sees – kids on their best behavior in various formats, so I don't necessarily expect him to have that good a grip on classroom reality. But still – "not okay for an adult to say 'get out'"? Surely someone has let him know what a middle school classroom can be like when he's not around? I've often thought there should be a requirement that every school principal and assistant principal spend a day a year subbing in a school where they were not known, to give them a reality dose. Sounds like it'd be a good idea for superintendents as well.

SHAKY SOCIOLOGY

The anti-suspension argument often seems to rely on some pretty shaky sociology. Take the SPLC report's conclusion that "It is difficult to argue that disciplinary removals result in improvements to the school learning climate when schools with higher suspension and expulsion rates average lower test scores than do schools with lower suspension and expulsion rates." In other words, they found that tougher schools have lower test scores! Suppose, for a moment, we were considering housing policy: Public housing administrators have at various times implemented regulations evicting law breakers from public housing projects. Maybe those policies were a good idea, maybe they were a bad idea – but would we judge them to have failed because the projects remain poorer and more dangerous than the average neighborhood?

A February 16, 2014 *New York Times* opinion piece, "Real Discipline in School" took the argument further – not only don't high suspension rates cure a school's problems, it argued, but "these practices increase dropout rates and arrest rates." The article didn't actually state how its authors reached this conclusion, but the online version referenced a 2011 report on Texas suspension policies. That report, *Breaking School Rules*, also found precisely the sorts of things you might expect – that students experiencing a greater amount of trouble in school tended to have lower grades and more trouble with the law; students classified as "emotionally disturbed" were more likely to be suspended; and that "schools that are successful in addressing those student behaviors that result in disciplinary action could potentially improve academic outcomes." But so far as backing up the opinion-writers' contention, the study actually concluded only that "Continued research and discussion can help determine whether these suspensions and expulsions are yielding other sought-after outcomes, such as better academic performance, higher rates of high school completion, [and] fewer juvenile justice contacts."

At times it almost seems that there's a sort of "good-enough-for-movement-work" philosophy about some of the arguments raised – that is to say, *we don't have to be that careful about what we actually say, because you know what we mean.* For instance, a December 26, 2013 *San Francisco Chronicle* opinion piece, "San Francisco schools need solutions, not suspensions" reported that "Last year, our district had nearly 2,000 suspensions; about 50 percent of these suspensions were of black students, despite their being 10 percent of the district's student population. As a result, black high school students receive on average 19 fewer instructional days annually than their peers." Did the authors mean to say that suspensions alone account for the 19 fewer days? I don't think so, because I doubt very much that this is the case. Did they want to actually mislead the reader? Again, probably not, but, on the other hand, precision does not seem to have been a big concern. (A note requesting clarification from the authors went unanswered.)

BETTER SOCIOLOGY

Happily, there is some better sociology out there on this difficult topic. When the SPLC study authors found that black students were suspended at a rate more than double the average of the 18 urban school districts they looked at, they found it "unlikely that poverty could sufficiently explain the gender and racial differences in these current data." Now, I happen to think that they got that right. Unfortunately, a certain narrowness of vision sets in and instead of considering the broader social or historical picture that might be a factor in this situation, they narrow their search to what they can find within the middle school walls. As a result their only recommendation – beyond the gathering and dissemination of more information – is to investigate the previously mentioned possibility of biases. The late John Ogbu, on the other hand, took a much broader view.

Ogbu was a Nigerian-born Anthropology Professor at the University of California at Berkeley who spent thirty five years studying the public school education of minorities in the U.S., during which he became persuaded of the importance of distinguishing between "voluntary" and "involuntary" minorities. He developed this distinction to answer the challenge sometimes emanating from immigrant groups – "We (Irish-Americans, Italian-Americans, etc.) had to struggle, but we made it. Why should they (African-Americans) be any different?" Voluntary minorities in Ogbu's scheme are immigrants who arrive in this country in search of a better life, a group that encompasses most of our hyphenated nationalities. Involuntary minorities include blacks brought here as slaves, Native Americans whose continent was taken from them, and Mexicans living in areas subsumed by the United States. When some of the nineteenth century European ancestors of current Americans were arriving to seek the American Dream, the ancestors of today's African-Americans were still living the American nightmare of slavery. Their descendants would live through another century of segregation and one new immigrant group after another would pass them on their way up the economic ladder.

Sociological theories won't help a student pass a test or a teacher quiet a classroom, we know. On the other hand, when you start mucking around in social policy, you've kind of got to have one. And what Ogbu has done is to provide a framework for understanding school realities that go deeper than the attitudes of individual teachers or administrators. There has traditionally been a hesitancy to engage in this for fear of appearing to "blame the victim," either by suggesting that black students are the cause of their own problems or perhaps even implying that as a group they are inherently less capable students. But in suggesting that we focus on the "involuntary minority" status of African-Americans when considering the situation of contemporary black students, Ogbu developed an approach that rests neither on the personal attitude of teachers nor on inherent racial characteristics of the student body, but on the real life weight that our history carries today. And while the other kinds of analysis may provide easier answers, everything I've seen suggests that Ogbu's is closer to describing the reality of the situation. Of course, as they say, a good analysis – and a few bucks – will get you a latte in today's world. But still, I figure closer to accurate has got to be better in the long run.

MANDELA

There's a lot about the anti-suspension movement that reminds me of Mandela – not the man but a proposal floated in Boston when I lived there that would have created a separate city by that name out of the neighborhoods where most of the black population lived. I never considered it a particularly good idea – the strongest argument for it seemed to be that it implicitly posed the question "You got a better idea?" to those who didn't support it – but I did appreciate the motivation. At least it represented a challenge to the status quo and the status of the city's black population certainly needed challenging and I think a lot of people kind of nodded along in support of the general idea of doing something. Mandela went on the ballot as an advisory question, it lost, and people went on to other things. Did the idea help anything in the end? I don't know, but it probably didn't hurt, anyhow

I think the anti-suspension effort gets a similar benefit of the doubt from a lot of people who are just glad to see somebody trying to do something. But, unlike Mandela, this campaign looks like it's got some legs and so we might want to think more seriously before just nodding along in support of its good intentions. I suspect that one of the reasons for the breadth of support the effort is drawing, from local school boards all the way up to the Obama Administration, is that it appears to be a solution that costs nothing – rewrite some rules and regulations and the problem will be gone. But to the extent that it's not a real solution, the tacit support we give it may only delay the search for more substantive solutions – ones which may cost money.

I've often been asked what I think would substantially help the situation of black students. After explaining that I think things like a true full-employment economy would probably do more to improve their lives than anything we might do inside schools, I'll say that the most important thing we can do to improve the situation inside the classroom is to increase the adult-to-student ratio. But if I go on to say that I've been in first and second grade classes where a five or six-to-one adult-to-student ratio is probably needed to keep all of the kids in the action (not necessarily teacher-to-student ratio, by the way; the adults might also be student teachers, aides, parents or other volunteers), some people's reaction is likely to be that something like that is not within the realm of possibility, so it's simply not to the point to talk about it. But my contention is no more or less true whether or not there's any likelihood of such ratios being effected. In the final analysis, the size of the problem cannot be whittled down simply to match the size of the cure deemed politically possible.

REAL SOLUTIONS?

This book primarily concerns my educational (and not-so educational) experiences, rather than my educational theories. Like anyone who spends time in schools, I have my own ideas about what works and what doesn't, my pet peeves and occasional disdain for what seems like fuzzy-headed thinking. The reader will have noticed many of them in these pages. And all of this matters because every child and every class matters.

But I will close by reiterating a point I made at the outset. These useful and meaningful discussions and debates about the right and wrong ways to teach are not really at the core of the dominant national discussion of education. Most, if not all of what I (and perhaps the reader) found deeply disturbing in my classroom experiences had little, if anything, to do with any national educational crisis and everything to do with a national social and economic crisis – the great and growing gap in income, wealth and opportunity.

My solution? Class-size reduction, of course. Adequate prenatal care, early childhood education and social services for poor children. Poverty reduction. Let me say that one again-- poverty reduction, whether by a commitment to a full-employment economy or some other means. And, in the meantime, maintaining public control and operation of public schools.

In other words, if we wish to dramatically improve the education of America's poor children, we will have to dramatically improve the lives of America's poor children.

BIOGRAPHY

Up until the publication of this book, Tom Gallagher was a substitute teacher. He has also been a Massachusetts State Representative, a United Nations Election Officer in East Timor, an Election Supervisor in Sarajevo, a freelance book reviewer, sold tickets for the San Francisco Opera, affixed Super Regular stickers to gas pumps, and done or been a few other things. He currently lives in San Francisco, but still considers Boston and New York home as well.

In the eyes of students past, Tom Gallagher has resembled George Carlin, Jack Nicholson, Frankenstein, Clint Eastwood, Woody Harrelson, Anthony Hopkins, Mr. Rogers, Arnold Schwarzenegger's father, and Red Foreman (the last a character from "That Seventies Show," which I've never seen.)

www.ingramcontent.com/pod-product-compliance
Lightning Source LLC
Chambersburg PA
CBHW021913180426
43198CB00034B/192